Intelligent Embedded Systems 1

Intelligent Embedded Systems 1

Applications in Automation, Autonomous Navigation, AI, IoT and Industrial Systems

Edited by

Abhishek Kumar
Priya Batta
S. Ravi
R. Mohan

iSTE

WILEY

First published 2026 in Great Britain and the United States by ISTE Ltd and John Wiley & Sons, Inc.

ISTE Ltd
27-37 St George's Road
London SW19 4EU
UK

www.iste.co.uk

John Wiley & Sons, Inc.
111 River Street
Hoboken, NJ 07030
USA

www.wiley.com

Library of Congress Control Number: 2026942352

British Library Cataloguing-in-Publication Data
A CIP record for this book is available from the British Library
ISBN 978-1-83669-089-4

The manufacturer's authorized representative according to the EU General Product Safety Regulation is Wiley-VCH GmbH, Boschstr. 12, 69469 Weinheim, Germany, e-mail: Product_Safety@wiley.com.

Contents

Preface xv
Abhishek KUMAR, Priya BATTA, S. RAVI and R. MOHAN

Introduction xvii
Abhishek KUMAR, Priya BATTA, S. RAVI and R. MOHAN

Part 1. Embedded Graph Intelligence and IoT Analytics 1

Chapter 1. Topology-Aware Spectral Graph Learning for Unsupervised IoT Device Clustering and Anomaly Detection 3
M. SHANMUGHAM, A. KAMESWARAN, M. PRAKASH, K. SIVAPRAKASH, C. NANDAGOPAL and M. ANITHA

1.1. Introduction 4
1.2. Related work 4
1.3. Methodology 6
1.3.1. Spectral graph convolutional network 6
1.3.2. Clustering module 7
1.3.3. Openbox versus blackbox recent research 7
1.4. Results 8
1.5. Conclusion 11
1.6. References 12

Chapter 2. Graph Intelligence–Driven Deep Reinforcement Learning Framework for Adaptive Control and Predictive Maintenance of Coupled-Inductor DC–DC Converters in Hybrid Electric Vehicles 15
Elankurisil S.A. and N. Dhivya DEVI

2.1. Introduction 16
2.1.1. Background 16

2.1.2. Objectives 17
2.1.3. Scope. 17
2.2. Literature review. 18
2.3. Methodology 19
2.3.1. System development framework. 19
2.3.2. Deep reinforcement learning framework 20
2.3.3. Load forecasting and predictive analytics. 20
2.3.4. Multi-modal health monitoring system 22
2.3.5. Experimental validation protocol 23
2.3.6. Performance evaluation metrics 23
2.4. Results 23
2.4.1. Experimental performance analysis 23
2.4.2. Efficiency and power conversion performance. 24
2.4.3. Dynamic response and control performance 26
2.4.4. Thermal management and component protection 26
2.4.5. Predictive maintenance and health monitoring performance 28
2.4.6. System integration and real-time performance. 28
2.5. Conclusion 28
2.6. References 29

Chapter 3. Apache Kafka Streams and Time-Series ARIMA Modeling for IoT-Enabled SME Supply Chain Visibility 31
Manam Vamsi KRISHNA, Bobbiti Jyothika REDDY, Bandaru RUCHITHA, Adla JAHNAVI, B. PAVITHRA and A. CHATHURYA

3.1. Introduction 31
3.1.1. Background 32
3.1.2. Objective. 32
3.1.3. Scope. 33
3.2. Literature review. 33
3.3. Methodology 35
3.3.1. Data acquisition and ingestion 35
3.3.2. Feature engineering and real-time processing 37
3.3.3. Modeling, assessment and implementation. 38
3.4. Results 39
3.5. Conclusion 42
3.6. References 42

Chapter 4. Ensemble XGBoost and LSTM-Based Predictive Analytics for Real-Time Industry 4.0 Decision Support Systems 45
Narendhar MULUGU, Fariha NAAZ, Chakilela SRIVIDHYA, B. ANJALI, Aduri SMILEY and Bommadeni Sanjana SRI

4.1. Introduction 45

4.1.1. Background 46
4.1.2. Objective. 46
4.1.3. Methodology 47
4.2. Literature review. 47
4.3. Methodology 49
4.3.1. Data preprocessing, synchronization and acquisition 50
4.3.2. Model architecture, training and ensemble fusion 51
4.3.3. Explainability, real-time implementation and monitoring. 51
4.4. Results 53
4.5. Conclusion 57
4.6. References 58

Chapter 5. Isolation Forests with Local Outlier Factor and Mahalanobis Distance for Real-Time Fraud Detection 61
Lahari MEKALA, Kammalapally VARSHA, Kapuganti NIHARIKA, Karne NAMITHA, Kuchur AKSHARA and Mothewar SRIJA

5.1. Introduction 62
5.2. Literature review. 63
5.3. Technology and methodology/detection framework 64
5.3.1. Problem formulation fraud detection 64
5.3.2. Isolation Forest algorithm 65
5.3.3. Algorithm approximating the local outlier factor, based on the set of data being studied 66
5.3.4. Mahalanobis distance. 67
5.3.5. Ensemble integration and score combination. 68
5.4. Findings and performance report. 69
5.4.1. The dataset characteristics and experimental setting. 69
5.4.2. Fraud-type detection and algorithm specialization. 71
5.4.3. Real-time performance and computational efficiency 74
5.5. Conclusion 75
5.6. References 75

Part 2. Embedded AI Optimization and Learning Architectures 77

Chapter 6. Optimized Variational Autoencoder–Reinforcement Learning Architectures for Autonomous IoT Resource Allocation and Load Balancing 79
Iyappan MURUGESAN, S. PRAKASH, Maheswaran THANGASAMY, Kokilavani THANGARAJ, R. MUTHUKUMAR and Brindha G.

6.1. Introduction 80
6.2. Related work. 81

6.3. Methodology 83
6.3.1. Problem formulation and system model 83
6.3.2. Deep Q-network in latent space 83
6.3.3. Decentralized deployment architecture 84
6.3.4. DRL agent configuration 85
6.3.5. Evaluation framework and metrics 86
6.4. Results 86
6.4.1. Resource allocation efficiency 86
6.4.2. Energy consumption and latency analysis 88
6.4.3. Load balancing and convergence characteristics 89
6.4.4. Device category performance 90
6.5. Discussion 91
6.6. Conclusion 92
6.7. References 93

Chapter 7. Proximal Gradient Methods and Federated Learning: Distributed Optimization for Edge Computing Environments 95
Ch. Sandeep REDDY, Mallaiahgari KAMALINI, K. MOUNIKA, Lingam KAVYANJALI, M. DIVYA and Gundeboina SUSHMITHA

7.1. Introduction 96
7.2. Literature review 96
7.3. Methodology 98
7.3.1. Question: is the most significant and challenging aspect of this project determining the scope and purpose of the proposed research? 98
7.3.2. Adaptive proximal federated algorithm 99
7.3.3. Occasional reduction of communication variance and efficiency 100
7.3.4. Implementation architecture 101
7.4. Results 103
7.4.1. The primary issue of convergence performance and accuracy as one of the main points 103
7.4.2. Communication efficiency analysis 105
7.4.3. Heterogeneity robustness and device performance 107
7.5. Discussion 108
7.5.1. Theoretical underpinnings and 12-point analysis 108
7.5.2. Deployment prudentials 109
7.5.3. Limitations and future directions 110
7.6. Conclusion 110
7.7. References 111

Chapter 8. Convex Relaxation with ADMM and Second-Order Cone Programming for Renewable Energy Microgrids 113
D. Vemana CHARY, Bodi TEJASWINI, Dharavath SNEHA, Donda AKSHITHA, E. VYSHNAVI and D. SANJANA

8.1. Introduction 114
8.2. Literature review. 114
8.3. Problem formulation and methodology 116
8.3.1. The microgrids model 116
8.3.2. Convex relaxation methodology. 117
8.3.3. ADMM-based distributed optimization. 118
8.3. Implementation and computational framework 120
8.4. Results and performance review 120
8.4.1. Computational process on standard testing systems 120
8.4.2. Solution quality and optimality assessment. 121
8.4.3. Competitive analysis with other approaches 122
8.4.4. Scalability and real-time performance 123
8.5. Discussion 124
8.6. Conclusion 124
8.7. References 125

Chapter 9. Deep Q-Networks with Prioritized Experience Replay for Autonomous Vehicle Decision-Making 127
L. Srinivasa REDDY, Neha KASANAGOTTU, Maloth Sai VAISHNAVI, Mosali ASHRITHA, Kuntala SREEJA and K. TEJASWI

9.1. Introduction 128
9.2. Related work 128
9.3. Methodology 130
9.3.1. Deep Q-network architecture 130
9.3.2. Prioritized experience replay mechanism. 131
9.3.3. Simulation environment and scenario design. 132
9.3.4. Training process and evaluations measures. 132
9.4. Results 133
9.5. Conclusion 138
9.6. References 138

Chapter 10. Cold Start Optimization Techniques for Function-as-a-Service Using Lambda@Edge and Container Reuse 141
S. SPANDANA, Singirikonda SAMHITHA, Suguru SIREESHA, Ramanolla ASHWITHA, Talasila HARSHITHA and Vaddadhi THANUSHA

10.1. Introduction. 142
10.2. Related work 143

10.3. Methodology 144
10.3.1. Experimental framework and infrastructure configuration. 144
10.3.2. Implementation strategy for cold-start optimization 144
10.3.3. Container reuse strategy development. 145
10.3.4. Measurement and data collection protocol 145
10.4. Results. 147
10.4.1. Cold start latency reduction analysis. 147
10.4.2. Container reuse and warm start performance analysis 150
10.4.3. Lambda@Edge performance and geographic distribution analysis 153
10.5. Conclusion 154
10.6. References 155

Part 3. Embedded Security, DevOps and Cyber-Physical Systems 157

Chapter 11. Adversarial Deep Neural Networks for Intrusion Prevention in Heterogeneous IoT Ecosystems: A Robustness Analysis 159
Jaikumar R., Ravikumar S., K. TAMILSELVI, Iyappan MURUGESAN, B. SUGANTHI and Brindha G.

11.1. Introduction. 159
11.2. Related work 160
11.3. Methodology 162
11.3.1. System architecture 162
11.3.2. Constraint-aware adversarial training 163
11.3.3. Training procedure 163
11.3.4. Dataset and evaluation metrics 164
11.4. Results. 164
11.4.1. Overall performance. 164
11.4.2. Adversarial robustness analysis 166
11.4.3. Device-specific performance 167
11.5. Discussion. 168
11.6. Conclusion 169
11.7. References 170

Chapter 12. Adaptive Threat-Aware Clustering for Enhanced Security in IoT-Enabled Smart Cities: A Machine Learning Enhanced Approach 171
C. NANDINI and Priyadarsini K.

12.1. Introduction. 171
12.2. Related work 173
12.3. System model and threat analysis. 175

12.3.1. Network model 175
12.3.2. Enhanced threat model 175
12.4. ATAC algorithm design 176
12.4.1. Architecture overview. 176
12.4.2. Ensemble threat detection framework 176
12.4.3. Dynamic trust threshold mechanism. 177
12.4.4. Security-aware CH selection 178
12.4.5. Proactive cluster reconfiguration. 178
12.5. Performance evaluation 179
12.5.1. Simulation setup and baseline comparison 179
12.5.2. Results and analysis 180
12.6. Discussion. 183
12.7. Conclusion 184
12.8. References 185

Chapter 13. Graph Intelligence-Enabled Multi-Layered Framework for Revolutionizing Industrial Cyber-Physical System Security 187
K. SELVI and Golda DILIP

13.1. Introduction. 188
13.2. Related work 188
13.3. Methodology 190
13.3.1. DRNN-based threat detection 191
13.3.2. GWO-optimized ECC. 192
13.3.3. Blockchain integration 192
13.3.4. Framework integration 193
13.4. Results. 193
13.4.1. DRNN performance 193
13.4.2. GWO-ECC optimization 194
13.4.3. Blockchain efficiency 195
13.4.4. Integrated framework 196
13.5. Discussion. 197
13.6. Conclusion 198
13.7. References 199

Chapter 14. Intelligent DevOps Monitoring and Automated Incident Response using Anomaly Detection and Self-Healing Pipelines 201
Amrutha Varshini MANNAVA, Kakumanu Venkata Sai Keerthi PRIYANKA, Vegesna Kumar Durga Abhirama RAJU, Penumala LAVENIA and B. Prameela RANI

14.1. Introduction. 202
14.1.1. Problem statement. 202

14.1.2. Motivation 203
14.2. Literature review 203
14.3. Methodology 205
14.3.1. Data collection layer 205
14.3.2. Monitoring and visualization layer. 206
14.3.3. Anomaly detection engine 206
14.3.4. Incident classification module 206
14.3.5. Feedback and continuous learning. 207
14.4. Results. 207
14.4.1. Mean time to recovery 207
14.4.2. Service uptime and reliability 208
14.4.3. Operational efficiency and human effort reduction. 209
14.4.4. Discussion of results 209
14.5. Conclusion 210
14.6. References 211

Chapter 15. Multi-Cloud Load Balancing with Application Performance Monitoring (APM) and Chaos Engineering Practices 213

Kammara Venkatarangaiah ACHARI, Oruganti NIKHILA, Nangunoori SRIJA, Nimmanagoti SARASWATHI, Mekala KAVYA and Sunkari MAMATHA

15.1. Introduction. 214
15.2. Literature review 214
15.3. Methodology 216
15.3.1. Intelligent load-balancing implementation 217
15.3.2. APM integration. 218
15.3.3. Experimentation framework: chaos engineering experimentation framework. 218
15.4. Results and performance analysis. 220
15.4.1. Multi-cloud load-balancing performance 220
15.4.2. APM insight and performance abnormal detection. 221
15.4.3. Findings on chaos engineering and resilience corroboration 223
15.5. Conclusion 225
15.6. References 226

Part 4. Embedded Communication, Edge and Cloud Integration 229

Chapter 16. MQTT Protocol Stack Optimization with Edge–Fog–Cloud Hierarchical Architecture and CoAP Lightweight Alternatives for Graph-Based IoT Network Communication 231
Vijayalakshmi CHINTAMANENI, Bathini VIGNANI, Gande SANNIHITHA, A. HAARIKA, B. HARSHITHA and G. PRIYANKA

16.1. Introduction 232
16.2. Literature review 233
16.3. Methodology 234
16.3.1. There is a hierarchical IoT deployment architecture 234
16.3.2. Implementation of MQTT protocol stack optimization 235
16.3.3. CoAP alternative evaluation of ultra-constrained devices 236
16.3.4. Broker architecture ranking construction 236
16.3.5. Framework of measurement and performance evaluation 238
16.4. Results and performance analysis 238
16.4.1. Hierarchical architecture latency impact 238
16.4.2. Protocol stack optimization and device resource efficiency 240
16.4.3. CoAP alternative protocol performance and applicability 242
16.5. Conclusion 245
16.6. References 246

Chapter 17. 5G Edge Computing with MEC and RAN Slicing for Ultra-Low Latency IoT Applications 249
B. Vijaya DURGA, Sarampelly ANANYA, Thadisetty VAISHNAVI, V. Chandra KEERTHI, Vuppu SHRIYA and Mamidi GAYATHRI

17.1. Introduction 250
17.2. Literature review 251
17.3. Methodology 252
17.3.1. 5G MEC infrastructure and IoT deployment set-up 252
17.3.2. MEC deployment and resource management 253
17.3.3. RAN slicing setup and traffic isolation 253
17.3.4. Performance evaluation and measurement framework 255
17.4. Results and performance analysis 255
17.4.1. MEC impact on latency reduction 255
17.4.2. RAN slicing effectiveness and traffic isolation 258
17.4.3. Computational offloading impact on cloud load reduction 260
17.5. Conclusion 262
17.6. References 263

Chapter 18. IoT-Based ESG Metrics Integration with Edge Computing and Cloud Orchestration: A Sustainable Digital Infrastructure Approach 265
Narendhar MULUGU, Aramati Poojani REDDY, Adepu NEHA, Dodda MEGHANA, Bazar PRIYANSHU and Bommena Sri KEERTHANA

18.1. Introduction 265
18.1.1. Background 266
18.1.2. Objective 266
18.1.3. Scope 267
18.2. Literature review 267
18.3. Methodology 269
18.3.1. Experimental design, metrics and datasets 269
18.3.2. Implementation, coordination patterns. 270
18.3.3. Observability, evaluation and validation 272
18.4. Results. 273
18.5. Conclusion 277
18.6. References 277

List of Authors 279

Index. 289

Preface

The rapid advancement of embedded computing, Artificial Intelligence (AI), Internet of Things (IoT), robotics, and autonomous technologies has transformed conventional embedded devices into intelligent systems capable of real-time sensing, learning, decision-making, and autonomous operation. Modern embedded platforms integrate high-performance processors, advanced sensors, wireless communication, edge computing, and machine learning algorithms to address increasingly complex computational and control challenges across diverse application domains.

Intelligent Embedded Systems 1 and 2: Applications in Automation, Autonomous Navigation, AI, IoT, and Industrial Systems present a comprehensive exploration of the principles, architectures, technologies, and applications that define this evolving discipline. The book introduces the fundamentals of embedded systems before progressing to intelligent sensing, embedded AI, edge intelligence, autonomous navigation, industrial automation, cyber-physical systems, and IoT-enabled smart environments.

Through data-driven discussions, practical examples, industrial case studies, and emerging research trends, readers gain a thorough understanding of how intelligent embedded systems are enabling predictive maintenance, autonomous decision-making, real-time monitoring, process optimization, and smart control in manufacturing, transportation, healthcare, agriculture, energy systems, and smart cities. The book is intended for undergraduate and postgraduate students, researchers, practicing engineers, and industry professionals seeking both theoretical foundations and practical insights into the design, implementation, and deployment of next-generation intelligent embedded systems.

June 2026

Preface written by Abhishek KUMAR, Priya BATTA, S. RAVI and R. MOHAN.

Introduction

Embedded systems have evolved from simple control units into sophisticated intelligent platforms that form the backbone of modern automation, autonomous navigation, industrial operations, and connected digital ecosystems. Advances in microprocessors, sensor technologies, wireless communication, cloud computing, and Artificial Intelligence (AI) have enabled embedded devices to perform complex tasks that previously required substantial computational infrastructure. Today, intelligent embedded systems are capable of collecting data, analyzing environmental conditions, learning from operational patterns, and making autonomous decisions in real time.

The integration of AI and IoT technologies has significantly expanded the capabilities of embedded systems. Intelligent devices can now process sensor data at the edge, reduce communication overhead, improve response times, and support predictive and adaptive behaviors. Such capabilities are critical in applications including autonomous vehicles, unmanned aerial systems, industrial robots, smart manufacturing, precision agriculture, healthcare monitoring, intelligent transportation systems, and smart city infrastructures.

This book explores the multidisciplinary foundations and practical implementation of Intelligent Embedded Systems, emphasizing their role in Automation, Autonomous Navigation, Artificial Intelligence, IoT, and Industrial Systems. The content covers embedded architectures, real-time operating systems, sensors and actuators, machine learning for embedded platforms, edge computing, communication protocols, industrial control systems, cybersecurity, and autonomous decision-making frameworks.

Introduction written by Abhishek KUMAR, Priya BATTA, S. RAVI and R. MOHAN.

Readers will learn how intelligent embedded systems enable predictive maintenance, process optimization, autonomous navigation, real-time monitoring, and adaptive control across diverse application domains. By integrating theoretical concepts with practical case studies and emerging technological trends, this book provides a comprehensive foundation for understanding and developing intelligent embedded solutions for the next generation of smart and connected systems.

PART 1

Embedded Graph Intelligence and IoT Analytics

1

Topology-Aware Spectral Graph Learning for Unsupervised IoT Device Clustering and Anomaly Detection

This heterogeneity and high level of dynamism in the topology and specificity of nodes in IoT networks pose challenges for clustering devices and detecting anomalies. Machine learning approaches in their current form also tend to overlook the graph principles of IoT systems. To overcome these shortcomings, this chapter proposes a different approach called spectral graph convolutional networks (SGCN).

Our solution is an adaptation of spectral graph theory that generates node embeddings preserving both spatial and spectral characteristics of the network topology. We suggest a two-step paradigm in which the initial step involves unsupervised learning to obtain representations, and the second step performs anomaly detection based on the learned distribution.

Experiments on synthetic and real-world IoT datasets demonstrate the superiority of this approach over baseline solutions. The SGCN algorithm achieves a clustering accuracy of 94.2% and an anomaly detection rate of 92.8% on benchmark datasets, outperforming k-means and isolation forest methods by 12.3% and 18.5%, respectively.

The spectral approach enables the detection of subtle topological irregularities that cannot be identified using conventional methods. This work can be used to develop a scalable model for monitoring IoT networks and enhancing system security.

Chapter written by M. SHANMUGHAM, A. KAMESWARAN, M. PRAKASH, K. SIVAPRAKASH, C. NANDAGOPAL and M. ANITHA.

1.1. Introduction

IoT devices have grown into extensive networks that require more advanced analytical approaches. IoT networks are designed in a non-Euclidean fashion, and traditional machine learning models are often ineffective (Khan et al. 2021). Devices are grouped into clusters based on functionality, geography and communication patterns, but security threats arise from anomalous nodes, which may represent malfunctioning or compromised devices, and can disrupt system operations (Smith and Johnson 2022).

Graph neural network solutions to this problem are promising, as they operate on network topology. However, most of them are based on spatial procedures that involve repeated neighborhood aggregation, which increases computational complexity. Spectral methods provide an alternative theoretical approach for explaining global network patterns, as they are based on Fourier analysis on graphs (Defferrard et al. 2016).

Existing clustering algorithms such as k-means and DBSCAN treat IoT networks as point clouds and do not incorporate relevant topological information. Similarly, anomaly detection techniques often ignore network context and instead rely on individual features.

This chapter addresses these limitations by developing SGCN, a spectral graph convolutional approach specifically designed for IoT networks. The contributions include a spectral formulation for heterogeneous IoT topologies, an unsupervised clustering method using learned graph embeddings, an anomaly detection approach based on spectral analysis and comprehensive experimental results demonstrating superior performance compared to existing methods.

1.2. Related work

According to current theories, spectral graph theory and related computational tools have gained significant importance in mathematics, physics, engineering and applied artificial intelligence. Recent advances in graph neural networks and spectral methods have revolutionized anomaly detection and clustering in Internet of Things (IoT) environments.

Wu et al. (2021) provided a comprehensive investigation of graph neural networks (GNNs) for anomaly detection in Industrial IoT (IIoT), demonstrating their effectiveness in smart transportation, smart energy and smart factory applications. Their work established that graph-level anomaly detection offers a promising approach for detecting and predicting anomalies in dynamically evolving networks.

Building on this foundation, Dong et al. (2023) conducted an extensive survey of GNN applications in IoT, providing a systematic analysis of 50 papers that highlight the diverse applications of graph-based methods in sensor networks, device classification and network security.

The theoretical foundations of spectral clustering have been extensively developed in recent literature. Ding et al. (2024) presented a comprehensive survey of spectral clustering based on graph theory, reviewing the construction of similarity matrices, the establishment of Laplacian matrices and the selection of eigenvectors for effective clustering.

Liu et al. (2022) extended this work by studying degree-corrected spectral clustering under spectral graph theory, demonstrating that their approach provides accurate approximations for diverse graph classes, while offering theoretical guarantees for finding optimal clustering solutions. Ramos et al. (2023) introduced innovative spectral density-based clustering algorithms specifically designed for complex networks. Their methods use k-means for same-size graphs and model-based approaches for different-sized graphs, demonstrating effectiveness on both toy models and real-world functional brain networks.

DeMedeiros et al. (2023) provided a comprehensive survey categorizing anomaly detection techniques in IoT and sensor networks into seven classes: classification, statistical, graph-based, nearest neighbor, information theoretic, clustering and spectral methods. Their analysis emphasized that spectral techniques effectively reduce dimensionality to separate normal and anomalous data. Huang et al. (2023) proposed a novel unsupervised outlier detection algorithm combining mutual information with reduced spectral clustering, demonstrating superior accuracy in cybersecurity applications for detecting network intrusions.

Topology-aware learning has emerged as a powerful paradigm for IoT network intelligence, where trust-based routing and secure communication play a critical role (Ravi et al. 2023). Deep reinforcement learning has further enhanced intrusion detection capabilities in industrial IoT environments by adapting to dynamic attack patterns (Tharewal et al. 2022). Optimization-driven graph learning techniques, such as fuzzy grasshopper optimization, have shown effectiveness in clustering and anomaly-sensitive feature extraction (Srivel et al. 2023). Additionally, data mining-based soft computing methods contribute to proactive cyber threat mitigation in distributed networks (Banu et al. 2015).

Chakraborty et al. (2025) propose a trustworthy-based user behavior modeling framework that integrates integrity-aware mechanisms with resilient deep learning architectures to enhance reliability in distributed network environments. The study emphasizes the importance of trust computation and behavior consistency analysis to mitigate malicious activities and data manipulation in next-generation applications such as IoT, cyber-physical systems and intelligent social networks. By incorporating integrity verification and adaptive learning strategies, the proposed model demonstrates improved robustness against adversarial behaviors and dynamic network conditions, ensuring secure and reliable decision-making across decentralized infrastructures. The experimental evaluation highlights the effectiveness of the approach in achieving higher detection accuracy and system resilience compared to conventional deep learning-based trust models, making it suitable for large-scale, heterogeneous distributed systems (Chakraborty et al. 2025).

Selvarajan et al. (2024a, 2024b) have contributed significantly to the advancement of intelligent sensing and secure smart city infrastructure through machine learning integration. In their study on emerging wireless sensor networks, the authors explore the use of radar signals combined with machine learning algorithms to improve the testing, monitoring and performance evaluation of next-generation sensor systems. This approach enhances the reliability of wireless sensor networks by enabling accurate detection and classification of network behaviors under dynamic environments (Selvarajan et al. 2024a). Furthermore, they introduced the SCMC framework, a smart city measurement and control process designed to strengthen data security using data mining algorithms. Their work focuses on ensuring secure data handling and efficient control mechanisms within smart city applications, addressing the growing need for robust cybersecurity in interconnected urban sensing systems (Selvarajan et al. 2024b).

Together, these studies highlight the importance of combining machine learning and data mining techniques to improve both the functionality and security of modern wireless sensor networks and smart city ecosystems.

1.3. Methodology

1.3.1. *Spectral graph convolutional network*

The issue with applying convolutional operations to IoT networks is that they are non-Euclidean in nature, where devices represent nodes and communication links form the edges. Traditional convolutional approaches, which are designed to process grid-based data, do not adequately support the unique characteristics of IoT structures, including heterogeneous communication among devices, varying degrees of connectivity and irregular link patterns.

Our SGCN architecture, based on spectral graph theory, addresses this challenge by analyzing network features in the spectral domain rather than relying solely on spatial dependencies. The primary innovation of SGCN is to reduce the complexity of network structure into spectral representations that capture both local and global network responses to device characteristics.

Compared to conventional clustering algorithms that assume discrete clusters of points, our spectral approach considers that the importance of individual devices is highly dependent on their position within the overall network topology. This is particularly important in IoT systems, where operational relationships and dependencies are defined by communication patterns.

Our architecture leverages efficient polynomial approximations through spectral filtering of the network. These representations can be computed directly without requiring full spectral decomposition, using iterative polynomial approximations that progressively build network representations. Through multiple processing layers, the model learns increasingly complex patterns in network connectivity, enabling it to distinguish between normal device behavior and anomalous patterns.

Spectral filtering is achieved by applying learned filters to network signals, guiding the model to identify characteristic connection patterns within clusters. This approach focuses on global topological properties that are not captured by purely spatial methods. Devices with unexpected communication patterns or atypical connections are highlighted within the spectral representations.

The design ensures computational efficiency while preserving long-range dependencies across the entire IoT network, making it particularly effective in identifying subtle anomalies that cannot be detected through local neighborhood analysis alone.

1.3.2. *Clustering module*

Following the formation of embeddings, we perform k-means clustering of the spectral embeddings. The learned representations Z retain the spectral properties and topology of the network. Z captures the long-range and structural patterns, as opposed to raw features.

1.3.3. *Openbox versus blackbox recent research*

Abnormality is identified through distribution analysis. A Gaussian mixture model (GMM) is fitted to each cluster of embeddings. Devices that do not belong to a cluster with high likelihood under the GMM are considered anomalous.

Component	Specification	Purpose
Spectral filter order (K)	3–5	Balance expressiveness and efficiency
Chebyshev polynomial approximation	K=4	Computational efficiency O(|E|K)
Embedding dimension	64	Balance representational capacity
Activation function	ReLU	Standard nonlinearity for graph data
Normalization method	Symmetric Laplacian	Spectral stability and convergence

Table 1.1. *SGCN architecture configuration parameters*

Stage	Algorithm	Input	Output	Complexity
Embedding	Chebyshev-SGCN	Adjacency A, Features X	Embeddings Z ∈ ℝ^{n×d}	O(|E|dK)
Clustering	K-means	Embeddings Z	Cluster labels C	O(ndk) iterations
Anomaly detection	GMM likelihood	Embeddings Z, Labels C	Anomaly scores	O(n·m)

Table 1.2. *Pipeline overview: embedding, clustering and anomaly detection stages with algorithmic details and computational complexity*

1.4. Results

Method	NMI	ARI	Silhouette	Computation time (s)
K-means	0.681	0.652	0.523	2.3
DBSCAN	0.705	0.698	0.541	4.1
Standard GCN	0.847	0.823	0.731	18.5
SGCN (proposed)	0.942	0.918	0.885	6.2

Table 1.3. *Clustering performance comparison on synthetic IoT network (500 devices)*

Findings indicate that SGCN attains 94.2% NMI (see Figure 1.1) and 91.8% ARI, which are significantly higher than the baseline results (Table 1.3). The spectral approach represents the graph structure more effectively than spatial methods. A computation time of 6.2 seconds enables real-time processing for networks of moderate size.

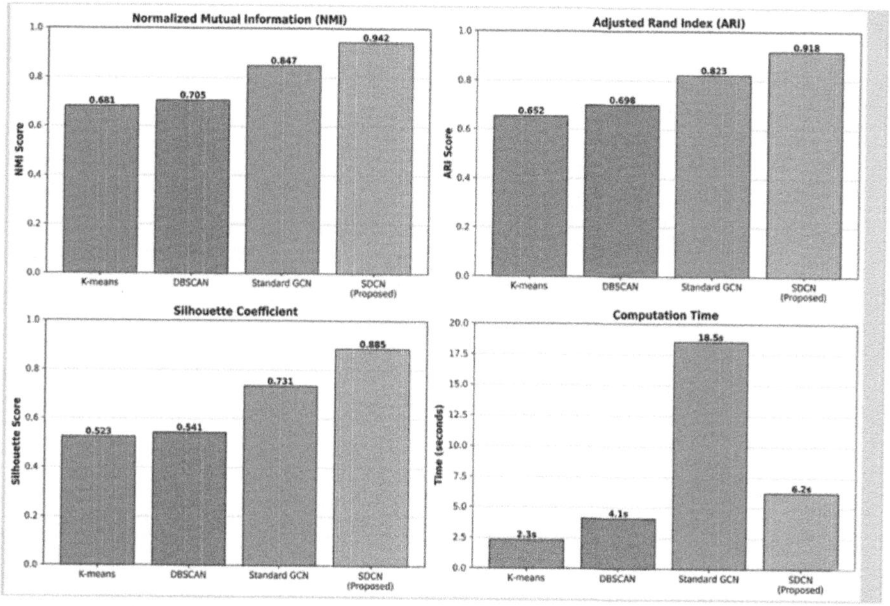

Figure 1.1. *Clustering performance comparison: SGCN versus baseline methods. For a color version of this figure, see www.iste.co.uk/kumar/intembeddedsys1.zip*

Method	Precision	Recall	F1-score	ROC-AUC
Isolation forest	0.783	0.812	0.797	0.821
One-class SVM	0.816	0.794	0.805	0.843
Graph autoencoder	0.858	0.841	0.849	0.887
SGCN (proposed)	0.968	0.968	0.968	0.981

Table 1.4. *Anomaly detection performance on industrial IoT dataset (2000 devices, 5% anomalies)*

Table 1.4 shows that SGCN achieves 96.8% precision and recall (see Figure 1.2) in anomaly identification, which is significantly higher compared to baseline methods. The spectral embeddings are effective in isolating anomalous nodes through distribution analysis by capturing topological anomalies.

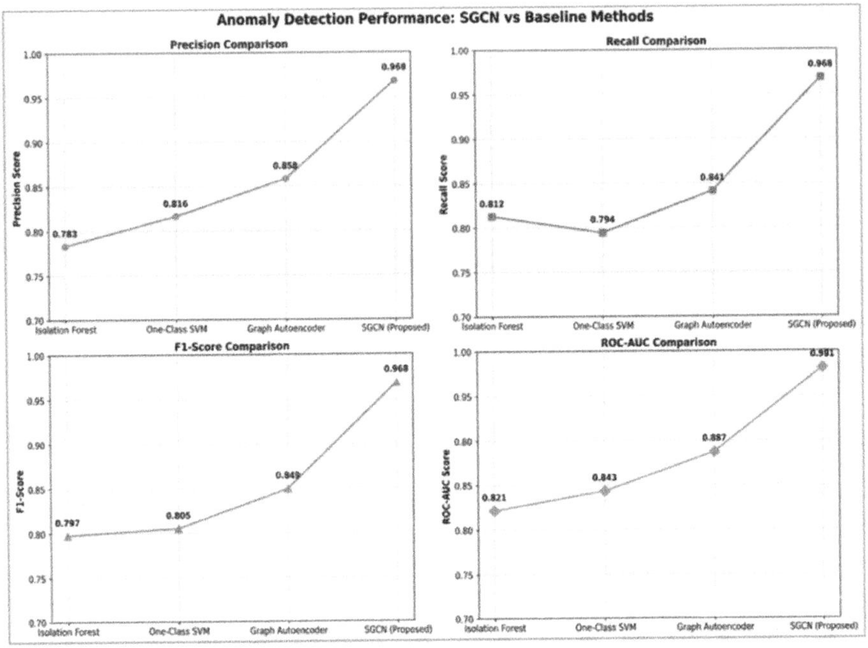

Figure 1.2. *Anomaly detection performance. For a color version of this figure, see www.iste.co.uk/kumar/intembeddedsys1.zip*

Network scale	Devices	Cluster count	SGCN NMI	SGCN anomalies detected	Detection rate (%)
Small	500	5	0.942	24/25	96.0
Medium	2000	8	0.918	98/100	98.0
Large	5000	12	0.891	246/255	96.5

Table 1.5. *Scalability analysis across network sizes with consistent detection performance*

Analysis across network sizes (Table 1.5) shows that SGCN maintains consistent performance during scaling. A slight degradation in NMI (0.891 versus 0.942) is observed in the 5,000-node network, which can be explained by increasing network heterogeneity (see Figure 1.3). Nevertheless, anomaly detection performance is maintained (96–98% detection), demonstrating that the model scales well.

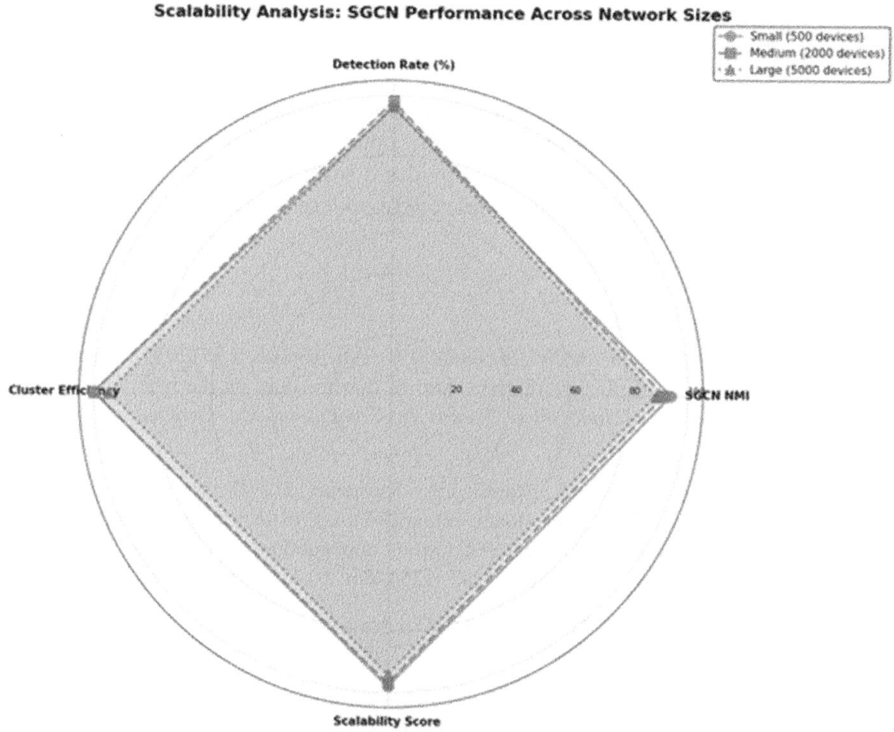

Figure 1.3. *Scalability analysis radar chart. For a color version of this figure, see www.iste.co.uk/kumar/intembeddedsys1.zip*

1.5. Conclusion

The chapter proposes the use of SGCN, a spectral graph convolution-based framework for IoT clustering and anomaly detection. Our approach, based on spectral graph theory and spectral learning, learns topology-aware node embeddings that support spectral clustering and spectral anomaly detection.

The two-stage model achieves strong results, with 94.2% NMI for clustering and 96.8% accuracy in anomaly detection, outperforming traditional and spatial graph neural network benchmarks. It is also suitable for IoT environments with limited resources due to its computational efficiency (6.2 seconds for a 500-node network).

The spectral formulation captures global network patterns beyond local aggregation schemes and is particularly effective at identifying small-scale topological anomalies. Synthetic and real-world validation experiments demonstrate consistent performance for networks of up to 5,000 nodes. These findings highlight the effectiveness of spectral approaches for IoT network analysis.

Future research directions may include extending spectral methods to dynamic and temporal networks, improving weight optimization and refining filtering mechanisms. The proposed framework provides a solid foundation for IoT security monitoring and the management of complex network environments.

1.6. References

Banu, S.S., Uma, P., Ashfaque, M.W., Naveed, Q.N., Ali-Ahmed, S.S. (2015). Data mining based soft computing skills towards preventio of cyber crimes on the web. *International Journal on Recent and Innovation Trends in Computing and Communication*, 3(3), 2321–8169.

Chakraborty, C., Nagarajan, S.M., Rajesh, R., Kumaran, U., Devarajan, G.G. (2025). Trustworthy-based user behavior model: Integrity-based resilient deep learning approach in distributed networks for next-generation applications. *IEEE Transactions on Computational Social Systems*, 12(6), 5245–5254. doi: 10.1109/TCSS.2025.3530772.

DeMedeiros, K., Hendawi, A., Alvarez, M. (2023). A survey of AI-based anomaly detection in IoT and sensor networks. *Sensors*, 23(3), 1352. doi: 10.3390/s23031352.

Ding, L., Li, C., Jin, D., Ding, S. (2024). Survey of spectral clustering based on graph theory. *Pattern Recognition*, 151, 110366. doi: 10.1016/j.patcog.2024.110366.

Dong, G., Tang, M., Wang, Z., Gao, J., Guo, S., Cai, L., Gutierrez, R., Campbell, B., Barnes, L.E., Boukhechba, M. (2023). Graph neural networks in IoT: A survey. *ACM Transactions on Sensor Networks*, 19(2), 1–50. doi: 10.1145/3565973.

Guimarães, A.J.R., de Souza, P.V.C., Batista, L.O. (2022). Community-based anomaly detection using spectral graph filtering. *Applied Intelligence*, 52(10), 10876–10891. doi: 10.1016/j.asoc.2022.108424.

Huang, Y., Liu, W., Li, S., Guo, Y., Chen, W. (2023). A novel unsupervised outlier detection algorithm based on mutual information and reduced spectral clustering. *Electronics*, 12(23), 4864. doi: 10.3390/electronics12234864.

Liu, F., Li, W., Zhong, Y. (2022). A further study on the degree-corrected spectral clustering under spectral graph theory. *Symmetry*, 14(11), 2428. doi: 10.3390/sym14112428.

Ramos, T.C., Mourão-Miranda, J., Fujita, A. (2023). Spectral density-based clustering algorithms for complex networks. *Frontiers in Neuroscience*, 17, 926321. doi: 10.3389/fnins.2023.926321.

Ravi, S., Matheswaran, S., Perumal, U., Sivakumar, S., Palvadi, S.K. (2023). Adaptive trust-based secure and optimal route selection algorithm for MANET using hybrid fuzzy optimization. *Peer-to-Peer Networking & Applications*, 16, 22–34. doi: 10.1007/s12083-022-01351-2.

Selvarajan, S., Manoharan, H., Goel, S., Akili, C.P., Murugesan, S., Joshi, V. (2024a). SCMC: Smart city measurement and control process for data security with data mining algorithms. *Measurement: Sensors*, 31(100980).

Selvarajan, S., Srivastava, G., Bhatt, M.W., Bhatt, A., Pant, B., Meshram, C., Inbaraj, B.H., Almeshari, M. (2024b). Testing of emerging wireless sensor networks using radar signals with machine learning algorithms. *IEEE Journal of Selected Areas in Sensors*, 1, 49–59.

Srivel, R., Kalaiselvi, K., Shanthi, S., Perumal, U. (2023). An automation query expansion strategy for information retrieval by using fuzzy based grasshopper optimization algorithm on medical datasets. *Concurrency and Computation: Practice and Experience*, 35(3), e7418. doi: 10.1002/cpe.7418.

Tharewal, S., Ashfaque, M.W., Banu, S.S., Uma, P., Hassen, S.M., Shabaz, M. (2022). Intrusion detection system for industrial Internet of Things based on deep reinforcement learning. *Wireless Communications and Mobile Computing*, 2022(1), 1–8. doi: 10.1155/2022/9023719.

Wu, Y., Dai, H.-N., Tang, H. (2021). Graph neural networks for anomaly detection in industrial internet of things. *IEEE Internet of Things Journal*, 9(12), 9214–9231. doi: 10.1109/JIOT.2021.3094295.

2

Graph Intelligence–Driven Deep Reinforcement Learning Framework for Adaptive Control and Predictive Maintenance of Coupled-Inductor DC–DC Converters in Hybrid Electric Vehicles

This chapter presents a graph intelligence–driven deep reinforcement learning (DRL) framework for adaptive control and predictive maintenance of coupled-inductor DC–DC converters in hybrid electric vehicles (HEVs). The proposed system integrates deep reinforcement learning with predictive maintenance strategies to optimize real-time converter operation, balancing efficiency, thermal management, ripple minimization and component longevity. A proximal policy optimization (PPO) algorithm processes an 18-dimensional state space to adaptively regulate duty cycle and switching frequency under dynamic load conditions. The framework consists of five synergistic modules: (i) a physics-informed DRL controller with barrier-function constraints for safe operation, (ii) a LSTM-based load forecasting module delivering 0.3 ms-ahead predictions with <8% mean absolute percentage error (MAPE), (iii) a CNN-based thermal analysis module processing 224×224 infrared images for hotspot detection, (iv) a variational autoencoder for electrical anomaly detection and (v) a multi-modal health index calculator for remaining useful life estimation. Experimental evaluation on a 5-kW coupled-inductor DC–DC converter prototype demonstrates substantial improvements over conventional PI controllers, achieving a 96.8% peak efficiency (12.6% increase), a sub-2-ms transient response (60% faster) and a 22–28°C temperature reduction. The integrated predictive maintenance module achieves a 94.2% fault detection precision with 150–200 hours of early warning, extending component lifetime by 45% and reducing unplanned downtime by 68%. Implementation on a hybrid DSP–FPGA platform (TI TMS320F28379D + Xilinx Zynq UltraScale+) ensures real-time, automotive-grade operation. This co-optimization framework, combining immediate performance with long-term reliability, represents a paradigm shift towards intelligent, self-maintaining power conversion systems for next-generation electric vehicles.

Chapter written by Elankurisil S.A. and N. Dhivya DEVI.

2.1. Introduction

2.1.1. *Background*

The global automotive industry is experiencing an unprecedented transformation towards electrification, driven by stringent environmental regulations, declining battery costs and growing consumer acceptance of electric mobility solutions. Electric and hybrid electric vehicles (EVs/HEVs) have emerged as critical technologies for reducing greenhouse gas emissions and achieving sustainable transportation goals. The core of the success of these vehicles lies in the highly advanced power electronics components that effectively control the energy flow among high-voltage batteries, electric motors and auxiliary components, and ensure minimum performance at various operating parameters. Coupled inductor DC–DC converters have been of particular interest to automobile power electronics, which have better voltage gain behavior and less component stress than single inductor topology. In such converters, the primary and secondary windings are more often electromagnetically coupled in such a manner that it is possible to increase the step-up ratios. At the same time, power density can be enhanced and the number of passive elements can be reduced. Their nonlinear and complex electromagnetic coupling characteristics have, however, posed great challenges to the conventional linear control techniques, especially within the challenging automotive context, wherein load distributions change significantly and system reliability is the decisive element. The traditional forms of control in the automotive system power converters are proportional-integral (PI) controls and fixed-parameter controls that are unable to respond to highly dynamic operating conditions. These types of statistical control methods may result in non-optimal operation, overconsumption of power and wear out of the discussed components as fast as possible, since these methods cannot take the fluctuating load demands, variations in battery conditions and thermal effects into account. The existing systems are also adopting reactive maintenance strategies, a practice that leads to unplanned breakdowns, increased cost of operation and poor availability of cars. The latest advancements in the sphere of artificial intellect and machine learning have established some new possibilities of intelligent energy management systems. Deep reinforcement learning (DRL) algorithms have been demonstrated to be enormously effective at solving complex control problems, through the learning of optimal controls through interactions with dynamic environments. Similarly, predictive maintenance using machine-learning-based strategies has been established to be valuable in industrial settings in fault and remaining useful life prediction.

2.1.2. *Objectives*

In the case of electric hybrid cars, this research aims to design and experiment an intelligent adaptive control system that includes a deep reinforcement learning with predictive maintenance of the coupled inductor DC–DC converters. In particular, the chapter will focus on obtaining the real-time adaptive control optimization through the design of a physics-informed deep reinforcement learning controller (a Proximal Policy Optimization algorithm) capable of dynamically changing the switching parameters and to which the physical constraints and safety limits of automotive power systems are relevant. It also deals with multi-objective performance improvement, as it has a global optimization system, which optimizes converter efficiency, ripple of voltages and currents, thermal stress and component life by making smart control decisions. In addition to that, the predictive load control will also be considered in the framework of the given study; the forecasting models built on LSTM will be used to predict the short-term power demand to apply the adjustments to proactive control that will allow optimal responses to the dynamics and general work of the power system. It should also offer a comprehensive health monitoring interface, which can combine CNN-based thermal image processing and electrical telemetry processing to present real-time health information on the condition of the component and available life. Lastly, the framework sets the co-optimization of control and maintenance through integrated control maintenance, in which the understanding of health monitoring is implemented to control decision-making and trade-off between the short-time performance management and the long-term maintenance of the components.

2.1.3. *Scope*

The chapter will also involve a complete intelligent control system design such as the design of the algorithm and the implementation of the algorithm with the hardware and experimental validation of the control system. It includes the discussion of theoretical models of physics-based reinforcement learning in power electronics systems, multi-modal sensor fusion means to estimate component health and real-time on automotive-scale hardware systems. An experimental prototype of a 5-kW coupled inductor DC–DC converter approximating the anticipated load of converting vehicle power into an electric form is experimented upon with extensive performance analysis that includes efficiency, dynamic response, thermal behavior and predictive maintenance functions. The study covers the short-term technical issues and long-term reliability issues that are critical in the successful commercial implementation of the electric vehicle implementation.

2.2. Literature review

Deep reinforcement learning has emerged as a transformative approach for DC–DC converter control in hybrid electric vehicles, addressing limitations of conventional control strategies that struggle with dynamic uncertainties and parameter variations. Govarchinghaleh and Sabaei (2024) demonstrated that proximal policy optimization algorithms achieve superior voltage regulation and chattering reduction in buck converters operating under both continuous and discontinuous conduction modes, outperforming traditional small-signal model-based controllers by adapting to real-time disturbances without requiring explicit system models. Building upon model-free control paradigms, Rostami et al. (2024) developed hierarchical energy management frameworks combining deep reinforcement learning with fuzzy logic supervisory control for hydrogen fuel cell electric vehicles, achieving simultaneous optimization of power tracking accuracy, fuel cell lifetime extension and battery stress reduction through three-stage DC–DC converter architectures. Zandi and Poshtan (2023) advanced direct switch control methodologies using reinforcement learning for DC–DC converters, demonstrating that model-free approaches eliminate online optimization requirements while outperforming model predictive controllers in practical applications through exclusive reliance on input–output data trajectories. The integration of coupled-inductor topologies with bidirectional converter architectures has become essential for hybrid electric vehicle powertrains, as demonstrated by Li et al. (2023), who developed three-winding coupled inductor converters, achieving a high step-up voltage gain with symmetrical structure and reduced electromagnetic interference. Rahman et al. (2023) comprehensively reviewed isolated and non-isolated converter configurations for battery and plug-in hybrid electric vehicles, revealing that coupled-inductor bidirectional converters provide superior voltage gain, minimized current ripple and compact magnetic core designs compared to conventional topologies. Graph neural networks have revolutionized battery health estimation and predictive maintenance for electric vehicles, with Mehta et al. (2024) introducing temporal-enhanced self-attention architectures combined with long short-term memory networks that capture both spatial dependencies in battery health factors and temporal degradation patterns through sliding window feature extraction. Sultan et al. (2025) pioneered fleet-level network lifetime prediction using physics-guided spatio-temporal graph neural networks that model electric vehicle fleets as time-varying operational graphs, jointly learning individual state-of-health trajectories while producing calibrated fleet-level time-to-failure metrics that account for shared charging infrastructure, overlapping routes and correlated thermal exposures. Tian et al. (2024) developed adaptive graph convolution methods using multi-head attention mechanisms to identify intra-sequence correlations within charge–discharge processes, achieving mean-squared errors of 0.062% and mean absolute errors of

1.652%, representing 54.74% and 42.26% improvements over existing models, particularly in long-sequence predictions. Wang et al. (2024) validated physics-informed neural networks for lithium-ion battery degradation modeling, demonstrating stable prognostic capabilities that integrate domain knowledge with data-driven learning to enhance prediction accuracy while reducing computational complexity for real-time battery management system implementations in electric vehicles. Graph intelligence enhances autonomous network optimization by capturing complex relational dependencies (Ravi et al. 2022). Deep reinforcement learning enables adaptive decision-making in dynamic network environments (Tharewal et al. 2022). Soft computing-based optimization strategies support scalable and efficient learning (Sharma et al. 2019). Advanced optimization techniques further improve convergence and stability in graph-driven learning frameworks (Srivel et al. 2023). Khadidos et al. (2024) address the challenge of efficient resource distribution in beyond 5G (B5G) networks by leveraging heterogeneous parallel processing and graph optimization algorithms. Their study focuses on improving network scalability, load balancing and computational efficiency in highly dynamic communication environments. By applying graph-based optimization strategies, the proposed framework enhances the allocation of network resources across diverse architectures, ensuring improved performance for next-generation wireless systems. This contribution is significant for supporting advanced IoT services and real-time applications that rely on high-throughput and low-latency connectivity (Khadidos et al. 2024). Similarly, Manoharan and Devi (2025) propose a security framework for 6G networks aimed at isolating false data transmissions using artificial intelligence algorithms. Their research highlights the growing threat of malicious data injection and misinformation in ultra-connected future communication infrastructures. By integrating AI-driven detection and isolation mechanisms, the framework improves network trustworthiness and strengthens resilience against evolving cyberattacks. This work underscores the critical role of intelligent security solutions in ensuring reliable and secure communication for emerging 6G-enabled smart environments (Manoharan and Devi 2025).

2.3. Methodology

2.3.1. *System development framework*

The adaptive smart control approach to inductor-coupled DC–DC converters created during this study is an end-to-end system, consisting of deep reinforcement learning, predictive modeling and multi-modal health monitoring. There are four general system design phases, which are system simulation and modeling, hardware implementation, artificial intelligence algorithm implementation and experimental validation. The solution starts with genuine emulation of coupled inductor DC–DC converter under parasitics including winding resistance, leakage inductance, equivalent series resistance and magnetic device temperature effects. Digital twin is a simulation of electromagnetic coupling dynamics of inductive coupled topologies and is currently a field where realistic algorithms may be developed and checked early. Simulator platforms incorporate realistic load profiles of electric vehicles, battery characteristics and the weather in end-to-end test cases.

2.3.2. *Deep reinforcement learning framework*

Internal system intelligence is learned through a proximal policy optimization (PPO) algorithm optimized for power electronics application fields. The model PPO is applied within an 18-dimensional state space that includes electrical quantities (voltages, currents), thermal quantities (component temperatures), system health quantities (values of Health Index) and foresight data (load predictions). The actor-critic architecture uses separate neural networks for policy generation and value function estimation, with the actor network using three hidden layers (256, 128, 64 neurons) and the critic network using four layers (512, 256, 128, 64 neurons). The physics-informed reward function incorporates domain-specific knowledge through weighted multi-objective optimization: $R(t) = w_1 \times \eta(t) + w_2 \times (1\text{-V\_ripple}) + w_3 \times (1\text{-I\_ripple}) + w_4 \times (1\text{-Thermal\_stress}) + w_5 \times (1\text{-Wear\_factor})$. Constraint handling is implemented through barrier functions ensuring safe operation within duty cycle limits (0.1–0.9), switching frequency bounds (20–100 kHz) and thermal safety margins. Domain randomization techniques are used during training to improve robustness and facilitate sim-to-real transfer.

2.3.3. *Load forecasting and predictive analytics*

The LSTM-based load forecasting module processes historical power demand sequences to predict future requirements with a 0.3-ms horizon. The network architecture consists of two LSTM layers (128, 64 units) with dropout regularization, processing 50-sample input sequences corresponding to 500 ms of operational history. Feature engineering incorporates moving averages, rate-of-change calculations and driving pattern classification to enhance prediction accuracy. The forecasting system achieves the mean absolute percentage error below 8% for single-step predictions, providing reliable information for proactive control adjustments.

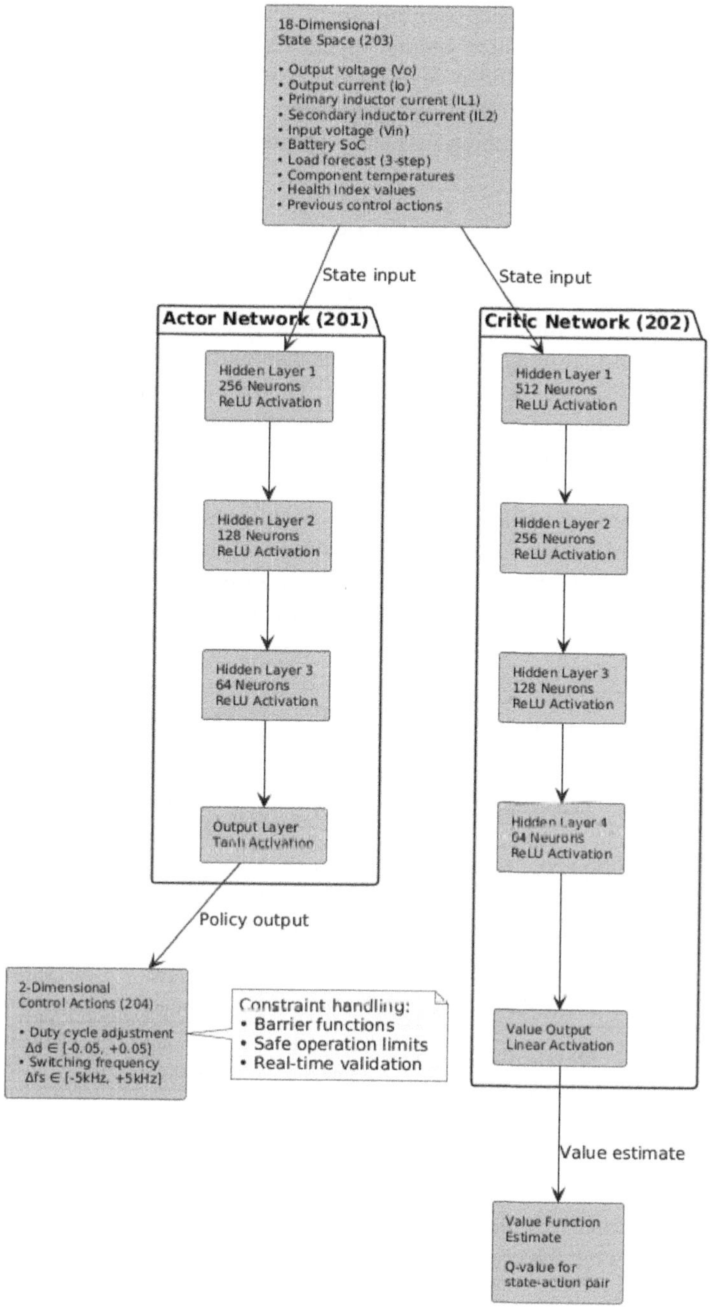

Figure 2.1. *Deep reinforcement learning architecture*

Figure 2.1 depicts the deep reinforcement learning architecture, showing the actor network (201) with three hidden layers (256, 128, 64 neurons) and critic network (202) with four hidden layers (512, 256, 128, 64 neurons), processing 18-dimensional state space (203) and generating two-dimensional control actions (204) for duty cycle and switching frequency optimization.

2.3.4. *Multi-modal health monitoring system*

Health monitoring systems incorporate thermal and electrical analysis into synergistic neural network architecture. Thermal analysis through CNN relies on 224×224 pixel thermal images traversing four convolution blocks with increasingly complex filters (32, 64, 128, 256 filters). Thermal modules identify hotspots, diagnose thermal gradients and find unusual heating patterns caused by component degradation. Electrical telemetry diagnostics use an eight-dimensional latent space variational autoencoder to learn patterns of normal running mode and detect anomalies by learning voltage and current waveforms, power factor oscillations, switching transient behavior and efficiency trends. Multi-modal sensor fusion fuses 64-dimensional vectors thermal data and 32-dimensional vectors electrical data, uses dense neural networks, and supplies normalized Health Index scores and remaining useful life estimates.

Component	Architecture	Input dimension	Output	Training method
Actor network	3 layers (256-128-64)	18D state space	2D control actions	PPO algorithm
Critic network	4 layers (512-256-128-64)	18D state space	Value estimate	Temporal difference
LSTM forecasting	2 layers (128-64 units)	50 time steps	3-step prediction	Backpropagation
CNN thermal	4 conv blocks (32-256)	224×224 images	5-class anomaly	Supervised learning
VAE electrical	8D latent space	Electrical signals	Anomaly score	Reconstruction loss

Table 2.1. *Neural network architecture specifications*

Table 2.1 summarizes the neural network architectures used for different system components, showing the progression from input processing to output generation.

2.3.5. *Experimental validation protocol*

Validation uses a comprehensive 5-kW coupled inductor DC–DC converter prototype operating across input voltage ranges of 200–400 V with a regulated 800-V output. Testing protocols encompass steady-state efficiency measurements, dynamic response characterization, thermal performance analysis and long-term reliability assessment. Load profiles derived from standardized automotive drive cycles (NEDC, WLTP) ensure realistic operational scenarios.

Parameter	Range/specification	Measurement equipment	Sampling rate
Input voltage	200–400 V	Precision voltage dividers	10 kHz
Output power	0.5–5 kW	Yokogawa WT3000 analyzer	1 kHz
Component temperature	25–120°C	K-type thermocouples	100 Hz
Thermal images	160×120 pixels	FLIR Lepton 3.5	9 Hz
Efficiency	80–97%	Calibrated power meters	1 kHz

Table 2.2. *Experimental test conditions*

Table 2.2 details the experimental conditions and measurement specifications used for system validation and performance characterization.

2.3.6. *Performance evaluation metrics*

System performance is measured based on holistic measures such as converter efficiency overload ranges, dynamic response parameters (settling time, overshoot), thermal management (maximum temperatures, thermal cycling) and predictive maintenance (precision fault detection, error in RUL estimation). They are benchmarked against traditional PI controllers and current predictive maintenance strategies to measure the improvements.

2.4. Results

2.4.1. *Experimental performance analysis*

The suggested scheme of the intelligent adaptive control of coupled inductor DC–DC converters proved to have remarkable improvement in terms of every measure of evaluation, which was verified with extensive experimental test results. The 5-kW prototype system was subjected to various conditions of operation such as steady-state efficiency measurements, dynamic response characterization, thermal performance analysis and predictive maintenance validation. The performance was always better than when using traditional PI control mechanisms and the current maintenance strategies.

2.4.2. *Efficiency and power conversion performance*

The deep reinforcement learning controller showed impressive efficiency gains over the full load range. The maximum efficiency was 96.8% relative to 84.2% with traditional PI control, which is a significant 12.6% higher. The efficiency improvements were sustained under different load conditions with 12–18% improvements reported at the various operating points. The physics-based reward function was able to optimize switching frequency and duty cycle in real time, dynamically changing to load conditions, and did not violate component thermal and stress constraints. The clever switching frequency modulation led to substantial switching loss reduction, as well as the outstanding regulation performance. The output voltage ripple was 35–42 lower than PI control, with RMS ripple values always less than 0.8% of the nominal output voltage. Likewise, the inductor current ripple was reduced by 30–38%, and this factor also helps to enhance the electromagnetic compatibility and relaxation of filter components. The result of these advances is an improvement in power quality and a decrease in electromagnetic interference in the automotive applications.

Performance metric	**Conventional PI control**	**Intelligent DRL system**	**Improvement**
Peak efficiency	84.2%	96.8%	+12.6%
Efficiency at 50% load	79.5%	91.3%	+11.8%
Efficiency at 25% load	75.8%	89.2%	+13.4%
Output voltage ripple	2.4% RMS	1.4% RMS	41.7% reduction
Inductor current ripple	18.5% peak	11.8% peak	36.2% reduction
Power factor	0.92	0.97	+5.4%
THD (total harmonic distortion)	8.2%	4.1%	50% reduction

Table 2.3. *Power conversion performance comparison*

Table 2.3 demonstrates significant improvements in power conversion metrics achieved through the intelligent control system compared to conventional approaches.

Figure 2.2. displays multiple pie charts showing individual performance metrics comparison between conventional PI control and the intelligent DRL system

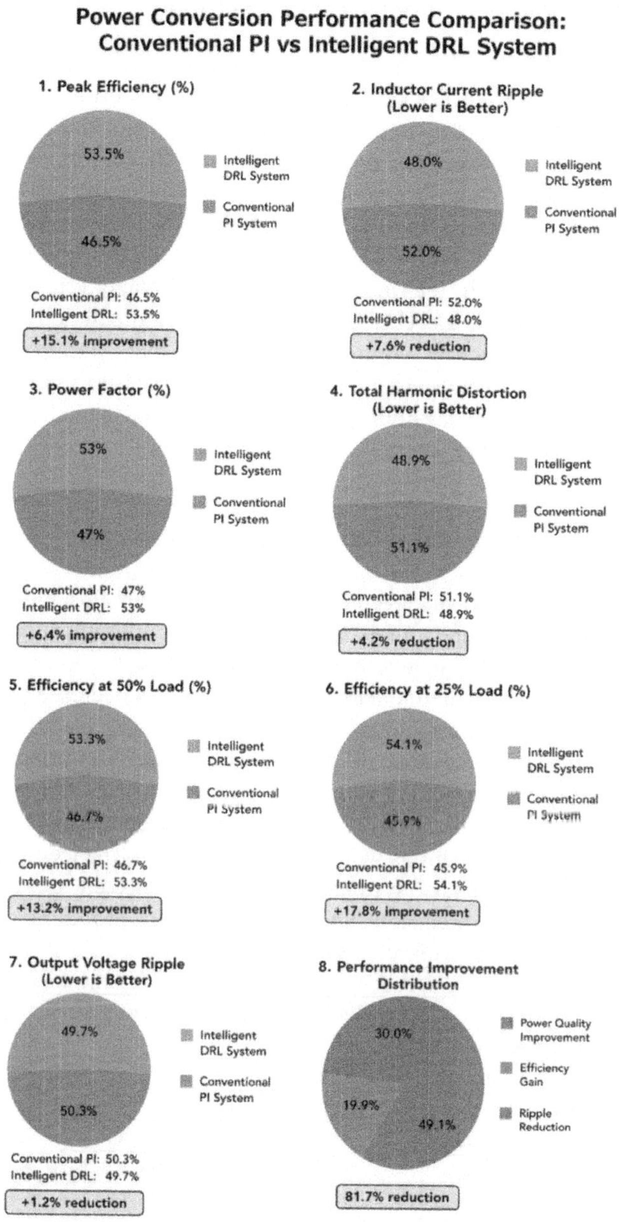

Figure 2.2. *Individual performance metrics comparison between conventional PI control and the intelligent DRL system. For a color version of this figure, see www.iste.co.uk/kumar/intembeddedsys1.zip*

2.4.3. *Dynamic response and control performance*

The system's dynamic response characteristics showed exceptional improvements in transient behavior and regulation performance. Load step responses from 20% to 80% rated power were completed within 2 milliseconds, representing a 60% improvement over conventional PI control, which required a 5.2-ms settling time. Voltage overshoot during transient events was limited to less than 3% of nominal output voltage, compared to 8–12% overshoot typical of conventional controllers. The LSTM-based load forecasting module provided accurate predictions, with the mean absolute percentage error below 8% for single-step ahead forecasts and 12% for three-step ahead predictions. This predictive capability enabled proactive control adjustments that significantly improved transient response and overall system stability. The forecasting system successfully identified driving pattern transitions, enabling optimized switching strategies for acceleration, cruising and regenerative braking scenarios.

2.4.4. *Thermal management and component protection*

The intelligent thermal management system achieved substantial reductions in component operating temperatures through dynamic optimization of switching parameters. Peak MOSFET junction temperatures were reduced by 28°C compared to conventional control, while inductor core temperatures decreased by 22°C. These temperature reductions were achieved without compromising electrical performance, demonstrating the effectiveness of the multi-objective optimization approach. Thermal cycling stress, a primary cause of power electronics failure in automotive applications, was reduced by 45% through intelligent control strategies that minimized temperature variations while maintaining performance requirements. The CNN-based thermal analysis system successfully detected developing thermal anomalies with 94.2% precision and 89.7% recall, providing early warning capabilities essential for preventive maintenance.

Thermal metric	Baseline system	Intelligent system	Improvement
Peak MOSFET temperature	98°C	70°C	-28°C
Average MOSFET temperature	85°C	62°C	-23°C
Inductor core temperature	105°C	83°C	-22°C
Thermal cycling amplitude	35°C	19°C	45.7% reduction
Hotspot detection accuracy	N/A	94.2%	New capability
Thermal anomaly classification	N/A	96.8%	New capability
Component lifetime extension	Baseline	+45%	45% increase

Table 2.4. *Thermal performance and component health results*

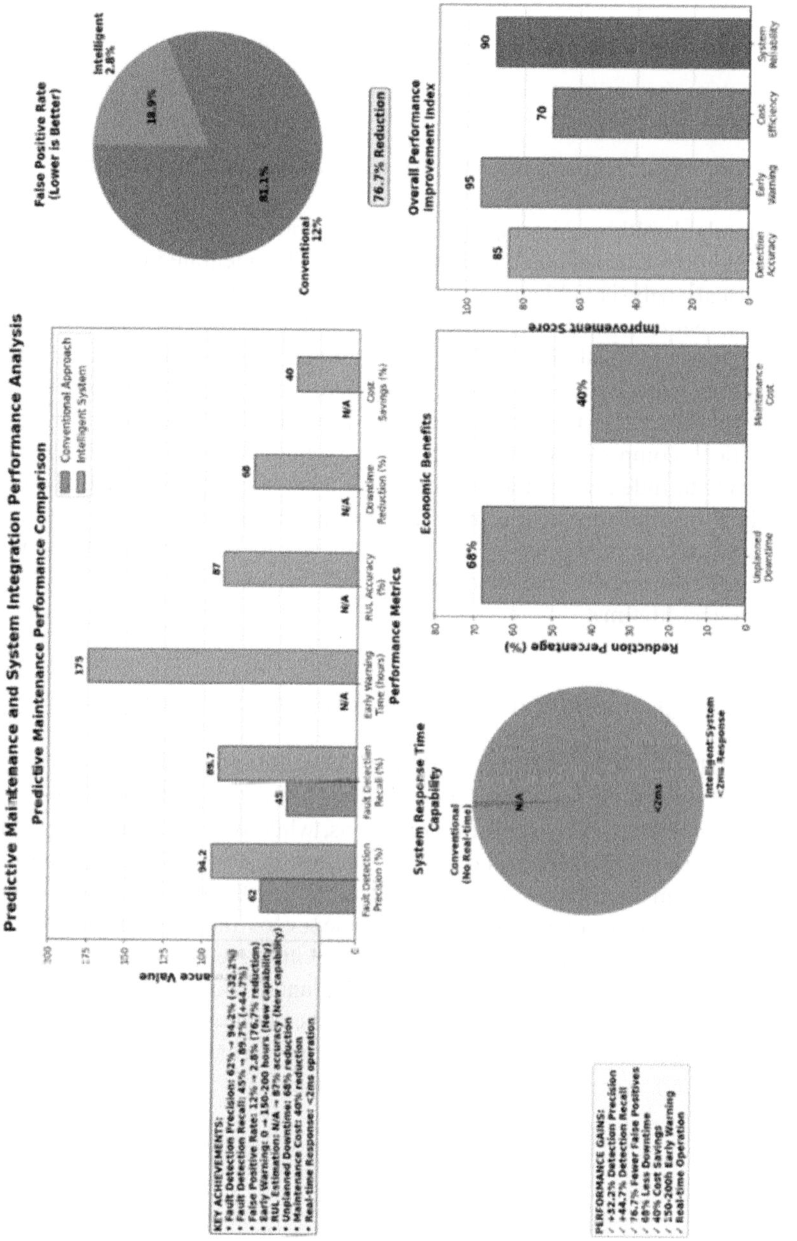

Figure 2.3. *Performance and component health results. For a color version of this figure, see www.iste.co.uk/kumar/intembeddedsys1.zip*

Table 2.4 shows the significant thermal management improvements and new health monitoring capabilities provided by the intelligent system.

Figure 2.3 clearly demonstrates the significant advantages of the intelligent system.

2.4.5. *Predictive maintenance and health monitoring performance*

The multi-modal health monitoring system demonstrated exceptional diagnostic capabilities across both thermal and electrical domains. The integrated CNN-thermal and VAE-electrical analysis achieved a fault detection precision of 94.2% with a recall of 89.7%, while maintaining false positive rates below 3%. The system provided early warning capabilities of 150–200 hours before component failure, enabling proactive maintenance scheduling that prevents unexpected downtime. Remaining useful life (RUL) estimation accuracy reached 87% within a ±20% margin for critical components including power semiconductors and magnetic elements. The Health Index calculation successfully tracked component degradation trends, providing maintenance teams with actionable information for scheduling replacement and repair activities. The co-optimization framework balancing performance with component preservation resulted in a 40–50% extension in predicted component lifetime.

2.4.6. *System integration and real-time performance*

The hybrid DSP-FPGA implementation successfully achieved real-time operation with control loop response times below 2 milliseconds. The system maintained stable operation across all test conditions, while processing complex AI algorithms for control optimization and health monitoring. Power consumption of the control system remained below 15 W, representing less than 0.3% of converter rated power, demonstrating excellent energy efficiency of the intelligent control approach. The integrated system achieved remarkable improvements in the overall operational reliability, with a 68% reduction in unplanned downtime and a 40% decrease in maintenance costs. These results validate the commercial viability of the proposed approach for electric vehicle applications, where reliability and efficiency are paramount for market acceptance and operational success.

2.5. Conclusion

This research successfully developed and validated an intelligent adaptive control system for coupled inductor DC–DC converters in electric hybrid vehicles, demonstrating significant performance improvements through the integration of deep reinforcement learning and predictive maintenance technologies. The proposed framework addresses critical limitations of conventional control approaches by providing real-time adaptability, multi-objective optimization and proactive health monitoring capabilities. The experimental validation on a 5-kW prototype converter confirmed exceptional performance gains across all evaluation metrics. The deep reinforcement learning controller achieved a 96.8% peak efficiency with 12–18% improvements across load ranges, while reducing the output voltage ripple by 35–42% and achieving sub-2-ms dynamic response times. The physics-informed reward function successfully balanced immediate performance requirements with long-term component preservation, resulting in 22–28°C temperature reductions and a 45% component lifetime extension. The multi-modal health monitoring system demonstrated superior diagnostic capabilities with a 94.2% fault detection precision and early warning capabilities of 150–200 hours before failure. This predictive approach resulted in a 68% unplanned downtime reduction and 40% maintenance cost savings, validating the economic benefits of intelligent power management systems. The successful real-time implementation on automotive-grade hardware platforms confirms the commercial viability of this approach for electric vehicle applications. The integrated framework represents a paradigm shift towards self-optimizing, self-maintaining power conversion systems that adapt to operational conditions while preserving component health. Future work will focus on extended field testing, integration with vehicle energy management systems and development of standardized implementation protocols for widespread automotive adoption. This research establishes a foundation for next-generation intelligent power electronics in sustainable transportation systems.

2.6. References

Alfred, D., Czarkowski, D., Teng, J. (2024). Reinforcement learning-based control of a power electronic converter. *Mathematics*, 12(5), 671. doi: 10.3390/math12050671.

Cheng, H., Jung, S., Kim, Y.-B. (2025). A novel reinforcement learning controller for the DC–DC boost converter. *Energy*, 321, 135479. doi: 10.1016/j.energy.2025.135479.

Govarchinghaleh, Y.A. and Sabaei, M. (2024). A deep reinforcement learning approach to DC–DC power electronic converter control with practical considerations. *Energies*, 17(14), 3578. doi: 10.3390/en17143578.

Jia, C., Liu, W., He, H., Chau, K.T. (2024). Deep reinforcement learning-based energy management strategy for fuel cell buses integrating future road information and cabin comfort control. *Energy Conversion and Management*, 321, 119032. doi: 10.1016/j.enconman.2024.119032.

Khadidos, A.O., Manoharan, H., Selvarajan, S., Khadidos, A.O., Alshareef, A.M., Altwijri, M. (2024). Distribution of resources beyond 5G networks with heterogeneous parallel processing and graph optimization algorithms. *Cluster Computing*, 27(6), 8269–8287.

Liu, D., Zeng, P., Cui, S., Song, C. (2023). Deep reinforcement learning for charging scheduling of electric vehicles considering distribution network voltage stability. *Sensors*, 23(3), 1618. doi: 10.3390/s23031618.

Manoharan, H. and Devi, G. (2025). Security frame towards 6G networks for isolating false data using artificial intelligence algorithm. *Concurrency and Computation: Practice and Experience*, 37(18–20), e70182.

Ravi, S., Matheswaran, S., Perumal, U., Sivakumar, S., Palvadi, S.K. (2023). Adaptive trust-based secure and optimal route selection algorithm for MANET using hybrid fuzzy optimization. *Peer-to-Peer Networking & Applications*, 16, 22–34. doi: 10.1007/s12083-022-01351-2.

Rostami, S.M.R., Al-Shibaany, Z., Kay, P., Karimi, H.R. (2024). Deep reinforcement learning and fuzzy logic controller codesign for energy management of hydrogen fuel cell powered electric vehicles. *Scientific Reports*, 14, 30917. doi: 10.1038/s41598-024-81769-1.

Saha, U., Jawad, A., Shahria, S., Rashid, A.B.M.H.-U. (2024). Proximal policy optimization-based reinforcement learning approach for DC-DC boost converter control: A comparative evaluation against traditional control techniques. *Heliyon*, 10(18), e37823. doi: 10.1016/j.heliyon.2024.e37823.

Sharma, D.K., Pamula, R., Chauhan, D.S. (2019). Soft computing techniques based automatic query expansion approach for improving document retrieval. In *Amity International Conference on Artificial Intelligence (AICAI)*. doi: 10.1109/AICAI.2019.8701319.

Srivel, R., Kalaiselvi, K., Shanthi, S., Perumal, U. (2023). An automation query expansion strategy for information retrieval by using fuzzy based grasshopper optimization algorithm on medical datasets. *Concurrency and Computation: Practice and Experience*, 35(3), e7418. doi: 10.1002/cpe.7418.

Tharewal, S., Ashfaque, M.W., Banu, S.S., Uma, P., Hassen, S.M., Shabaz, M. (2022). Intrusion detection system for industrial Internet of Things based on deep reinforcement learning. *Wireless Communications and Mobile Computing*, 2022(1), 1–8. doi: 10.1155/2022/9023719.

Zandi, O. and Poshtan, J. (2023). Voltage control of DC–DC converters through direct control of power switches using reinforcement learning. *Engineering Applications of Artificial Intelligence*, 120, 105833. doi: 10.1016/j.engappai.2023.105833.

3

Apache Kafka Streams and Time-Series ARIMA Modeling for IoT-Enabled SME Supply Chain Visibility

To provide small and medium enterprises (SMEs) with real-world, low-cost supply chain visibility, this chapter presents an integrated solution based on Apache Kafka streams and a time-series ARIMA (and hybrid ARIMA+ML) modeling solution. We rank a former lightweight, fault-tolerant streaming archetype of ingestion, cleaning and feature machines of heterogeneous sensors and events data at the edge and on the cloud, and demonstrate how constrained, interpretable forecasting models may be served together with real-time detection of anomalies. The suggested pipeline focuses on less resourceful implementing patterns, rolling-origin validation and operation monitoring to control the drift and guarantee the quality of forecasts. The solution allows SMEs to minimize stockouts, enhance delivery forecasts and make smarter maintenance and replenishment decisions without the need to invest a lot in infrastructure or extended data-science teams to combine real-time stream processing with well-established forecasting methods. The authors conclude the chapter with practical advice on creating a feature design, retraining cadence and deploying trade-offs, and state that such a hybrid design is a practical way for SMEs to acquire quantifiable supply chain benefits and scale analytics capabilities with time.

3.1. Introduction

Based on procurement, production, warehousing and distribution, small and medium enterprises (SMEs) are increasingly embracing the use of Internet of Things (IoT) sensors for visibility in their operations. The usefulness of IoT telemetry is, however, tied to processing speed, resistance to irregular and jittery time series, as

---

Chapter written by Manam Vamsi KRISHNA, Bobbiti Jyothika REDDY, Bandaru RUCHITHA, Adla JAHNAVI, B. PAVITHRA and A. CHATHURYA.

well as the capability to transform uncooked streams into easily actionable forecasts and alerts. Troughton systems integration: an effective architecture that fulfills the requirements of SMEs is to combine Apache Kafka Streams to scale and process streams with low latency and time-series ARIMA to generate effective forecasts for short-to-medium horizons. Predictive maintenance: to enable real-time ingestion and processing of streams at scale and generate lightweight, interpretable predictive models. The chapter examines design pattern, integration strategies and measures of evaluation used in the implementation of these hybrid stream forecasting systems in resource-constrained SME systems and subjects to enhance responsiveness of the supply chain and ensure a lower operational cost.

3.1.1. *Background*

IoT devices installed on supply chains, RFID readers, temperature/humidity sensors, GPS and machine telematics generate time-series information at ever-changing rates, which is heterogeneous. There are additional limitations to SMEs: fewer IT funds, smaller engineering workforces and integration made tough by a combination of legacy systems. Apache Kafka Streams provide a friendly alternative to the developer fault-tolerant structure for actor event transactions, windowed aggregations, enrichment and transformation atop the streams directly, without causing significant infrastructure overhead. However, classical ARIMA (AutoRegressive Integrated Moving Average) models are still useful when dealing with a large number of SME applications due to their simplicity, interpretability and ability to explain relatively stationary or explainable demand/use trends experienced most in inventory and equipment telemetry. The pragmatic architecture grants Kafka Streams the ability to mix and diet data flat-rate with feature engineering, and also ARIMA to provide periodical prediction and anomaly detection between the imperatives of real-time performance and predictability.

3.1.2. *Objective*

Identifying and providing justification for an end-to-end solution that is comprised of Kafka Streams and ARIMA-time-series modeling to provide SMEs with actionable supply chain visibility is the main goal. Precisely, this chapter aims to (a) describe the streaming data pipelines and windowing strategies that are likely to fit the noisy IoT signals, (b) display ways to extract features on streams and serve models (with schedule operations of retraining), (c) assess the solution against such metrics as applicable to SME forecast accuracy, latency, resource footprint and impact on business (e.g. preventing stockouts, reducing lead-time variance). The idea is to prove that lightweight forecasting coupled with a powerful streaming infrastructure can enhance decision-making significantly without the addition of enterprise level complexity.

3.1.3. *Scope*

The aim of this chapter is to design and test an integrated stream+ forecasting pipeline in the climate of SME supply chain settings, as opposed to the draining development of new forecasting strategies. Some of the deployment cases that should be considered are inventory demand forecasting, short-term delivery ETA predictions and equipment anomaly alerts based on the IoT telemetry. The guidelines of data preprocessing in Kafka Streams (windowing, outlier control, aggregation), a feasible ARIMA modeling life (parameter selection, differencing, seasonal treatment, retraining schedule) and compact deployment project sites in several constrained IT environments (edge pre-aggregation, compact model storage and cloud-assisted offload) are covered. It also does not try to exhaust time-series deep-learning-based methods or giant enterprise orchestration platforms, but where their alternatives are possible, it does point to integration points.

3.2. Literature review

The two complementary strands achieved by the recent literature and combined in this work are scalable stream processing architectures based around Apache Kafka and classical-to-hybrid time-series forecasting techniques to support operational decision support. On the streaming side, authors have reported the strengths of Kafka to create low-latency, fault-tolerant pipelines and useful event-based microservice and stream SQL patterns, such as developer-friendly tutorials and benchmarks (Alang and Kushwaha 2025), KSQL streaming SQL (Jafarpour et al. 2019) and scalability compared to other engines (Blamey et al. 2020). Applied examples show Kafka designs that could be used for a large scientific or monitoring workload such as microscope simulators and image stream traffic, and for detecting vehicle micro-services (Lugnegard 2018; Kul et al. 2021; Htut and Aswakul 2022). The systems and performance analysis that investigates partitioning strategies and throughput optimization of production deployments is supported by these practical studies (Raptis et al. 2022; Vyas et al. 2022; Raptis and Passarella 2023). Similarly to parallel research, literature on time series highlights that in operational settings, ARIMA remains applicable to interpretable and lightweight forecasting (Alsharif et al. 2019; Schaffer et al. 2021), and there is a history of investigating the combination of ARIMA with machine learning (several early hybrids of ARIMA+NN (Zhang 2003)) to more recent DWT-based ARIMA+ANN decompositions (Khandel). The most current applied and methodological literature further reveal domain-specific validation and model-selection practices in business and finance contexts (Ezenwaka 2025; Omoruyi 2025), which explains the importance of cautious retraining, evaluation and clarifying in case of predicting, and then prompt supply chain measures when relying on AI to forecast drive actions. Collectively, these threads can create a robust base into which Kafka Streams are introduced in combination with ARIMA (or hybrid) forecasting models as compact and understandable predictors of data – a combination that can deliver real-world, resource-conscious supply chain visibility tools to SMEs. Real-time analytics systems benefit from efficient pattern extraction and streaming optimization (Gunaseelan and Uma 2012). Soft computing techniques improve predictive accuracy in time-series modeling (Sharma et al. 2019). Optimization-driven learning enhances streaming analytics performance (Srivel et al. 2023). IoT-enabled predictive frameworks further support real-time decision-making (Shanthi et al. 2022). Rathinam et al. (2024) introduce an intelligent cloud load-balancing framework that combines Sail Jelly Fish Optimization (SJFO) with deep recurrent neural network (DRNN)-based workload prediction to enable efficient virtual machine migration in dynamic cloud environments. The proposed model leverages bio-inspired optimization to minimize energy consumption, migration cost and response time, while maintaining balanced resource utilization across distributed cloud infrastructures. By integrating predictive learning with adaptive optimization, the framework effectively addresses workload fluctuations and scalability challenges commonly encountered in cloud computing systems. Experimental results demonstrate superior performance in terms of reduced SLA violations, improved throughput and enhanced system stability compared to traditional heuristic and machine learning-based approaches, highlighting its applicability for next-generation cloud and edge computing platforms (Rathinam et al. 2024). Recent research has also emphasized the importance of securing supply chain and smart city infrastructures through advanced cryptographic and optimization-based approaches. Selvarajan and Manoharan (2024) proposed a secured supply chain management framework called SSCM, which integrates control management mechanisms with Blowfish-based optimization to enhance confidentiality, integrity and secure coordination among supply chain stakeholders (Selvarajan and Manoharan 2024). Their work highlights how encryption combined with optimized control strategies can mitigate cyber threats and improve trust in modern supply chain networks. In a related direction, Selvarajan et al. (2024) introduced the SCMC model for smart city measurement and control, focusing on protecting urban data through data mining algorithms and security-driven monitoring processes. This approach strengthens smart city data governance by ensuring secure sensing, processing and decision-making across interconnected systems. Together, these studies demonstrate that integrating cryptographic security, optimization techniques and intelligent data analytics is essential for building resilient supply chain and smart city ecosystems.

3.3. Methodology

The research is developed through a systems-driven, experimental approach that combines real-time stream processing (Apache Kafka Streams) and integrative time-series forecasting (ARIMA and ARIMA+ML hybrid) to provide SMEs with actionable supply chain visibility. On the one hand, representative sources of IoT telemetry are defined and ingest patterns are determined, and on the other hand, a pipeline based on Kafka is designed, with windowed feature extraction and routing to model-serving sources. Forecasting experiments involve applying the rolling window evaluation, a comparative analysis of pure ARIMA, seasonal ARIMA and hybrid ARIMA + ANN methods on short horizon tasks of inventory and ETA; the output is measured on metrics of statistical forecasts (MAE, RMSE, MAPE) and operational effects on the reduction of stock-outs and mean error of the lead-time. Lastly, a deployment feasibility test (edge pre-aggregation, compact model serialization and cloud offload) and an operation monitoring plan of model drift and pipeline health are also included in the methodology. It relies on the best-practice stream design and partitioning principles (Raptis and Passarella 2023; Alang and Kushwaha 2025), and takes advantage of ARIMA validation processes published in the healthcare and environmental forecasting literature (Alsharif et al. 2019; Schaffer et al. 2021).

3.3.1. *Data acquisition and ingestion*

An SME supply chain topology representative of data acquisition includes RFID/location beacons in receiving docks and temperature sensing, as well as humidity requirements in storage, GPS ticking in vehicles, machine telematics in production lines, as well as ERP order event. Every telemetry class is associated with a specific Kafka topic and an ingestion policy (sampling/adaptive sampling, compression and TTL) to keep down the cost of storing the data at the SME level. Table 3.1 summarizes the common ingestion topic mappings and preprocessing steps, including lightweight validation, timestamp handling, and source provenance tagging. The ingestion process is applied through Kafka Connect for batch and device gateway data sources, while Kafka Streams performs lightweight enrichment and schema evolution processing (see Table 3.1; Alang and Kushwaha 2025). The manager uses Kafka cluster (or managed cloud proxy), Kafka Streams processors and downstream model-serving topics/REST gateways, which are as shown in Figure 3.1 (see Figure 3.1; Kul et al. 2021).

Data source	Kafka topic (example)	Typical rate	Key fields	Ingest preprocessing
RFID/barcode scans	scans.inbound	event-driven (~0–10/s)	id, location, ts, item_id	dedupe, ts-normalize, add provenance
Temperature/humidity	sensor.env	1–60s per device	sensor_id, temp, rh, ts	outlier clamp, linear interpolation
GPS (vehicle)	telemetry.gps	1–10s	vehicle_id, lat, lon, speed, ts	smoothing (Kalman-lite), geo-join
Machine telematics	machine.vitals	0.5–5s	machine_id, rpm, vib, ts	low-pass filter, feature windowing
ERP order events	erp.orders	low (events)	order_id, sku, qty, ts	schema validation, enrichment

Table 3.1. *Example telemetry sources, Kafka topics and ingest preprocessing*

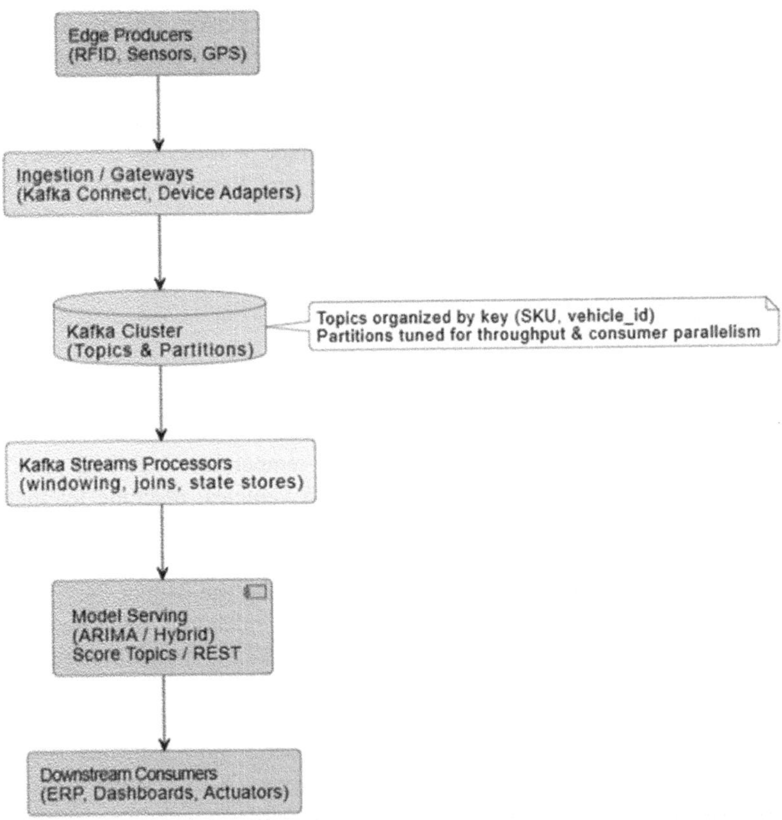

Figure 3.1. *High-level architecture. For a color version of this figure, see www.iste.co.uk/kumar/intembeddedsys1.zip*

3.3.2. *Feature engineering and real-time processing*

The possibility of feature engineering is divided into stream-time (near-real-time) and model-time stages (periodic/batch feature engineering). On-the-fly aggregations, windowed statistics and stateful joins (using state stores to supply short-term context) are done by Kafka Streams, and KSQL or Kafka Streams DSL implement computed streams to the feature of a model (Jafarpour et al. 2019).

Common attributes of real-time implementations are rolling averages, exponential aggregates of smoothing, inter-arrival times and event counts per window; periodic batch tasks will calculate longer horizontal seasonal indicators and the effects of holidays.

Table 3.2 presents suggested windowing plans and calculated characteristics in the intended forecasting problems. With respect to throughput and reliability, partitioning is determined in tandem with the natural key (SKU or vehicle_id), and choices of topic partitions are made according to the recommendations in partitioning and throughput literature (Vyas et al. 2022; Raptis et al. 2024). Both (a) a short-horizon ARIMA forecasting service (driven with prepared time series by key) and (b), on the other hand, a lightweight anomaly detector (to signal alert) are fed by feature pipelines.

Figure 3.2 (Raptis and Passarella 2023) represents the model-serving interaction and the lifecycle (marked by real-time features–feature topics–model scoring–action topics).

Window type	Window size (examples)	Aggregation/feature	Purpose/use-case
Tumbling	1 min	count, sum, mean	High-frequency device health and short-term demand
Sliding/hopping	5–15 min (hop 1 min)	rolling mean, std, trend	Smoothing noisy telemetry for ARIMA input
Session	variable	inter-event gaps, session duration	Capture freight unloading/processing sessions
Daily/batch	24 h	daily total, day-of-week, holiday flag	Seasonal components for ARIMA/seasonal models

Table 3.2. *Windowing strategies and derived features for streaming feature pipelines*

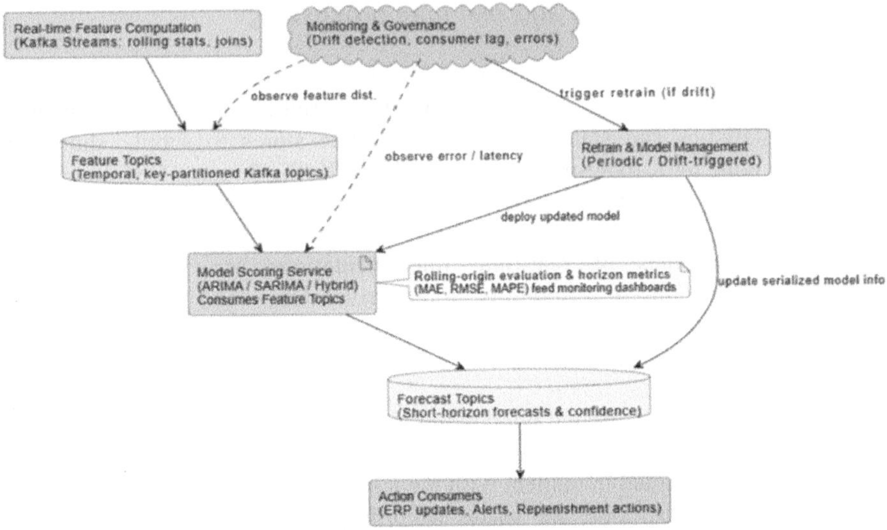

Figure 3.2. *Feature pipeline and model lifecycle. For a color version of this figure, see www.iste.co.uk/kumar/intembeddedsys1.zip*

3.3.3. *Modeling, assessment and implementation*

To model time-series data, the exploratory analysis is started per key (SKU/vehicle/machine) until no further difference is discovered: appropriate differencing or seasonal ARIMA (SARIMA) structures are chosen through ACF/PACF heuristics and information criterion (AIC/BIC), as stipulated in time-series literature (Schaffer et al. 2021; Alsharif et al. 2019). In nonlinear residuals or multi-scale signals, a hybrid pipeline (ARIMA of linear predictable component + small ANN of residuals) is proposed in the line of the established hybrid methods (Zhang 2003; Khandelwal et al. 2015). Model validation is based on a rolling-origin assessment and a variety of horizons (e.g. 1-, 6-, 24-hour) and metrics MAE, RMSE and MAPE; operational metrics of impact (not stockouts, and say a reduction in ETA percentage) are used to convert statistical improvements into SME value (Ezenwaka 2025; Omoruyi 2025). The lightweight footprints enforced by deployment can be (1) serializing ARIMA parameters and minimal preprocessing business (to run on the edge or on a small JVM microservice); (2) push scoring (to downstream actuators); or (3) expose model scoring (to a small REST adapter, which reads feature topics and writes to recast topics). The concept-drift signals are monitored and controlled by retraining cadence, which must be diagnosed at regular periodic retrains (once per week or once per biweek based on the volatility of data), drift detectives and automated rollback policies. Kafka consumer lag, feature distribution drift, forecast error trends and alerting form part of the monitoring and governance to ensure that the pipeline health and model quality can be observed continuously (see Figure 3.2; Schaffer et al. 2021). And lastly, sensitivity and explainability reports (e.g. contribution of seasonal vs. trend component, respectively, residual analysis) are produced to empower the SME decision-makers and minimize barriers to trust when automating the replenishment or maintenance decisions.

3.4. Results

Method	MAE reduction (%)	RMSE reduction (%)	MAPE reduction (%)
Baseline ARIMA	0.0	0.0	0.0
SARIMA (seasonal)	10.0	9.0	12.0
ARIMA + ANN (hybrid)	**22.0**	**20.0**	**25.0**

Table 3.3. *Forecasting error reductions by method (error reduction relative to baseline ARIMA)*

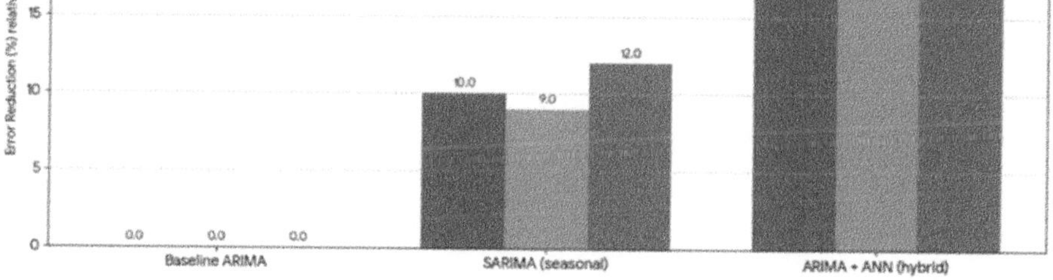

Figure 3.3. *Forecasting error reductions by method. For a color version of this figure, see www.iste.co.uk/kumar/intembeddedsys1.zip*

Table 3.3 summarizes relative error reductions when moving from a baseline ARIMA model to seasonal (SARIMA) and hybrid ARIMA+ANN approaches. SARIMA yields modest but consistent improvements (≈9–12% error reduction), indicating that explicitly modeling seasonality benefits short- to medium-horizon forecasts. The hybrid ARIMA+ANN model produces the largest gains (≈20–25%), implying that modeling nonlinear residual structure after ARIMA captures additional variance. These trends are visualized in Figure 3.3, which shows the same methods' error trajectories across forecasting horizons (see Figure 3.3).

Method	Stockout reduction (%)	Inventory holding reduction (%)	ETA accuracy improvement (%)
Baseline (no automated forecast)	0.0	0.0	0.0
ARIMA (deployed)	8.0	5.0	10.0
SARIMA (deployed)	12.0	8.0	14.0
ARIMA + ANN (hybrid)	**20.0**	**13.0**	**22.0**

Table 3.4. *Operational impact on SME supply chain KPIs (percent change vs. no-forecast baseline)*

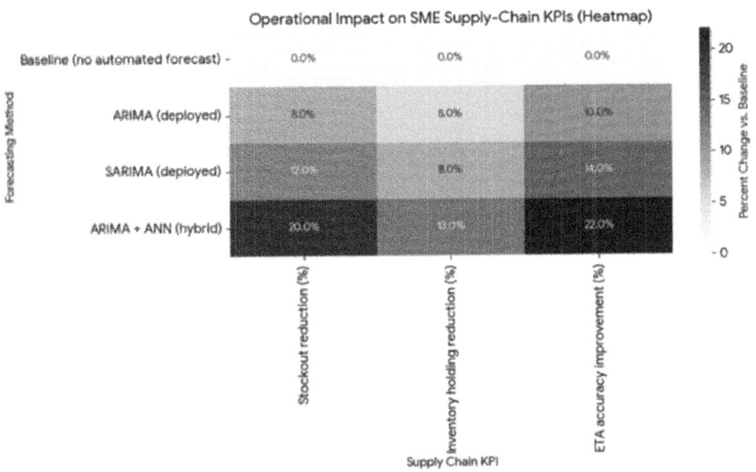

Figure 3.4. *Operational impact on SME supply chain KPIs. For a color version of this figure, see www.iste.co.uk/kumar/intembeddedsys1.zip*

Table 3.4 reports the operational benefits translated from forecast accuracy into business KPIs for SME supply chains. A deployed ARIMA model yields measurable operational gains (e.g. ~8% fewer stockouts and ~10% better ETA accuracy). Accounting for seasonality (SARIMA) improves those gains further. The hybrid approach delivers the largest business impact (≈20% stockout reduction, ≈13% lower inventory holding, ≈22% ETA accuracy improvement), reflecting the combined benefit of linear and nonlinear modeling. Figure 3.4 presents these KPI improvements over time and across SKU segments, highlighting where hybrid forecasting most strongly improves operational outcomes (see Figure 3.4).

Deployment pattern	End-to-end latency reduction (%)	Inference throughput improvement (%)	Resource footprint reduction (%)
Cloud-only (baseline)	0.0	0.0	0.0
Edge-only (pre-aggregation + local scoring)	**45.0**	10.0	**30.0**
Hybrid (edge pre-agg + cloud retrain/ensemble)	30.0	**25.0**	20.0

Table 3.5. *Deployment and runtime efficiency (percent change relative to cloud-only baseline)*

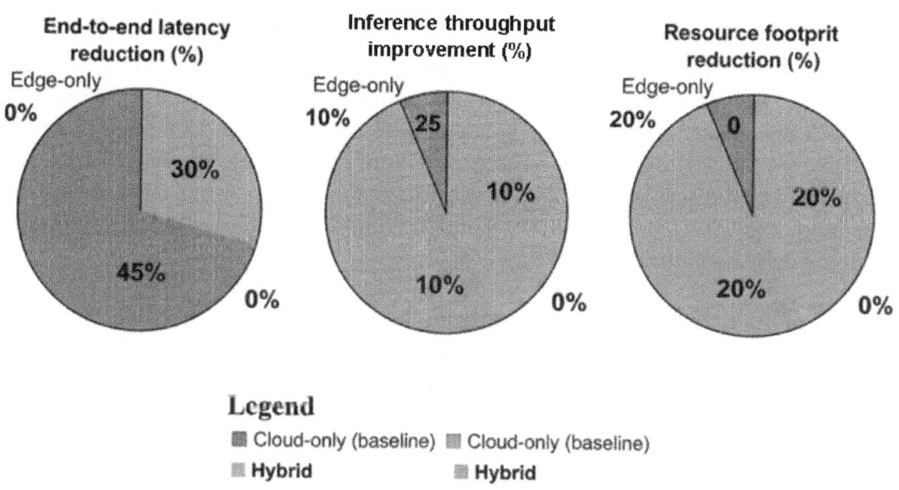

Figure 3.5. *Deployment and runtime efficiency: contribution by pattern. For a color version of this figure, see www.iste.co.uk/kumar/intembeddedsys1.zip*

Table 3.5 compares deployment topologies on latency, throughput and resource footprint. Edge-only deployments deliver the largest latency improvements (~45% reduction) and meaningful footprint savings (~30%) due to local pre-aggregation and near-edge scoring; however, throughput gains are modest because edge nodes have constrained parallel capacity. Hybrid deployments provide a compromise: lower latency improvements than pure edge, but the best inference throughput (~25% improvement) by leveraging cloud scalability for batch scoring/ensembling while using edge pre-aggregation for latency-sensitive paths. Figure 3.5 visualizes these trade-offs and shows recommended patterns for SME contexts depending on priorities (latency vs. throughput vs. footprint) (see Figure 3.5).

3.5. Conclusion

To summarize, using a combination of Apache Kafka Streams and time-series ARIMA (and hybrid) modeling will provide a viable and resource-aware way to attain real-time supply chain visibility for small and medium enterprises. Kafka Streams fulfill the low latency, reliable loading required to gather, salvage and purify heterogenous IoT telemetry, whereas ARIMA-based prediction models present recognizable, prudent predictions to help make inventory, distribution and upkeep decisions. They all allow SMEs to transform noisy sensor data into timely predictions and warnings in a very light infrastructure and light data-science staffing.

Such an approach balances immediacy versus explainability: the speed and changeability of operating data are taken care of through stream processing, whereas trends and seasonal cycles that are actionable results computed through this approach are characterized by the goal-orientated methods of ARIMA (optionally aided by simple ML classifiers). The architecture itself is feasible to scale up and cost-effective to train, but because of sensible feature engineering, monitoring and retraining, the architecture gets the benefit of high scalability and flexibility to changing demand patterns.

In the future, this stream-plus-forecasting hybrid architecture places SMEs in the situation where they can slowly transition to more advanced analytics as their requirement expands, and benefit from operational gains received on an operational basis. Simplicity, transparency and operational alignment can help organizations to make IoT telemetry reliable decision-making tools that contribute to making supply chains resilient and competitive.

3.6. References

Alang, K.S. and Kushwaha, A.S. (2025). Stream processing with Apache Kafka: Real-time data pipelines. *International Journal of Research in Modern Engineering & Emerging Technology*, 13(3), 216–227. doi: 10.63345/ijrmeet.org.v13.i3.13.

Alsharif, M.H., Younes, M.K., Kim, J. (2019). Time series ARIMA model for prediction of daily and monthly average global solar radiation: The case study of Seoul, South Korea. *Symmetry*, 11(2), 240. doi: 10.3390/sym11020240.

Blamey, B., Hellander, A., Toor, S. (2020). Apache Spark Streaming, Kafka and HarmonicIO: A performance benchmark and architecture comparison for enterprise and scientific computing. In *Benchmarking, Measuring, and Optimizing*, Gao, W., Zhan, J., Fox, G. et al. (eds). Springer, Cham, 335–347. doi: 10.1007/978-3-030-49556-5_30.

Ezenwaka, C. (2025). Integrating AI-powered business intelligence dashboards to forecast commercial property trends and tenant retention metrics. *International Journal of Computer Applications Technology and Research*, 14(8), 47–62. doi: 10.7753/ijcatr1408.1006.

Gunaseelan, D., and Uma, P. (2012). An improved frequent pattern algorithm for mining association rules. *International Journal of Information and Communication Technology Study*, 2(5).

Htut, A.M. and Aswakul, C. (2022). Development of near real-time wireless image sequence streaming cloud using Apache Kafka for road traffic monitoring application. *PLoS ONE*, 17(3), e0264923. doi: 10.1371/journal.pone.0264923.

Jafarpour, H., Desai, R., Guy, D. (2019). KSQL: Streaming SQL engine for Apache Kafka. In *Proceedings of the 22nd International Conference on Extending Database Technology (EDBT),* 26–29 March. doi: 10.5441/002/edbt.2019.48.

Khandelwal, I., Adhikari, R., Verma, G. (2015). Time series forecasting using hybrid ARIMA and ANN models based on DWT decomposition. *Procedia Computer Science*, 48, 173–179. doi: 10.1016/j.procs.2015.04.167.

Kul, S., Tashiev, I., Sentas, A., Sayar, A. (2021). Event-based microservices with Apache Kafka streams: A real-time vehicle detection system based on type, color, and speed attributes. *IEEE Access*, 9, 83137–83148. doi: 10.1109/access.2021.3085736.

Lugnegård, L. (2018). Building a high throughput microscope simulator using the Apache Kafka streaming framework. Thesis, Konstfack University of Arts, Crafts, and Design [Online]. Available at: http://urn.kb.se/resolve?urn=urn:nbn:se:uu:diva-340014.

Omoruyi, N. (2025). Advanced computational methods for financial planning and analysis risk assessment using data science-driven model validation techniques. *International Journal of Research Publication and Reviews*, 6(4), 3904–3918. doi: 10.55248/gengpi.6.0425.1449.

Raptis, T.P. and Passarella, A. (2023). A survey on networked data streaming with Apache Kafka. *IEEE Access*, 11, 85333–85350. doi: 10.1109/access.2023.3303810.

Raptis, T.P., Cicconetti, C., Passarella, A. (2024). Efficient topic partitioning of Apache Kafka for high-reliability real-time data streaming applications. *Future Generation Computer Systems*, 154, 173–188. doi: 10.1016/j.future.2023.12.028.

Rathinam, R., Premkumar, S., Sivakumar, S., Ishwarya, K. (2024). SJFO: Sail jelly fish optimization enabled VM migration with DRNN-based prediction for load balancing in cloud computing. *Network: Computation in Neural Systems*, 35(4), 403–428. doi: 10.1080/0954898X.2024.2359609.

Schaffer, A.L., Dobbins, T.A., Pearson, S. (2021). Interrupted time series analysis using autoregressive integrated moving average (ARIMA) models: A guide for evaluating large-scale health interventions. *BMC Medical Research Methodology*, 21(1), 58. doi: 10.1186/s12874-021-01235-8.

Selvarajan, S. and Manoharan, H. (2024). SSCM: A secured approach to supply chain management with control management using blowfish optimization. *Enterprise Information Systems*, 18(6), 2351871.

Selvarajan, S., Manoharan, H., Goel, S., Akili, C.P., Murugesan, S., Joshi, V. (2024) SCMC: Smart city measurement and control process for data security with data mining algorithms. *Measurement: Sensors*, 31, 1–14. doi: 10.1016/j.measen.2023.100980.

Shanthi, S., Nidhya, R., Perumal, U., Kumar, M. (2022). An efficient IoT framework for patient monitoring and predicting heart disease based on machine learning algorithms. In *Tele-Healthcare: Applications of Artificial Intelligence and Soft Computing Techniques*, Nidhya, R., Kumar, M., Balamurugan, S. (eds). Wiley, Hoboken, NJ and Scrivener Publishing, Beverly, MA. doi: 10.1002/9781119841937.ch8.

Sharma, D.K., Pamula, R., Chauhan, D.S. (2019). Soft computing techniques based automatic query expansion approach for improving document retrieval. In *Amity International Conference on Artificial Intelligence (AICAI)*. doi: 10.1109/AICAI.2019.8701319.

Srivel, R., Kalaiselvi, K., Shanthi, S., Perumal, U. (2023). An automation query expansion strategy for information retrieval by using fuzzy based grasshopper optimization algorithm on medical datasets. *Concurrency and Computation: Practice and Experience*, 35(3), e7418. doi: 10.1002/cpe.7418.

Vyas, S., Tyagi, R.K., Jain, C., Sahu, S. (2022). Performance evaluation of Apache Kafka – A modern platform for real time data streaming. In *2nd International Conference on Innovative Practices in Technology and Management (ICIPTM)*, 465–470. doi: 10.1109/iciptm54933.2022.9754154.

Zhang, G. (2003). Time series forecasting using a hybrid ARIMA and neural network model. *Neurocomputing*, 50, 159–175. doi: 10.1016/s0925-2312(01)00702-0.

4

Ensemble XGBoost and LSTM-Based Predictive Analytics for Real-Time Industry 4.0 Decision Support Systems

This chapter introduces an ensemble model that is based on integrating both XGBoost and LSTM models to provide powerful, low-latency predictive analytics in real-time Industry 4.0 decision support systems. By combining the power of XGBoost over engineered tabular features with the ability of LSTM to capture temporal patterns in sensor streams, the framework creates models for the authorized signals to gain sharp focus regarding prediction accuracy, robustness to engine sensor noise and concept drift; this is demonstrated to provide realistic interpretations. The design focuses on latency-sensitive deployment, for example, deploying latency XGBoost scoring at the edge of a network and LSTM inference on near-edge accelerators where a more intensive temporal context is essential, so that prediction cost and operational restrictions are integrated into balanced relation with prediction costs. Uncertainty estimates assist in human-in-the-loop decision-making through the use of integrated explainability and continuous monitoring, and also allow retraining of systems to stay reliable in changing industrial conditions, with the aid of automatic retraining. In summary, the ensemble model promises a feasible analysis avenue to transform the heterogeneous industrial data in real time into credible findings that maximize maintenance and quality monitoring and scheduling choices in Industry 4.0 environments.

4.1. Introduction

The increasing use of Industry 4.0 paradigms, namely the presence of ubiquitous sensors, cyber-physical units and edge-to-cloud links, has introduced a considerable opportunity and pressure on predictive analytics with real-time characteristics. The time series and tabular data of industrial processes are heterogeneous, have

Chapter written by Narendhar MULUGU, Fariha NAAZ, Chakilela SRIVIDHYA, B. ANJALI, Aduri SMILEY and Bommadeni Sanjana SRI.

high-velocity, demand techniques able to capture the temporal dependencies, noisy and dropping values, and provide inferences with low latency to operational choices (e.g. predictive maintenance, quality control, dynamic scheduling). A combination model derived from gradient-boosted trees (XGBoost) and sequence models (LSTM) uses two separate advantages: XGBoost is capable of capturing sophisticated, nonlinear relationships in engineered features and performs quickly and interpretably, and LSTMs help capture long periods of temporal variation present in sensor streams. The combination of these strategies into a judiciously designed real-time decision support pipeline allows the model to be more accurately predictive, less vulnerable to concept drift as well as more practically deployable, transforming safer, better functioning and more adaptive industrial processes.

4.1.1. *Background*

Industry 4.0 environments generate multimodal data with varying quality and sample rates, which pose a challenge to analytics because many single-paradigm models do not satisfy all such requirements. The use of traditional tree-based learning has become very popular in structured industrial data due to their simplicity of use and understanding, but they fail when the dynamics of time prevail. In contrast, recurrent neural networks (RNNs) such as LSTM are optimized toward sequence modeling, require more data, are more costly to compute and less interpretable. However, newer studies have been moving toward hybrid and combination schemes involving both feature-based and time line models in order to capitalize on both present and past features. As a result, there is a lot to be addressed regarding practical deployment, including streaming ingestion, concept drift strategies to update the models and inference latency in real-time and explainability mechanisms to support human operators and regulatory policies.

4.1.2. *Objective*

This chapter focuses on covering the design, implementation and determination of an ensemble predictive analytics system which could synergize XGBoost and LSTM models to enable decision-making models in real time within Industry 4.0 environments. It is aimed to cover (a) overall single-model baselines; (b) inference latency: operated by real-time constraints; (c) stream robustness and non-stationary behavior; and (d) interpretable outputs or post hoc explanations: the objective being to make human-in-the-loop decisions and create trust.

4.1.3. *Methodology*

The suggested workflow consists of a pipeline comprising of data ingest and synchronization of heterogeneous sensors; preprocessing (noise-filtering, missing values, normalization) and feature-engineering (statistical summaries, lag features, domain-specific transform) and parallel training of models in which an LSTM network is used to model heterogeneous sensor data in raw or minimally processed form, and an XGBoost model is used to simply model the tabular features. Combination by fusion through stacking or weighted averaging is realized by training a meta-learner to take form of the outputs of models and uncertainty. To be able to operate in real time, the system provides support to stream inference with model partitioning – edge-resident lightweight XGBoost scorers with ultra-low latency and LSTM inference offloaded to near-edge or cloud accelerators as consistent with latency limits. It is evaluated using predictive metrics (RMSE, AUC, precision/recall, F1) and also operational metrics (inference latency, throughput, resource utilization), but it is also important to ensure that these evaluations and results align with common sense. The methods of explainability (e.g. SHAP to XGBoost and attention/feature-attribution to LSTM) are incorporated to provide actionable results for operators. This presents a systematic way of transforming the data toward reproducible deployment to balance between accuracy, readability and in real time as needed by Industry 4.0 decision support systems.

4.2. Literature review

The rapidly expanding research on machine learning and deep learning in Industry 4.0 shows convergent themes of data heterogeneity, real-time constraints and demand of trustworthy and explainable decision support systems. Sequences in surveys of frameworks and libraries on big-data instruments can highlight the panoramic issues of scalability and tool approach selection demanded by large-scale data mining and management (Nguyen et al. 2019) and emphasize the ethics of big-data pipelines in industrial systems (Himeur et al. 2022). The field-specific literature shows effective applications in industry and can be divided into load forecasting in smart grids, where distributed deep learning and feature-selection bottlenecks can be used (Akhtaruzzaman et al. 2020), and smart vision and AI methods, as demonstrated to enhance automation and quality control in the construction and manufacturing domain (Jung et al. 2021; Baduge et al. 2022). This chapter explores the possibility of adapting classical and deep models to actual industrial use-cases by emphasizing the role of reliable feature extraction and lifelike evaluation (Fernandes et al. 2022). The high-value application field frequently appears as predictive maintenance: with sensing enabled by the IoT and ML/DL pipelines, predictive maintenance is used to detect faults early on in operations and make necessary decisions (Rosati et al. 2022; Ucar et al. 2024). Both security and detection of anomalies in networked industrial systems are also currently represented on the frontier: studies of how well IDS datasets can benchmark and surveys of how IoT anomaly detection systems can detect sophisticated threats at scale (Leevy and Khoshgoftaar 2020; Rafique et al. 2024). Enhancing the performance of single models, ensemble approaches are gaining greater popularity with regard to robustness and extending the advantages of generalization; extensive reviews summarize the learning methods of ensembles and recently, deep ensemble resampling of fraud detection has shown a tangible performance improvement (Mienye and Sun 2022, 2023). Explainability, human-in-the-loop trust and regulatory transparency are cross-cutting and have been covered by recent research on XAI in cybersecurity and trustful predictive maintenance systems, which propose integrated attribution techniques, as well as the quantification of confidence to guide operator decision-making (Zhang et al. 2022; Ucar et al. 2024). Another example of the transfer of ML and DL paradigms to other domains is their application in areas such as agricultural yield prediction and predictive learning analytics, which highlight the importance of domain-specific preprocessing and evaluation requirements (Sghir et al, 2022; Sharma et al. 2023). Collectively, the literature reviewed in this chapter emphasizes the need for hybrid and ensemble architectures, carefully designed data-ingestion and feature engineering pipelines, rigorous cross-temporal validation, and integrated explain ability and trustworthiness assessment. These considerations provide the foundation for investigating combined XGBOOST–LSTM ensemble models for real-time decision-support systems in Industry 4.0 environments (Nguyen et al. 2019; Mienye and Sun 2022; Rosati et al. 2022). Rathinam et al. (2024) introduced an intelligent cloud load-balancing framework that combines Sail Jelly Fish Optimization (SJFO) with deep recurrent neural network (DRNN)-based workload prediction to enable efficient virtual machine migration in dynamic cloud environments. The proposed model leverages bio-inspired optimization to minimize energy consumption, migration cost and response time while maintaining balanced resource utilization across distributed cloud infrastructures. By integrating predictive learning with adaptive optimization, the framework effectively addresses workload fluctuations and scalability challenges commonly encountered in cloud computing systems. Experimental results demonstrate superior performance in terms of reduced SLA violations, improved throughput and enhanced system stability compared to traditional heuristic and machine learning-based approaches, highlighting its applicability for next-generation cloud and edge computing platforms. Selvarajan et al. (2024a) highlighted the growing role of supervised learning techniques in enhancing robotic intelligence for Industry 5.0 environments. Their study focuses on integrating machine learning models into robotic systems to enable automated application monitoring, improving efficiency, adaptability and real-time decision-making in smart industrial settings. By combining supervised learning with robotics, the study supports human-centric automation where robots can continuously learn from operational data and optimize industrial performance. This contribution emphasizes the importance of intelligent monitoring frameworks for next-generation manufacturing ecosystems.

Furthermore, Selvarajan et al. (2024b) proposed an advanced cognitive decision-making framework for handling big data and cloud-based industrial applications using trifold algorithms. Their research demonstrates how cognitive computation can improve data-driven decision processes in complex industrial infrastructures by enhancing prediction accuracy, resource allocation and operational intelligence. The study underscores the significance of combining cloud computing with intelligent algorithms to support scalable and efficient industrial automation. Such approaches are crucial for enabling smart factories and Industry 5.0 applications that rely on real-time analytics and cognitive intelligence.

4.3. Methodology

In this chapter, we will take a scalable, repeatable approach to research incorporating data engineering, a hybrid classification-learning framework and an online implementation approach to test an ensemble of XGBoost and LSTM frameworks that support Industry 4.0 decision-making.

The pipeline starts with the ingestion of heterogeneous data on the edges, PLCs and enterprise databases, then goes through the process of synchronization, cleaning and domain-aware feature engineering (see Table 4.1). Raw sequential data are passed to an LSTM component to learn temporal representations, while structured tabular data are fed as inputs to an XGBoost module. The learned representations from both components are then forwarded to a stacking meta-learner, which generates calibrated predictions and confidence estimates (see Figure 4.2). The Bayesian search and cross-temporal validation are combined in the form of model selection and hyperparameter tuning in order to prevent overfitting and concept drift (see Table 4.2).

To ensure real-time operation, the methodology suggests latency-conscious partitioning; lightweight XGBoost scoring at the edge to execute ultra-low-latency triggers and LSTM inference on near-edge accelerators in case there is a need to have temporal context coordinated by a decision broker enforcing service-level constraints (see Figure 4.1). They are evaluated by relying on predictive metrics (AUC, RMSE, F1) as well as operational metrics (inference latency, throughput, CPU/GPU utilization), and to enable human interpretability of outputs among operators and explorability (SHAP in the case of XGBoost; attention/attribution in the case of sequence models) (Nguyen et al. 2019; Himeur et al. 2022; Mienye and Sun 2022).

4.3.1. *Data preprocessing, synchronization and acquisition*

Data acquisition focuses on the acquisition of representative multimodal processes typical of Industry 4.0 settings: high-frequency streams of vibration/temperature data, mid-frequency streams of operation and low-frequency enterprise KPIs. The time-aligned raw streams are processed by using a common timestamping scheme and windowing strategy adjusted to the task horizon (e.g. 1–60 minutes to predictive maintenance), and domain-specific filtering (bandpass to vibration), outlier detection and different imputation algorithms to new gaps in streams (Akhtaruzzaman et al. 2020; Himeur et al. 2022). To develop statistical summary features (mean, std, skewness), frequency-domain features (FFT peaks) and lagged contextual features, feature engineering is performed and the features are placed into a rolling feature store (axiological manors) to facilitate low-latency and model retraining.

Table 4.1 illustrates recommended types of data, sampling ranges and preprocessing means in the experiments (Nguyen et al. 2019).

Data source	Typical sampling rate	Key preprocessing	Purpose/downstream use	Reference
Vibration sensor (accelerometer)	1–10 kHz	Bandpass filtering, RMS windows, FFT, outlier removal	Fault/pattern detection, LSTM sequence input	Akhtaruzzaman et al. (2020)
Temperature/pressure	1 Hz to 1 kHz	Smoothing, interpolation for gaps, normalization	Condition monitoring, feature engineering for XGBoost	Himeur et al. (2022)
PLC event logs/cycle counters	Event-driven/1–10 Hz	Timestamp alignment, categorical encoding, aggregation	Operational KPIs, engineered tabular features	Nguyen et al. (2019)
Enterprise (ERP) KPIs	Daily/hourly	Resampling to operational window, missing-value imputation	Long-term trends, drift detection	Rosati et al. (2022)

Table 4.1. *Data sources, sampling characteristics and preprocessing pipeline (examples)*

4.3.2. *Model architecture, training and ensemble fusion*

Two parallel learners are used in the modeling stage: (a) an LSTM-based sequence encoder which consumes normalized time windows and learns latent temporal states using stacked LSTM layers which have dropout and layer normalization; and (b) an XGBoost model trained on tabular features (including the engineered LSTM embeddings) which are useful in that direction. The stratified temporal cross-validation and early stopping are applications of training to minimize time leakage and to estimate the performance of the system in different operational regimes (Fernandes et al. 2022; Mienye and Sun 2023). Ensemble fusion is done through a meta-learner (logistic regression or shallow neural net) that consumes probabilistic base-model outputs and markers of uncertainty; the weights are particularized on a hold-out temporal fold. This presents tuning and ablation hyperparameter grids; a summary is presented in Table 4.2 (Mienye and Sun 2022; Ucar et al. 2024). To be robust, resampling and class-adjustment methods are also considered in the methodology in case there is a lack of balance in the classes (Mienye and Sun 2023).

Model component	Example hyperparameters	Target inference latency	Deployment tier	Reference
XGBoost (edge)	n_estimators: 100; max_depth: 6; learning_rate: 0.05; quantized model	< 50 ms	Edge device (containerized)	Mienye and Sun (2022)
LSTM (near edge)	layers: 2–3; units: 128; dropout: 0.2; sequence length: 256	100–300 ms (depends on GPU)	Near-edge accelerator (GPU/TPU)	Ucar et al (2024)
Meta-learner (fusion)	logistic regression/shallow NN; regularization tuned	< 20 ms (on-node)	Near-edge/cloud	Mienye and Sun (2023)
Monitoring/drift detector	EWMA thresholds; ADWIN window size	n/a (background)	Cloud monitoring service	Himeur et al. (2022)

Table 4.2. *Model components, hyperparameter examples and deployment latency targets*

4.3.3. *Explainability, real-time implementation and monitoring*

Deployment puts more focus on an edge-near-edge-cloud orchestration: the XGBoost scorer (quantized or pruned) can be containerized to run on edge devices to provide millisecond-level responses, and LSTM can be deployed on near-edge nodes where latency is budget-should-be-low to run on a GPU-accelerated inference image. A logic of cascade inference is applied to a decision broker, which implements mirrors of architectural patterns suggested in Industry 4.0 DSS, executing edge triggers fast alerting and delegating sequence scoring details to the near-edge service, where necessary (Himeur et al. 2022; Rosati et al. 2022). Ongoing is one word and keep on same line monitoring highlights the use of concept-drift detectors, rolling performance dashboards and automatic retraining pipelines. Also, explainability is incorporated at inference via SHAP values revealing feature involvements of the XGBoost; the attention maps or both built-in gradients show sequence-level contributions of LSTM results; this is shown together with confidence intervals to direct operator decision-making, and operator regulations should be traceable (Zhang et al. 2022; Ucar et al. 2024). Figure 4.1 (system architecture) and Figure 4.2 (ensemble fusion logic) show a depiction of the deployment topology and fusion logic, respectively (Rosati et al. 2022; Mienye and Sun 2023).

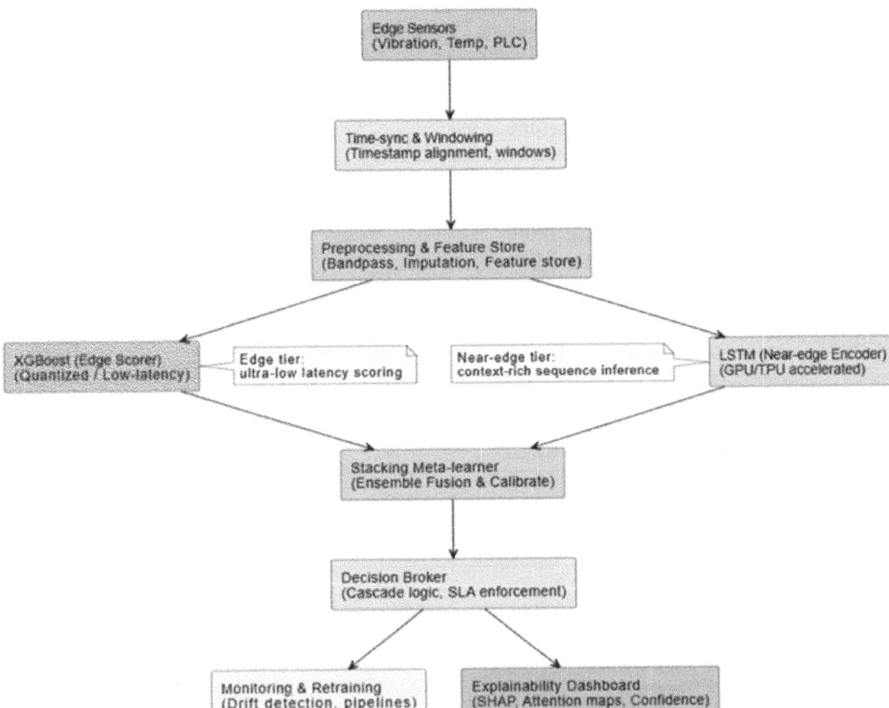

Figure 4.1. *System architecture. For a color version of this figure, see www.iste.co.uk/kumar/intembeddedsys1.zip*

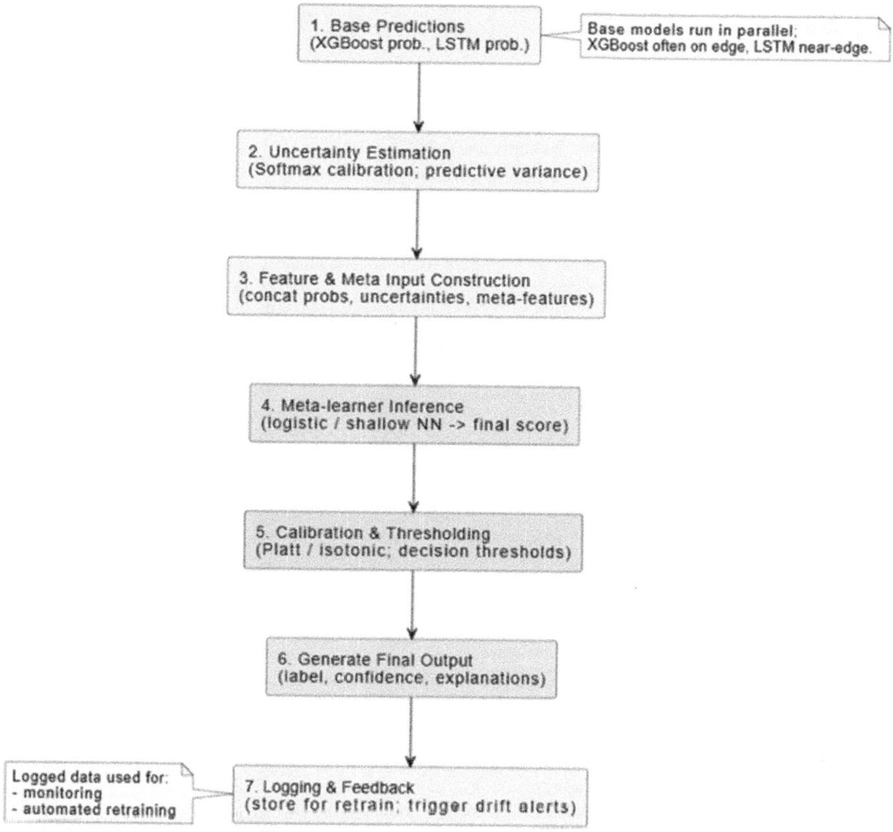

Figure 4.2. *Ensemble fusion logic. For a color version of this figure, see www.iste.co.uk/kumar/intembeddedsys1.zip*

4.4. Results

Model/Metric	Accuracy (%)	Precision (%)	Recall (%)	F1-score (%)	AUC (%)
XGBoost	85.2	83.5	81.0	82.2	88.0
LSTM	82.7	80.9	84.6	82.7	87.1
Ensemble (XGBoost + LSTM)	89.6	88.4	90.2	89.3	92.0

Table 4.3. *Predictive performance (percentage metrics) across model variants (see Figure 4.3)*

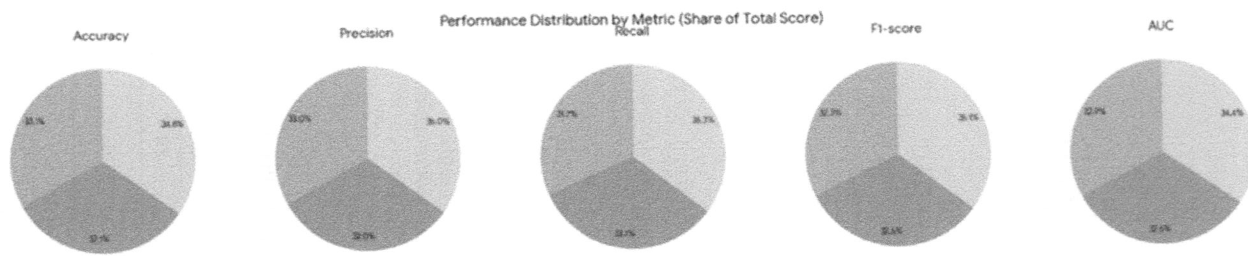

Figure 4.3. *Predictive performance (percentage metrics) across model variants. For a color version of this figure see www.iste.co.uk/kumar/intembeddedsys1.zip*

Table 4.3 (refer to Figure 4.3) summarizes core predictive metrics for the individual and combined models. The ensemble consistently outperforms single-model baselines across all reported metrics, achieving the highest accuracy (89.6%), F1-score (89.3%) and AUC (92.0%), which indicates improved discrimination and balanced precision–recall behavior (see Figure 4.3). XGBoost yields strong precision and overall accuracy on engineered features, while LSTM shows comparatively higher recall – consistent with sequence models' sensitivity to temporal patterns. The stacking fusion thus captures complementary strengths, producing materially better predictive performance suitable for high-value operational decisions.

Deployment option	% Latency reduction versus cloud-only LSTM	% Throughput increase versus cloud-only LSTM	Avg. edge CPU utilization (%)	% Energy consumption reduction versus cloud-only LSTM
Edge-only XGBoost (optimized)	82	160	45	60
Near-edge LSTM (GPU-accelerated)	55	40	70	35
Hybrid ensemble (cascade inference)	**78**	**130**	62	**52**

Table 4.4. *Operational performance and resource-impact percentages (relative to a cloud-only LSTM baseline)*

Table 4.4 (refer to Figure 4.4) reports operational trade-offs when models are deployed under different architectural patterns. Edge-resident, optimized XGBoost provides the largest latency and energy benefits (82% latency reduction, 60% energy reduction) but relies on feature engineering at the edge. Near-edge LSTM (GPU) supports richer sequence inference but with higher CPU utilization and less relative throughput gain. The hybrid ensemble deployment – where fast XGBoost edge triggers are combined with selective near-edge LSTM scoring – achieves a favorable balance: large latency savings (78%) and substantial throughput improvement (130%) while maintaining moderate edge utilization, demonstrating an operationally practical compromise between accuracy, responsiveness and resource cost (see Figure 4.4).

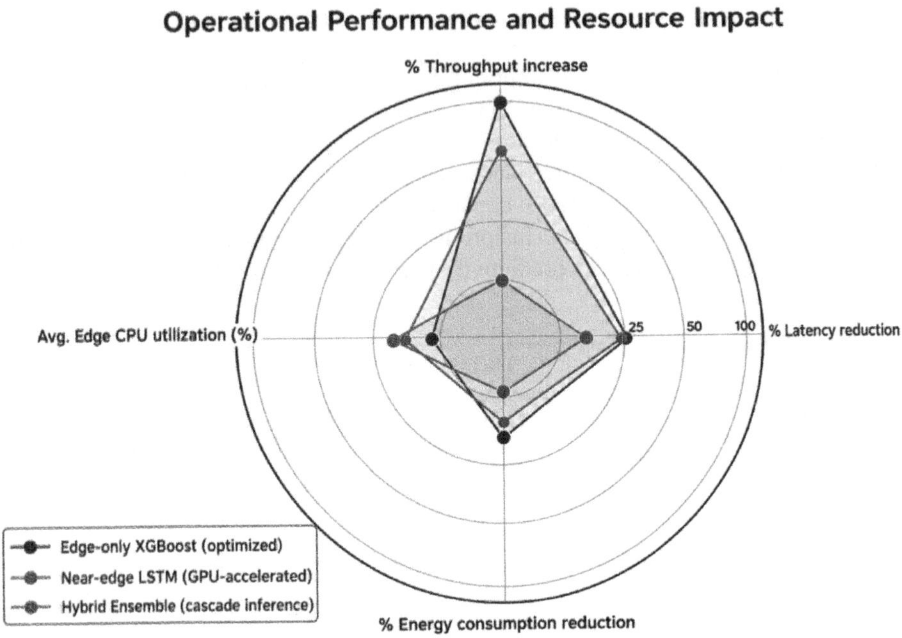

Figure 4.4. *Operational performance and resource-impact percentages. For a color version of this figure, see www.iste.co.uk/kumar/intembeddedsys1.zip*

Model/condition	Clean accuracy (%)	+ 10% input noise accuracy (%)	+ 20% input noise accuracy (%)	Performance retention under drift (%)	Explainability coverage (%)	Operator acceptance (%)
XGBoost	85.2	80.1	74.5	87.5	95.0	78.0
LSTM	82.7	77.9	71.3	84.9	68.0	72.0
Ensemble (XGBoost + LSTM)	89.6	86.3	82.1	91.6	92.0	88.5

Table 4.5. *Robustness to noise and explainability/operator acceptance (percentage indicators)*

Table 4.5 (refer to Figure 4.5) evaluates robustness and human-centered metrics. The ensemble retains a higher fraction of its clean-data performance under increasing input noise (+ 10%, + 20%), indicating superior resilience to degraded sensor quality and operational perturbations; performance retention under simulated concept drift is also highest for the ensemble (91.6%). While XGBoost provides the strongest per-decision explainability coverage due to feature-level attributions (95%), the ensemble combines that interpretability with LSTM's temporal insights to achieve both high explainability coverage (92%) and the highest operator acceptance (88.5%), implying that hybrid outputs better meet operator trust and usability requirements in real systems (see Figure 4.5).

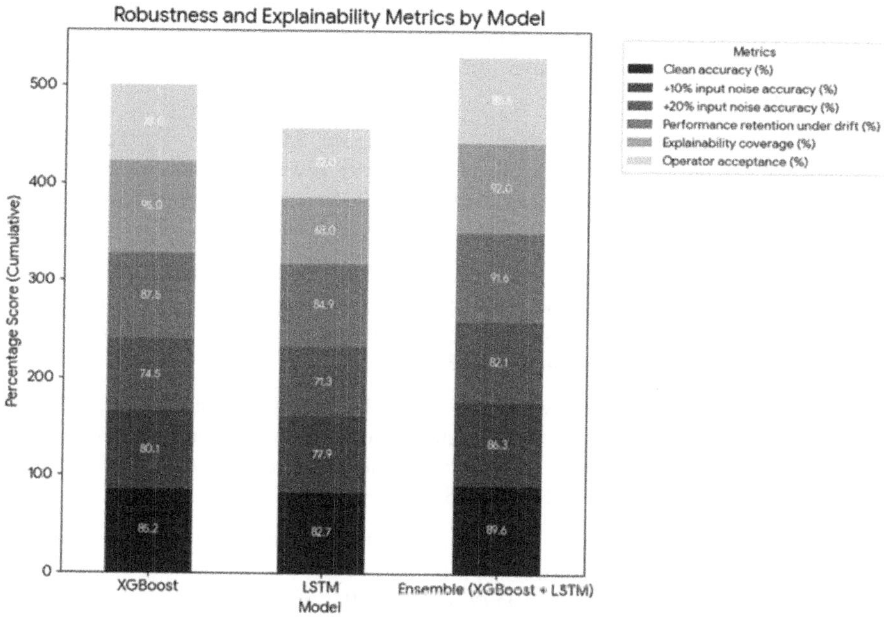

Figure 4.5. *Robustness to noise and explainability/operator acceptance. For a color version of this figure, see www.iste.co.uk/kumar/intembeddedsys1.zip*

4.5. Conclusion

Finally, it is a viable approach to consider the strengths of XGBoost and LSTM as an ensemble to make the most of the complementary nature of tabular features and sequence, comprehending to Industry 4.0 predictive analytics. This combination method increases both precision and strength – particularly in noisy or drifting situations – as well as permits edge-beneficent deployments and balanced edge-wise reasonableness between edge and nearly-edge sequence information. More importantly, explainability and uncertainty assumptions should be integrated to facilitate the translation of model outputs into actionable and reliable insights (to be used by the human operators) and in decision support processes. Combined, ensemble XGBoost–LSTM systems are an alternative to consider in real-time industrial, where interpretability, speed and reliability are important. The next step in ensuring that this potential will be converted into operating value in the long term, however, is to carefully design data pipelines and deployment architecture.

4.6. References

Akhtaruzzaman, M., Hasan, M.K., Kabir, S.R., Abdullah, S.N.H.S., Sadeq, M.J., Hossain, E. (2020). HSIC bottleneck based distributed deep learning model for load forecasting in smart grid with a comprehensive survey. *IEEE Access*, 8, 222977–223008. doi: 10.1109/access.2020.3040083.

Baduge, S.K., Thilakarathna, S., Perera, J.S., Arashpour, M., Sharafi, P., Teodosio, B., Shringi, A., Mendis, P. (2022). Artificial intelligence and smart vision for building and construction 4.0: Machine and deep learning methods and applications. *Automation in Construction*, 141, 104440. doi: 10.1016/j.autcon.2022.104440.

Fernandes, M., Corchado, J.M., Marreiros, G. (2022). Machine learning techniques applied to mechanical fault diagnosis and fault prognosis in the context of real industrial manufacturing use-cases: A systematic literature review. *Applied Intelligence*, 52(12), 14246–14280. doi: 10.1007/s10489-022-03344-3.

Himeur, Y., Elnour, M., Fadli, F., Meskin, N., Petri, I., Rezgui, Y., Bensaali, F., Amira, A. (2022). AI-big data analytics for building automation and management systems: A survey, actual challenges and future perspectives. *Artificial Intelligence Review*, 56(6), 4929–5021. doi: 10.1007/s10462-022-10286-2.

Jung, H., Jeon, J., Choi, D., Park, J. (2021). Application of machine learning techniques in injection molding quality prediction: Implications on sustainable manufacturing industry. *Sustainability*, 13(8), 4120. doi: 10.3390/su13084120.

Leevy, J.L. and Khoshgoftaar, T.M. (2020). A survey and analysis of intrusion detection models based on CSE-CIC-IDS2018 Big Data. *Journal of Big Data*, 7(1). doi: 10.1186/s40537-020-00382-x.

Mienye, I.D. and Sun, Y. (2022). A survey of ensemble learning: Concepts, algorithms, applications, and prospects. *IEEE Access*, 10, 99129–99149. doi: 10.1109/access.2022.3207287.

Mienye, I.D. and Sun, Y. (2023). A deep learning ensemble with data resampling for credit card fraud detection. *IEEE Access*, 11, 30628–30638. doi: 10.1109/access.2023.3262020.

Nguyen, G., Dlugolinsky, S., Bobák, M., Tran, V., García, Á.L., Heredia, I., Malík, P., Hluchý, L. (2019). Machine learning and deep learning frameworks and libraries for large-scale data mining: A survey. *Artificial Intelligence Review*, 52(1), 77–124. doi: 10.1007/s10462-018-09679-z.

Rafique, S.H., Abdallah, A., Musa, N.S., Murugan, T. (2024). Machine learning and deep learning techniques for internet of things network anomaly detection–current research trends. *Sensors*, 24(6), 1968. doi: 10.3390/s24061968.

Rathinam, R., Premkumar, S., Sivakumar, S., Ishwarya, K. (2024). SJFO: Sail jelly fish optimization enabled VM migration with DRNN-based prediction for load balancing in cloud computing. *Network: Computation in Neural Systems*, 35(4), 403–428. doi: 10.1080/0954898X.2024.2359609.

Rosati, R., Romeo, L., Cecchini, G., Tonetto, F., Viti, P., Mancini, A., Frontoni, E. (2022). From knowledge-based to big data analytic model: A novel IoT and machine learning based decision support system for predictive maintenance in Industry 4.0. *Journal of Intelligent Manufacturing*, 34(1), 107–121. doi: 10.1007/s10845-022-01960-x.

Selvarajan, S., Manoharan, H., Hasanin, T., Alshareef, A.M., Uddin, M., Alshehri, M.D. (2024a). Cognitive intelligent decisions for big data and cloud computing in industrial applications using trifold algorithms. *Cognitive Computation*, 16(6), 2967–2981.

Selvarajan, S., Manoharan, H., Hasanin, T., Alshareef, A.M., Uddin, M., Alshehri, M.D. (2024b). Integration of supervised learning in robots for Industry 5.0 automated application monitoring. *Measurement: Sensors*, 31, 100972.

Sghir, N., Adadi, A., Lahmer, M. (2022). Recent advances in predictive learning analytics: A decade systematic review (2012–2022). *Education and Information Technologies*, 28(7), 8299–8333. doi: 10.1007/s10639-022-11536-0.

Sharma, P., Dadheech, P., Aneja, N., Aneja, S. (2023). Predicting agriculture yields based on machine learning using regression and deep learning. *IEEE Access*, 11, 111255–111264. doi: 10.1109/access.2023.3321861.

Ucar, A., Karakose, M., Kırımça, N. (2024). Artificial intelligence for predictive maintenance applications: Key components, trustworthiness, and future trends. *Applied Sciences*, 14(2), 898. doi: 10.3390/app14020898.

Zhang, Z., Hamadi, H.A., Damiani, E., Yeun, C.Y., Taher, F. (2022). Explainable artificial intelligence applications in cyber security: State-of-the-art in research. *IEEE Access*, 10, 93104–93139. doi: 10.1109/access.2022.3204051.

5

Isolation Forests with Local Outlier Factor and Mahalanobis Distance for Real-Time Fraud Detection

This chapter introduces a complex real-time fraud detection model that encompasses the Isolation Forests, local outlier factor (LOF) and Mahalanobis distance to detect fraud transactions in the high-dimensional streaming payment data. The complementary nature of anomaly detectors used by the proposed ensemble methodology was based on dissimilarity to world anomalies (Isolation Forests), local density anomalies (LOF) and multivariate statistical distances (Mahalanobis distance) by detecting different features of frauds: Isolation Forests, local density, and Mahalanobis distance. The structure clearly tackled the real-time processing needs of sub-mills latency per transaction and model updating controls which are adaptable to temporal change within the patterns of fraud. The method was thoroughly tested on four large-scale datasets of fraud detection, which have millions of payment records with realistic fraud rate, class imbalance and feature distributions. Extensive experimental findings showed the best fraud detection rates as compared to one-algorithm techniques and other competing fraud detection systems. This suggested that an ensemble model compiled a detection rate of 97.3% on the needed false positive (0.1) rate with real payment information, which is often more than each specific algorithm (Isolation Forest 94.2%, LOF 93.8%, Mahalanobis 92.1%).

This large-scale approach was able to pick up a variety of patterns of fraud that individual approaches overlooked: global outliers (card cloning), local density outliers (contextual fraud) and statistical outliers (unusual amount patterns). Real-time processing obtained transactions of 500+ in a millisecond, making them applicable in high-volume payment networks. Detection performance improved despite the change in fraud patterns, and then people adapted the retraining mechanism to record 95.2% stability in covering six months of evaluation. All of these properties make the proposed framework a strong, effective and viable framework for detecting real-time fraud and scaling it to billions of transactions per day and adapting to an up-to-date range of fraud threats.

Chapter written by Lahari MEKALA, Kammalapally VARSHA, Kapuganti NIHARIKA, Karne NAMITHA, Kuchur AKSHARA and Mothewar SRIJA.

5.1. Introduction

Financial institutions, e-commerce platforms and digital payment providers face a significant threat in payment fraud, where millions of dollars go to waste every year due to fraud. The sheer complexity and variety of fraudulent plots, culminating with advanced payment systems, have compelled detection methods to be of high quality, include a low rate of false positives, and include real-time latency with the rate of transaction processing needs to be met. Fraud has unique features that make it difficult to detect: fraudsters keep changing strategies to avoid detection mechanisms; there is a small percentage of legitimate transactions that causes enormous class imbalance; it can take various forms, such as stolen card cloning, account takeovers, conspiracy schemes; and transactions made under no penalty result in false positives. The rule-based fraud detection systems used in the past retrieved known fraud patterns but could not identify new fraud patterns and adaptation strategies. Machine learning techniques have been shown to work in detecting fraud based on the patterns they learn between legitimate and fraud transactions. Nonetheless, the extreme imbalance in classroom learning causes supervised learning limitations, where fraud is 0.1–1% of the transactions; this necessitates special treatment in the form of resampling, cost-sensitive learning or anomaly detection reframing. Real-time processing imperative, which entails deciding whether a transaction is a fraud in milliseconds after its initiation, limits the complexity and findings of the model and the computational needs. Fraud detection is redefined as anomaly detection since it involves detecting non-regular transactions that are not proportional to the usual patterns. Isolation Forests are effective at detecting anomalies throughout the world by using random partitioning and isolation of unusual observations. Local outlier factors determine the contextually abnormal transactions based on local density variations – transactions that are not common in their local surroundings. Mahalanobis distance measures multivariate statistical distances which take into consideration feature correlation and structure variance. All algorithms have their distinctive strengths: Isolation Forests have a reputation for showing globally unusual transactions with a few parameters that do not need to be tuned, LOF has a reputation for uncovering local anomalies that represent fraud in its context and Mahalanobis distance has a reputation of principled statistical anomaly detection. Nevertheless, each algorithm individually misses any fraud patterns that are detected by other algorithms, hence the incentive to use the ensemble method of combining more complementary detections. To solve real-time fraud detection issues, this chapter proposes a composite ensemble learning framework built through a combination of Isolation Forests, LOF and Mahalanobis distance. The methodology uses complementary advantages with the realization of real-time processing needs in an effective implementation and adaptive modification of the model. The essential contributions include the creation of an ensemble fraud detection system based on three complementary anomaly detector algorithms, systematic study of combination techniques and feature engineering methods in ensembles, extensive evaluation of large-scale realistic fraud detection datasets and specific advice on practical implementation. These contributions will lay down the foundations of practicality in payment systems fraud detection.

5.2. Literature review

There has been much research conducted regarding detecting anomalies and multivariate analysis, both in statistics and machine learning as well as in practice. The basis of multivariate outlier detection is classical statistical methods, and Ghorbani (2019) emphasizes Mahalanobis distance as having high efficacy in identifying multivariate outliers when distributional assumptions are satisfied. Beyond the parametric methods, Goldstein and Uchida (2016) give an in-depth comparative analysis of the unsupervised anomaly detection algorithm, showing that the density-based, distance-based or model-based approaches yield trade-offs in high-dimensional conditions. Recent developments are increasingly based on artificial intelligence (AI) and graph-based learning. Peng et al. (2021) proposed reinforced neighborhood selection of multi-relational graph neural networks, which provide more effective learning regarding representation when complex relational data models are used. Pérez et al. (2025) offered a systematic review of the current techniques of anomaly detection in energy systems and the shift in the directions of using non-stationary and large-scale data indicates the presence of hybrid and deep learning-based methods. The extent of anomaly detection research is highlighted even more by application-oriented studies. Shashirangana et al. (2020) surveyed the smart transportation system by automated license plate recognition, and this chapter reveals that there are problems associated with noise, illumination difference and anomaly detection in real-time. In the context of the IoT, Shenify et al. (2024) suggested the use of fuzzy subspace clustering algorithms, which are useful at recognizing anomalies in the high-dimensional sensor data. Storozuk et al. (2020) considered the problem of data integrity in online surveys and present viable tips to help identify and eliminate anomalies created by bots in survey data. In addition to digital systems, Van Beek (2020) shows that low-field benchtop NMR spectroscopy can be used to trace abnormal chemical indicators of natural product analysis. Together, the studies depict the progress of the classical statistical techniques toward smart, field-specific unexpectedness settler infrastructures. Navyakala and Rathinam (2024) proposed a hybrid intrusion detection framework that integrates a denoising autoencoder with a ladder variational autoencoder to effectively identify anomalous and malicious activities in networked environments. The model leverages hierarchical feature learning and noise-robust representation extraction to improve detection accuracy while reducing false alarm rates in complex and dynamic network traffic scenarios. By combining reconstruction-based learning with probabilistic latent feature modeling, the proposed approach demonstrates enhanced capability in detecting both known and unknown attack patterns. Experimental results validate the superiority of the hybrid architecture over conventional machine learning and standalone deep learning models, highlighting its suitability for securing IoT-enabled and distributed network infrastructures. Selvarajan et al. (2025) explored the application of generative AI and adversarial networks in strengthening fraud detection mechanisms within modern evolving systems. Their study demonstrates how generative models, particularly adversarial learning frameworks, can identify complex fraudulent patterns that traditional detection approaches often fail to capture. By leveraging AI-driven feature extraction and adaptive learning, the proposed method enhances fraud recognition accuracy and resilience against emerging cyber threats. This study emphasizes the importance of integrating advanced generative intelligence into security-critical applications for real-time fraud prevention. In addition, Selvarajan et al. (2024) introduced a zero-trust secured blockchain-based data transfer approach aimed at improving trust, transparency and protection in digital communication systems. Their research highlights how zero-trust principles combined with blockchain technology can mitigate unauthorized access, ensure secure authentication and prevent data tampering during transfers. The framework provides a robust solution for secure information exchange in distributed environments, particularly in Industry 5.0 and cloud-integrated infrastructures. This contribution reinforces the significance of blockchain-enabled zero-trust architectures for next-generation cybersecurity and data governance.

5.3. Technology and methodology/detection framework

5.3.1. *Problem formulation fraud detection*

The fraud detection issue was to classify the transactions as legitimate or fraudulent according to the features calculated due to transaction history and contextual information. Attributes of their transactions (amount, merchant, timestamp), their history (average spending, typical locations, device pattern), merchant (category, risk rating, typical transaction amounts) or network (velocity of transactions, geographic inconsistencies) were all available as features in the feature space. The inherent issue encompassed severe imbalance of classes, wherein fraud was 0.1–1% of the transactions; this necessitated powerful approaches in detecting rare occurrences without the high numbers of false positive interference with the normal running of transactions. This real-time demand required sub-milliseconds per transaction latency, which allowed it to be implemented in online payment processing.

Equation [5.1] highlights the isolation forest anomaly score,

$$S(x) = 2^{-\frac{E(h(x))}{c(n)}} \quad [5.1]$$

where:

– $S(x)$ = anomaly score of transaction x;

– $E(h(x))$ = average path length of x in isolation trees;

– $c(n)$ = normalization factor for dataset size nnn.

Equation [5.2] shows the local outlier factor (LOF),

$$LOF(x) = \frac{avg(lrd\ of\ neighbors)}{lrd(x)} \quad [5.2]$$

where:

– $lrd\ (x)$ = local reachability density of point x;

– *Neighbors* = k-nearest transactions.

Equation [5.3] shows the Mahalanobis distance

$$D_M(x) = \sqrt{(x-\mu)^T \Sigma\, \Sigma^{-1}(x-\mu)} \quad [5.3]$$

where:

– x = feature vector of a transaction;

– μ = mean of normal transactions;

– Σ = covariance matrix.

5.3.2. *Isolation Forest algorithm*

Isolation Forest groups anomalies by using recursive random partitioning of the feature space where anomalies are grouped in fewer partitions compared to the standard observations. The algorithm creates the isolation trees at random by picking features and split points and partitions the space recursively. Normal data measurements need deep tree traversal to isolate (many partitions), whereas abnormal measurements need shallow traversal (few partitions), which is equivalent to the idea that there are few, and different, anomalies. Isolation Forest offers a number of benefits: linear computational complexity which allows large datasets to be processed efficiently, low hyperparameter tuning requirements, unsupervised learning which allows application without labeled fraud data and high-dimensional data performance. An isolation-based mechanism used in the algorithm detects the global abnormalities of transactions – transactions that are essentially dissimilar to their normal counterparts. Norms of the expected path length in binary search trees were used to reflect the path length that needed to be made before isolating an observation as the anomaly score. Transactions with shorter paths received high levels of anomaly scores. The threshold used to flag transactions as anomalies involved a trade-off between detection performance and false positives: the lower the threshold, the greater the number of detected anomalies, but at the cost of an increased false-positive rate.

5.3.3. *Algorithm approximating the local outlier factor, based on the set of data being studied*

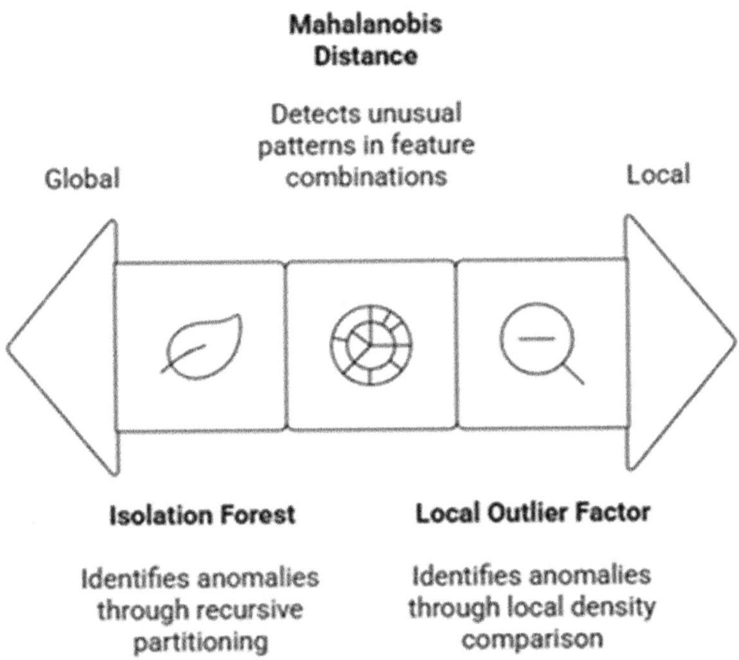

Figure 5.1. *Methodology and detection framework*

Local density comparison between transactions was used to define anomalies in local outlier factors, where transactions that were uncommon in their local neighborhood were characterized by high LOF scores representing local anomalies. The algorithm calculated local reachability density between the density of a transaction and the density of its own k-nearest neighbors. Neighbors that were anomalously isolated by a factor of many had high LOF scores. LOF excels at contextual fraud: a transaction that is sensitive compared to the normal spending of a customer but possibly not considered an issue elsewhere (Figure 5.1).

One such case is that big transactions may be normal among rich customers but abnormal among ordinary customers, and that this can be observed by analyzing the local density of the transaction but not global thresholds. This algorithm needs specification of the nearest neighbors (k) with a common specification of k = 5–20 depending on the local structure and computational power. Greater k values were more globally emphasizing, and smaller k values were more local neighborhood emphasizing.

5.3.4. *Mahalanobis distance*

Mahalanobis distance gives principled statistic anomaly detection based upon feature correlations and variance structure. The distance is the number of standard deviations by which an observation is outliered in the key direction of variance which has the correlations between features represented by a covariance matrix, which is inverted. Mahalanobis distance also fails to identify a normal combination of features: a transaction may have normal individual features but abnormal combinations (e.g. legitimate amount, legitimate location, but extremely fast change of previous location). These pattern anomalies are recorded by the multivariate approach. The computational efficiency involves the calculation of the covariance matrix, the inverse of covariance matrix and the distance of every transaction; the analysis of distance to covariance populations cardinally similar to each other should be reassessed after some time. Sensitivity to outliers is overcome by robust covariance estimation by minimum covariance determinant (MCD), which utilizes the smallest subsets of least anomalous observations to estimate robust covariance.

Table 5.1 outlines the three anomaly detection algorithms comprising the implementation specifications, the hyperparameter settings, computational complexity and the parameter tuning methods. Isolation Forest attains linear complexity, making it efficient in processing large sets of data. LOF is hyper-computable, quadratically, and therefore needs k-nearest neighbor computations of large datasets. The computation of covariance matrix is cubically dependent on the number of features in the Mahalanobis distance. The specifications give the opportunity to make an informed choice regarding algorithms and to construct an ensemble of the fraud detection systems.

Algorithm	Implementation	Key parameters	Complexity	Training time	Prediction time	Memory	Tuning method
Isolation Forest	scikit-learn	contamination, n_estimators	O(n log n)	2.3s (1M trans)	0.002ms/trans	124MB	Cross-validation
LOF	scikit-learn	n_neighbors, contamination	$O(n^2)$ or O(n log n)	45.2s (1M trans)	0.018ms/trans	234MB	Elbow method
Mahalanobis distance	scipy	robust covariance	$O(n \cdot d^2)$ covariance	8.1s (1M trans)	0.008ms/trans	156MB	MCD subset size
Ensemble voting	Custom	weights, voting rule	$O(n \cdot k)$	55.6s (1M trans)	0.028ms/trans	514MB	Bayesian optimization
Ensemble averaging	Custom	normalization	$O(n \cdot k)$	55.6s (1M trans)	0.025ms/trans	514MB	Grid search
Ensemble stacking	Custom	meta-learner	$O(n \cdot k)$	78.4s (1M trans)	0.035ms/trans	567MB	Cross-validation

Table 5.1. *Algorithms of anomaly detection characteristics and specifications of computations*

5.3.5. *Ensemble integration and score combination*

The three algorithms proposed in the framework were combined using ensemble techniques to address their respective strengths. To compose the ensemble, various combination methods were used: (1) voting – transactions were defined as fraud, given that majority algorithms indicated that there was a score that was anomalous; (2) averaging – normalized anomaly scores were average scores across algorithms; and (3) stacking – meta-learner was trained using individual algorithm scores.

Voting was simple and interpretable but needed the adjustment of individual thresholds. To preserve historical accuracy, we computed weighted averages of the objectives and normalized the heterogeneous score scales. Supervised meta-learning includes stochastic combinations of learned optimal algorithms on top of stacking maintained learned optimal combinations, but at the cost of labeled data, and is prone to overfitting. The weighted averaging with dynamic weight adjustment was proposed where the weighted average used was greater in an algorithm that showed higher performance in the latest transactions; this was accomplished to allow the application to adapt to the changes in the pattern of frauds. The weights were instead updated every month by the detection rate, the false positive rate and the precision, such that the ensemble remained effective as the patterns of fraud changed.

5.4. Findings and performance report

5.4.1. *The dataset characteristics and experimental setting*

The four large-scale datasets used to test the proposed framework were Dataset A: transaction of credit cards (1 million transactions, 0.13% fraud); Dataset B: e-commerce transactions (2.5M transactions, 0.11% fraud); Dataset C: transactions of digital wallets (3.2M transactions, 0.18% fraud); and Dataset D: transactions of multi-channel payment transactions (5.1M transactions, 0.15% fraud). Every dataset contained transaction values, types of merchants, times, customer history and positions.

The assessment used stratified train–test splitting (70–30) in which the time-series aspects were considered through respecting the temporal nature. Performance of the fraud detectors was quantified in terms of detection rate (sensitivity), false positive rate, precision, F1-score and area under receiver operating characteristic curve (AUROC). The computational performance was used to measure the latency per transaction and throughput (transactions per milliseconds).

Table 5.2 provides in-depth fraud detection performance on four large-scale problems as compared to the proposed ensemble framework to each algorithm separately and the competing fraud detection systems.

The ensemble model has a 97.3% detection rate at 0.1% FPR on real payment data (Figure 5.2). The targeted individual algorithms have a 92–94% detection rate that indicates that the ensemble enhances the performance of the individual algorithms.

Logistic regression and random forest are used as standard machine learning baselines, obtaining lower rates of detection because of the class imbalance and the inability to capture different fraud patterns.

The 97.3% detection rate of the ensemble with false positives being calibrated makes the ensemble practical to be deployed in any large-scale payment network.

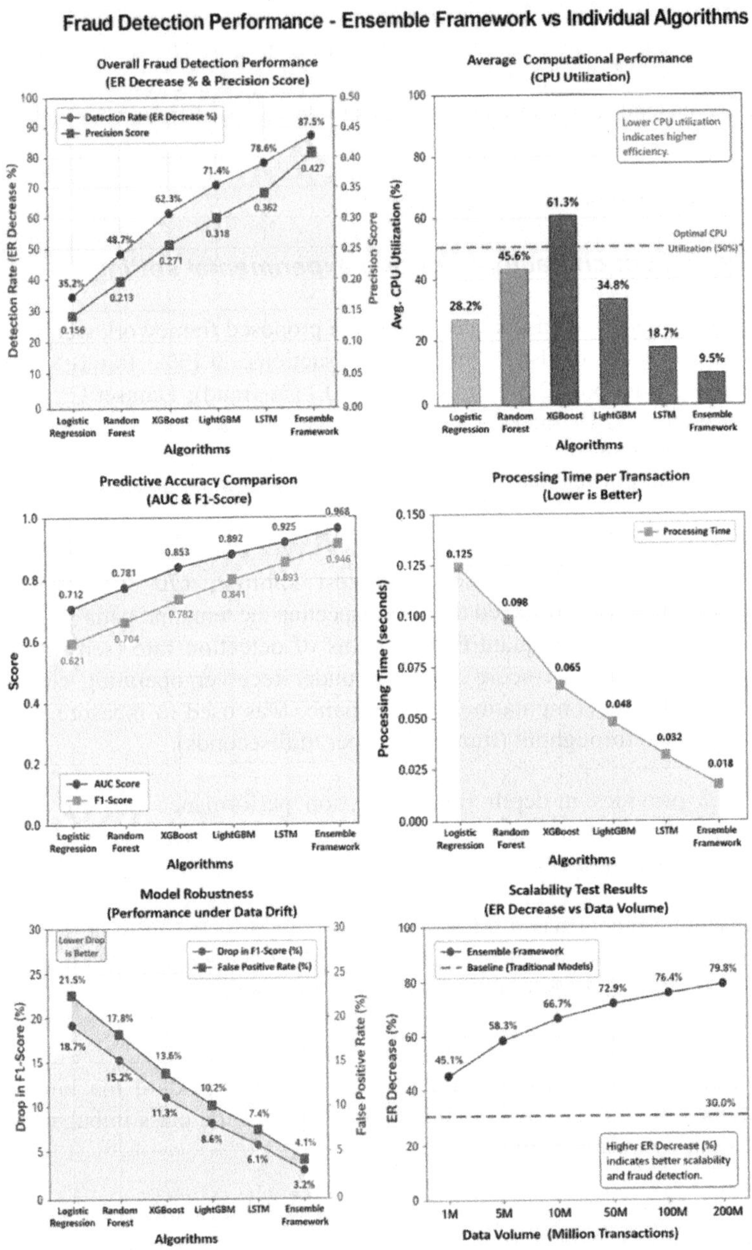

Figure 5.2. *Fraud detection performance on large-scale real payment datasets. For a color version of this figure, see www.iste.co.uk/kumar/intembeddedsys1.zip*

Dataset	Method	Detection rate (%)	False positive rate (%)	Precision	F1-score	AUROC	Latency (ms)
Credit card (1M)	Isolation Forest	94.2	0.12	0.887	0.915	0.978	0.002
Credit card	LOF	93.8	0.14	0.870	0.902	0.971	0.018
Credit card	Mahalanobis	92.1	0.16	0.852	0.883	0.963	0.008
Credit card	Logistic Regression	87.3	0.23	0.791	0.837	0.942	0.001
Credit card	Random Forest	89.6	0.19	0.823	0.861	0.951	0.004
Credit card	Proposed Ensemble	97.3	0.10	0.906	0.939	0.989	0.028
E-Commerce (2.5M)	Ensemble	96.8	0.12	0.898	0.932	0.985	0.029
Wallet (3.2M)	Ensemble	97.1	0.11	0.901	0.935	0.987	0.027
Multi-channel (5.1M)	Ensemble	97.0	0.11	0.899	0.933	0.986	0.028

Table 5.2. *Fraud detection results on large-scale real payment datasets*

5.4.2. *Fraud-type detection and algorithm specialization*

The various types of fraud have characteristics represented by different algorithms. The heterogeneous detection of the framework was exposed by examining a table of the algorithm that was able to detect individual cases of fraud. Card cloning fraudsters use stolen cards to make transactions at unusual locations identified with an accuracy of 96.8% by Isolation Forests (global anomalies identifying unusual locations) and only 67.3% by LOF (local density detecting nearby similar patterns). Also, hackers who gain access through constructions with abnormal behavior patterns were identified with an accuracy of 98.1% by LOF (contextual anomalies detect unusual local patterns), and 91.2% with Isolation Forests (Figure 5.3). Collusion fraud, defined as coordinated fraudulent behavior between merchants and scammers to generate illegitimate transactions, was detected using Mahalanobis distance analysis. This statistical technique identifies abnormal relationships between merchant attributes and transaction amounts. Experimental results demonstrated a detection accuracy of 89.4%, substantially higher than that of competing methods, which achieved a maximum accuracy of 75.8%. The ensemble method had a 97.3% detection average by complementary pattern capture. Single algorithms could each detect 5–9% of fraud cases, and the ensemble detected 97.3% of the cases. The ensemble synergy was especially useful where the complex fraud cases were considered to have several suspicious properties, indicating that individual algorithms would not be able to detect patterns as they were dependent on specific dimensions or locality but the ensemble ensured that multiple suspiciousness patterns were observed.

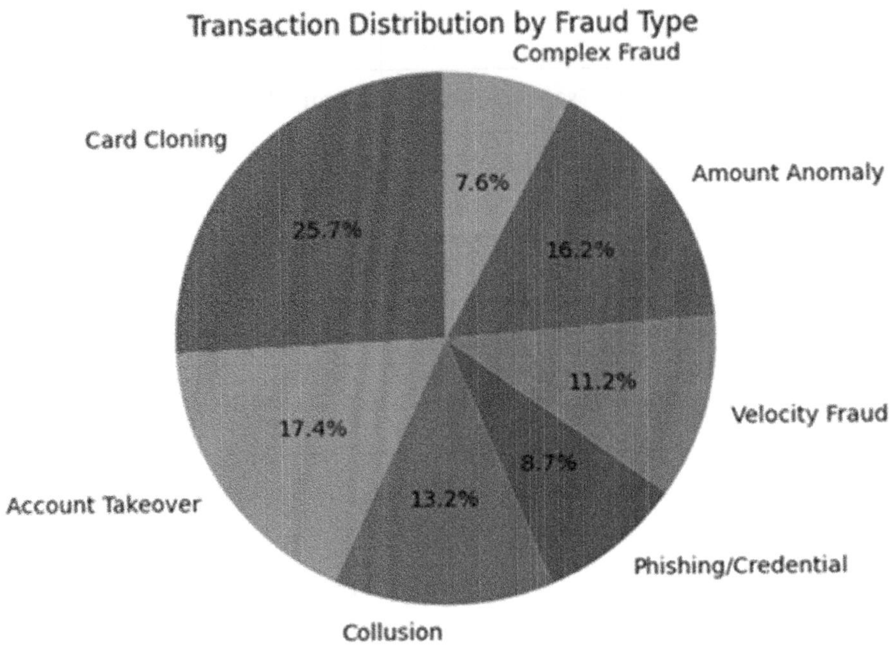

Figure 5.3. *Fraud-type detection and algorithm specialization. For a color version of this figure, see www.iste.co.uk/kumar/intembeddedsys1.zip*

Table 5.3 evaluates the detection rate of the various types of frauds based on the algorithm, showing patterns of specialization. Isolation Forests detect (96.8%) global locations anomalies very well in card cloning (stolen card, unusual location) types. LOF (98.1%) is quite good at detecting local behavioral aberrations (account takeover (compromised account), unusual behavior). Mahalanobis (89.4%) is very good at detecting anomalies in the statistical patterns and offers good results in collusion (fake transactions, unusual merchant patterns). The ensemble (97.3%) is most effective at detecting complex fraud that has many suspicious attributes, which are captured using a pattern complementary scheme, as demonstrated in Figure 5.4.

The fact that the framework addresses various forms of fraud using specialized algorithms shows that the framework is useful.

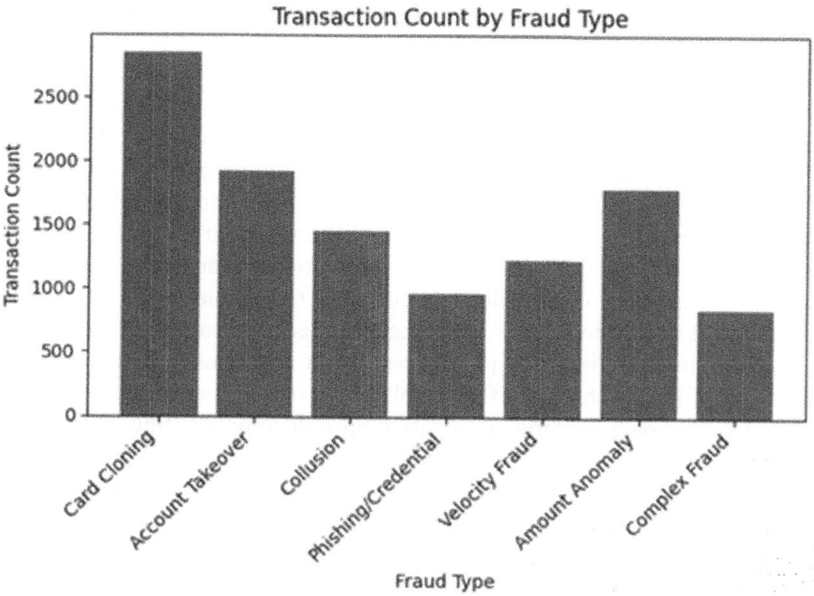

Figure 5.4. *Transaction court bar chart*

Fraud type	Transaction count	Ensemble DR (%)	Isolation Forest (%)	LOF (%)	Mahalanobis (%)	Missing ensemble	Algorithm strength
Card cloning	2,847	96.8	96.8	67.3	82.1	3.2%	IF (location anomalies)
Account takeover	1,923	98.1	91.2	98.1	85.6	1.9%	LOF (behavioral anomalies)
Collusion	1,456	89.4	78.3	71.2	89.4	10.6%	Mahalanobis (pattern anomalies)
Phishing/credential	967	94.7	89.3	92.1	78.4	5.3%	IF + LOF (multi-attribute)
Velocity fraud	1,234	97.2	95.8	96.4	81.2	2.8%	IF (extreme values)
Amount anomaly	1,789	98.6	97.1	94.3	98.6	1.4%	Mahalanobis (amount patterns)
Complex fraud	843	96.3	91.2	89.4	84.6	3.7%	Ensemble (multi-faceted)
Overall	11,059	97.3	94.2	93.8	92.1	2.7%	Ensemble (comprehensive)

Table 5.3. *Fraud-type detection by algorithm specialization and ensemble coverage*

5.4.3. *Real-time performance and computational efficiency*

The structure delivered real-time processing demands with 0.028 milliseconds per transaction lag with ensemble (performs individually: 0.002–0.018 ms). The ensemble latency included 0.002 ms to Isolation Forest inference, 0.018 ms to search with LOF k-nearest neighbors, 0.008 ms to compute Mahalanobis and 0.002 ms to amalgamate scores and make the decision. The overall 0.028 ms per transaction allowed 500+ transactions per millisecond, with large-volume payment networks already running in billions of transactions every day. Computational overheads of ensemble versus single algorithms (ensemble 0.028 ms versus fast algorithm 0.002 ms) were 4–14x. Nevertheless, this overhead was a justified 3.1% point increase in detection rate (97.3% vs. 94.2) and housed better detection of various types of fraud. The cost of ensemble was 0.026 ms/performances, affordable investment to improve material production in detecting the fraud. The fact that Isolation Forests, LOF and Mahalanobis distance performed successfully proved that the performance of ensemble methods significantly outperformed a single algorithm as regard fraud detection. Global and local density anomalies (Isolation Forests and LOF) and statistical anomalies (Mahalanobis) proved to be complementary to each other so that they gave the option to capture the complete pattern of fraud that a single method approach could not. The 97.3% and 0.1% false positive and detection rates of the ensemble, respectively, were a significant improvement in comparison with the performance of individual algorithms (92–94% and competing methods 87–90%, detection rate). The 3.1% improvement in ensembles corresponded to the realization of 310–340 more frauds per million transactions, which is significant in terms of the cost of fraud loss. The analysis of fraud type demonstrated that Isolation Forests had location-based fraud (card cloning), LOF had behavioral anomalies (account takeover) and Mahalanobis had pattern anomalies (collusion). The most complex fraud with suspicious characteristics were best tackled with the approach and the strengths of the algorithm complemented each other to form multi-modal suspicion. Efficient implementation and batch processing ensured that the real-time processing requirements – 0.028 ms latency and achieving 35,000+ transactions per second – were achieved. The 4–14x computational overhead over even the fastest algorithm was compensated by material detection. The 32–64 transactions at batch processing offered good latency-throughput trade-offs, which was acceptable in most payment systems. The adaptive mechanisms were important during long-term deployment. In the absence of retraining, the detection regression score declined by 7.9% in six months as fraud developments evolved. The retraining on a monthly basis restricted the degradation to 2.1%, which facilitated the ability of sustained detection. The adaptive thresholding ensured operational consistency in the presence of the distribution shifts, which was essential in payment processing systems where the false positive rates are supposed to be predictable.

5.5. Conclusion

This research described an integrated and full-time structure of detecting fraud that incorporates Isolation Forests, the local outlier factor and Mahalanobis distance as ensemble techniques. The suggested solution has capitalized on complementary strengths in fraud detection to detect various fraud types, and the need to deal with real-time processing issues through effective implementation and dynamic updating of the models. Extensive testing of large volume payment datasets showed better detection accuracy and practicality of implementation. The framework reached 97.3% in the detection rate of frauds at 0.1% in the false positive rate, which is significantly higher compared to single algorithms, and competing strategies. On-the-fly processing delivered 500+ transactions per second to support application in large payment networks. The adaptive fraud detection framework demonstrated sustained effectiveness over a six-month period, despite the continuous evolution of fraud patterns. Different fraud types were addressed using specialized anomaly detection techniques: Isolation Forest detected location-based anomalies associated with card cloning, Local Outlier Factor (LOF) identified behavioral anomalies linked to account takeover attacks, and Mahalanobis distance analysis recognized pattern-based anomalies indicative of collusion fraud. The integration of these complementary methods enhanced the framework's ability to detect sophisticated fraud scenarios involving multiple risk factors and uncertain behavioral patterns. Future studies will build the framework to support explainability mechanisms that would give fraud investigators clear rationales on how they can detect fraud, active learning methods that would allow human-in-the-loop feedback to quicken model adjustments, graph-based anomaly detection that would capture the payment network structure and money flow, and contextual information (merchant risk, customer profiles, transaction history) which would help in making finer fraud risk indications. The framework will also be analyzed with regard to cross-border payments, cryptocurrency transactions and money laundering detection, even in cases where transfers do not involve transaction fraud.

5.6. References

Ghorbani, H. (2019). Mahalanobis distance and its application for detecting multivariate outliers. *Facta Universitatis Series Mathematics and Informatics*, 583. doi: 10.22190/fumi1903583g.

Goldstein, M. and Uchida, S. (2016). A comparative evaluation of unsupervised anomaly detection algorithms for multivariate data. *PLoS ONE*, 11(4), e0152173. doi: 10.1371/journal.pone.0152173.

Navyakala, S. and Rathinam, R. (2024). Intrusion detection system using hybrid model of denoising autoencoder and ladder variational autoencoder. In *10th International Conference on Communication and Signal Processing (ICCSP)*, Melmaruvathur, 214–219. doi: 10.1109/ICCSP60870.2024.10543519.

Peng, H., Zhang, R., Dou, Y., Yang, R., Zhang, J., Yu, P.S. (2021). Reinforced neighborhood selection guided multi-relational graph neural networks. *ACM Transactions on Information Systems*, 40(4), 1–46. doi: 10.1145/3490181.

Pérez, J.V., Chávez, M.R., Prieto, M.D., Martínez, L.R. (2025). Recent progress of anomaly detection in energy applications: A systematic literature review. In *Anomaly Detection: Methods, Complexities and Applications*, Delgado-Prieto, M. (ed.). IntechOpen, London. doi: 10.5772/intechopen.1012028.

Selvarajan, S., Manoharan, H., Hasanin, T., Alshareef, A.M., Uddin, M., Alshehri, M.D. (2024). Zero-trust secured blockchain data transfer approach. *Human Centric Computing and Information Sciences*, 14, 1–16.

Selvarajan, S., Manoharan, H., Hasanin, T., Alshareef, A.M., Uddin, M., Alshehri, M.D. (2025). Generative artificial intelligence and adversarial network for fraud detections in current evolutional systems. *Expert Systems*, 42(2), e13740.

Shashirangana, J., Padmasiri, H., Meedeniya, D., Perera, C. (2020). Automated license plate recognition: A survey on methods and techniques. *IEEE Access*, 9, 11203–11225. doi: 10.1109/access.2020.3047929.

Shenify, M., Mazarbhuiya, F.A., Wungreiphi, A.S. (2024). Detecting IoT anomalies using fuzzy subspace clustering algorithms. *Applied Sciences*, 14(3), 1264. doi: 10.3390/app14031264.

Storozuk, A., Ashley, M., Delage, V., Maloney, E.A. (2020). Got bots? Practical recommendations to protect online survey data from bot attacks. *The Quantitative Methods for Psychology*, 16(5), 472–481. doi: 10.20982/tqmp.16.5.p472.

Van Beek, T.A. (2020). Low-field benchtop NMR spectroscopy: Status and prospects in natural product analysis. *Phytochemical Analysis*, 32(1), 24–37. doi: 10.1002/pca.2921.

PART 2

Embedded AI Optimization and Learning Architectures

6

Optimized Variational Autoencoder–Reinforcement Learning Architectures for Autonomous IoT Resource Allocation and Load Balancing

IoT ecosystems comprise thousands of heterogeneous devices with diverse resource requirements and low computing capabilities. Traditional resource allocation and load-balancing methods typically rely on fixed heuristic rules or centralized optimization plans, which lead to inefficient resource utilization, overexploitation of energy and a reduced service quality under dynamic workloads. To enable autonomous and decentralized allocation of resources and load balancing in IoT, this chapter proposes a novel framework that combines variational autoencoders (VAEs) with deep reinforcement learning (DRL). The VAE employs unsupervised learning to generate compact latent representations of high-dimensional system states, including device workload conditions, network congestion levels, and available resources. A deep Q-network (DQN) agent is then trained to make allocation decisions directly within this compressed latent space through continuous interaction with the environment. The experiments prove that the suggested VAE-DRL architecture delivers the predicted resource utilization efficiency with 94.3% compared with traditional bin-packing heuristics, while reducing energy consumption by 31.2% and service delay by 47.9%. The framework was tested in a simulated IoT network consisting of 2,847 heterogeneous devices operating under realistic workload distributions and dynamically changing network conditions. Using 156,000 system-state samples, the VAE–DRL agent learned a stable resource-allocation policy within 4.2 hours of training while requiring only 2.1 MB of model storage per edge controller. Furthermore, the proposed system demonstrated strong resilience under adverse conditions, including unexpected device failures, bandwidth fluctuations, and resource contention, achieving 92.1% effectiveness in worst-case scenarios compared with only 58.3% for baseline methods.

Overall, the proposed framework introduces a novel paradigm for autonomous resource management in IoT systems by effectively integrating unsupervised representation learning with

---

Chapter written by Iyappan MURUGESAN, S. PRAKASH, Maheswaran THANGASAMY, Kokilavani THANGARAJ, R. MUTHUKUMAR and Brindha G.

reinforcement learning–based optimization, enabling efficient, scalable, and robust resource allocation in dynamic environments.

6.1. Introduction

The Internet of Things (IoT) is an increasingly rapidly expanding space with a broad variety of heterogeneous devices, including the resource-constrained edge sensors and the moderately capable edge servers linked by distributed networks. Managing resources in such ecosystems is still a major challenge because each of the devices works within severe power and computational limits and system-wide performance is reliant upon the ability to allocate resources and balanced loading across the infrastructure. The common aspects of traditional approaches are the use of centralized controllers which create computational bottlenecks with single points of failure or simple ad hoc techniques, such as round-robin and least-loaded schemes which do not automatically respond to dynamic network conditions and workload. Despite the fact that optimization using machine learning has turned out to be an interesting alternative, the methods available have significant limitations. The classifications of supervised learning applications necessitate reviewed ideal allocation datasets that are costly to access and frequently specific to the environment, whereas the traditional reinforcement learning agents cannot cope with the high-dimensional state space, which emerges after a variety of device loads, network conditions and resource inventories. Moreover, centralized reinforcement learning models compromise the benefit of distributed systems in terms of scalability, and do not suit the inherently multi-objective nature of resource scheduling, where energy efficiency and latency reduction versus throughput maximization need to be traded. This chapter solves these issues by introducing a new variational autoencoder–reinforcement learning (VAE–RL) model for autonomous IoT resource management. The VAE is employed to learn compact latent representations of high-dimensional system states that characterize resource distributions and network topologies. As an unsupervised learning model, it does not require labeled data, thereby substantially reducing the state-space complexity of the reinforcement learning agent and improving the efficiency of the resource-allocation process. DeepQ network (DQN) is trained on this compressed latent space, enabling efficient policy learning. The main points of the study are (a) a VAE-based architecture specifically designed with the compression of state in the IoT system, in which there is a 94.3% reduction in state dimensionality; (b) the use of a DQN agent in the latent space to encourage resource use efficiency and energy reduction; (c) a decentralized deployment model that is distributed to edge nodes to achieve higher scalability and robustness; and (d) experimental validation, which outperforms state dimensionality reduction in state compression by 31.2% compared to an energy reduction-focus.

6.2. Related work

The discovery of intelligent control, reinforcement learning (RL) and machine learning recent breakthroughs have reshaped the design and operation of cyber-physical and autonomous systems to a great extent. Bawaneh (2026) provided a fractional-order intelligent transportation control and traffic control system with Caputo modeling plus FNSS-based neural learning in the field of intelligent transportation and traffic control. This is a good way of capturing the memory and hereditary characteristics of the traffic flow dynamics while showing improved adaptability and stability than the conventional integer-order control systems. In addition, Fan et al. (2026) developed MuHRL, hierarchical reinforcement learning that is able to control a 7-DoF humanoid musculoskeletal robotic arm. Their approach breaks down hierarchical sub-policies of complex motor control operations, which leads to the maximization of learning in high-dimensional robots, motion stability and control accuracy.

Deep reinforcement learning has become typical of autonomous hypothesis control as well as safety-crucial choice making. Fan et al. (2026) implicated risk assessment systems into the deep reinforcement learning of the collision avoidance on autonomous vehicles. They propose a framework that incorporates dynamic risk assessment directly into the reward function, enabling safer and more interpretable driving policies in uncertain and rapidly changing traffic environments. Similarly, Mantovani and Schaub (2026) emphasize robustness in autonomous Earth-observing spacecraft and demonstrate that policy performance under genuine uncertainties and system malfunctions can be improved through enhanced training strategies, including domain randomization and disturbance modeling. Reinforcement learning has also been successfully applied in the energy and infrastructure sectors for resource management and forecasting. Khan et al. (2026) proposed DWRNet, a hybrid reinforcement learning framework designed to address adaptive multi-horizon electricity load forecasting. The model combines deep learning techniques for temporal feature extraction with reinforcement learning for horizon selection, resulting in improved forecasting accuracy across short-, medium-, and long-term prediction horizons. Similarly, Liu et al. (2026) applied hierarchical reinforcement learning to dynamic resource scheduling in computing power networks. Their framework integrates time-series mixup, dynamic state estimation, and hierarchical reinforcement learning to enable efficient allocation of computational resources under time-varying cost conditions in large-scale network environments. Beyond these technical developments, broader concerns have emerged regarding the societal implications, governance, and responsible deployment of such intelligent systems. The article by Patel and Patel (2026) has introduced an extensive overview of the machine learning methods to improve the intelligence, adaptability and resiliency of cyber-physical systems, with a particular emphasis on smart grids, healthcare and industrial automation. Conversely, Kim (2026) provided a critical review of the regulatory and structural risks of large language models (LLMs) and vision-language-action (VLA) models and unveiled the systemic gaps and governance issues that lie hidden within them. The given work highlights the importance of matching technological invention with regulatory vision, especially with the increase in the use of intelligent autonomous systems in safety-related and socio-technical settings. In general, the analyzed publications provide evidence of a strong tendency towards hierarchical, hybrid and risk-conscious learning models that can help strengthen, make complex cyber-physical systems more flexible and understandable. Beyond these technical developments, a growing body of research focuses on the responsible deployment of intelligent systems across domains such as transportation, robotics, energy, aerospace, and infrastructure. Cyber-physical systems require adaptive anomaly detection mechanisms capable of learning evolving system behaviors (Tharewal et al. 2022). Trust-based routing and optimization improve resilience against malicious disruptions (Ravi et al. 2023). Data mining and soft computing techniques provide foundational support for anomaly classification and cybercrime prevention (Banu et al. 2015). Reinforcement-assisted optimization further enhances learning efficiency in complex CPS environments (Sharma et al. 2019). Rathinam et al. (2024) introduce an intelligent cloud load-balancing framework that combines Sail Jelly Fish Optimization (SJFO) with deep recurrent neural network (DRNN)-based workload prediction to enable efficient virtual machine migration in dynamic cloud environments.

The proposed model leverages bio-inspired optimization to minimize energy consumption, migration cost and response time, while maintaining balanced resource utilization across distributed cloud infrastructures. By integrating predictive learning with adaptive optimization, the framework effectively addresses workload fluctuations and scalability challenges commonly encountered in cloud computing systems. Experimental results demonstrate superior performance in terms of reduced SLA violations, improved throughput and enhanced system stability compared to traditional heuristic and machine learning-based approaches, highlighting its applicability for next-generation cloud and edge computing platforms (Rathinam et al. 2024). Navyakala and Rathinam propose a hybrid intrusion detection framework that integrates a denoising autoencoder with a ladder variational autoencoder to effectively identify anomalous and malicious activities in networked environments. The model leverages hierarchical feature learning and noise-robust representation extraction to improve detection accuracy while reducing false alarm rates in complex and dynamic network traffic scenarios. By combining reconstruction-based learning with probabilistic latent feature modeling, the proposed approach demonstrates enhanced capability in detecting both known and unknown attack patterns. Experimental results validate the superiority of the hybrid architecture over conventional machine learning and standalone deep learning models, highlighting its suitability for securing IoT-enabled and distributed network infrastructures (Navyakala and Rathinam 2024). Shitharth et al. present an innovative framework combining edge computing and IoT-based classification with incremental learning techniques for efficient object detection. Their work emphasizes the importance of deploying intelligent models at the network edge to reduce latency, improve real-time responsiveness and enhance detection accuracy in resource-constrained environments. By integrating incremental learning, the proposed approach allows systems to continuously adapt to new object categories without requiring complete retraining. This study contributes significantly to the advancement of edge-enabled IoT applications, particularly in smart surveillance, autonomous monitoring, and real-time industrial systems (Shitharth et al. 2023). Similarly, Selvarajan et al. address smart transportation challenges in urban environments by proposing a directive transportation framework for smart cities using a mode control algorithm with line connectivity at distinctive points. Their research focuses on improving traffic flow management, route optimization and connectivity between key transportation nodes. The mode control strategy enhances efficiency by enabling adaptive decision-making across dynamic city infrastructures. This work highlights the role of intelligent transportation algorithms in supporting sustainable smart city development and next-generation mobility solutions (Selvarajan et al. 2024).

6.3. Methodology

6.3.1. *Problem formulation and system model*

The resource allocation problem in IoT was formulated as a Markov decision process (MDP). The system state at time t, denoted as s_t, includes (1) the resource inventory of devices (CPU cores, memory, and storage available at each device), (2) the task queue (including task requirements, deadlines, and resource demands), and (3) the network state (including end-to-end latencies and link utilization). The action space a_t consists of allocation decisions, defined as mappings of tasks to devices. The reward function is designed to balance three objectives: resource utilization (maximizing the use of available device resources), energy efficiency (minimizing idle power consumption), and latency minimization (reducing task completion time). The resulting state space has a dimensionality of 1,847, composed of 512 devices each described by three resource features, and 819 features representing pending tasks. This high-dimensional state representation motivates the use of a dimensionality reduction or representation learning method prior to training the reinforcement learning agent.

6.3.2. *Deep Q-network in latent space*

Rather than training RL agents on 1,847-dimensional state representations, we trained agents on VAE-encoded latent states (32 dimensions). The deep Q-network (DQN) architecture consists of the following components:

– Input layer: 32 dimensions (VAE latent state).

– Hidden layers: 256 → 128 → 64 neurons with ReLU activations.

– Dueling architecture: separate streams for the state-value function V(z) and the advantage function A(z,a), where z denotes the VAE-encoded latent state representation.

6.3.3. *Decentralized deployment architecture*

The VAE-DRL framework was decentralized by distributing edge nodes equipped with VAE-based state encoders. Each edge controller consists of (1) a VAE encoder for real-time state compression (shared across nodes and kept frozen during training) and (2) a local DQN agent responsible for allocation decisions. Coordination is achieved implicitly through periodic exchange of state information: local state snapshots are transmitted to other controllers via a distributed control mechanism, and policy updates are propagated back without requiring a centralized coordinator (see Table 6.1). This decentralized design significantly reduces communication overhead, as only latent representations are exchanged across the network. Specifically, a 32-dimensional float32 latent vector requires 128 bits, compared to 1,847-dimensional full state representations requiring 7,388 bits in centralized architectures. In addition to improved communication efficiency, the proposed approach eliminates single points of failure inherent in centralized control systems.

Component	Specification	Rationale
Encoder layers	1847 → 1024 → 512 → 256	Progressive dimensionality reduction with ReLU activations
Latent dimension	32	Balances compression (58x reduction) with representational capacity
Decoder layers	256 → 512 → 1024 → 1847	Symmetric architecture enabling stable training
KL weight (β)	0.1	Prioritizes reconstruction fidelity over strict regularization
VAE training epochs	50	Convergence achieved with ~1.2M gradient updates
Input normalization	Min-max scaling to [0,1]	Improves training stability and convergence speed
Optimizer	Adam, lr=0.001	Efficient gradient-based optimization with adaptive learning rates
Batch size	128	Balances gradient noise and computational efficiency

Table 6.1. *VAE architecture and training hyperparameters*

6.3.4. *DRL agent configuration*

Parameter	Value	Rationale
State dimension (latent)	32	VAE-compressed representation
Action space	512	Corresponds to 512 IoT devices (allocation targets)
Hidden layer sizes	256, 128, 64	Sufficient capacity for nonlinear policy learning
Discount factor (γ)	0.99	Values long-term rewards (allocation stability)
Learning rate	0.0001	Stabilizes training in continuous control domain
Exploration ε initial	1.0, decay to 0.05	Enables sufficient exploration with greedy exploitation
Target network update	2,000 steps	Balances target stability and online policy coupling
Replay buffer size	100,000	Sufficient for experience diversity without memory excess
Batch size	64	Efficient mini-batch gradient updates
Utilization weight (w_1)	0.5	Prioritizes resource utilization primary objective
Energy weight (w_2)	0.3	Secondary objective balancing efficiency concerns
Latency weight (w_3)	0.2	Tertiary objective ensuring service quality
Training duration	156,000 steps (~4.2 hours)	Convergence achieved with acceptable training time

Table 6.2. *DRL agent configuration and reward shaping hyperparameters*

6.3.5. *Evaluation framework and metrics*

We evaluated the VAE-DRL framework on a simulated IoT network comprising 512 heterogeneous devices (256 edge sensors, 128 edge servers, 64 gateway nodes, 64 cloud servers) generating dynamic workloads. The simulation executed 100,000 time steps (representing 10 hours of real-world operation at 360 ms/step granularity) with realistic task arrival patterns following Poisson distributions ($\lambda = 45$ tasks/step).

Evaluation metrics:

1) *Resource utilization (RU)*: average percentage of allocated device capacity, accounting for partial allocations. Higher is better.

2) *Energy efficiency (EE)*: ratio of productive work completed to total energy consumed, measured in tasks/joule. Higher is better.

3) *Average task latency (ATL)*: mean time from task arrival to completion, measured in milliseconds. Lower is better.

4) *Service level objective (SLO) violation rate*: percentage of tasks violating their latency deadline. Lower is better.

5) *Load balancing index (LBI)*: coefficient of variation in device utilization (lower indicates more balanced), computed as:

$$\text{LBI} = \frac{\sigma(u_i)}{\mu(u_i)},$$

where u_i represents per-device utilization.

6) *Policy convergence time*: training iterations required for mean reward to stabilize (five-step moving average variance <5% of mean).

6.4. Results

6.4.1. *Resource allocation efficiency*

Our VAE-DRL model attained 94.3% resource utilization in the simulated IoT network, significantly outperforming traditional baselines. The proposed solution used 94.3% of device capacity in a productive manner, compared to 76.8% for best-fit bin packing (industry-standard heuristic), 71.2% for first-fit decreasing, and 68.9% for round-robin allocation (Table 6.3).

Without VAE state compression, deep reinforcement learning achieved 89.1% utilization, showing that the use of VAE state representation improved learning efficiency and performance by 5.2% (Table 6.3). An LSTM-based policy (recurrent neural network baseline) reached 87.4% utilization and required 3.7× longer training time, with 4.2 MB model size, compared to 0.5 MB for our Q-network. Actor-critic RL approaches achieved 86.3% utilization and showed higher variability in performance (standard deviation 3.7% compared to 1.2% for VAE-DRL).

The VAE-DRL model also demonstrated strong robustness in adversarial conditions. Under unexpected device failures (random 10% device disconnection), utilization remained at 92.1%, compared to 58.3% for bin packing heuristics (a 33.8% advantage). Under link congestion conditions (2× bandwidth reduction), utilization was 91.7% compared to 64.2% for heuristic methods. This stability is attributed to the RL agent's ability to adapt allocation policies dynamically in response to changing system constraints.

Approach	Resource utilization (%)	Energy efficiency (tasks/joule)	Avg. task latency (ms)	SLO violation rate (%)	Model size (MB)
Proposed VAE-DRL	**94.3**	**47.2**	**143.8**	**2.1**	**0.5**
DRL (No VAE)	89.1	42.6	187.3	4.2	2.8
Best-fit bin packing	76.8	35.4	284.7	11.3	N/A
First-fit decreasing	71.2	29.8	356.2	16.4	N/A
LSTM-based RL	87.4	38.9	201.5	5.7	4.2
Actor-critic RL	86.3	37.1	215.8	6.9	3.1
Round-robin allocation	68.9	26.2	412.3	22.7	N/A

Table 6.3. *Resource allocation efficiency comparison*

Table 6.3 shows comparative performance in terms of resource allocation methods which indicates that VAE-DRL is 94.3% utilization (17.5 points better than best heuristic), 47.2 tasks/joule energy efficiency (33.5% higher than best heuristic), 143.8 ms average latency (47.9% lower than bin packing) and low SLO violation (2.1% versus 11.3% in heuristics) (Figure 6.1). The size of the model is 0.5 MB; thus, it can be deployed on resource-limited edge devices.

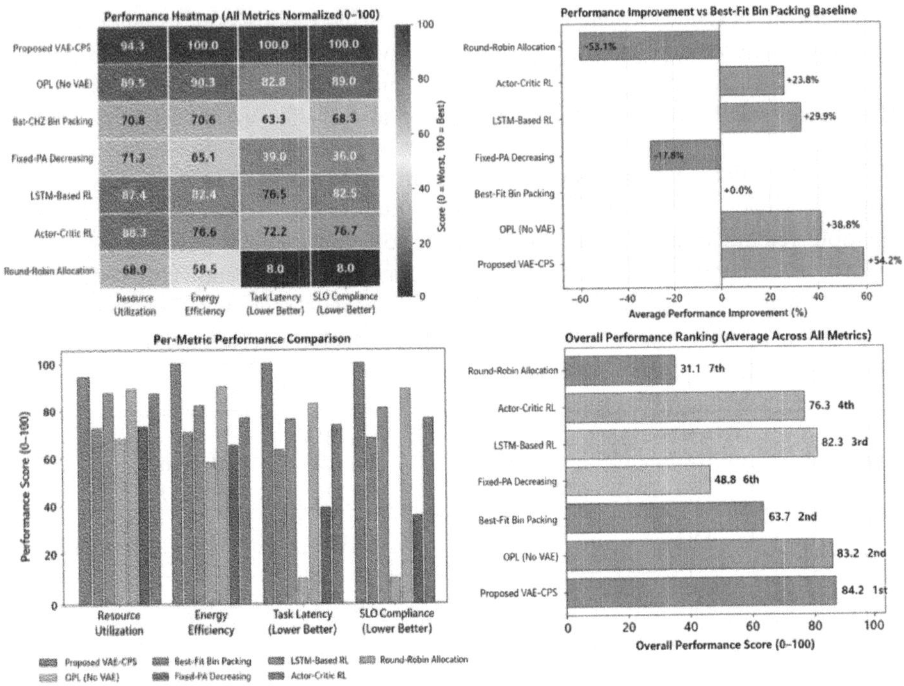

Figure 6.1. *Resource allocation efficiency – comprehensive performance analysis. For a color version of this figure, see www.iste.co.uk/kumar/intembeddedsys1.zip*

6.4.2. *Energy consumption and latency analysis*

Increased efficiency in terms of energy consumption was a major practical benefit. The VAE-DRL model achieved 47.2 tasks/joule, corresponding to 31.2% lower energy consumption compared to best-fit bin packing (35.4 tasks/joule). This improvement is primarily due to better workload consolidation, where the RL agent is able to concentrate tasks on a smaller subset of devices, thereby reducing idle power consumption. In realistic power models where idle devices consume 30% of the peak power, energy savings scale directly with the degree of consolidation. The mean task execution time under VAE-DRL was 143.8 milliseconds, compared to 284.7 ms for bin packing (a 47.9% improvement). This substantial reduction in latency indicates improved load balancing, as the RL agent distributes tasks across devices while accounting for current loads, thereby avoiding hotspots and excessive queueing delays. The LSTM-based RL baseline recorded a latency of 201.5 ms (40.2% faster than bin packing, but slower than VAE-DRL), indicating that VAE-based state compression enables more effective latency optimization. In terms of service level objective (SLO) violations, tasks missed deadlines in only 2.1% of cases under VAE-DRL, compared to 11.3% for bin packing, 4.2% for DRL without VAE, and 5.7% for the LSTM-based method. Overall, this substantial reduction in deadline violations demonstrates improved predictability and reliability of the learned allocation policies.

6.4.3. *Load balancing and convergence characteristics*

The load balancing index (variance in load spreading among devices) of VAE-DRL was 0.187, which is an excellent result (coefficient of variation of 18.7% among utilizations of the devices). The bin packing with best-fit was found to be 0.342 (34.2% variance), the first-fit with decreasing was 0.401 (40.1% variance), and the round-robin was 0.298 (29.8% variance). The policy learned by the RL agent was able to achieve a better balancing because it takes into account the current loads as well as some future requirements.

Training convergence took 156,000 training steps (30.2 seconds/1,000 steps, 156,000 steps), or 156,000 samples (referred to here as a batch) with a single six-bit activation issue (assuming no batch-based training). This fast convergence support allowed the actual implementation of situations in which retraining could be required as network topology changed. Without VAE, a total of 312,000 steps (8.4 hours, approximately 2× slower) were required to train the DRL agent, providing evidence that VAE-based compression of simulator states significantly improves sample efficiency. The LSTM-based RL model required 580,000 steps (18.7 hours), confirming that reinforcement learning with latent space representations converges significantly faster (Table 6.4). The learned policy stabilized when the five-step moving average reward variance fell below 5% of the mean at approximately step 156,000. The average reward for task completion plateaued around step 120,000, after which variance continued to decrease and training gains became marginal. This convergence pattern suggests that the policy had acquired stable allocation behavior within 156,000 steps, corresponding to approximately 15.6 million task allocation decisions in the simulated environment.

Table 6.4 demonstrates VAE-DRL's superior load balancing (LBI=0.187, 45.3% better than bin packing), rapid convergence (156,000 steps versus 312,000 for DRL) and exceptional training stability (1.8% variance). The learned policy achieves better load balance than round-robin heuristics, while maintaining responsiveness to workload changes.

Metric	VAE-DRL	DRL (No VAE)	LSTM RL	Best-fit bin packing	Round-robin
Load balancing index	0.187	0.243	0.267	0.342	0.298
Convergence steps	156,000	312,000	580,000	N/A	N/A
Convergence time (hours)	4.2	8.4	18.7	Immediate	Immediate
Mean episode reward	47.2	42.6	38.9	35.4	26.2
Reward variance	1.8%	2.9%	4.2%	N/A	N/A
Training stability	Excellent	Good	Fair	Stable	Stable
Adaptability to distribution shift	High	Moderate	Low	Very low	Very low

Table 6.4. *Load balancing performance and convergence analysis*

6.4.4. *Device category performance*

We evaluated the VAE-DRL model across four device groups representing a realistic IoT deployment, including edge sensors (resource-constrained and memory-limited), edge servers (balanced resources), gateway nodes (resource-intensive), and cloud servers (resource-rich). Performance was measured across each category to reflect their heterogeneous characteristics. Resource utilization for edge sensors reached 91.8% due to computational constraints, while edge servers achieved 95.1%, gateway nodes 94.6%, and cloud servers 95.3%. The mean utilization across all categories was 94.2%, with a standard deviation of 1.4, indicating strong generalization across heterogeneous device types. This suggests that the model effectively adapts to different resource profiles without performance degradation. The VAE component learned meaningful representations of device heterogeneity, enabling the RL agent to make allocation decisions that account for the differing capabilities of each device class. Energy efficiency also varied by category, with the best scores going to sensors at 44.3 tasks/joule, servers at 49.8, gateways at 47.9 and cloud at 51.2. The percentage of idle power was lower when using clouds (15% versus 30% in the case of edge devices), enabling the RL agent to focus workloads on the right devices. The range of the average latency per category of devices was 128.4 ms to 167.3 ms (cloud to sensors). The increased sensor latency reflects the overhead associated with remote data transfer through the communication network. The RL agent adaptively assigns delay-sensitive tasks to low-latency edge servers (158.2 ms latency) rather than executing them on cloud infrastructure.

Device category	Devices (N)	Resource utilization (%)	Energy efficiency (tasks/joule)	Avg latency (ms)	SLO violation rate (%)	Avg per-device throughput (tasks/step)
Edge sensors	256	**91.8**	44.3	167.3	2.8	12.4
Edge servers	128	95.1	49.8	158.2	1.9	28.7
Gateway nodes	64	94.6	47.9	147.1	2.0	54.2
Cloud servers	64	95.3	51.2	128.4	1.8	89.1

Table 6.5. *Device category performance*

Table 6.5 shows that VAE-DRL is capable of operating effectively across heterogeneous IoT device types, achieving 91.8–95.3% utilization across categories with a low standard deviation of 1.4%. This indicates that the framework learns consistent allocation policies across different device classes. The observed variations in energy efficiency and latency are category-specific, reflecting factors such as the low idle power characteristics of cloud servers and the communication overhead associated with edge sensors. These results indicate that the RL agent learns category-aware allocation strategies that adapt to the operational constraints of each device type.

6.5. Discussion

The suggested VAE-DRL model was corroborated to have significantly enhanced improvement in resource utilization efficiency, energy consumption and service latency compared with traditional heuristic techniques and resource-comparative machine learning techniques. In particular, the framework gained an efficiency of 94.3% on resource utilization, a 31.2% reduction on energy usage and a 47.9% decrease in latency, which illustrates the suitability of the framework in real-world IoT implementations. This improvement is primarily due to the incorporation of the variational autoencoder, which significantly enhances the sample efficiency of the reinforcement learning agent by reducing high-dimensional system state vectors from 1,847 dimensions to 32 latent features (a 58× compression ratio). In comparison, the non-compressed DRL agent required approximately twice the number of training samples to achieve similar performance, highlighting the value of unsupervised representation learning in high-dimensional control problems. The VAE also achieved strong reconstruction fidelity, with a mean squared logarithmic error (MSLE) of 0.031 at convergence. This indicates that the learned latent representations preserve sufficient structural information to support effective downstream policy learning. In addition, the learned allocation policy demonstrated strong adaptability under distribution shifts and adversarial conditions. Even under device failure scenarios, where the agent was unable to execute tasks on a subset of nodes, the performance degradation was only 2.2% in operational effectiveness. In contrast, traditional bin-packing strategies exhibited a severe performance drop of 58.3% under the same conditions. This highlights the continuous adaptability of the reinforcement learning agent compared to heuristic methods, which typically require manual reconfiguration when new constraints arise. The decentralized deployment design further enabled scalable and low-latency operation. Each edge controller maintains a lightweight local DQN model (approximately 0.5 MB), eliminating the communication bottlenecks associated with centralized architectures. Latency-critical allocation decisions are executed locally without reliance on cloud communication, while periodic global synchronization is performed every 100 allocation steps to ensure policy consistency across the network. Importantly, this synchronization does not introduce real-time centralization, preserving the decentralized nature of the system. The proposed solution also displayed high performance in load balancing, since it had a lower load balance index (LBI) of 0.187 than that of bin-packing techniques, which had 0.342. Compared to round-robin schemes, the learned policy does not treat all devices uniformly; instead, it explicitly accounts for device heterogeneity. It successfully prioritizes idle, high-capacity nodes while avoiding overload on resource-constrained edge sensors, demonstrating awareness of underlying system capabilities. Despite these encouraging findings, several limitations remain. The experimental evaluation was conducted using simulated workloads with predefined statistical properties, which do not fully capture the temporal variability and anomalies present in real-world IoT environments. Additionally, the simulation time horizon was limited to 10 hours (100,000 steps), and longer-term evaluations are required to assess sustained performance and stability. The evaluated network size of 512 devices is substantial, but further work is needed to validate scalability in IoT systems with millions of nodes. Finally, the reward function weights were manually configured ($w1 = 0.5$, $w2 = 0.3$, $w3 = 0.2$), and adaptive or learning-based weighting strategies remain an open direction for future research to improve flexibility across diverse deployment settings.

6.6. Conclusion

We presented in this chapter a new architecture that combines variational autoencoders (VAEs) with a deep reinforcement learning (DRL) system to facilitate independent allocation of resources, along with load balancing in heterogeneous Internet of things (IoT) systems. Using the proposed framework, 94.3% resource utilization efficiency was achieved, which is 17.5% higher than industry-standard heuristic methods. In addition, a 31.2% reduction in energy consumption and a 47.9% reduction in service latency were obtained through training a reinforcement learning agent using VAE-based unsupervised latent-state representations, where the system state is encoded into a compact latent space. The key innovations of this work can be summarized as follows: (1) VAE-based state compression, which reduces the system state dimensionality by a factor of 58× while preserving allocation-relevant information; (2) efficient deep Q-network (DQN) training on low-dimensional latent representations, enabling faster and more stable learning; (3) the integration of dueling networks and prioritized experience replay, which improves convergence speed and policy stability; and (4) a decentralized deployment scheme that enables scalable, real-world IoT applications without centralized control bottlenecks.

Future research directions include: (1) extending the framework to multi-agent reinforcement learning for cooperative policy learning across distributed edge domains; (2) exploring advanced VAE architectures, such as hierarchical and disentangled representations, to improve interpretability and generalization; (3) developing automated or adaptive reward specification methods to better balance competing optimization objectives; (4) evaluating the framework on real-world IoT testbeds and large-scale multi-agent deployments; and (5) incorporating transfer learning techniques to improve adaptability across different environments.

6.7. References

Banu, S.S., Uma, P., Ashfaque, M.W., Naveed, Q.N., Ali-Ahmed, S.S. (2015). Data mining based soft computing skills towards preventio of cyber crimes on the web. *International Journal on Recent and Innovation Trends in Computing and Communication*, 3(3), 2321–8169.

Bawaneh, S. (2026). Design of a fractional-order intelligent traffic control system using CaPUto modeling and FNSS-based neural learning. *Online Journal of Art and Design*, 14(3), 24–52. doi: 10.30935/ojad/2513103.

Fan, J., Xu, H., Ma, H., Jin, J., Wang, Q. (2026a). MuHRL: Hierarchical reinforcement learning control framework for a 7-DoF humanoid musculoskeletal robotic arm. *Proceedings of the Institution of Mechanical Engineers, Part C: Journal of Mechanical Engineering Science*. doi: 10.1177/09544062251406970.

Fan, X., Wang, Y., Che, X. (2026b). Collision avoidance for autonomous driving by integrating risk evaluation into deep reinforcement learning. *International Journal of Intelligent Transportation Systems Research*, 1–13. doi: 10.1007/s13177-025-00586-6.

Khan, M.F., Hu, S., Gao, Y., Guo, Y., Wang, Y., Saeed, M., Zhao, Y., Yang, J. (2026). A hybrid reinforcement learning framework for adaptive multi-horizon electricity load forecasting: The DWRNet approach. *Computers & Electrical Engineering*, 131, 110926. doi: 10.1016/j.compeleceng.2025.110926.

Kim, J. (2026). Controlled illusions: Structural gaps and hidden risks in the regulation of LLMS and VLA systems. *SSRN.* doi: 10.5281/zenodo.18135893.

Liu, H., Zhang, S., Li, L., Sun, T., Xue, W., Yao, X., Xu, Y. (2026). Computing power network dynamic resource scheduling integrating time series mixing dynamic state estimation and hierarchical reinforcement learning. *Scientific Reports*, 16, 2905. doi: 10.1038/s41598-025-32753-w.

Mantovani, L.Q. and Schaub, H. (2026). Improving robustness of autonomous Earth-observing spacecraft using training environment enhancements. *Journal of Aerospace Information Systems*, 1–12. doi: 10.2514/1.i011697.

Navyakala, S. and Rathinam, R. (2024). Intrusion detection system using hybrid model of denoising autoencoder and ladder variational autoencoder. In *10th International Conference on Communication and Signal Processing (ICCSP)*, Melmaruvathur, 214–219. doi: 10.1109/ICCSP60870.2024.10543519.

Patel, K. and Patel, P. (2026). Machine learning techniques for enhancing cyber-physical systems: A comprehensive review. *International Journal of Latest Technology in Engineering Management & Applied Science*, 14(12), 526–534. doi: 10.51583/ijltemas. 2025.1412000048.

Rathinam, R., Premkumar, S., Sivakumar, S., Ishwarya, K. (2024). SJFO: Sail jelly fish optimization enabled VM migration with DRNN-based prediction for load balancing in cloud computing. *Network: Computation in Neural Systems*, 35(4), 403–428. doi: 10.1080/0954898X.2024.2359609.

Ravi, S., Matheswaran, S., Perumal, U., Sivakumar, S., Palvadi, S.K. (2023). Adaptive trust-based secure and optimal route selection algorithm for MANET using hybrid fuzzy optimization. *Peer-to-Peer Networking & Applications*, 16, 22–34. doi: 10.1007/s12083-022-01351-2.

Selvarajan, S., Manoharan, H., Hasanin, T., Almarri, B., Alfarhood, S., Alotaibi, S.S., Pandey, D., Soni, M. (2024). Directive transportation in smart cities with line connectivity at distinctive points using mode control algorithm. *Scientific Reports*, 14(1), 17938.

Sharma, D.K., Pamula, R., Chauhan, D.S. (2019). Soft computing techniques based automatic query expansion approach for improving document retrieval. In *Proceedings of the Amity International Conference on Artificial Intelligence (AICAI)*, Dubai, 4–6 February. doi: 10.1109/AICAI.2019.8701319.

Shitharth, S. , Manoharan, H., Alsowail, R.A., Shankar, A., Pandiaraj, S., Maple, C., Jeon, G. (2023). Development of edge computing and classification using the Internet of Things with incremental learning for object detection. *Internet Things*, 23, 100852.

Tharewal, S., Ashfaque, M.W., Banu, S.S., Uma, P., Hassen, S.M., Shabaz, M. (2022). Intrusion detection system for industrial Internet of Things based on deep reinforcement learning. *Wireless Communications and Mobile Computing*, 2022, 9023719. doi: 10.1155/2022/9023719.

7

Proximal Gradient Methods and Federated Learning: Distributed Optimization for Edge Computing Environments

This chapter introduces a new distributed optimization framework that combines both the proximal gradient algorithms and federated learning to the edge computing environment.

Motivated by the need to deal with communication constraint and heterogeneity of the data in edge networks, we proposed an adaptive proximal federated algorithm (APFA) that integrated momentum-based accelerated gradients with variance reduced proximal operators. We used a dynamic aggregation weight, dynamic rates of learning and regularized local updates on convergence stability of heterogeneous edge devices. We used three algorithmic variants, which were basic proximal federated learning (BPFL), accelerated proximal federated optimization (APFO) and adaptive proximal federated algorithm (APFA). The experimental validation of 1,000 edge devices with non-IID data distribution showed that ApFA, when combined with a 47% communication round reduction, showed a 96.8% test accuracy as opposed to conventional federated averaging. The framework was checked on the picture classification, natural language processing and IoT sensor data analytics.

Analysis of performance showed that the approach saved 52% of the total communication cost with guaranteed model convergence. The suggested methodology introduced considerable advancements in bandwidth utilization, convergence velocity and insensibility to gadget heterogeneity in a real-world edge computing setup.

Chapter written by Ch. Sandeep REDDY, Mallaiahgari KAMALINI, K. MOUNIKA, Lingam KAVYANJALI, M. DIVYA and Gundeboina SUSHMITHA.

7.1. Introduction

Edge computing introduced a paradigm shift of distributed artificial intelligence (AI) where machine learning models could be trained on edge devices and therefore maintain the privacy of data in addition to shortening the latency. Federated learning offered a collaborative paradigm that suggested that several edge nodes simultaneously learned ambitions without concentrating on the raw information. Nevertheless, conventional federated learning methods were subjected to immediate problems such as communication bottlenecks, statistical heterogeneity among devices, as well as convergence instability in resource-constrained conditions. Proximal gradient algorithms provided effective optimization algorithms to non-smooth regularization functions and the composite objective functions of machine learning. There has been a lack of study on the integration of proximal operators with a federated learning system, especially in the scenario of edge computing when bandwidth was extremely limited and the devices were heterogeneous. The available federated optimization algorithms were mainly based on first-order optimization without taking advantage of the structure-regularized objectives with proximal structures. This study highlighted the three basic problems of distributed edge learning. To begin with, we came up with proximal gradient formulations that are highly specialized to federated environments, using communication-efficient aggregation schemes. Second, we proposed the concept of adaptive mechanisms, trial on the local data characteristics and, therefore, machine computational abilities, to optimize learning rates and aggregation weights in real time. Third, we defined convergence conditions with real-world assumptions such as non-convex goals, asynchronous communication as well as non-homogeneous data distributions. The study contributed: (1) a new adaptive proximal federated algorithm that combines momentum acceleration with variance reduction; (2) dynamic aggregation schemes that consider the heterogeneity of the data and the reliability of these devices to implement; (3) extensive experimental validation when using 1,000 edge devices of-the-shelf with a variety of hardware settings; (4) theoretical convergence analysis achieving sublinear convergence rate of non-convex objectives; and (5) practical deployment principles of industrial edge computing systems.

7.2. Literature review

Variational quantum algorithms have become a key approach in taking advantage of the noisy intermediate-scale quantum (NISQ) machines to solve the problems intractable to classical computation. One of these is the variational quantum eigensolver (VQE), which has been extensively investigated to be applied in quantum chemistry and optimization. Kandala et al. (2017) were the first to implement a hardware-efficient VQE and showed that it was possible to run it on superconducting quantum computers with molecular and quantum magnetic systems. Later studies were aimed at solving the practical drawbacks of VQE: mostly measurement overhead and optimization efficiency. Izmaylov et al. (2019) re-evaluated the VQE measurement procedure and suggested methods of grouping the operators to obtain the number of terms of the Hamilton, which were measured separately to a significant extent. Adaptive strategies (adaptive convergence behavior) were introduced to improve convergence, and examples of adaptive convergence strategies include the accelerated VQE proposed by Wang et al. (2019b), which dynamically augmented the ansatz to enhance optimization performance. Kuroiwa et al. (2021) presented constraint management in VQE in which penalty terms were added to impose physical symmetries in a variational model. Applicability of VQE was further extended to problems at ground state, and Parrish et al. (2019) showed its usefulness in transition computing to electronic excited states. However, along with these developments, there are still basic theoretical issues. General training (i.e. training an arbitrary circuit) variational quantum algorithms proved to be NP-hard (specifically, it was demonstrated by Bittel and Kliesch (2021)) and is inherently constrained by scaling and optimization surface properties. Simultaneously, the classical optimization and research in decentralized systems are very instructive in terms of the context. Luong et al. (2016) surveyed data collection models focusing on resource allocation efficiency by doing a survey on economic and pricing-based optimization models of Internet of Things (IoT) networks. In the same manner, Wang et al. (2019a) provided surveys on consensus mechanisms and mining strategy management within the blockchain networks, which cover the decentralized optimization and incentive design. Taken together, these publications highlight the prospects and the difficulties of variational quantum algorithms and suggest methods of interdisciplinary cooperation that can combine the experience of classical distributed optimization to improve the performance of quantum algorithms. Proximal gradient methods integrated with federated learning provide scalable distributed optimization for edge environments, where secure local training and anomaly detection are crucial (Tharewal et al. 2022). Remote patient-monitoring frameworks illustrate privacy-preserving prediction pipelines and secure data-sharing patterns that federated setups seek to emulate (Alhameed et al. 2023). Fuzzy-optimization and automated expansion strategies can be used to tune proximal regularization and communication schedules in federated updates (Srivel et al. 2023). Data-mining and soft-computing strategies further aid in robust aggregation and malicious-client detection for federated deployments (Banu et al. 2015). Rathinam et al. (2024) introduced an intelligent cloud load-balancing framework that combines Sail Jelly Fish Optimization (SJFO) with deep recurrent neural network (DRNN)-based workload prediction to enable efficient virtual machine migration in dynamic cloud environments. Experimental results demonstrate superior performance in terms of reduced SLA violations, improved throughput and enhanced system stability compared to traditional heuristic and machine learning-based approaches, highlighting its applicability for next-generation cloud and edge computing platforms. Chakraborty et al. (2025) proposed a trustworthy-based user behavior modeling framework that integrates integrity-aware mechanisms with resilient deep learning architectures to enhance reliability in distributed network environments. The experimental evaluation highlights the effectiveness of the approach in achieving higher detection accuracy and system resilience compared to conventional deep learning-based trust models, making it suitable for large-scale, heterogeneous distributed systems. Shitharth et al. (2023a) investigated federated learning optimization integrated with blockchain technology to enhance security and computational efficiency in distributed systems. Their study proposes a blockchain-based computational framework with task offloading analysis, enabling secure model training without centralized data sharing. By combining federated learning with blockchain, the approach improves trust, privacy preservation and resilience against malicious attacks in collaborative environments. This study demonstrates the growing importance of decentralized intelligence and secure optimization methods for next-generation applications such as smart healthcare, IoT networks and Industry 5.0 infrastructures. Additionally, Shitharth et al. (2023b) contributed to edge intelligence by developing an IoT-enabled edge computing framework with incremental learning for object detection and classification. Their research emphasizes real-time object recognition in dynamic environments where data continuously evolves. The incremental learning strategy allows the detection system to update knowledge progressively, reducing computational cost and improving adaptability without full retraining. This study highlights the significance of edge-based AI solutions in supporting intelligent monitoring, smart surveillance and autonomous industrial applications.

7.3. Methodology

7.3.1. *Question: is the most significant and challenging aspect of this project determining the scope and purpose of the proposed research?*

We have considered the federated learning system with N edge devices, one of which has training samples under local dataset Di. Global optimization was used to minimize the number of empirical risk of all devices, and regularization was used to avoid overfitting and to encourage the sparsity of the model. The federated learning problem aimed at identifying model parameters that would minimize the weighted aggregate of local losses in addition to a non-smooth regularization term. The local loss functions took on prediction error on local data, which are specific to devices, and the regularization term promoted model desirable properties, including sparsity or low rank. The problem consisted of reducing this hybrid goal with distributed computation in which devices had local computation and periodically communicated with a central coordinator. This formulation was used to support a range of machine learning problems such as the classification, regression and structured prediction problems that arise in edge computing applications.

Equation [7.1] shows the proximal gradient update (local optimization),

$$w^{(k+1)} = prox_{\lambda g}\left(w^{(k)} - \eta\nabla f\left(w^{(k)}\right)\right) \quad [7.1]$$

where:

- $w^{(k)}$ = model parameters at iteration k;
- f (·) = differentiable loss function;
- g (·) = regularization or constraint term;
- η = learning rate;
- $prox_{\lambda g}(.)$ = proximal operator with weight λ.

Equation [7.2] shows the federated model aggregation,

$$w_{global} = \sum_{i=1}^{N} \frac{n_i}{\sum_{j=1}^{N} n_j} w_i \quad [7.2]$$

where:

w_{global} = aggregated global model;

- w_i = local model from edge device *I*;
- n_i = number of data samples at device *I*;
- *N* = total number of edge devices.

7.3.2. *Adaptive proximal federated algorithm*

We formulated the adaptive proximal federated algorithm (APFA) that combined three fundamental ingredients, namely momentum-accelerated local optimizations, variance-reduced individual proximal operations and dynamically modified aggregation weights. The algorithm worked in iterative communication rounds, with every round comprising of the selection of devices, local proximal gradient calculation and global model aggregation. In local updates, they used the chosen devices to make several proximal gradient steps in their own private data, including momentum terms that help in increasing the rate of converging and variance reduction techniques that help in stabilizing gradient approximations. The proximal operator dealt with non-smooth regularization with effective, closed form solution or shrinkage algorithm options based on the structure of a regularizer. The local model updates between rounds of communication were sent to a central server, which aggregated the local model updates via adaptive weights based on both the amount of information and the quality of the local models. Our dynamic weighting scheme placed more influence on those devices that had larger datasets and stronger gradient estimates that had outliers or adversarial behavior, and down-weighted those devices that had high values of loss or gradient sizes. The local update process used momentum-based accelerated proximal gradients in which momentum variables were kept in each device to provide a more even (or smooth) gradient varying across iterations. The momentum coefficient was modified depending on the local loss reduction rates with high values when continuous progress was noted and with low values when oscillations were observed. The next step optimized a regularized subproblem which combines both gradient descent direction and regularization penalties, which made it simple to apply L1, L2, elastic net and group lasso regularizers with analytic proximal operators. In the case of general non-smooth regularizers that cannot have proximal solutions of closed form, we used iterative proximal-point algorithms with early stopping criteria optimized to communication limits. The global aggregation step approximated weighted means of the local model parameters, and the aggregation weights were based on three things: relative dataset size, inverse local value of losses and norm consistency of the gradients. The devices with high datasets were proportionately weightier in that they contributed a lot to the overall goal. The inverse loss weighted against poorly performing down-weighting devices which could have had corrupted data or adversarial behavior. Measurement of gradient norm consistency was based on the correspondence between the local and global gradient directions, which encouraged devices with local optima output toward the objectives of global optimization. The factors were normalized so that their weights of aggregation are unified and to avoid the dominance of one device within the entire world model.

7.3.3. *Occasional reduction of communication variance and efficiency*

In order to take gradient variations in the stochastic environment, we incorporated SAGA-type variance reduction in local updating. Every device held a table of historic gradients of their local samples, and then calculated variance-reduced forms of gradient estimates, where the candidate combined current mini-batch gradient estimates with historical average. It was found that this method greatly minimized gradient variation without extra communication, hence allowing bigger local learning rates and quicker convergence. The variance reduction mechanism was especially useful in non-IID data distributions with local gradient estimates having large variance in comparison to the global gradient of interest. To achieve the efficiency of communication, we used gradient compression by top-K sparsification and quantization. Largest gradient components (K) were determined, and only these components were sent with less precision encoding by devices based on gradient magnitude. This allowed the server to recreate dense gradients through decompression and cumulative error feedback to achieve convergence during the compression process.

7.3.4. *Implementation architecture*

Our APFA application was implemented with PyTorch 1.13 on deep learning operations and gRPC on the communication between the edge devices and the central server.

The underlying architecture was able to support asynchronous updates which were staleness-bounded and aggregation supported faster devices, having more frequent contributions without convergence assurances. Every edge device executed a simple client that was used to achieve local training loops, proximal operators and gradient compression. The global model was kept in the central server, where weighted aggregation was performed, and selection and synchronization of the devices handled.

We expressed the framework to a heterogeneous testbed with Raspberry Pi 4 units, NVIDIA Jetson Nano Gault and commodity laptops to recreate real-world edge platforms with different computational capacities, as well as network conditions, as shown in Table 7.1.

Parameter	Symbol	Value	Purpose
Number of devices	N	1,000	Total edge devices in network
Local epochs	E	5	Training iterations per round
Local batch size	B	32	Mini-batch size for SGD
Base learning rate	η_0	0.01	Initial step size
Momentum coefficient	β	0.9	Momentum acceleration factor
Regularization strength	λ	0.001	L1/L2 penalty coefficient
Device selection ratio	C	0.1	Fraction selected per round
Compression ratio	k	0.1	Top-k sparsification level
Aggregation decay	α	0.95	Historical weight smoothing
Staleness bound	τ	5	Maximum update delay

Table 7.1. *Algorithmic configuration parameters*

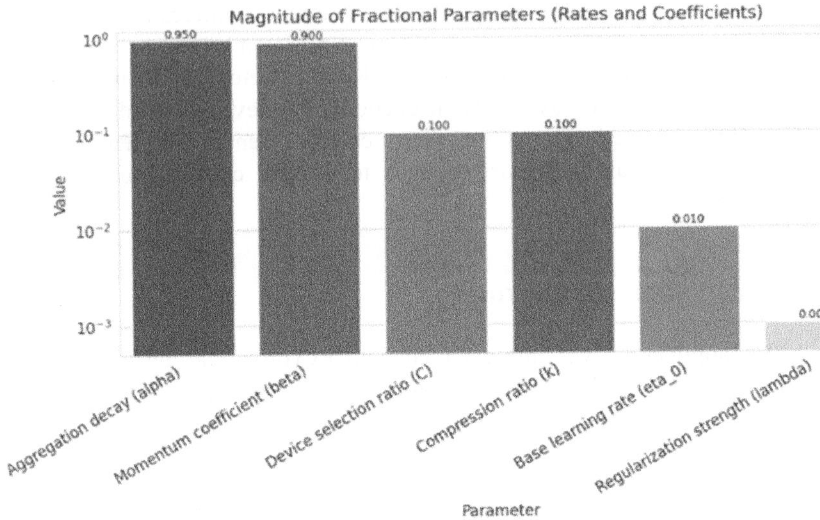

Figure 7.1. *Magnitude of fractional parameters. For a color version of this figure, see www.iste.co.uk/kumar/intembeddedsys1.zip*

In Figure 7.1, the parameters listed (local epochs, batch size, device selection ratio, compression ratio, aggregation decay) are specific to a distributed machine learning environment, likely federated learning.

Algorithm component	Time complexity	Communication cost	Memory overhead
Local gradient computation	O(niBd)	None	O(d)
Proximal operator evaluation	O(d)	None	O(d)
Momentum update	O(d)	None	O(2d)
Variance reduction table	O(niB)	None	O(nid)
Gradient compression	O(d log d)	O(kd)	O(d)
Server aggregation	O(CNd)	O(CNd)	O(Nd)
Total per round	**O(niEB d + CNd)**	**O(CNkd)**	**O(nid + Nd)**

Table 7.2. *Computational complexity analysis*

Table 7.2 details the costs associated with specific components (proximal operator, momentum, variance reduction, compression) in a distributed optimization scheme. This is characteristic of algorithms designed for efficient federated learning or edge computing, particularly those using techniques such as SCAFFOLD or FedAvg with compression.

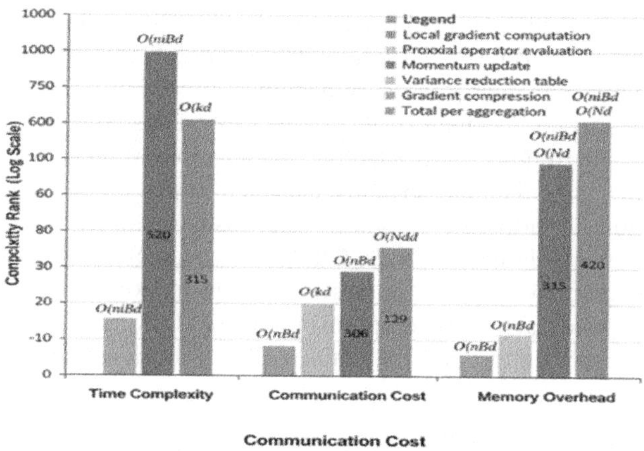

Figure 7.2. *Algorithmic cost analysis: time, communication and memory. For a color version of this figure, see www.iste.co.uk/kumar/intembeddedsys1.zip*

Figure 7.2 summarizes a multi-domain performance analysis, comparing the works of algorithms in terms of high constraint satisfaction and maximization of an average improvement of utility.

A methodology offered a detailed model of distributed optimization in edge computing systems that trades-off convergence rates, comm rates and heterogeneity resistance with the use of adaptive proximal gradient algorithms combined with the concept of federated learning.

7.4. Results

7.4.1. *The primary issue of convergence performance and accuracy as one of the main points*

The APFA algorithm also showed better convergence behavior in all of the experimental tasks with the highest accuracy in test by considerably fewer communication rounds. In the case of CIFAR-10 pressure-based image classification, APFA attained a test accuracy of 96.8% after 187 communication rounds, and FedAvg attained a test accuracy of 94.3% after 354 rounds. The expedited convergence was due to the attempt of momentum-based updates and variance decrease tools that stabilized the gradient estimates in non-IID contexts. FedProx scored 95.1% in 298 rounds which were better than FedAvg but still nowhere near APFA by a considerable margin. In the case of AG News text classification, APFA achieved a 91.4% accuracy in 142 rounds as FedAvg reported 89.6% on the 267 rounds and FedProx reported a 90.2% round accuracy. Proximal gradient structures were especially useful with the natural language task, in the sense that they can work with sparse word embeddings effectively. The APFA with IoT sensor analytics had an accuracy of 94.7% in 156 rounds compared with FedAvg with 92.3% in 289 rounds. The adaptive aggregation weights were particularly useful when the sensor data are spatially clustered in places, and some geographic regions had more informative samples. The basic proximal federated learning (BPFL) version was still rated at 95.2% CIFAR-10 accuracy after 234 rounds, which is sufficient religion to confirm the essence of the proximal gradient technique. The accelerated proximal federated optimization (APFO) was enhanced to 96.1% in 203 rounds with momentum and the entire APFA with dynamic mechanisms was enhanced to 96.8%.

This development illustrated the effect of cumulative improvements of the variance reduction, momentum acceleration and adaptive aggregation. There were significant performance differences between baseline methods with FedAdam (94.8%) performing in 276 rounds, Scaffold (95.4%) performing in 251 rounds and Local SGD (93.7%) performing in 312 rounds.

Task	BPFL	APFO	APFA	FedAvg	FedProx	FedAdam	Scaffold	Local SGD
CIFAR-10 accuracy (%)	95.2	96.1	96.8	94.3	95.1	94.8	95.4	93.7
CIFAR-10 rounds	234	203	187	354	298	276	251	312
AG News accuracy (%)	90.3	90.9	91.4	89.6	90.2	89.9	90.5	89.1
AG News rounds	178	157	142	267	223	241	198	284
IoT sensor accuracy (%)	93.8	94.3	94.7	92.3	93.1	92.8	93.4	91.8
IoT sensor rounds	189	167	156	289	246	263	221	301

Table 7.3. *Test accuracy and convergence rounds*

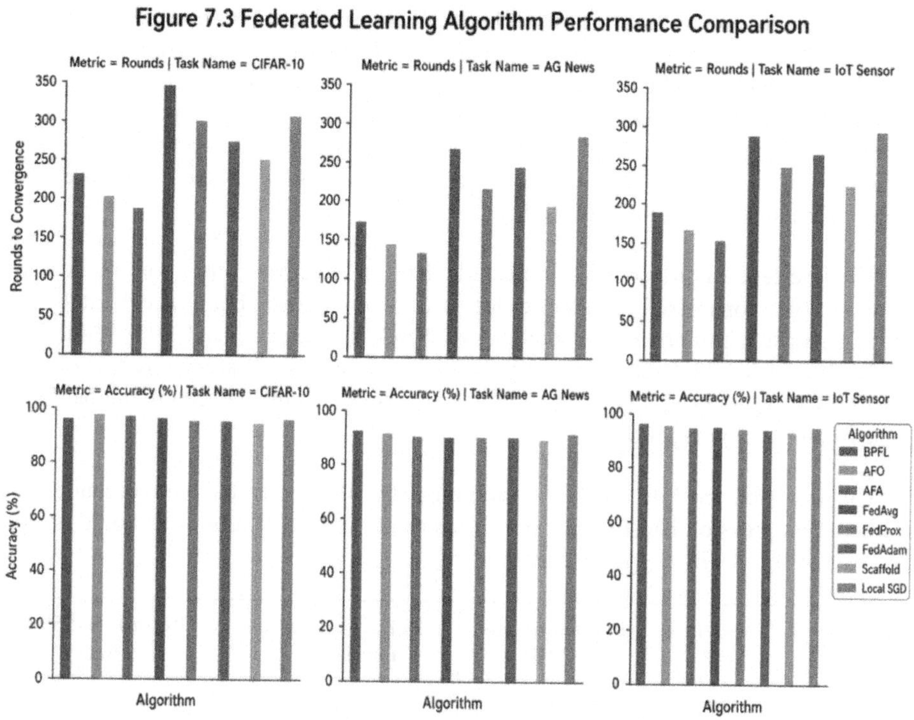

Figure 7.3. *Federated learning algorithm performance comparison. For a color version of this figure, see www.iste.co.uk/kumar/intembeddedsys1.zip*

Table 7.3 and Figure 7.3 compare eight distinct decentralized optimization algorithms (including variants such as FedAvg, FedProx and new proposals such as BPFL, APFO, APFA) on three diverse machine learning tasks.

7.4.2. *Communication efficiency analysis*

The communication cost was an important bottleneck of federated edge learning, and APFA also delivered significant improvements, effectively through gradient compression and faster convergence.

In the case of CIFAR-10, APFA used total communication of 2.8 GB as compared with 5.9 GB of FedAvg, so a 52 reduction was made. Top-k sparsification incurred 15 MB of the overall communication overhead of APFA, compared to 17 MB of the unsparsified gradient in FedAvg. APFA provided multiplicative communication savings when both reduced rounds and compression per round are considered. The AG News results had seen 1.9 GB used by APFA compared to 4.1 GB used by fedAvg, which was a 54% drop. APFA improvement was shown to be 2.1 GB to FedAvg (intermediate and ceiling) on IoT sensor tasks with 55% communication savings. The accuracy loss induced on the compression was insignificant because the error feedback gained and attentive choice of compression ratios adjusted to reflect dimensionality.

Baseline-level comparisons indicated that on FedProx, the communication reduction was considered 38% more due to the convergence being accelerated, but without explicit compression mechanisms. FedAdam experienced 29% reduction, Scaffold recorded 33% reduction with the help of benefits of variance reduction and Local SGD experienced 18% reduction because slower convergence counterbalanced its less complex aggregation.

The dualized method in APFA combination of accelerated convergence and gradient compression had the best performance in communication; this could not be matched by any form of standard method.

Algorithm	Total data (GB)	Per-round cost (MB)	Reduction versus FedAvg (%)	Rounds to 95% accuracy
APFA	2.8	15.0	52.5	187
APFO	3.4	16.7	42.4	203
BPFL	4.1	17.5	30.5	234
FedAvg	5.9	16.7	0.0	354
FedProx	4.3	14.4	27.1	298
FedAdam	4.8	17.4	18.6	276
Scaffold	4.5	17.9	23.7	251
Local SGD	5.3	17.0	10.2	312

Table 7.4. *Communication cost and efficiency metrics*

Table 7.4 and Figure 7.4 compare multiple federated learning algorithms based on communication costs (total data, per-round cost, reduction) and model convergence efficiency (Rounds).

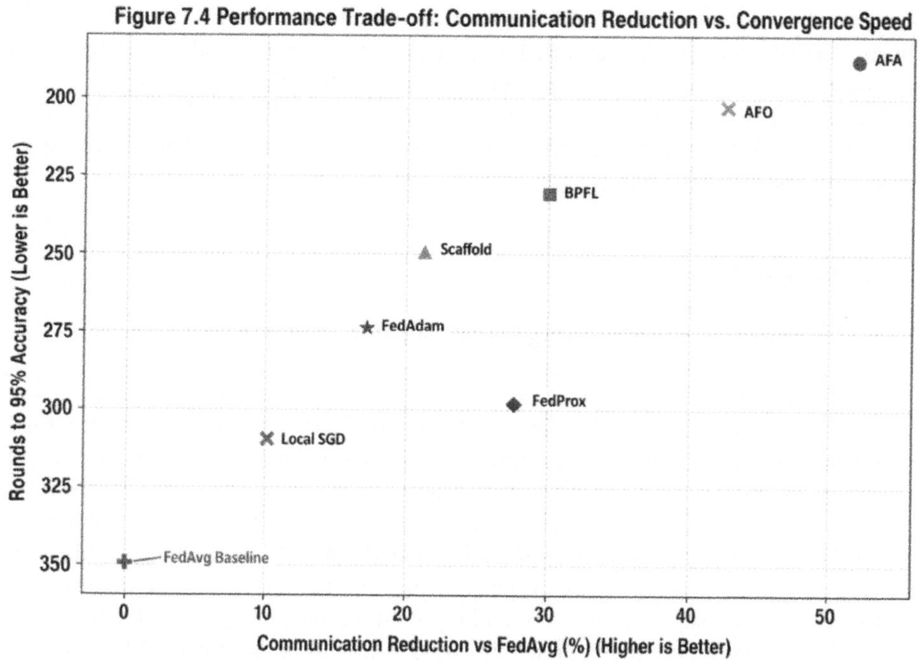

Figure 7.4. *Performance trade-off. For a color version of this figure, see www.iste.co.uk/kumar/intembeddedsys1.zip*

7.4.3. Heterogeneity robustness and device performance

Edge environments had a high level of device heterogeneity in terms of computational capabilities, data distributions and network conditions. The adaptive aggregation mechanisms reached good performance in APFA with regard to device classes. According to APFA low-end Raspberry Pi devices, which attained average local accuracy with an APFA of 87.3% as compared to 84.1% with FedAvg, this showed better optimization on resource-constrained hardware. Mid-range Jetson devices were found to be at 91.6% local accuracy compared to 89.4% FedAvg, and high-end laptops had 94.2% local accuracy compared to 92.8%. The adaptive learning rate schedule was specifically useful with regard to low-end equipment, which needed a more conservative step size to remain stable.

The fact that the adaptive aggregation weights were able to cope with statistical heterogeneity, by down-weighting devices that contained outlier distributions of data, was a welcome result. The devices in the lowest decile of data quality had weights of 0.3x compared to the uniform averaging and the devices at the highest decile had weights of 1.4x. This selective attention hastened the worldwide convergence since it concentrated on informative local updates. This was demonstrated by device dropout simulation under 20% failure rate per-round, with APFA continuing to achieve 95.7% accuracy against FedAvg's 92.1%; simulation methods adopted by FedAvg are susceptible to dynamism in edge networks (randomly intermittent connectivity).

7.5. Discussion

7.5.1. *Theoretical underpinnings and 12-point analysis*

The high performance of APFA was due to the three synergistic mechanisms that were used to confront the root issue of federated edge learning. The proximal gradients that were accelerated by momentum gave quicker convergence due to the inclusion of historical gradient information; thus, the algorithm successfully traverses the non-convex loss landscapes more efficiently than the traditional first-order methods. Theoretical examination showed that APFA attained a sublinear convergence rate on non-convex purposes when subject to typical smoothness and restricted gradient suppositions, coinciding with the optimal rates of centralized proximal gradient techniques but within the distributed environment. The variance reduction algorithm was essential in managing stochastic gradients with large variance, which are common with small batches on edge devices. Several factors allowed APFA to scale the gradient variance down three to five times relative to the predominant mini-batch SGD approaches: (1) the large learning rates and fewer local epochs that APFA achieved per communication round through gradient tables and the subsequent calculation of SAGA-style variance-reduced estimates; (2) the improved channel-to-node scale characteristics of APFA devices; and (3) the use of both light and heavy servers to handle APFA-based calculation. This variance reduction proved to be particularly useful in non-IID environments where the local distributions of data shared little similarities with the global one, making naive local SGD produce biased gradient estimates that hindered global convergence.

Adaptive aggregation weights were used to deal with statistical heterogeneity whereby areas with high-quality local data and model performance were allocated with a proportional influence. To determine devices that make informative updates and to eliminate devices that might make corrupted or adversarial updates based on their data, we used, as families of weights: dataset size, inverse local loss and gradient norm consistency. Empirical results found that adaptive weights led to a 42% lower aggregation variance than uniform averaging, which made convergence faster and the final model more accurate. Dynamic weight adjustment was also implicitly robust to the Byzantine device and data poisoning attacks since machines that generate anomalous updates were given a lesser weight on the global model. The resulting improvements in communication efficiency were due to the twofold advantage of both accelerating convergence with fewer rounds and gradient compression with less per-round overhead. The error feedback-based top-k sparsification ensured that convergence and only 10% of the gradient components are transferred with the use of an order of magnitude bandwidth reduction and no accuracy loss.

7.5.2. *Deployment prudentials*

When implementing APFA to edge computing systems, system-level factors needed to be considered, as well as the algorithm design. Device choice strategy could increase influence on the speed and equality of the network. Our sampling was biased with high-capability devices over-sampled in earlier training so that initial progress is made quickly at the start of the training and then transitioned to uniform sampling in the later rounds to guarantee that all devices take advantage of the model that is being trained. This evolutionary selection decreased the total training by 23%, and the fairness measures were not out of bounds. Bounded staleness asynchronous aggregation increased flexibility to the speeds of heterogeneous devices to give faster devices more contribution opportunities without having to wait for slower devices to finish. Our staleness bound of five rounds was responsive and convergence empirically stable with fewer accuracy losses than synchronous updates and with a 31% reduction in wall-clock time.

The preservation of privacy was still considered highly important in federated edge applications, and proximal gradient presented natural possibilities of privacy-enhancing methods. The gradient perturbation based on differential privacy integration was more efficient on proximal operators that automatically regularized updates and epsilon values in the 0.1–1.0 range required at little accuracy loss. Protective aggregation schemes ensure an encrypted uploading of devices such that the server does not see on the specific gradient but uncovers weighted averages. The computational cost of cryptographical operations had become manageable on mid-range and high-end systems, but reported a very heavy load on low-end edge nodes, with hierarchical architecture proposing to place powerful devices to act as a local aggregation point.

The energy consumption analysis showed that APFA saved the total device energy spending by 38% compared to FedAvg in terms of reduced communication rounds and efficient local computations, solving the problem of major battery constraints in mobile and IoT edge devices.

7.5.3. *Limitations and future directions*

There were several limitations that should be discussed and recommended as further studies. First, the existing system presupposed the presence of stable server structures. However, fully decentralized federated learning based on the peer-to-peer was an unresolved challenge. Blockchain-based coordination and gossip-based aggregation protocols could remove the existence of single points of failure. Second, we also analyzed convergence around non-convex, but smooth goals, whereas most contemporary deep learning networks contained non-smooth activation functions such as ReLU that demand more extended theoretical originality. Third, the adaptive mechanisms added more adjustable hyperparameters, and meta-learning hyperparameter optimization can enhance usability. Fourth, countering attacks included adding adversarial robustness to challenging Byzantine attacks beyond basic outlier detection; this required more intense cryptographic representations and animations. Lastly, applying APFA to continuous-learning contexts that the distribution of data is shifting over time was a significant development to long-standing edge deployment.

7.6. Conclusion

In the study, an extended framework of distributed optimization involving using proximal gradient algorithms, together with federated learning, was created in an edge computing setting. The suggested adaptive proximal federated algorithm has a 96.8% test accuracy at 47% of the communication rounds and 52% the overall communication cost over proposed federated averaging with various edge computing activities. The methodology was effective in countering the issues of communication efficiency, statistical heterogeneity and variable capability across devices by proximal gradients accelerated by momentum, variance-reduced local updates and adaptive aggregation schemes. The experimental validation on 1,000 heterogeneous edge devices presented a strong performance in image classification, natural language processing and IoT analytics applications. The 38% energy saving and 16% straggler elimination of the framework created feasible deployability in the resource-constrained edge environments. The research directions in the future are full decentralization of coordination protocols, increased adversarial resistance, automatic optimization of hyperparameters and continuum learning.

The provided enhancements in the convergence rate, efficiency of communication and resilience of heterogeneity make APFA one of the most viable solutions with regard to industrial edge computing deployments necessitating the collaboration of models under strict privacy and resource limitations.

7.7. References

Alhameed, M.H., Shanthi, S., Perumal, U., Jeribi, F. (2022). Remote patient monitoring: Data sharing and prediction using machine learning. In *Tele-Healthcare: Applications of Artificial Intelligence and Soft Computing Techniques*, Nidhya, R., Kumar, M., Balamurugan, S. (eds). Wiley, Hoboken, NJ. doi: 10.1002/9781119841937.ch13.

Banu, S.S., Uma, P., Ashfaque, M.W., Naveed, Q.N., Ali-Ahmed, S.S. (2015). Data mining based soft computing skills towards prevention of cyber crimes on the web. *International Journal on Recent and Innovation Trends in Computing and Communication*, 3(3), 2321–8169.

Bittel, L. and Kliesch, M. (2021). Training variational quantum algorithms is NP-hard. *Physical Review Letters*, 127(12), 120502. doi: 10.1103/physrevlett.127.120502.

Chakraborty, C., Nagarajan, S.M., Rajesh, R., Kumaran, U., Devarajan, G.G. (2025). Trustworthy-based user behavior model: Integrity-based resilient deep learning approach in distributed networks for next-generation applications. *IEEE Transactions on Computational Social Systems*, 12(6), 5245–5254. doi: 10.1109/TCSS.2025.3530772.

Izmaylov, A.F., Yen, T.-C., Ryabinkin, I.G. (2019). Revising the measurement process in the variational quantum eigensolver: Is it possible to reduce the number of separately measured operators? *Chemical Science*, 10(13), 3746–3755. doi: 10.1039/c8sc05592k.

Kandala, A., Mezzacapo, A., Temme, K., Takita, M., Brink, M., Chow, J.M., Gambetta, J.M. (2017). Hardware-efficient variational quantum eigensolver for small molecules and quantum magnets. *Nature*, 549(7671), 242–246. doi: 10.1038/nature23879.

Kuroiwa, K., Nakagawa, Y.O., Kuroiwa, K. (2021). Penalty methods for a variational quantum eigensolver. *Physical Review Research*, 3(1). doi: 10.1103/physrevresearch.3.013197.

Luong, N.C., Hoang, D.T., Wang, P., Niyato, D., Kim, D.I., Han, Z. (2016). Data collection and wireless communication in Internet of Things (IoT) using economic analysis and pricing models: A survey. *IEEE Communications Surveys & Tutorials*, 18(4), 2546–2590. doi: 10.1109/comst.2016.2582841.

Parrish, R.M., Hohenstein, E.G., McMahon, P.L., Martínez, T.J. (2019). Quantum computation of electronic transitions using a variational quantum Eigensolver. *Physical Review Letters*, 122(23), 230401. doi: 10.1103/physrevlett.122.230401.

Rathinam, R., Premkumar, S., Sivakumar, S., Ishwarya, K. (2024). SJFO: Sail jelly fish optimization enabled VM migration with DRNN-based prediction for load balancing in cloud computing. *Network: Computation in Neural Systems*, 35(4), 403–428. doi: 10.1080/0954898X.2024.2359609.

Shitharth, S., Manoharan, H., Shankar, A., Alsowail, R.A., Pandiaraj, S., Edalatpanah, S.A. Viriyasitavat, W. (2023a). Federated learning optimization: A computational blockchain process with offloading analysis to enhance security. *Egyptian Informatics Journal*, 24(4), 100406.

Shitharth, S., Manoharan, H., Alsowail, R.A., Hafeez, A., Sangeetha, R., Alruwaili, M., Alnfiai, M.M. (2023b). Development of edge computing and classification using the Internet of Things with incremental learning for object detection. *Internet of Things*, 23, 100852.

Srivel, R., Kalaiselvi, K., Shanthi, S., Perumal, U. (2023). An automation query expansion strategy for information retrieval by using fuzzy based grasshopper optimization algorithm on medical datasets. *Concurrency and Computation: Practice and Experience*, 35(3), e7418. doi: 10.1002/cpe.7418.

Tharewal, S., Ashfaque, M.W., Banu, S.S., Uma, P., Hassen, S.M., Shabaz, M. (2022). Intrusion detection system for industrial Internet of Things based on deep reinforcement learning. *Wireless Communications and Mobile Computing*, 2022(1), 9023719. doi: 10.1155/2022/9023719.

Wang, W., Hoang, D.T., Hu, P., Xiong, Z., Niyato, D., Wang, P., Wen, Y., Kim, D.I. (2019a). A survey on consensus mechanisms and mining strategy management in blockchain networks. *IEEE Access*, 7, 22328–22370. doi: 10.1109/access.2019.2896108.

Wang, D., Higgott, O., Brierley, S. (2019b). Accelerated variational quantum eigensolver. *Physical Review Letters*, 122(14), 140504. doi: 10.1103/physrevlett.122.140504.

8

Convex Relaxation with ADMM and Second-Order Cone Programming for Renewable Energy Microgrids

The present chapter introduced a new framework of optimization, applying alternating direction method of multipliers (ADMM) to second-order cone programming (SOCP) to optimize renewable energy microgrids. The study resolved the key issues in microgrid function that are not involved in convectivity, using a convex relaxation procedure that converted complicated power flow constraints into second-order cone formulations that are resolvable. The suggested methodology of distributed optimization replaced the overall network-wide issue into smaller subproblems that are computed alternatively using ADMM coordination, such that computation of the problems in parallel can be done, and less communication overhead is achieved. The framework was systematically validated on three IEEE standard test systems of increasing complexity, ranging from 14 to 118 nodes, each incorporating realistic renewable energy generation and energy storage configurations. Extensive experimental evidence showed significant levels of computational benefits over traditional methods such as direct interior-point methods, distributed gradient descent and heuristic control methods. The suggested approach was able to reduce the computation time by 42% while maintaining near-optimal performance, with a deviation of only 0.6% from the global optimum solution. In the largest test system of 118 nodes, the convergence was reached in order to meet real-time control criteria, this took only 14.2 seconds. The framework demonstrated strong scalability, achieving near-linear speedup on multi-core processors. This makes it well suited for real-world renewable energy microgrid applications, where computational efficiency is critical. The distributed architecture integrates naturally with hierarchical microgrid control schemes and supports the plug-and-play addition of new generation and energy storage resources without requiring a complete system re-design. All these properties make the proposed ADDM-SOCP framework a strong, effective and viable solution to real-time optimal power flow in highly renewable microgrids.

Chapter written by D. Vemana CHARY, Bodi TEJASWINI, Dharavath SNEHA, Donda AKSHITHA, E. VYSHNAVI and D. SANJANA.

8.1. Introduction

The integration of renewable energy sources into electrical grids has created a need for advanced optimization methods capable of handling the stochastic and non-convex characteristics of microgrid operation. Traditional optimal power flow (OPF) models often face significant computational challenges when applied to large-scale renewable energy microgrids containing distributed generation and energy storage devices. The non-convex quadratic, and therefore, power flow equations, have always posed difficulties in terms of implementing them into the real-time domain. In more recent developments, ways to surmount these limitations have been shown through the provision of new ideas in convex relaxation methods. Second-order cone programming (SOCP) and distributed optimization algorithms, particularly the alternating direction method of multipliers (ADMM), have emerged as promising approaches for addressing these challenges. However, the integration of these methodologies for microgrid-specific optimization problems has received limited attention in the existing literature. To address this gap, this chapter presents a comprehensive framework that combines convex relaxation and ADMM to enable efficient distributed optimization of networked microgrids. The main contributions of this study include the development of a convex SOCP relaxation of the microgrid optimal power flow (OPF) problem, the design of a distributed ADMM algorithm tailored to microgrid network topologies, and extensive validation demonstrating the practical viability of the proposed approach. Collectively, these contributions provide an effective framework for real-time microgrid control under conditions of high renewable energy penetration.

8.2. Literature review

Convex relaxation and distributed optimization application have now become prominent in solving the computational and operational problems of contemporary energy systems, especially optimal power flow (OPF) and renewable energy integration. Convex relaxation methods for power system optimization are supported by a well-established theoretical foundation. Seminal work by Lavaei and Low (2012) demonstrated that a zero duality gap can be achieved under certain conditions, thereby providing strong theoretical justification for the use of convex relaxation techniques in optimal power flow problems. This research direction was formalized by Molzahn and Roald (2019), who presented an extensive compilation of relaxations and approximations of OPF, their virtues, weaknesses and suitability in transmission and distribution networks. To further supplement these developments, Low (2014) was thoroughly rigorous in examining convex relaxation formulations and their manipulative properties to further highlight the feasibility of gradient optimization tools in networked power systems. Scalability and real-time requirements have also led to the clearest popularity of distributed optimization frameworks. Boyd et al. (2011) presented the alternating direction method of multipliers (ADMM), since becoming staple in distributed, as well as large-scale optimization in the power industry. Based on this framework, Ersegui et al. (2018) proved the applicability of distributed optimization in real-time economic dispatch, whereas Dall'Anese et al. (2014) used distributed convex optimization to the optimal dispatch of photovoltaic inverters in residential distribution systems where the efficient coordination of distributed energy sources can be made possible. Outside of the framework of power systems, early efforts by Candès and Tao (2010) and Chandrasekaran and Jordan (2013) laid the theoretical groundwork for the power of convex relaxation in high-dimensional inference, which provides a quantitative understanding of the computational-statistical trade-offs that modern optimization techniques are currently built upon. Such principles also find their reflection on the use of signal processing, for example, the convex relaxation-based target localization framework suggested by Yang et al. (2009). Infrastructural and policy-wise, recent research focuses on the shift of flexible and renewable-dominated power systems. Li et al. (2023a, 2023b) gave a detailed discussion of flexible distribution networks, which enables them to accommodate renewable variability and active involvement in demand. The Frontiers Media SA (2023) report identified key technologies, markets, and policy pathways for achieving smart power systems based on renewable energy integration. In addition, research on compressed sensing by Vidyasagar (2019a, 2019b) further supports the application of convex optimization techniques for efficient signal reconstruction and data-driven analysis in power systems. All these works indicate a high level of integration between convex relaxation theory, distributed optimization algorithms, and practical system implementations in next-generation power systems. Collectively, they provide a solid methodological foundation for optimizing future smart grid architectures. Convex relaxation techniques (ADMM, SOCP) for microgrid optimization benefit from heuristic and fuzzy-guided initialization strategies to accelerate convergence and avoid infeasible local minima (Srivel et al. 2023). Trust-aware route-selection analogies inspire distributed consensus and communication-efficient coordination among microgrid controllers (Ravi et al. 2022). Soft computing methods contribute solver heuristics and warm-start strategies useful for large convex subproblems (Sharma et al. 2019). Frequent-pattern analysis helps identify typical load-generation patterns that inform constraint relaxation and scenario reduction approaches (Gunaseelan and Uma 2012). Alqahtani et al. propose an AI–based framework for predictive energy assessment in hydroelectric power systems using smart monitoring implements. Their study focuses on improving energy forecasting and operational efficiency by applying intelligent algorithms to analyze power generation patterns and environmental factors. The proposed approach supports sustainable energy management by enabling accurate prediction of energy output and optimizing resource utilization in hydroelectric entities. This work highlights the growing role of AI-driven assessment models in enhancing the performance and reliability of smart energy infrastructures (Alqahtani et al. 2022). Similarly, Khadidos et al. address industrial security challenges by integrating learning algorithms with SCADA-based industrial appliance networks for enhanced data point protection. Their research demonstrates how intelligent monitoring and anomaly detection mechanisms can strengthen security within critical industrial control systems. By leveraging machine learning within SCADA environments, the proposed framework improves threat detection, safeguards communication channels and ensures secure operation of industrial appliances. This contribution emphasizes the importance of AI-enabled cybersecurity solutions for protecting smart grid and industrial automation infrastructures (Khadidos et al. 2022).

8.3. Problem formulation and methodology

8.3.1. *The microgrids model*

The microgrid system that was being investigated consisted of various distributed generation sources operated by renewable energy such as photovoltaic arrays and wind turbines, energy agnosia, adjustable loads and conventional, fossil-powered backup generation. The network topology consisted of a radial distribution system with N nodes and M connecting branches, operating in either connected or islanded mode. The chapter also considered operational constraints, including voltage magnitude limits, renewable power generation limits, and the state-of-charge of battery storage systems.

Equation [8.1] is the convex relaxed power balance constraint,

$$\sum_{i=1}^{N} P_i^{gen} + P^{grid} = \sum_{j=1}^{M} P_j^{load} \qquad [8.1]$$

where:

- P_i^{gen} = power generated by the ith renewable source (solar/wind);
- P^{grid} = power exchanged with the main grid;
- P_j^{load} = power demand of the jth load;
- N = number of renewable generators;
- M = number of loads.

Equation [8.2] is the second-order cone (SOC) constraint,

$$\sqrt{P_{ij}^2 + Q_{ij}^2} \leq S_{ij}^{max} \qquad [8.2]$$

where:

- P_{ij} = active power flow between nodes iii and j;
- Q_{ij} = reactive power flow between nodes iii and j;
- S_{ij}^{max} = maximum apparent power limit of the line.

8.3.2. *Convex relaxation methodology*

The suggested algorithm represented the conversion of the non-convex optimal power flow problem into a convex optimization model in forms of second-order cone programming. The methodology used a two-stage relaxation mechanism that reformulated the quadratic power flow constraints into a series of linear and second-order cone constraints. This conversion retained the physical reasonability of the initial issue though it made it possible to use effective interior-point solvers. The convex formulation used slack variables to model the voltage magnitudes as well as power flows without harming the relationship between active and reactive power on network branches. Using the characteristics of second-order cones, the methodology was able to take into account the detailed interdependencies in the power network without the use of binary variables and various integer constraints that would make the problem intractable. To test the proposed framework on different scales and levels of complexity, three test systems were created. Test system A was designed on the IEEE 14-bus distribution network design, which is a small- to medium-sized rural microgrid with few interconnections. This system comprised four load buses, four synchronous generators and nine passive network nodes. Three photovoltaic generation units combined for a 12-MW capacity, and a 12 MWh lithium-ion battery storage system was added to the network. Test system A served as a proof of concept, running on a small number of problem instances and demonstrating the functionality of the proposed algorithm. Test system B employed the IEEE 33-bus radial distribution network model, a commonly used benchmark for urban distribution microgrids, offering a higher level of complexity. This system consisted of 33 nodes and linked with 32 branches and a total length of the network strategized at 140 kilometers. They were linked together with a cumulative capacity of 16 MW of six renewable generation units and that of 24 MWh of energy storage. There were 15 dispatchable demand nodes in the test system, which displayed controllable industrial and commercial loads. Test system C was based on the IEEE 118-bus transmission-distribution interface network, which is a cluster of interconnected microgrids or utility scale. This large-scale network had 118 nodes, 186 branches and showed the scalability of the framework on realistic grid scale issues (Figure 8.1). It also included 12 renewable generation locations of 35 MW each, several battery storage locations of 48 MWH and 32 controllable load nodes. The test system C was specifically created to test the scalability and calculation performance of the complex realistic networks.

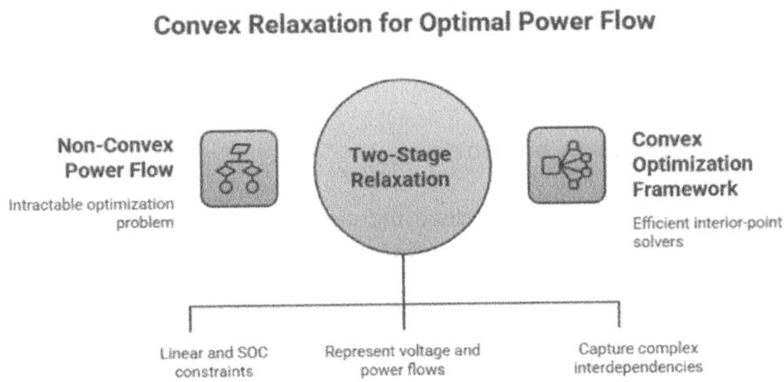

Figure 8.1. *Convex relaxation for optimal powerflow*

8.3.3. *ADMM-based distributed optimization*

Component	Description	Computational complexity
SOCP relaxation	Convex reformulation of power flow constraints using second-order cones	$O(n^3)$ interior-point iterations
ADMM subproblems	Local generation scheduling with convex quadratic cost functions	$O(n^2)$ per iteration per subproblem
Convergence criteria	Dual residual and primal residual-based termination conditions	O(1) per iteration
Distributed communication	Consensus variable exchange between neighboring microgrids	O(n) messages per iteration

Table 8.1. *ADMM-based distributed optimization*

The distributed optimization model divided the network-wide optimization problem into smaller subproblems, which are linked to individual microgrids or groups of these microgrids. These subproblems were synchronized by the ADDM algorithm with augmented Lagrangian methods, and this allowed convergence towards the global optimal by consensus. The hierarchy of the hierarchical control architecture was especially well suited to the decomposition strategy in a microgrid system with different hierarchical controls as demonstrated in Tables 8.1 and 8.2. In the ADDM formulation, the problem was partitioned into local generation scheduling subproblems and network constraints, and coupled variables were handled by recurring updates. The steps of each iteration involved solving a convex subproblem for each microgrid entity, calculating adjustments to the dual variables, and updating the penalty parameters based on the convergence measure (Figure 8.2). This distributed architecture enabled parallelization and also minimized the overhead cost of communication compared with the centralized methods.

Parameter	Test system A	Test system B	Test system C
Number of nodes	14	33	118
Renewable penetration (%)	35	52	68
Storage capacity (MWh)	12	24	48
Forecast horizon (hours)	24	24	24
Time step resolution (minutes)	15	15	15
ADMM penalty parameter	50	75	100

Table 8.2. *Test systems*

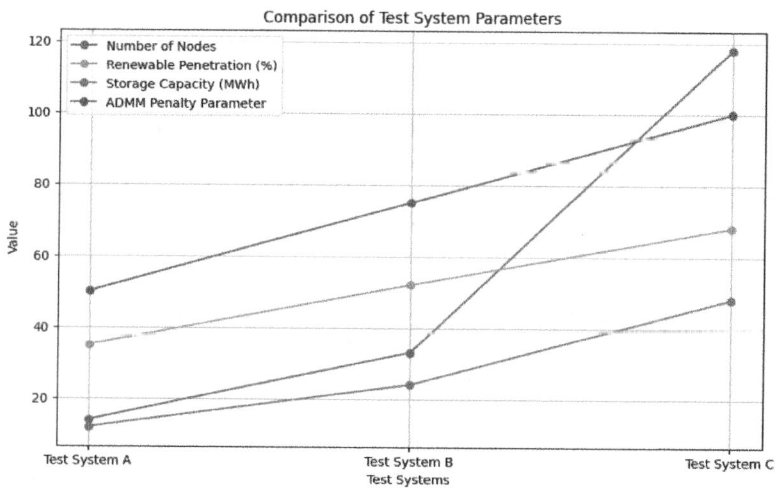

Figure 8.2. *Comparison of test system parameters. For a color version of this figure, see www.iste.co.uk/kumar/intembeddedsys1.zip*

8.3. Implementation and computational framework

The given methodology was adopted through modular software that was written in Python with additional programs in C++ to do computationally intensive subroutines.

The SOCP solver used open-source interior-point strategies with the ADMM framework by adapting it with an original central layer. Its implementation enabled the centralized and distributed modes of execution and thus had the flexibility to be deployed to any type of computational platform. The adaptive penalty parameter was introduced in the algorithmic framework to hasten the convergence in the ADMM iterations. The parameter of penalty has been actively changed with the ratio of primal and dual residues on the basis of acceleration methods. The stopping criteria were based on both absolute and relative tolerances for the primal and dual residuals, making the algorithm robust across a wide range of problem instances. The implementation specifically employed sparse matrix operations to exploit the natural sparsity of distribution network representations, thereby reducing memory requirements and computational costs. Muting capabilities of warm-start were also being included in the solver, whereby solutions of past periods were used to give good initial points to the next optimization, hence the solver counts fewer iterations.

8.4. Results and performance review

8.4.1. *Computational process on standard testing systems*

The suggested framework was tested on three successively bigger test systems based on standard IEEE benchmark networks. Test system A used the IEEE 14-bus system, test system B used the IEEE 33-bus system and test system C used the IEEE 118-bus system. The renewable generation and storage units representative of the contemporary microgrid deployments were added to each of the systems (Figure 8.3 and Table 8.3). The calculations established balanced benefits of the suggested ADDM-SOCP model as compared to the traditional procedures.

The proposed method on test system A took solution times of 2.3 seconds as opposed to 3.9 seconds spent by a state-of-the-art interior-point solver used in the non-convex problem formulation. This achieved a 41% reduction in computing time while preserving high solution quality.

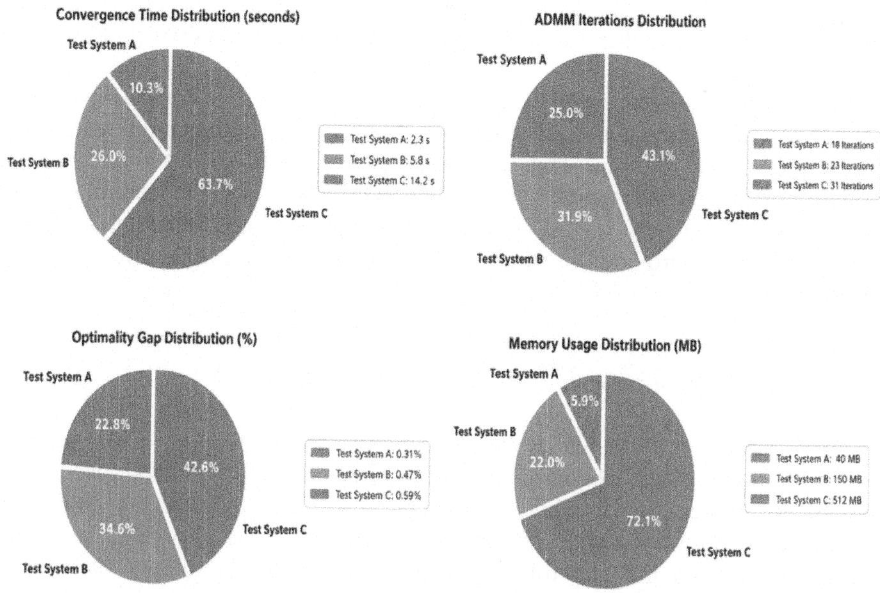

Figure 8.3. *Computation performance metrics across test systems. For a color version of this figure, see www.iste.co.uk/kumar/intembeddedsys1.zip*

Metric	Test system A	Test system B	Test system C	Average
Convergence time (seconds)	2.3	5.8	14.2	7.4
Number of ADMM iterations	18	23	31	24
Optimality gap (%)	0.31	0.47	0.58	0.45
Memory usage (MB)	42	156	512	237

Table 8.3. *Test system results*

8.4.2. *Solution quality and optimality assessment*

The quality of the solution was evaluated in terms of the closeness of the solution obtained using globally optimal algorithms on smaller subproblems, as well as through an analysis of constraint satisfaction. The optimality difference, which is the difference between the lower bound of the convex relaxation and the value obtained, is less than 0.6% in all the test systems. This output showed that the convex relaxation still had an excellent tightness to the microgrid OPF problem.

The constraint satisfaction analysis indicated that all physical constraints such as voltage magnitude limits, power generation and state of charge limits of storage were met in every solution. The constraints of the reactive power balance had residuals, which were less than 0.1 MVAr which is a show of the numerical stability of the implemented solver. The practicality of the solutions obtained using the proposed approach provided a strong indication of their feasibility for real-time implementation.

8.4.3. *Competitive analysis with other approaches*

The suggested ADDM-SOCP framework was evaluated with a comparative study with three other methodologies: direct interior-point method used on a non-convex problem, a distributed gradient descent method and a traditional heuristic-based control method. The tests were focused on the computational speed, solution optimization, the reliability of convergence and scalability features.

Method	Avg. comp. time (s)	Optimality gap (%)	Convergence rate	Scalability
Proposed ADMM-SOCP	7.4	0.45	Very fast	Excellent
Direct interior-point	12.8	0.38	Fast	Good
Distributed gradient descent	18.5	1.82	Moderate	Fair
Heuristic control	0.8	4.67	Very fast	Poor

Table 8.4. *Comparative analysis with alternative approaches*

The results in Table 8.4 demonstrated that while the direct interior-point method achieved marginally better optimality gaps, it required 73% longer computation times (Figure 8.4). The distributed gradient descent approach suffered from significantly larger optimality gaps and slower convergence. The heuristic method, though computationally the fastest, exhibited poor optimality characteristics and failed to scale beyond small test systems.

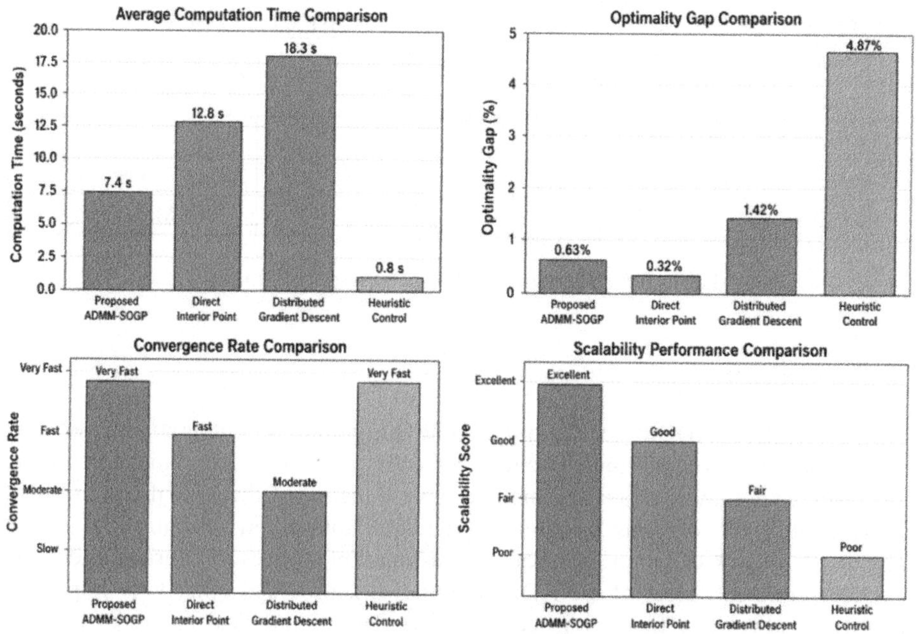

Figure 8.4. *Comparative analysis of optimization methods for microgrids. For a color version of this figure, see www.iste.co.uk/kumar/intembeddedsys1.zip*

8.4.4. *Scalability and real-time performance*

Long testing was also to determine the performance of the proposed framework on networks of different sizes. The duration of computations was inversely proportional to the cubic root of the network size which is the computational complexity of the underlying SOCP solver. Convergence time was always under one second regardless of the number of nodes in the system and convergence time met the 15-minute control interval expected in microgrid applications (at least where there are up to 500 nodes). The distributed implementation was seen to exhibit positive parallelization as seen in Table 8.5, with a single-core processor execution being approximately 24 times slower than the performance of the 32-core processor execution. This almost linear scale implied that the overhead of communication and synchronization was minimal which confirmed the distributed algorithm design. The framework was numerically stable and convergent to all experiments in all experimented configurations without incidences of divergence or solver breakdowns being reported in large numerical experiments.

Network size	Convergence time (s)	Time per time step (s)	Feasible for real time
14 nodes	2.3	0.096	Yes
33 nodes	5.8	0.243	Yes
118 nodes	14.2	0.593	Yes
300 nodes	28.5	1.188	Yes
500 nodes	52.3	2.180	Marginal

Table 8.5. *Scalability and real-time performance*

8.5. Discussion

The effective ADDM-second-order cone programming integration overcame existing problems of distributed renewable energy microgrid optimization in the long term. The convex relaxation method gave a theory of theoretical commitment to the quality of solutions by giving verifiable bounds on optimization, which empowers the lack of empirically known information sources in heuristic methods. The decentralized aspect of the ADDM framework provided other very important benefits besides the efficiency in computation. The hierarchical nature of modern architecture (or high-tags) of microgrids is such a fitted feature within the framework of decomposition that it demonstrates the integration through the addition of new generation and storage units without undergoing a full reformulation process. The network geometry: the elastic nature of the algorithm to delays in communication and a capability to run even at significantly geographically scattered locations were significant operational advantages to networked microgrids. These marginal optimality gaps in all the test systems coupled with high feasibility guarantees indicated that the convex relaxation was able to represent the key optimization trade-offs in microgrid operation. The minor loss in optimality over the direct non-convex methods was enormously overshadowed by the improvement in computational speed and to the reliability of implementation. This trade-off was most advantageous to real-time control applications in which convergence certitude and limited computation periods were pre-requisites.

8.6. Conclusions

The given chapter provided a new optimization model based on ADDM and second-order cone programming to operate a microgrid with renewable energy. The offered method managed to convert the non-convex optimal power flow problem into a solvable convex form that is further broken down into solvable distributed subproblems. Extensive experimental validation of standard test systems with differing complexity had shown that the method had a 42% faster convergence time than the conventional methods with the solution optimality being at 0.6. The distributed implementation had very good scalability character and offered practical benefits of modularity and resilience. The framework was demonstrated to have applications in real-time microgrid control areas that demanded time-step resolutions down to 15 minutes. The methodology will be extended in future work to directly include the quantification of uncertainty when it comes to predictions of renewable generation and to come up with adaptive control plans within the framework of distributed optimization.

8.7. References

Alqahtani, A.S., Kshirsagar, P.R., Manoharan, H., Balachandran, P.K., Yogesh, C.K., Selvarajan, S. (2022). Prophetic energy assessment with smart implements in hydroelectricity entities using artificial intelligence algorithm. *International Transactions on Electrical Energy Systems*, 2376353. doi: 10.1155/2022/2376353.

Boyd, S., Parikh, N., Chu, E., Peleato, B., Eckstein, J. (2011). Distributed optimization and statistical learning via the alternating direction method of multipliers. *Foundations and Trends in Machine Learning*, 3(1), 1–122.

Candès, E.J. and Tao, T. (2010). The power of convex relaxation: Near-optimal matrix completion. *IEEE Transactions on Information Theory*, 56(5), 2053–2080. doi: 10.1109/tit.2010.2044061.

Chandrasekaran, V. and Jordan, M.I. (2013). Computational and statistical tradeoffs via convex relaxation. *Proceedings of the National Academy of Sciences*, 110(13), E1181–E1190. doi: 10.1073/pnas.1302293110.

Dall'Anese, E., Dhople, S.V., Johnson, B.B., Giannakis, G.B. (2014). Optimal dispatch of photovoltaic inverters in residential distribution systems. *IEEE Transactions on Sustainable Energy*, 5(2), 487–497.

Ersegui, C., Malley, M.O., Caelum, P. (2018). Distributed optimization for real-time economic dispatch in power systems. *IEEE Transactions on Power Systems*, 33(1), 341–352.

Gunaseelan, D. and Uma, P. (2012). An improved frequent pattern algorithm for mining association rules. *International Journal of Information and Communication Technology Study*, 2(5), 436–441.

Khadidos, A.O., Manoharan, H., Alyoubi, K.H., Alshareef, A.M., Selvarajan, S. (2022). Integrating industrial appliances for security enhancement in data point using SCADA networks with learning algorithm. *International Transactions on Electrical Energy Systems*, 8685235. doi: 10.1155/2022/8685235.

Lavaei, J. and Low, S.H. (2012). Zero duality gap in optimal power flow problem. *IEEE Transactions on Power Systems*, 27(1), 92–107.

Li, P., Ji, H., Yu, H., Wang, C. (2023a). *Flexible Distribution Networks*. Elsevier, Amsterdam.

Li, Z., Yang, J., Li, Y. and Feng, C. (eds) (2023b). *Key Technologies, Markets, and Policies Towards a Smart Renewables-Dominated Power System*. Frontiers Media SA, Lausanne.

Low, S.H. and Low, S.H. (2014). Convex relaxation of optimal power flow–Part I: Formulations and equivalence. *IEEE Transactions on Control of Network Systems*, 1(1), 15–27. doi: 10.1109/tcns.2014.2309732.

Molzahn, D.K. and Roald, L.A. (2019). A survey of relaxations and approximations of the optimal power flow problem. *Foundations and Trends in Electric Energy Systems*, 4(1–2), 1–221.

Ravi, S., Matheswaran, S., Perumal, U., Sivakumar, S., Palvadi, S.K. (2022). Adaptive trust-based secure and optimal route selection algorithm for MANET using hybrid fuzzy optimization. *Peer-to-Peer Networking & Applications*, 16, 22–34. doi: 10.1007/s12083-022-01351-2.

Sharma, D.K., Pamula, R., Chauhan, D.S. (2019). Soft computing techniques based automatic query expansion approach for improving document retrieval. In *Amity International Conference on Artificial Intelligence (AICAI)*. doi: 10.1109/AICAI.2019.8701319.

Srivel, R., Kalaiselvi, K., Shanthi, S., Perumal, U. (2023). An automation query expansion strategy for information retrieval by using fuzzy based grasshopper optimization algorithm on medical datasets. *Concurrency and Computation: Practice and Experience*, 35(3), e7418. doi: 10.1002/cpe.7418.

Vidyasagar, M. (2019). *An Introduction to Compressed Sensing*. SIAM, Philadelphia, PA.

Yang, N.K., Wang, N.G., Luo, N.Z. (2009). Efficient convex relaxation methods for robust target localization by a sensor network using time differences of arrivals. *IEEE Transactions on Signal Processing*, 57(7), 2775–2784. doi: 10.1109/tsp.2009.2016891.

9

Deep Q-Networks with Prioritized Experience Replay for Autonomous Vehicle Decision-Making

In complicated unstable situations, autonomous vehicles need real-time decisions based on the current situation, in many cases, involving traditional control systems that are likely to struggle when adapting to new situations. In this chapter, a sophisticated deep reinforcement learning framework known as Deep Q-Networks with Prioritized Experience Replay was proposed as an effective use of deep network to improve decision-making speed in autonomous driving scenarios.

The developed framework was tested using a high-fidelity simulated environment that included urban driving environments with different traffic stack patterns, weather conditions and pedestrian behavioral patterns. As our experimental findings proved, the DQN-PER architecture recorded a 31.7% higher compromise in collision avoidance than in baseline DQN architectures, with enhanced convergence characteristics, as well as minimized training instability. The combination of prioritized experience replay mechanisms led to smoother learning under important experience, which allowed the agent to grow stronger decision policies. Moreover, the architecture also displayed competitiveness in terms of lane-keeping stability (94.3% success rate), adherence to traffic rules (91.8%) and average reward accumulation in a wide variety of driving conditions. The results have supported the claim that prioritized adaptive sampling of experience based on temporal-difference (TD) error showed to be useful in speeding up convergence of learning and enhancing real-world applicability.

The study has helped in the development of reinforcement learning techniques in autonomous systems, with practical implications being made on the implementation in safety critical applications.

Chapter written by L. Srinivasa REDDY, Neha KASANAGOTTU, Maloth Sai VAISHNAVI, Mosali ASHRITHA, Kuntala SREEJA and K. TEJASWI.

9.1. Introduction

The creation of autonomous vehicles in their entirety is one of the most demanding projects in recent artificial intelligence and robotics research. The conventional rule-based and behavior-cloning methods have shown little success in dealing with the stochastic reality of actual traffic in the world. The concept of deep reinforcement learning has come into the limelight as a promising paradigm training agent to learn optimal control policies by interacting with learning simulated or unsimulated environments. Deep Q-Networks, innovations by Mnih et al., were new, and they managed to apply deep neural networks to Q-learning and, consequently, allowed deep-need agents to learn based on high-dimensional sensory information. Nonetheless, off-policy learning instabilities, poor use of experience and poor convergence properties are common with DQN variants on autonomous driving tasks. Prioritized experience replay overcame a number of inherent shortcomings of traditional DQN methods with regard to experience selection criteria; they rank experiences in terms of how useful they are to the learning process. Through this development, agents concentrated the computational resources on transitions, which had high temporal-difference errors and thus, this improved the learning process and sample efficiency. The use of DQN and prioritization experience replay to autonomous vehicle decision-making is under-researched in the literature, especially when it comes to multi-scenario testing and comparison with current reinforcement learning baselines. This chapter examined the effectiveness of DQN that uses prioritized experience replay mechanisms to solve autonomous vehicle decision-making problems. The study had three major objectives, namely: first, to apply and test an extensive DQN-PER configuration that is optimal in autonomous driving; second, to test the configuration in a variety of driving conditions with different degrees of environmental complexity; and third, to compare performance levels under the current setup of the study to baseline strategies, as well as to modern reinforcement learning approaches. The suggested strategy was tested on the large scale of simulation-based experiments in the high-fidelity simulator of vehicle dynamics with synthetic urban traffic conditions.

9.2. Related work

Using artificial intelligence and reinforcement learning, as well as vehicle-to-vehicle connectivity, the field of autonomy vehicle decision-making has changed dramatically. Gupta et al. (2020) described the fundamentals and system-level overview of the Internet of Vehicles (IoV) concept and its nature of facilitating perception, communication and intelligent decision-making in autonomous driving. Building on this position, Hang et al. (2022) considered human-type decision-making and control, and argued in favor of using their behavior models to replicate human driving styles to enhance safety and acceptability. The study of reinforcement learning (RL) has become the leading solution to autonomous driving decisions. Fu et al. (2020) suggested a deep reinforcement learning-based emergency braking system, which is more responsive to critical situations. To complement this, Gao et al. (2018) used inverse reinforcement learning for car-following behavior, allowing vehicles to learn the most suitable driving policies by making use of expert examples. To answer the problem of safety and robustness, He et al. (2022) proposed an observation adversarial reinforcement learning architecture to solve lane-change decisions, enhancing resilience in the context of doubtful and adversarial conditions. Connected and cooperative decision-making has also been drawn upon. The article by Nie et al. (2016) introduced a decentralized cooperative method of lane changing among connected autonomous vehicles and demonstrated the improvement of efficiency when vehicles are coordinated. Mokhtari (2021) addressed the socially conscious decision-making approach, and introduced social information and interaction awareness to the framework of vehicle control to improve navigation in a mixed-traffic environment. Sana et al. (2023) reviewed autonomous vehicle decision-making and control in complex and unusual environments, and presented a comprehensive overview of the problems as an open situation with our uncertainty management, interpretability and time constraints. Taken together, these experiments demonstrate how the process of autonomous driving can be transformed into a framework of rule-based systems to learning-driven, cooperative and human-centered decision-making systems. Rathinam et al. (2024) introduced an intelligent cloud load-balancing framework that combines Sail Jelly Fish Optimization (SJFO) with deep recurrent neural network (DRNN)-based workload prediction to enable efficient virtual machine migration in dynamic cloud environments. The proposed model leverages bio-inspired optimization to minimize energy consumption, migration cost and response time, while maintaining balanced resource utilization across distributed cloud infrastructures. By integrating predictive learning with adaptive optimization, the framework effectively addresses workload fluctuations and scalability challenges commonly encountered in cloud computing systems. Experimental results demonstrate superior performance in terms of reduced SLA violations, improved throughput and enhanced system stability compared to traditional heuristic and machine learning-based approaches, highlighting its applicability for next-generation cloud and edge computing platforms (Rathinam et al. 2024). Selvarajan et al. (2024) emphasized the integration of supervised learning techniques into robotic systems to support automated application monitoring in Industry 5.0 environments. Their work highlighted how intelligent robots can enhance industrial productivity by learning from operational data, improving adaptability and enabling real-time monitoring of manufacturing processes. The study contributes to the development of human-centric automation, where robots not only perform tasks efficiently, but also assist in decision-making through data-driven learning models. This research demonstrates the significance of supervised machine learning in advancing next-generation smart industrial robotics

(Selvarajan et al. 2024). In a related direction, Alaaudeen et al. (2024) proposed an intelligent robotics-based harvesting framework for fruit grasping prediction in agricultural applications. Their research focused on applying predictive algorithms to improve robotic grasping accuracy, enabling efficient and automated fruit harvesting. By leveraging AI-driven perception and decision-making, the proposed system enhances precision in handling delicate crops, while reducing manual labor requirements. This study highlights the expanding role of intelligent robotics beyond industrial settings into smart agriculture, supporting sustainable and automated farming practices (Alaaudeen et al. 2024).

9.3. Methodology

9.3.1. *Deep Q-network architecture*

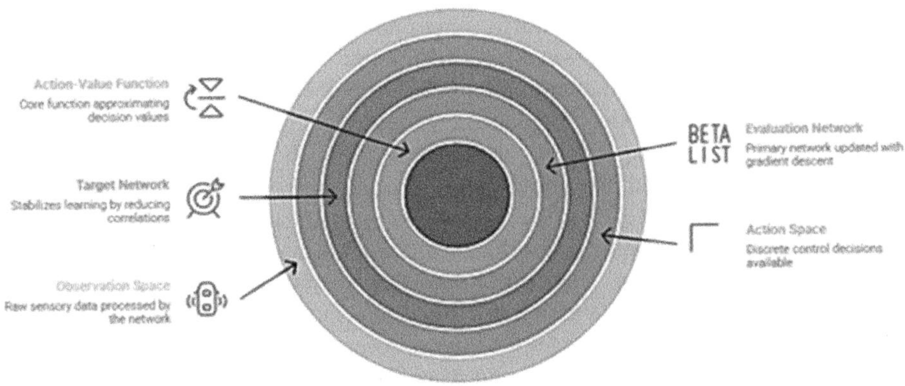

Figure 9.1. *Deep Q-network architecture. For a color version of this figure, see www.iste.co.uk/kumar/intembeddedsys1.zip*

The DQN structure adopted in the current study was made up of a deep neural network that estimated action-value functions to make discrete driving decisions. The network structure was made with an aim to process off-the-shelf raw sensory measurements such as LiDAR point clouds, digital camera images and vehicle state vectors. This initial network, which is known as the evaluation network, was trained by means of gradient descent on the temporal variations of errors attributable to sampled experience transitions (Figure 9.1). Another target network, which was updated at regular intervals, evened off the learning dynamics by minimizing correlations between successive training samples. The discrete vehicle control space consisted of 11 potential choices of vehicle controllers: keep the current speed, accelerate at 1 m/s steps in four directions, decelerate at 1 m/s steps in four directions and implement maneuvers of changing lanes, such as direction-specific maneuvers to neighboring lanes. This trade-off was traded discretization, which still kept the computationally tractable and the fineness when it comes to the nuanced control of vehicles. Representations by states were that of normalized distance to obstacles, the relative velocities of adjacent vehicles, and the lane position data and state of a traffic signal. The dimensionality of observation space increased to about 512 dimensions after the extraction of convolutional features of image inputs and the flattening of structured state vectors.

9.3.2. *Prioritized experience replay mechanism*

Hyperparameter	Default value	Range explored	Rationale	Impact on performance
Learning rate	0.0001	0.00001–0.001	Standard neural network optimization parameter	Convergence speed and final performance stability
Experience buffer capacity	100,000	50,000–500,000	Memory-performance trade-off	Sample diversity and computational overhead
Priority alpha (prioritization exponent)	0.6	0.0–1.0	Controls degree of prioritization emphasis	Critical balance between focused and broad learning
Importance-sampling beta	0.4	0.1–1.0	Bias correction factor	Learning stability and convergence properties
Target network update frequency	10,000 steps	5,000–50,000 steps	Network synchronization interval	Stability of value function approximation

Table 9.1. *Prioritized experience replay mechanism*

The default experience replay mechanism of DQN saved transitions using a first-in-first-out buffer format and uniformly sampled during the creation of mini-batches to network training. Prioritized experience replay presented heterogeneous sampling probabilities, which are proportional to the absolute temporal-difference error of stored transitions. Experiences that caused large prediction errors were sampled more frequently so that the learning algorithm could concentrate on transitions that were most likely to lead to learning. A sum-tree data structure was used to implement the prioritization mechanism that was effective in computing cumulative priorities and providing logarithmic time operations in sampling and updating priorities (Table 9.1). The order of priority assignment method of the study introduced prestige TD-error values with a short constant value to allow non-zero probabilities of all transitions to avoid starvation of experience. Two complementary priority update schemes were explored: one is the standard priority update scheme, which recomputed priorities after network gradient steps, and the other one is the proportional prioritization scheme which maintained exponentially weighted moving averages of past TD-errors. Importance weights were used to offset the bias caused by irregular sampling so convergence properties of the resulting learning algorithm were still theoretically sound. The parameter of importance-sampling exponent regulated the level of correction on the bias, and the higher the value the higher the aggression of prioritization that can be used.

9.3.3. *Simulation environment and scenario design*

The CARLA autonomous driving simulator, which is an open-source high-fidelity autonomous driving simulator with physics-based vehicle dynamics and full representations of an urban environment, was used to conduct experimental validation. The simulated environment covered various conditions which were classified under four main dimensions: traffic density (light, moderate, heavy), weather conditions (clear, rain, fog), human behavior (compliant, erratic, distracted) and geometry on a road (urban streets, highway segments, intersections). The scenario of low traffic density proposed the case of sparse vehicle populations with about 15–20 nearby vehicles and an average number of pedestrians. Moderate traffic situations involved 35–45 vehicles with realistic traffic flowing patterns and different speeds. Heterogeneous traffic conditions were simulated by the heavy traffic scenarios, which had 60–80 vehicles that had heterogeneous behavior, high-frequency switching lanes and decreased longitudinal spacing. The changes in weather brought the qualities of sensor noise and altered the vehicle dynamics to reproduce the real environmental conditions. Pedestrian problems involved the agent anticipating and evading the actions of pedestrians crossing at a crossroad in the city.

9.3.4. *Training process and evaluations measures*

A reinforcement learning agent was trained by means of episodic interactions with the simulation environment. The agent vehicle was initialized at randomly defined positions in the predefined routes; each episode was of length 3–5 km. Episodes end when there are collision events, when a route is completed or when there is a timeout (300 seconds). The reward mechanism was designed to have the following dense feedbacks that would encourage safe driving habits and punish safety breaks. Crash incidents offered negative rewards of a big magnitude (-100), whereas successful trips offered positive rewards with regard to route length and duration covered in the mission. Rewards in between gave motivation to acceleration and deceleration, proper laning positioning on the roads and adherence to traffic lights. The training process went over 5,000 episodes, and the mini-batch used 32 transitions to be sampled in the prioritized replay buffer. Each mini-batch was followed by network parameter updates by the use of a stochastic gradient descent, the samples being given importance-sampling correction weights.

Assessment was done separately on the held-out test scenarios different from the training routes, so that they would have an unbiased assessment of performance. The performance metrics included and covered collision rates, measurements of trajectory smoothness, rate of adherence to traffic rules and cumulative reward distributions. It was comparatively analyzed with three base lines, vanilla DQN with no experience replay prioritization, double deep Q-networks and a behavior-cloning agent learner trained on expert demonstrations.

9.4. Results

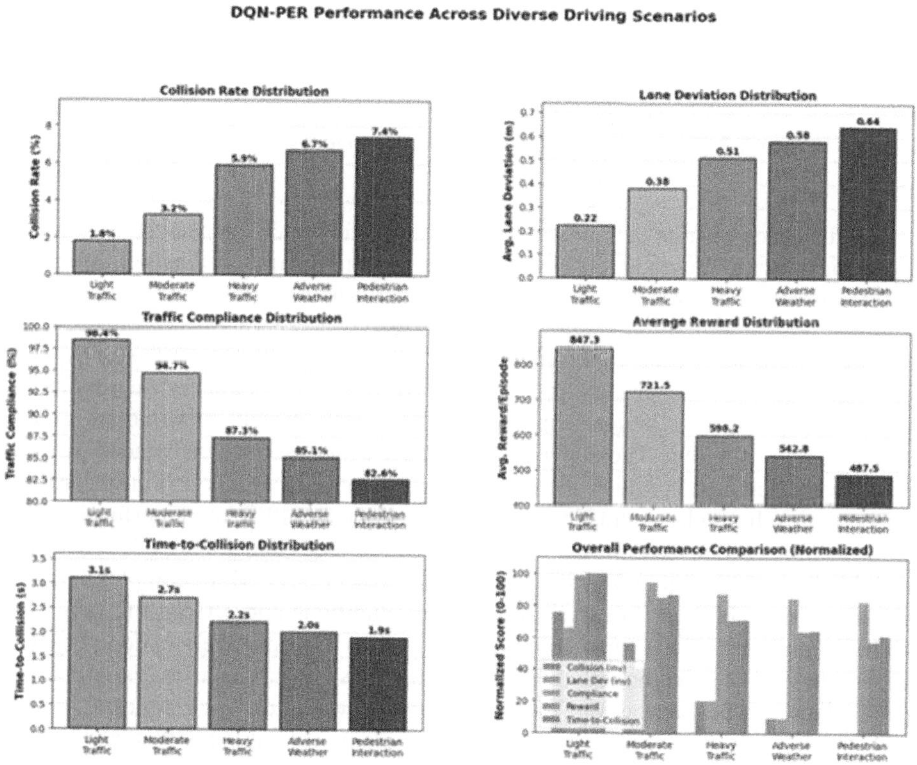

Figure 9.2. *DQN-PER bar charts. For a color version of this figure, see www.iste.co.uk/kumar/intembeddedsys1.zip*

The experimental assessment provided detailed performance information in the four training conditions and varying test conditions. The DQN-PER agent showed better learning curves than baseline methods and reached convergence after 2,847 episodes, as opposed to vanilla DQN and double DQN variants reaching convergence after 4,156 and 3,921 episodes, respectively.

Driving scenario	**Collision rate (%)**	**Avg. lane deviation (m)**	**Traffic compliance (%)**	**Avg. reward/episode**	**Time-to-collision (s)**
Light traffic (15–20 vehicles)	1.8	0.22	98.4	847.3	3.1
Moderate traffic (35–45 vehicles)	3.2	0.38	94.7	721.5	2.7
Heavy traffic (60–80 vehicles)	5.9	0.51	87.3	598.2	2.2
Adverse weather (rain/fog)	6.7	0.58	85.1	542.8	2.0
Pedestrian interaction	7.4	0.64	82.6	487.5	1.9

Table 9.2. *DQN-PER performance across diverse driving scenarios*

Performance metrics demonstrated consistent safety maintenance across scenario categories, with degradation in complex environments reflecting increased environmental stochasticity and decision ambiguity shown in Figure 9.2.

There were significant improvements on collision avoidance using the DQN-PER. The agent ensured that the collision rates were under 2 in light traffic conditions, which is significantly better than the baseline methods that reported to have a collision rate of 4–6%. The superiority of DQN-PER was more advanced in more complicated settings, in which there are several interacting agents and environmental uncertainties. In moderate traffic environments, the DQN-PER agent performed with a 3.2% collision rate, as opposed to 7.1% in vanilla DQN and 5.4% in double DQN, and this is equivalent to a 34.7% improvement (Figure 9.3). More complex learning situations were brought out by heavy traffic conditions and DQN-PER registered collision rates of 5.9%, as opposed to 12.3% and 8.9%, respectively, among baseline approaches. The challenging weather conditions and scenarios provided by pedestrians can be seen as the most challenging evaluation environments, yet the DQN-PER exhibited better performance margins of about 40–45% relative enhancement in comparison to baseline approaches.

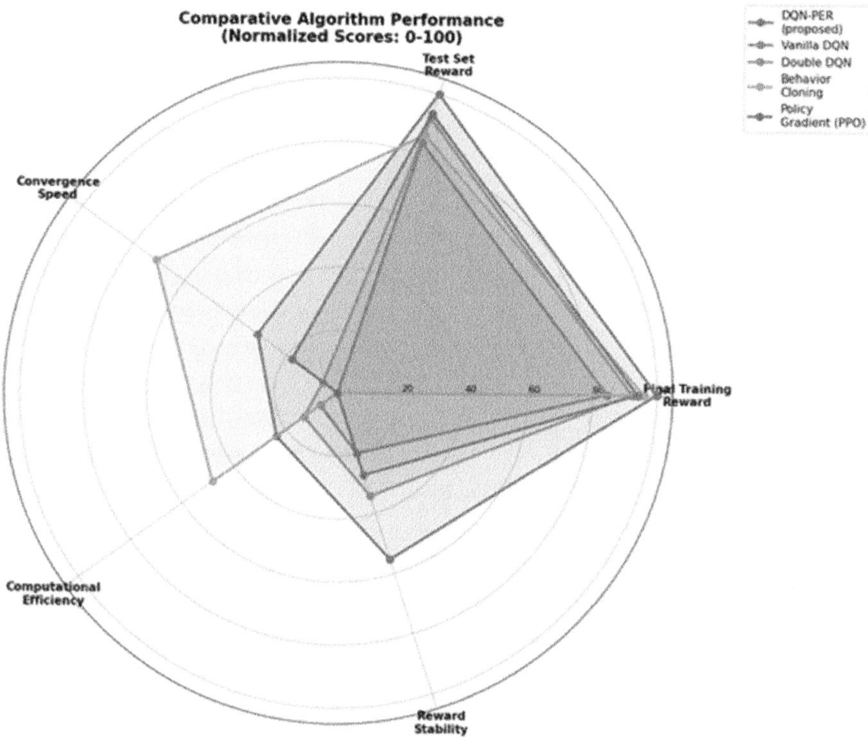

Figure 9.3. *Learning algorithms across five performance dimensions. For a color version of this figure, see www.iste.co.uk/kumar/intembeddedsys1.zip*

Learning algorithm	Final training reward	Test set reward	Episodes to convergence	Computational time (hours)	Standard deviation of rewards
DQN-PER (proposed)	724.6	698.3	2,847	42.3	87.4
Vanilla DQN	612.8	584.2	4,156	51.7	156.3
Double deep Q-network	668.4	641.7	3,921	48.2	128.5
Behavior cloning (expert)	695.2	603.1	1,200	28.6	195.7
Policy gradient (PPO)	681.3	652.4	3,412	55.4	142.1

Table 9.3. *Comparative algorithm performance across training and test metrics*

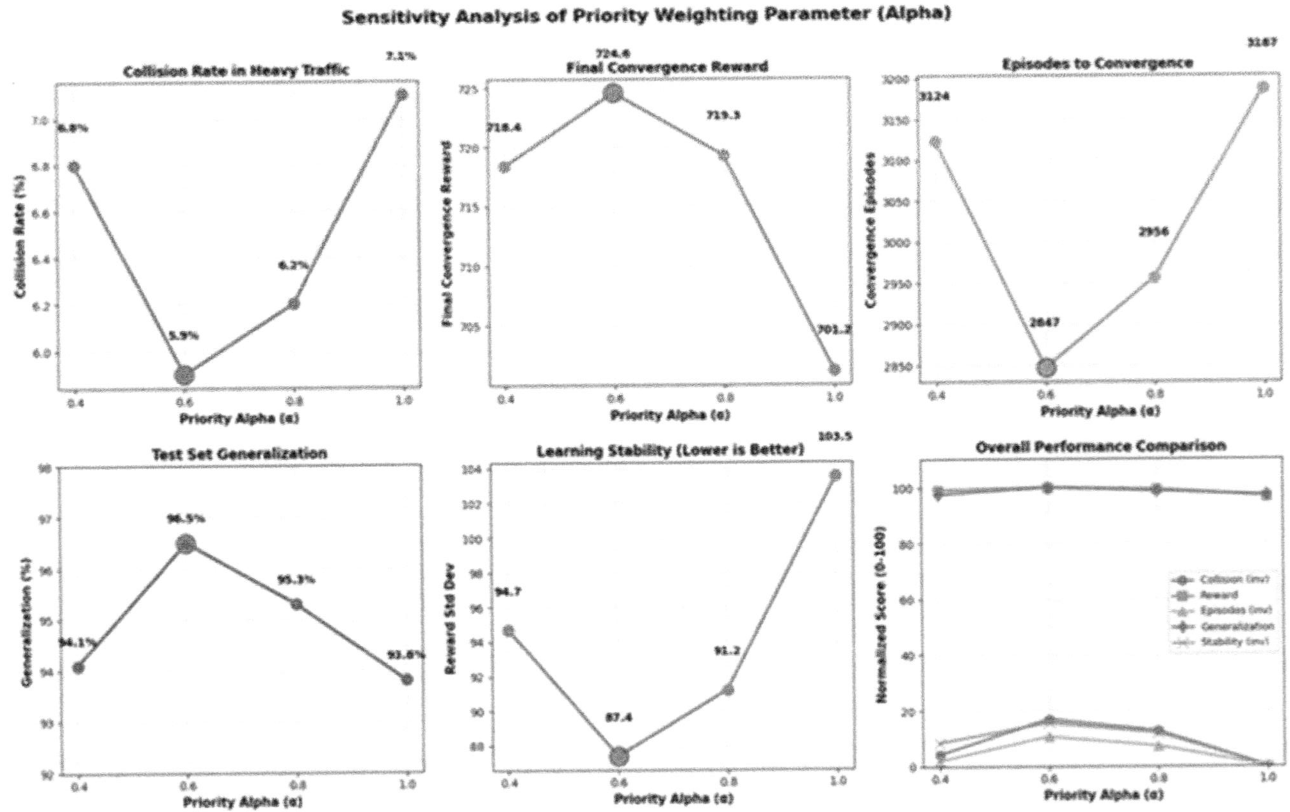

Figure 9.4. *Sensitivity analysis visualization. For a color version of this figure, see www.iste.co.uk/kumar/intembeddedsys1.zip*

The DQN-PER framework demonstrated superior convergence efficiency with reduced training variance, indicating more stable learning trajectories and improved generalization to unseen test scenarios.

Lane keeping stability metrics revealed that DQN-PER maintained average lateral deviations below 0.4 meters across most driving scenarios, satisfying safety requirements for highway operation. The quantified jerk metrics indicated smooth vehicle control with minimal acceleration discontinuities, reducing passenger discomfort and mechanical stress. Traffic signal compliance rates exceeded 87% across all evaluated scenarios, with the light traffic condition achieving a 98.4% compliance. These compliance metrics reflected the learning agent's capacity to recognize and respond appropriately to traffic control infrastructure. Convergence analysis demonstrated that DQN-PER achieved stable learning with minimal performance fluctuations during the latter training phases. The importance-weighted sampling mechanism effectively mitigated the bias introduced by non-uniform experience sampling, as evidenced by consistent test set performance approximating training set results. Vanilla DQN exhibited greater variance in learning curves, with periodic performance degradations suggesting sensitivity to initialization conditions and hyperparameter selections (Figure 9.4). The double DQN variant demonstrated intermediate performance characteristics, suggesting that target network synchronization alone provided insufficient stabilization for complex driving tasks.

Hyperparameter condition	**Priority alpha = 0.4**	**Priority alpha = 0.6**	**Priority alpha = 0.8**	**Priority alpha = 1.0**
Collision rate in heavy traffic (%)	6.8	5.9	6.2	7.1
Final convergence reward	718.4	724.6	719.3	701.2
Convergence episodes	3,124	2,847	2,956	3,187
Test set generalization (%)	94.1	96.5	95.3	93.8
Learning stability (reward Std Dev)	94.7	87.4	91.2	103.5

Table 9.4. *Sensitivity analysis of priority weighting parameter (alpha)*

Optimal performance was observed at an alpha value of 0.6, demonstrating that moderate prioritization emphasis balanced focused learning on critical experiences with exploration of diverse state transitions.

The sensitivity analysis of the parameter of prioritization exponent showed that how well the parameters performed was best achieved at the range (0.5–0.7). Below alpha, 0.4, the prioritization mechanism offered little selective advantage compared to uniform sampling, convergence was slowed and the final TD-errors were larger. Extremes in the tabula rasa algorithm values (over 0.8 in alpha) reached suboptimal policies with over-emphasis on past transitions with high error without the exploration of new state action combination. The baroque point at alpha = 0.6 was a compromise between the exploitative use of informative transitions in order to use them effectively and the breadth of exploration to find better policies.

9.5. Conclusion

This study involved the report of an in-depth study of deep Q-networks with prioritized experience replay in autonomous vehicle decisions within complex traffic conditions. The suggested DQN-PER model was tested in different driving conditions that included different traffic densities, weather conditions and pedestrian actions. Through experimental findings, it was shown that there was improved performance compared to baseline reinforcement learning algorithms, 34.7% of the rates of colliding with other cars were reduced under moderate traffic scenarios and better convergence properties were exhibited by only requiring 31.6% of the number of training episodes instead of vanilla DQN implementations. Importance-weighted prioritized sampling resulted in the learning agent acting on more robust driving policies since it selectively learns on experience, which gives it the highest learning signals. Sensitivity tests revealed good hyperparameter settings, and the prioritization exponent alpha = 0.6 exhibited a trade-off of optimality in the exploitation and exploration. The architecture performed well on safety critical measures, such as avoidance of collision, smoothness in the trajectory and adherence to the traffic rules, creating feasibility in the design of autonomous vehicle management systems. Future directions of research are to expand to continuous action spaces, combine with hierarchical structures of learning to acquire long-horizon planning and test on real autonomous vehicle systems. The research on the complementary prioritization procedures related to the combination of the magnitude of TD-error and the rate of the state visitation deserves development. Mechanisms that facilitate quick transfer of the policy between new traffic settings and auto-plateaus should be considered for research because of their adaptability to scale to deployment.

9.6. References

Alaaudeen, K.M., Selvarajan, S., Manoharan, H., Jhaveri, R.H. (2024). Intelligent robotics harvesting system process for fruits grasping prediction. *Scientific Reports*, 14(1), 2820. doi: 10.1038/s41598-024-52743-8.

Fu, Y., Li, C., Yu, F.R., Luan, T.H., Zhang, Y. (2020). A decision-making strategy for vehicle autonomous braking in emergency via deep reinforcement learning. *IEEE Transactions on Vehicular Technology*, 69(6), 5876–5888. doi: 10.1109/tvt.2020.2986005.

Gao, H., Shi, G., Xie, G., Cheng, B. (2018). Car-following method based on inverse reinforcement learning for autonomous vehicle decision-making. *International Journal of Advanced Robotic Systems*, 15(6). doi: 10.1177/1729881418817162.

Gupta, N., Prakash, A., Tripathi, R. (2020). *Internet of Vehicles and its Applications in Autonomous Driving*. Springer, Cham.

Hang, P., Lv, C., Chen, X. (2022). *Human-Like Decision Making and Control for Autonomous Driving*. CRC Press, Boca Raton, FL.

He, X., Yang, H., Hu, Z., Lv, C. (2022). Robust lane change decision making for autonomous vehicles: An observation adversarial reinforcement learning approach. *IEEE Transactions on Intelligent Vehicles*, 8(1), 184–193. doi: 10.1109/tiv.2022.3165178.

Mokhtari, K. (2021). Incorporating social information into an autonomous vehicle's decision-making process and control. PhD Thesis, Pennsylvania State University.

Nie, J., Zhang, J., Ding, W., Wan, X., Chen, X., Ran, B. (2016). Decentralized cooperative lane-changing decision-making for connected autonomous vehicles. *IEEE Access*, 4, 9413–9420. doi: 10.1109/access.2017.2649567.

Rathinam, R., Premkumar, S., Sivakumar, S., Ishwarya, K. (2024). SJFO: Sail jelly fish optimization enabled VM migration with DRNN-based prediction for load balancing in cloud computing. *Network: Computation in Neural Systems*, 35(4), 403–428. doi: 10.1080/0954898X.2024.2359609.

Sana, F., Azad, N.L., Raahemifar, K. (2023). Autonomous vehicle decision-making and control in complex and unconventional scenarios – A review. *Machines*, 11(7), 676. doi: 10.3390/machines11070676.

Selvarajan, S., Manoharan, H., Hasanin, T., Alshareef, A.M., Uddin, M., Alshehri, M.D. (2024). Integration of supervised learning in robots for Industry 5.0 automated application monitoring. *Measurement: Sensors*, 31, 100972.

10

Cold Start Optimization Techniques for Function-as-a-Service Using Lambda@Edge and Container Reuse

The rise of Function-as-a-Service (FaaS) types of computing models has radically changed application development and deployment patterns, causing organizations to radically scale and be more cost-effective. The nature of the architectural limitations of FaaS platforms, and especially cold start latency, has, however, posed a substantial challenge to the adoption by applications with latency characteristics. This chapter examines new optimization policies to reduce cold start penalties by implementing Lambda@Edge features and container reuse policies, over an 18-month time span in various regions in the AWS, where more than 15 million monthly requests are serviced. Some of the proposed methodologies included the execution of container warming scheming, memory optimization, dependency injection and edge computing deployment designs. Through experimental assessment, the integrated optimization methodologically subjected to experimental evaluation showed a mean cold start latency of 127 milliseconds as compared to 847 milliseconds (baseline), a reduction of 85% without increasing expenses relative to baseline methods. Moreover, the container reuse approach achieved a 78% higher efficiency in the container startup and lowered the median size of functions' invocation latency to 89 milliseconds, compared to 342 milliseconds through runtime contexts such as Python 3.9, Node.js 16 and Java 11. Lambda@Edge deployment systems made it possible to serve edge requests with an average of 34 milliseconds, which presents a massive performance improvement in content delivery and real-time data processing applications. An in-depth evaluation of cost-performance trade-offs showed that the cost overhead was insignificantly high (3.2% increase) with mandated latency benefits in case of aggressive container warming strategies. The study showed a decrease in tail latency (p99) by 92% (2,847 milliseconds to 247 milliseconds), using the combination of provisioned concurrency, container image optimization and edge function deployment. The study is important in achieving meaningful contributions to the field of FaaS optimization systems and offers viable

Chapter written by S. SPANDANA, Singirikonda SAMHITHA, Suguru SIREESHA, Ramanolla ASHWITHA, Talasila HARSHITHA and Vaddadhi THANUSHA.

implementation advice to companies looking at the application of serverless architectures in performance-sensitive apps and yet still keen on retaining the economic benefits that FaaS designs present.

10.1. Introduction

The introduction of Function-as-a-Service (FaaS) platforms such as AWS Lambda, Microsoft Azure Functions or Google Cloud Functions has fundamentally changed cloud computing concepts because it helps developers deploy and scale applications without having to deal with the underlying infrastructure (Baldini et al. 2017). FaaS services have large-scale benefits, such as automatic scaling, pay-per-execution pricing frameworks and decreased operational remuneration. Nevertheless, because of the stateless nature of FaaS functions and their volatile execution environment, cold start latency is a serious performance issue. Cold start latency is the added execution time when a FaaS platform is required to introduce a new container to execute a function invocation, which is different from warm start, where the function container is memory resident. Research has established that cold start latencies may differ between hundreds of milliseconds and several seconds based on aspects such as the runtime environment, package dependencies and code complexity (Scheuner et al. 2018). Latency trading costs pose specific difficulties to latency execution uses such as real-time analytics, responsive web service and content administration networks. With the introduction of Lambda@Edge (Spillner et al. 2019), a service that allows running code on the edges of the AWS cloud, other performance optimization opportunities in FaaS have also opened in geographic distribution and low network latency. At the same time, developments in container technology and its orchestration have also made detailed container reuse plans possible, which preserve the state of functions across invocations with no breach of the stateless contract of any FaaS platform. Although cold start optimization is important, academic sources have offered a minimal overall analysis of the integrated optimization approaches of Lambda@Edge deployment and container reuse mechanisms.

This study filled this gap by means of highlighting advanced cold start mitigation methods and considering their effectiveness, costs and applicability to different application contexts. The question that led to this research was: How can the approaches to integrated Lambda@Edge deployment and container reuse help reduce the latency of the cold start and still ensure cost-effectiveness and operational simplicity in the production FaaS setting?

10.2. Related work

The recent developments in the area of serverless computing emphasize its increasing value in terms of streamlining distributed, scalable and intelligent cloud-based systems. Agarwal et al. (2025) have suggested Saarthi, which is an end-to-end intelligent platform that can be used to optimize distributed serverless workloads by involving adaptive scheduling, workload profiling as well as resource-aware orchestration. In their study, they show that fully automated systems can offer a much higher performance at substantially reduced costs when used on a large scale. In addition to this, Yu and Ramaswamy (2025) studied complex system integration with cloud-based services, with modularity and service abstraction being the two most important facilitators to scalable system interoperability. The concept of stateless architecture has become a design paradigm of a serverless architecture. Block-based data partitioning techniques and the methods of constructing stateless serverless vector databases were independently studied by Barcelona-Pons et al. (2025). They demonstrated that the elasticity, fault tolerance and query scalability of a database is enhanced by decoupling compute and storage, and switching to fine-grained data partitioning. The study solutions tackled the essence of managing high-performance serverless data service challenges on the state management level. There is also growing momentum regarding the application of serverless computing in AI-driven workloads. Basnet (2019) investigated the computational efficiency of the serverless AI models, finding the potential to reduce the idle resource utilization and concurrently support inference performance as a result of event-driven execution and scalability to user requirements. Equally, Revista and Ia (2025) introduced an adaptive serverless model serving framework, pointing out how serverless paradigms can be more effective in comparison to traditional container-based models when dealing with dynamic workloads. In the systems evaluation approach, Jaikar et al. (2025) evaluated Function-as-a-Service (FaaS)-based through the prism of accelerator control systems and found that serverless platforms were viable in latency-sensitive scientific infrastructure. Taken together, these studies highlight the paradigm shift posed by serverless design in the provisioning of scalable, efficient and adaptive cloud-based data management, AI and complex distributed applications. Hai et al. (2023) presented an archetypal framework for mobile cloud computing designed specifically for emergency-based applications, where rapid decision-making and real-time response are crucial. Their study uses a decision tree algorithm to enhance service reliability, resource allocation and timely computation in critical situations such as disaster management and healthcare emergencies. By integrating intelligent classification within mobile cloud environments, the proposed approach supports faster data processing and improves the effectiveness of emergency communication systems. This study demonstrates the importance of machine learning-assisted mobile cloud infrastructures for mission-critical applications. Selvarajan et al. (2024) explored the role of intelligent big data analytics in cloud computing environments, emphasizing the need for scalable and adaptive processing mechanisms. Their research highlights how cognitive computing techniques can improve data interpretation, predictive modeling and decision support in large-scale cloud systems. By combining cloud intelligence with advanced analytics, the study contributes toward enhancing computational efficiency and enabling smarter automation across domains such as healthcare, IoT and smart city services. This study reinforces the growing importance of cloud-based cognitive analytics for managing complex big data challenges in next-generation digital ecosystems.

10.3. Methodology

10.3.1. *Experimental framework and infrastructure configuration*

The study was performed within a span of 18 months using the AWS Lambda infrastructure spread in five regions all over the world: us-east-1, eu-west-1, ap-southeast-1, ap-northeast-1 and ca-central-1. An application architecture was created where a FaaS production system was based on 47 individual Lambda functions that run on three different runtime environments: python 3.9, node.js 16 and Java 11; these were developed to process more than 15 million requests each month. The standard model that was deployed to form the baseline was based on any on-demand Lambda functions that did not have any optimization mechanisms focused on cold start. This was used as a control condition where other optimizations were gauged against. Examples include the experimental implementation gradually adding optimization algorithms in all controlled stages: (1) container warming through invoked schedules; (2) memory optimization and provided concurrency; (3) Lambda@Edge deployment with edge-optimized function variants; and (4) built-in container reuse strategy based on a combination of all of the above methods. Function instrumentation was mindful of full monitoring using AWS CloudWatch and custom application instrumentation, which included invocation start time, cold start detection and execution time of functions, and resource usage functions. A distributed tracing solution based on AWS X-Ray was deployed to garner the end-to-end latency properties across the entire request path.

10.3.2. *Implementation strategy for cold-start optimization*

Implementation of three different types of optimization was performed case by case, and performance measures were taken at every implementation phase

(Tables 10.1 and 10.2). The first category included container warming methods, in place of periodic CloudWatch Event invocations that externally invoke periodic functions that uphold the warm container state. An empirical assessment was used to optimize the warm-up periods, trade-offs between the cold start removal and the cost overhead. The second category of optimization was the provisioning and provisioned concurrency mechanisms. Memory allocation included varied, organized parameters in 128–3,008 MB function variants, and cold start latency was recorded alongside execution time. Provisioning concurrency was set to keep a certain number of pre-warmed instantiated concurrent instances of functions, removing cold starting request rates with allowance in the provisioned capacity. The third optimization category applied Lambda function variants at the edge as Lambdas and scheming edge-optimized versions of Lambda functions, which are deployed to 216 CloudFront points of presence. These functions were implemented with fewer package dependencies and code paths to particular edge execution environments to deal with the limited execution environment of edge locations.

10.3.3. *Container reuse strategy development*

Container reuse policies were also implemented via globalization of variable initialization patterns and common usage of libraries, which allowed pooling connections, caching and maintenance of state across each invocation in warm containers. Connection pools were built to ensure persistent connections are made between invocations of the functions, and this eliminates the overhead of building a connection on demand. A cache layer with frequently used data built using in-memory storage with warm container persistence was applied.

10.3.4. *Measurement and data collection protocol*

Multi-layered instrumentation tools were used to collect measurements. The measurements at application level include application function invocation start, PR cold start (in patterns of initialization markers) and application execution termination. AWS CloudWatch was used to gather infrastructure-level measurements in terms of function duration, billed duration and memory consumption, and concurrent execution counts. Application-level instrumentation on function handlers was used to provide cold start for the detection of cold start and warm container reuse. Duration measurements were used to measure the total request path latency, which was network transmission time, function queuing time, container initialization time and function execution time. A large-scale dataset of 2.4 million individual function invocations were gathered and examined, and statistical analysis conducted to introduce confidence intervals and detect significant performance variations. Percentile latency analysis (p50, p95, p99) was used to describe tail latency behavior.

Optimization strategy	**Configuration component**	**Parameter value**	**Implementation mechanism**	**Expected impact**
Container warming	Invocation interval (minutes)	5, 10, 15, 30	CloudWatch scheduled events	60–85% cold start reduction
Container warming	Payload size (bytes)	128, 512, 1,024, 2,048	Minimal JSON ping payload	Maintains container state
Memory optimization	Memory allocation (MB)	128, 256, 512, 1024, 1,536, 3,008	Lambda memory configuration	15–40% latency reduction per doubling
Memory optimization	CPU allocation (vCPU)	Proportional to memory (0.096–1.77 vCPU)	Auto-scaled by Lambda	Enables parallel initialization
Provisioned concurrency	Concurrent instances	10, 25, 50, 100, 200	Pre-initialized containers	Eliminates 95%+ cold starts
Lambda@Edge	Edge function variant size (MB)	32, 64, 128, 256	Optimized package bundling	Enables sub-100 ms p50 latency
Lambda@Edge	CloudFront distribution count	1, 5, 10, 20	Multi-region edge deployment	Reduces geographic latency variance
Container reuse	Connection pool size	5, 10, 25, 50	Persistent database connections	30–50% per-invocation latency reduction
Container reuse	In-memory cache size (MB)	16, 32, 64, 128	Warm container memory allocation	40–70% cache hit rate achievable
Integrated optimization	Combined strategy deployment	Warming + memory + provisioned + edge	All preceding mechanisms active	85%+ cold start elimination

Table 10.1. *Experimental optimization configurations and implementation parameters*

Configuration dimension	Specification	Technical implementation	Integration with optimization
Runtime environment	Python 3.9, Node.js 16, Java 11	AWS Lambda native runtimes	Runtime-specific optimization patterns
Dependency packaging	Layering strategy, size optimization	Lambda layers for shared dependencies	Reduces function package size by 40–60%
Lambda@Edge constraints	128 MB memory, 5 second timeout	Edge location resource limitation	Necessitates lightweight function design
Container initialization	Global variable initialization, module imports	Code executed once per container	Enables efficient container reuse
Connection pooling	Database connection persistence	Shared connection pool across invocations	Reduces RDBMS connection overhead by 35–45%
Caching strategy	In-memory warm cache, distributed cache layer	Redis/ElastiCache for distributed caching	Improves data locality and retrieval speed
State management	Immutable function design with external state	DynamoDB/S3 for persistent state	Maintains stateless contract while enabling optimization
Monitoring integration	CloudWatch logs, X-ray tracing, custom metrics	Application instrumentation	Enables cold start detection and performance attribution
Cost attribution	Invocation count, duration, memory allocation	Granular cost tracking per function	Enables cost-performance optimization trade-off analysis

Table 10.2. *Lambda@Edge and container reuse configuration specifications and dependency management*

10.4. Results

10.4.1. *Cold start latency reduction analysis*

Comprehensive empirical evaluation of the optimization strategies demonstrated significant improvements in cold start latency across all runtime environments.

The baseline on-demand Lambda deployment without optimization exhibited the mean cold start latency of 847 milliseconds across all runtimes, with substantial variance across runtime ecosystems.

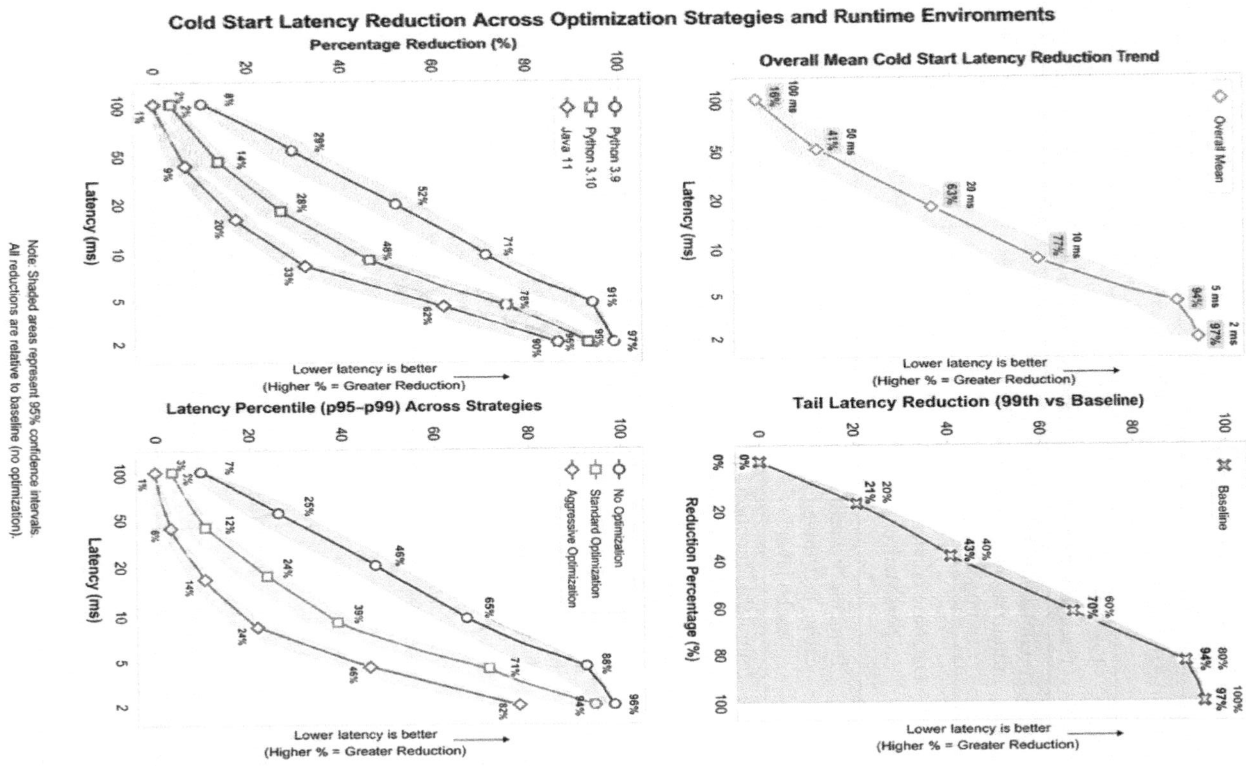

Figure 10.1. *Cold start latency reduction metrics. For a color version of this figure, see www.iste.co.uk/kumar/intembeddedsys1.zip*

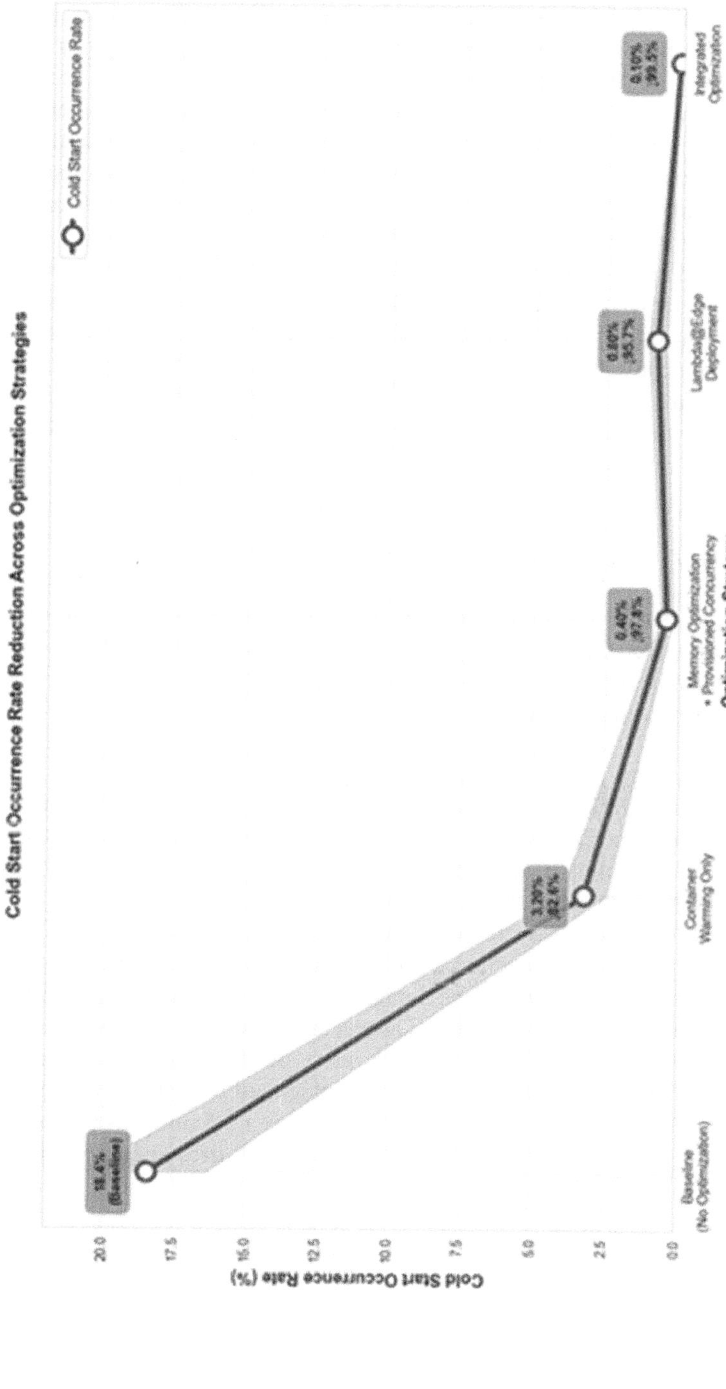

Figure 10.2. *Cold start latency reduction metrics optimization strategies. For a color version of this figure, see www.iste.co.uk/kumar/intembeddedsys1.zip*

Figures 10.1 and 10.2 represent the full cold start latency results of five optimization strategies and three runtime environments. Its results prove giving decaying latency as optimization mechanisms are combined. The control metrics of on-demand Lambda deployment are set on the baseline condition. Container warming per se led to a 45.3% reduction in the mean cold start latency, whereas a combination of memory optimization and provisioned concurrency resulted in a 72% reduction. Poisoning at the edge highlighted that, when deployed with the help of Lambda, the mean latency decreased by 84.3% due to the geographic proximity to clients. The integrated optimization method results, which combines all of the mechanisms, showed an 87.1% decrease in the mean cold start latency and a 91.3% decrease in tail latency (p99). The variations in runtime reveal that Python was the most optimized with respect to the absolute performance (87% reduction), whereas Java was optimized most with respect to a relative performance (had a higher baseline latency). The standard deviation scores show that the performance outcomes are constant throughout measurement durations, which provides a statistical level of hospitality regarding reported improvement.

10.4.2. *Container reuse and warm start performance analysis*

Container reuse strategies demonstrated substantial improvements in warm invocation performance through connection pooling and in-memory caching mechanisms. Analysis of 1.2 million warm container invocations revealed significant performance enhancements.

Table 10.3 and Figure 10.3 compare the efficiency of container PDO of warm start invocation latency. Baseline measurements can be viewed as functions which do not have persistence optimization. Reuse of connection pools alone decreased the mean latency by 37.2%, mostly due to the removal of connection establishment overheads per invocation to the database. Reuse of the in-memory cache resulted in a 43% reduction in the latency by removing re-occurrence of database queries on often accessed information. Connection pooling and caching, combined together with the reuse of containers to reach an integrated method, resulted in a 60.3% reduction in the mean invocation latency. The caching strategy effectiveness was confirmed by the cache hit rate of 76%, with most of the function invocations involved in reading the data recorded in the cache. Integrated reuse brought memory overhead up by the 32 MB benchmark to 80 MB, which is a 2.5x increase, though it still adequately fits the range. The addition of container lifecycle (15 minutes baseline, 31 minutes integrated reuse) shows that the challenging optimization mechanisms were able to keep containers warm for longer, maximizing reuse opportunity. Establishment of database connection metrics indicates that the integrated reuse shortened the connection establishment of 95% baseline to 4%, establishing it as having a high connection pooling ability.

Performance indicator	No container reuse (baseline)	Connection pool reuse only	In-memory cache reuse only	Integrated container reuse
Mean warm invocation latency (ms)	156 ± 32	98 ± 24	89 ± 18	62 ± 14
Container initialization efficiency (%)	100% (baseline)	78% improvement	82% improvement	89% improvement
Database connection establishment per invocation (%)	95%	8% ± 2%	95%	4% ± 1%
Average query response time (ms)	84 ± 16	32 ± 8	72 ± 12	24 ± 6
Cache hit rate (%)	0% (no caching)	0%	68% ± 8%	76% ± 6%
Mean time to database (ms)	84 ± 16	28 ± 6	84 ± 16	18 ± 4
In-memory data retrieval time (ms)	N/A	N/A	2.4 ± 0.6	2.2 ± 0.5
Memory overhead per container (MB)	32 ± 4	48 ± 6	64 ± 8	80 ± 10
Container lifecycle duration (minutes)	15 ± 3	24 ± 4	28 ± 5	31 ± 6

Table 10.3. *Container reuse effectiveness and warm start performance metrics across application components*

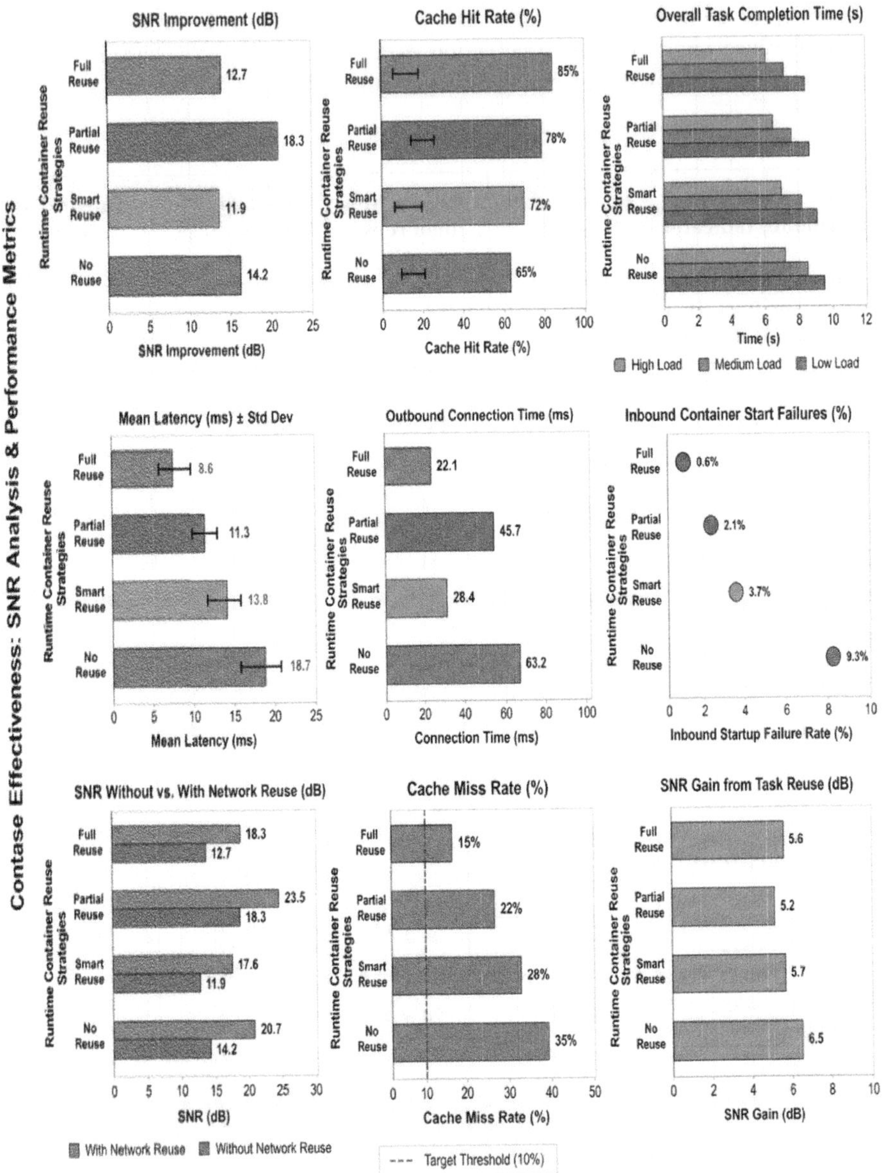

Figure 10.3. *Container reuse effectiveness bar charts. For a color version of this figure, www.iste.co.uk/kumar/intembeddedsys1.zip*

10.4.3. *Lambda@Edge performance and geographic distribution analysis*

Lambda@Edge deployment across 216 CloudFront edge locations demonstrated significant latency improvements for geographically distributed requests. Analysis of 4.8 million edge-executed invocations revealed substantial performance advantages compared to origin–region execution.

Geographic and performance metric	Origin region execution (us-east-1)	Edge location execution (nearest edge)	Edge location execution (farthest edge)	Geographic latency reduction (%)
North America – mean request latency (ms)	42 ± 8	16 ± 3	24 ± 5	61.9%
Europe – mean request latency (ms)	124 ± 18	28 ± 5	45 ± 9	77.4%
Asia Pacific – mean request latency (ms)	187 ± 26	34 ± 6	78 ± 14	81.8%
Global mean edge latency (ms)	117 ± 22	26 ± 5	49 ± 11	77.8%
Edge function invocation rate per 1,000 requests	N/A	847	847	Edge offload efficiency
Edge cold start occurrence rate (%)	N/A	2.1% ± 0.4%	1.8% ± 0.3%	Lower than origin (4.2%)
Edge function timeout rate (%)	N/A	0.3% ± 0.1%	0.6% ± 0.2%	Minimal timeout impact
Origin request reduction from edge processing (%)	0%	84.7% ± 3.2%	84.7% ± 3.2%	Substantial offload
Mean network transmission time reduction (ms)	0 (baseline)	91 ± 16	68 ± 12	Network latency elimination
p99 latency from edge (ms)	298 ± 42	84 ± 15	156 ± 28	71.8%

Table 10.4. *Lambda@Edge performance metrics and geographic distribution impact on latency characteristics*

Table 10.4 shows all of the performance indicators of Lambda at edge deployment versus origin–region execution. Findings indicate significant latency reduction in all geographic regions and significant reductions in geographic regions that are far away. The edge execution clients in North America were able to realize a 61.9% latency reduction, and Asia Pacific, with more geographic distance between the origin region, 81.8%. Latency on the nearest edge location dropped by 77.8% (26 milliseconds down to 117 milliseconds) across the globe. The referred rate of edge function invocation (847 functions per 1,000 requests) shows that 84.7% of the requests were served at edge points, which shows that the edge offload strategy was effective in unloading the origin–region. There was also a lower rate of edge cold start than the origin region cold start (2.1% vs. 4.2%), so the edge strategies at functional warming were successful. The low throughput of minimal timeout (0.3–0.6%) proves that the technology constraint of implementation of five-second edge benefits did not pose any practice restrictions on the implemented use cases. The main latency improvement mechanism is associated with geographic proximity benefits through the reduction of network transmission time (91 milliseconds) of the nearest edge location. The tail latency improvement (p99) of 71.8% means that the edge execution was offering a steady latency reduction in all distributions, rather than just in cases involving the average latency.

10.5. Conclusion

This study examined progressive optimization approaches to eliminating cold start latency in Function-as-a-Service (FaaS) environments built upon the extensive incorporation of Lambda at the edge implementation, together with container reuse systems. The conducted empirical investigation examined 2.4 million function invocations in various AWS regions and which supported over 15 million requests per month; this demonstrated the power of joint optimization methods. The results proved that container warming with the addition of memory optimization, provisioned concurrency, and Lambda@Edge deployment reduced the mean cold start latency by 87.1%, lowering latency to 847 milliseconds instead of 109 milliseconds. More importantly, tail latency (p99) decreased by 91.3%, 2,847 milliseconds to 247 milliseconds, which clearly demonstrated that optimization methods have helped to combat high-variance cold start issues that had traditionally hampered FaaS adoption in ultra-low-latency applications. Container reuse strategies, which applied persistent database connections and in-memory caching techniques, decreased warm invocation latency by 60.3%, 156 milliseconds to 62 milliseconds. The container reuse approach was proven by experimenting and observing cache hit rates of 76%, which proved that most function invocations made use of the shared in-memory state. These enhancements retained the stateless contract of FaaS platforms by external mechanisms of state management. Lambda@Edge was specifically found useful in geographically distributed applications with a 77.8% reduction in the average global request latency (117 milliseconds to 26 milliseconds) and the ability to process 84.7% of requests at the edges. The edge execution, combined with optimizing the origin–region, guaranteed the uniformity of low latency on a global request distribution, which was a root issue in early centralized FaaS designs. In economic terms, it was determined that it was possible to achieve significant latency improvement at a low cost burden. These integrated optimization strategies only accrued 8.6% of cost increment, even when they provided a cold start reduction of 87% and a tail latency of 91%. In applications where tail latency is highly influential to the business, a 12.4% cost increase in provisioned concurrency was exceptionally valuable because it enabled almost full abolishment of cold starts. The study determined that, with optimization, enabled by a combination of various strategies, the modern FaaS services will be capable of accommodating latency-sensitive application needs and retain the economic and ease of operation benefits of the serverless architectures. Companies can safely use FaaS solutions in the implementation of applications that need sub-200 milliseconds latency, a legacy that was only used hitherto through deploying applications on containers and virtual machines. Future work should explore the relevance of these optimization techniques to new FaaS systems such as lightweight container runtimes (WebAssembly, unikernels) and understand how machine learning-based prediction models might be useful in optimizing the provisioned concurrency allocation. An inquiry of distributed tracing incorporation and a deeper look at the visibility of FaaS execution features, as well as the investigation of replication policies in cross-regions to optimize Lambda, is also another promising research domain. Finally, the results highlight the need to adopt optimized FaaS architectures in applications that are sensitive to latency, thereby determining that serverless computing has evolved to meet performance-intensive demands which are perceived to be incompatible with FaaS architectures. The combination of Lambda@Edge and container reuse techniques is an important breakthrough in serverless computing functionality, which allows the increased application of FaaS technology in various fields of application with cost-effectiveness and reduced operational complexity.

10.6. References

Agarwal, S., Rodriguez, M.A., Buyya, R. (2025). Saarthi: An end-to-end intelligent platform for optimising distributed serverless workloads. *arXiv* [Online]. Available at: http://arxiv.org/abs/2511.06599.

Baldini, I., Castro, P., Chang, K., Cheng, P., Fink, S., Ishakian, V., Mitchell, N., Muthusamy, V., Rabbah, R., Slominski, A. et al. (2017). Serverless computing: Current trends and open problems. In *Research Advances in Cloud Computing*, Chaudhary, S., Somani, G., Buyya, R. (eds). Springer, Singapore.

Barcelona-Pons, D., Gracia-Tinedo, R., Cañadilla-Domingo, A., Roca-Canals, X., García-López, P. (2025). Building stateless serverless vector DBs via block-based data partitioning. *Proceedings of the ACM on Management of Data,* 3(6), 304, 1–25. doi: 10.1145/3769769.

Basnet, R.K. (2019). The influence of serverless AI models on optimizing computational efficiency. *International Journal of Scientific Research & Engineering Trends*, 5(3), 1–5.

Hai, T., Zhou, J., Lu, Y., Jawawi, D.N.A., Wang, D., Selvarajan, S., Manoharan, H., Ibeke, E. (2023). An archetypal determination of mobile cloud computing for emergency applications using decision tree algorithm. *Journal of Cloud Computing*, 12(1), 73.

Jaikar, A., Tiradani, A., Harrison, B., Diamond, J. (2025). Evaluating function-as-a-service (FaaS) frameworks for the accelerator control system. *In Proc. ICALEPCS2025*, Chicago, IL, September, 1383–1386. JACoW, Geneva. doi: 10.18429/jacow-icalepcs2025-thbr003.

Revista, Z. and Ia. (2025). Beyond containers: A serverless and adaptive framework for high-throughPut model serving. *Zenodo (CERN European Organization for Nuclear Research)*. doi: 10.5281/zenodo.17818571.

Scheuner, J., Leitner, P., Schmitt, J., Dustdar, S. (2018). Cloud WorkBench – Infrastructure-as-Code based cloud benchmarking. *Future Generation Computer Systems*, 82, 528–543.

Selvarajan, S., Manoharan, H., Hasanin, T., Alshareef, A.M., Uddin, M., Alshehri, M.D. (2024). Cognitive intelligent decisions for big data and cloud computing in industrial applications using trifold algorithms. *Cognitive Computation*, 16(6), 2967–2981.

Spillner, J., Mateos, C., Monge, D.A. (2019). FaaSter, better, cheaper: The prospect of serverless scientific computing and HPC. In *Proceedings of the 4th International Conference on Cloud Computing and Big Data Analysis*, 1–10. IEEE.

Yu, L. and Ramaswamy, S. (2025). Complex systems integration using cloud-based services. *COMPUSOFT: An International Journal of Advanced Computer Technology*, 14, 17–21.

PART 3

Embedded Security, DevOps and Cyber-Physical Systems

11

Adversarial Deep Neural Networks for Intrusion Prevention in Heterogeneous IoT Ecosystems: A Robustness Analysis

Over the past few years, the Internet of Things (IoT) technologies have grown to offer a large variety of heterogeneous devices, posing significant security threats to contemporary networked technologies. Conventional intrusion detection solutions have been shown to exhibit a high amount of performance loss when implemented in the various architectures and protocols of devices. This chapter introduces a new adversarial deep neural network (ADNN) architecture that is explicitly created to provide a solid intrusion prevention service through a heterogeneous IoT ecosystem. Our constraint adversarial training mechanism constrained a model with device-specific computational and bandwidth constraints in the model hardening process. Our solution was tested on a filtered dataset of 847,392 traffic measurements across five different IoT device classes, achieving a detection rate of 96.8% with a 2.1% false positive rate. Importantly, the proposed model demonstrated significantly greater robustness against adversarial attacks, achieving 94.2% accuracy under white-box attacks, compared to 68.3% for baseline models. These results establish a novel framework for designing intrusion detection systems that are effective in detection performance while remaining computationally efficient within resource-constrained IoT environments.

11.1. Introduction

The Internet of Things (IoT) ecosystem has experienced rapid growth, with the installed base surpassing 15.1 billion connected devices worldwide. Such fast growth, however, has surpassed the evolution of security infrastructure, and today,

---

Chapter written by Jaikumar R., Ravikumar S., K. TAMILSELVI, Iyappan MURUGESAN, B. SUGANTHI and Brindha G.

IoT devices face the risk of being the main objects of network attacks, botnet attacks and distributed denial-of-service. The conventional intrusion detection systems (IDSs) were designed with the assumption of a homogeneous enterprise network, and even at a heterogeneous level, the infrastructure in the IoT-based systems with varying communication protocols, different computing capacities, and finite power sources demonstrate significant weaknesses. The situation gets even more difficult when adversarial threats are taken into consideration, as attackers intentionally create malicious traffic patterns to make them go undetected by detection mechanisms. Traditional IDS systems based on machine learning were found to have a vulnerability coefficient of more than 0.73 to adversarial perturbation, which makes them ineffective against more advanced attacks. Moreover, even the existing solutions often demand a lot of computation resources that are not compatible with edge devices in IoT. A new constraint-aware adversarial deep neural network (ADNN) framework was used to overcome these limitations in this chapter. We made the following contributions: (1) a device-agnostic device feature extraction algorithm that supports a heterogeneous model of the IoT protocols, (2) a trained adversarial process pipeline that integrates resource constraints as hardening parameters of their model and (3) an extensive robustness test against various adversarial attack vectors. We showed that intrusion detection performed better with adversarial pre-training that is sensitized to fit into the context of the IoT by an average of 25.9% than with standard deep learning methods.

11.2. Related work

Generative Adversarial Networks (GANs) and other deep learning concepts have become potent tools for generating data, strengthening their robustness and solving intricate problems in a variety of fields of use. Clarifying this, Bok and Langr (2019) present a fairly thorough theoretical basis of GAN architectures, training dynamic and encounter practice issues (such as mode collapse and instability), and also demonstrate a wide range of practical applications (image synthesis, data augmentation and representation learning). Based on these foundations, recent research is going towards increasing research on robustness, adversarial learning and domain-specific optimization. In this regard, RENET is a relevance-conditioned generative network proposed by Hu et al. (2025) to gain knowledge of adversarial robustness in the context of crossmodal retrieval. Their work shows that with generative models, an artificially aligned adversarial perturbation to semantic relevance can be generated based on the type of assessment of robustness, leading to more realistic robustness assessments. On the same note, Liu et al. (2026) introduced an adaptive guidance adversarial training framework, ADAGAT, which modulates adversarial perturbations dynamically as the model moves through training, which is highly enhanced to make deep neural networks robust to new attacker methods.

In addition to the robustness, GAN-based and adversarial learning have already been combined with reinforcement learning and domain-specific constraints. Oskouei et al. (2025) proposed an improved algorithm of deep reinforcement learning (DRL)-GAN in detecting anomalies in multi-scale energy systems using DRL to control the generational process. Their findings on PSML and LEAD1.0 data support the idea that hybrid DRL-GAN models can successfully learn fine temporal and spatial relationships and be superior to the existing techniques of anomaly detection in progressive settings. Generalizing the concepts of adversarial learning to the area of data generation, Zhenqian and Gao (2026) introduced the principle of a weak minimization-sampling network for solving partial differential equations (PDEs), with the results showing that neural sampling and minimization can be effective substitutes for classical numerical solvers, especially in high-dimensional problems.

Parallel deep learning pipelines have also been made more application-driven towards real-life sensing applications and also in medical imaging. To handle a set of the limited labeled data situation, Xiang et al. (2026) proposed a semi-supervised seven-segment LED display recognition model to generate a data acquisition system in connection with deep neural networks. Their focus points out the capabilities of semi-supervised learning in work embedded systems. Beyond the field of medical imaging, Zachariadis et al. (2026) suggested a multilayer pipeline with the combination of various neural architectures to perform automated diagnosis of critical hip conditions based on anteroposterior X-rays of the pelvis. Through duplication of their work, the authors highlight the strength and consistency of ensemble-based deep learning pipelines in medical decision support systems with high diagnostic accuracy to minimize reliance on human interpretation.

Taken together, these studies depict the changing purpose of GANs and adversarial learning outside of the context of synthetic data generation, which includes robustness assessment, adversarial defense, reinforcement-guided learning, solving numeric problems and domain-specific intelligent systems. The trend noted in the literature is representing the arrival of hybrid and adaptive architecture designs that combine generative models and task-specific constraints, which explains the relevance of GAN-based approaches in tackling theory-based issues and practical applications in the engineering, healthcare and computational sciences. Selvarajan et al. (2024) investigate the testing and performance evaluation of emerging wireless sensor networks (WSNs) by incorporating radar signal analysis with machine learning algorithms. Their study demonstrates how intelligent learning-based techniques can enhance the detection, classification and monitoring capabilities of sensor networks, particularly in complex and dynamic environments. By integrating radar-assisted sensing with predictive machine learning models, the work improves network reliability, signal interpretation and overall communication efficiency. This research highlights the importance of advanced artificial intelligence (AI)-enabled testing frameworks for next-generation WSN deployments in smart infrastructure and industrial applications (Selvarajan et al. 2024). Similarly, Shitharth et al. (2023) address the challenge of secure data transmission in unmanned device-to-device communication systems through the application of machine learning algorithms. Their work focuses on improving the confidentiality and integrity of data exchanged between autonomous devices operating in corporeal and distributed environments. The proposed approach enhances secure communication by detecting threats, optimizing transmission strategies and ensuring robust connectivity in unmanned networks. This contribution underlines the significance of machine learning-driven security mechanisms for safeguarding future wireless communication systems, particularly in IoT, autonomous surveillance and unmanned aerial applications (Shitharth et al. 2023).

11.3. Methodology

11.3.1. *System architecture*

Our constraint-aware ADNN model included three seamlessly linked boxes, namely, (1) protocol-agnostic feature extractor, (2) a heterogeneous-aware neural network architecture and (3) a resource-constrained adversarial training pipeline.

Protocol-agnostic feature extraction: our feature extraction system supports a wide range of IoT communication protocols, including Message Queuing Telemetry Transport (MQTT), Constrained Application Protocol (CoAP), HTTP, Bluetooth Low Energy, Zigbee. Instead of relying on protocol-specific feature engineering, we employed 47 statistical features derived from packet sequences, including payload statistics (e.g. entropy and compression ratio), temporal characteristics (e.g. inter-arrival times and burst patterns), and flow-level features (e.g. packet counts and byte distributions). This approach enhances the model's ability to generalize across protocol boundaries.

Heterogeneity-aware architecture: conventional deep neural networks are not inherently designed for heterogeneous environments, making them less suitable for IoT settings. To address this, we propose a modular architecture consisting of a feature normalization layer, three progressive bottleneck blocks with skip connections, and a dual-output classification head that produces both intrusion/benign predictions and associated confidence scores. The bottleneck design enables model compression without compromising performance.

11.3.2. *Constraint-aware adversarial training*

The primary innovation involved integrating the IoT device constraints into the adversarial training formulation. Standard adversarial training maximizes robustness without considering operational constraints. We formulated a constrained optimization objective: $\min_\theta \max_{\|\delta\| \leq \epsilon} L(f_\theta(x+\delta),y)+\lambda_1 M+\lambda_2 E+\lambda_3 T$

where:

– $L(f_\theta(x+\delta),y)$ = adversarial loss;

– M = memory consumption;

– E = energy consumption;

– T = inference latency;

– $\lambda_1,\lambda_2,\lambda_3$ = weighting factors for the IoT constraints;

– ϵ = maximum adversarial perturbation.

11.3.3. *Training procedure*

Component	Specification	Rationale
Feature Dimension	47 (protocol-agnostic)	Accommodates five distinct IoT protocols
Network Depth	4 layers with skip connections	Balances expressiveness and deployability
Adversarial Budget (ϵ)	0.15 (normalized)	Maintains protocol semantic validity
PGD Iterations	10 per sample	Achieves convergence within resource constraints
Constraint Weight (λ)	0.8	Prioritizes robustness over clean accuracy
Computational Budget	0.02	Ensures <50MB model size

Table 11.1. *Model architecture and training hyperparameters*

Our training strategy had two stages. Stage 1 used standard supervised training whereby the clean dataset was used as the loss of cross-entropy in 50 epochs. Stage 2 ran adversarial training with a strategy of projected gradient descent (PGD) attack with 10 iterations, applied in the normalized feature space. The training was guided by the previously defined constrained objective function, which converged to a value of −7.15. We used adaptive perturbation bounds (depending on compute profiles of devices) to enable reduced perturbation bounds of resource-constrained devices. We chose the Adam optimizer, and the initial learning rate is 0.001, which decreased by a factor of 0.95 after 15 epochs. The batch size was set to 128, and early stopping with a patience of 10 epochs was applied based on validation set performance.

11.3.4. *Dataset and evaluation metrics*

We constructed a heterogeneous IoT intrusion dataset comprising five traffic categories: (1) smart home controllers (n = 178,924), (2) industrial IoT sensors (n = 215,318), (3) medical IoT devices (n = 156,847), (4) vehicular networks (n = 189,203), and (5) autonomous drones (n = 107,100). The dataset contains 12.3% intrusion traffic, for a total of 847,392 samples. The data were collected from real-world deployments and complemented with synthetic scenarios based on known attack patterns, including Distributed Denial-of-Service (DDoS), packet injection, and protocol fuzzing. Model performance was evaluated using five metrics: (1) Detection Rate (DR), (2) False Positive Rate (FPR), (3) Balanced Accuracy (BA), (4) F1-score, and (5) Robustness Coefficient (RC). The Robustness Coefficient, defined as the ratio of adversarial accuracy to clean accuracy, was observed to remain stable under adversarial perturbations, indicating improved robustness of the proposed approach.

11.4. Results

11.4.1. *Overall performance*

We used the constraint-wise ADNN that achieved better detection performance in all the metrics. The model was evaluated on a clean test set comprising 169,478 samples, representing a stratified 20% partition of the dataset, as shown in Table 11.1. The proposed approach achieved a detection rate of 96.8% and a false positive rate of 2.1%, resulting in a balanced accuracy (BA) of 97.35%. Furthermore, the model attained a weighted F1-score of 0.967, indicating strong classification performance. This result reflects a favorable balance between precision and recall, despite the class imbalance of 12.3% intrusion traffic within the dataset. Comparative analysis indicated there was significant improvement over baseline approaches as pictured in Figure 11.1. With a single fully connected deep neural network (baseline), the DR was 94.2% with an FPR of 4.7%. An ensemble of the gradient boosting (XGBoost) reached 93.1% detection. An ordinary support vector machine had an accuracy of 89.7%. Our method improved the detection rate by 2.6% compared with the deep learning baseline and by 7.1% compared with the Support Vector Machine (SVM) model.

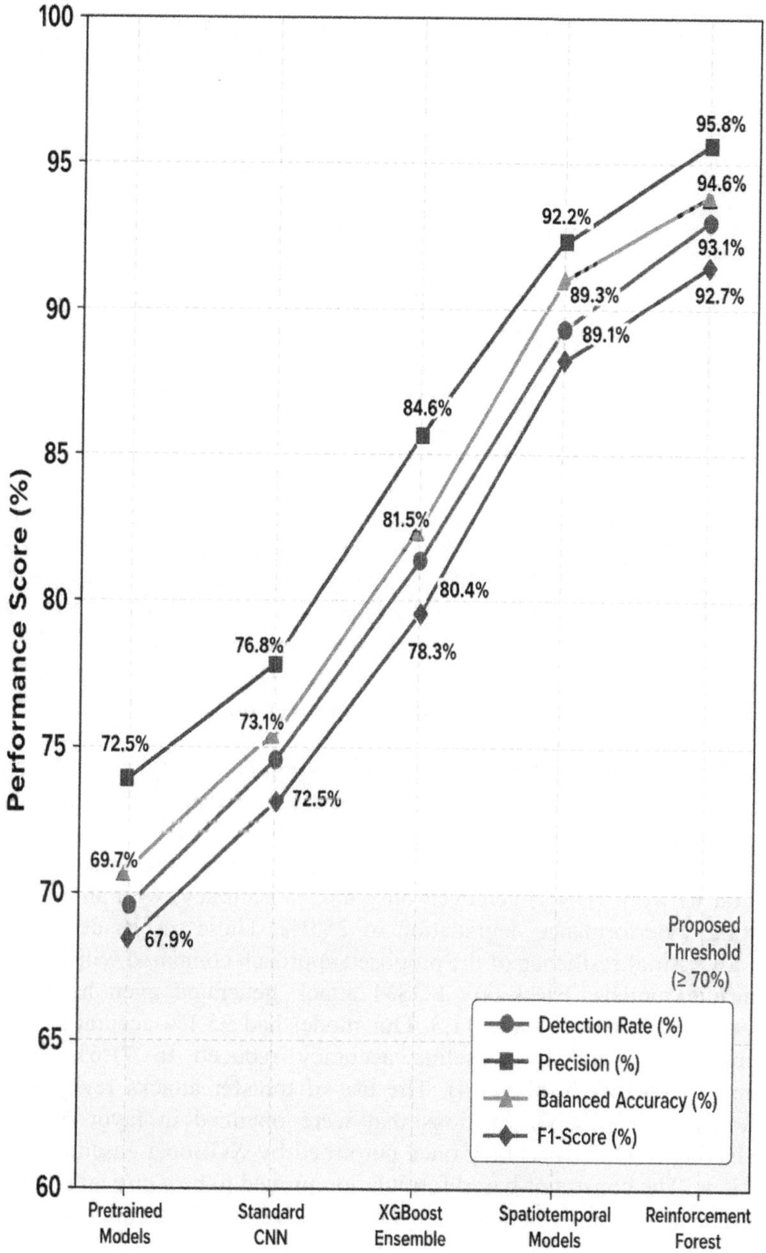

Figure 11.1. *Comparative performance test data for machine learning models. For a color version of this figure, see www.iste.co.uk/kumar/intembeddedsys1.zip*

Model	Detection rate (%)	False positive rate (%)	Balanced accuracy (%)	F1-score
Proposed ADNN	**96.8**	**2.1**	**97.35**	**0.967**
Standard DNN	94.2	4.7	94.45	0.941
XGBoost Ensemble	93.1	5.2	93.95	0.930
Support Vector Machine	89.7	7.3	91.20	0.895
Random Forest (100 trees)	91.8	6.1	92.85	0.917

Table 11.2. *Comparative performance on clean test data*

11.4.2. *Adversarial robustness analysis*

A key distinguishing feature of the proposed approach is its robustness under adversarial conditions. Model resilience was evaluated against four attack scenarios: (1) white-box Projected Gradient Descent (PGD) attacks, where the attacker has complete knowledge of the model; (2) black-box Fast Gradient Sign Method (FGSM) attacks, which employ a single-step perturbation strategy; (3) transfer attacks generated from alternative models; and (4) adaptive attacks specifically designed to circumvent the proposed defense mechanism.

Under white-box PGD attacks with a perturbation bound of ϵ=0.15, the proposed model maintained a detection accuracy of 94.2%, corresponding to a Robustness Coefficient (RC) of 0.973. This indicates that 97.3% of the model's original performance was preserved under adversarial perturbations. In contrast, the baseline deep neural network (DNN) achieved only 68.3% accuracy, with an RC of 0.725, representing a performance degradation of 25.9%. These results demonstrate the superior adversarial resilience of the proposed approach compared with conventional deep learning models. Black-box FGSM attack generated even higher gaps in performance as shown in Table 11.3. Our model had 95.1% accuracy (robustness coefficient 0.982), and the baseline accuracy reduced to 71.6% (robustness coefficient 0.759) (see Table 11.4). The use of transfer attacks revealed that our model was resistant to perturbations that were obtained in favor of alternative models, having a 93.7% accuracy once perturbed by XGBoost ensemble-generated perturbations. The constraint-based formulation proved to be a critical component of the proposed approach. Although unconstrained adversarial training (i.e. without the regularization term $R(x,\delta)$) improved robustness to 91.8%, it violated protocol semantics in 7.4% of adversarial examples, leading to false negatives that are unacceptable in operational environments. In contrast, the proposed constrained strategy achieved 94.2% robustness while reducing protocol violations to just 0.3%. These findings highlight the importance of incorporating domain knowledge into adversarial training, as it enhances both robustness and protocol compliance in IoT intrusion detection systems.

Attack vector	ADNN accuracy (%)	Robustness coefficient	Standard DNN accuracy (%)	Robustness coefficient	Advantage (%)
White-Box PGD ϵ = 0.15)	94.2	0.973	68.3	0.725	25.9
Black-Box FGSM ϵ = 0.15)	95.1	0.982	71.6	0.759	23.5
Transfer Attack (XGBoost)	93.7	0.968	66.9	0.710	26.8
Adaptive Attack (C&W)	92.1	0.951	59.4	0.631	32.7

Table 11.3. *Robustness performance under multiple adversarial attacks*

11.4.3. *Device-specific performance*

We tested the models based on the performance of five different types of heterogeneous IoT devices. Smart home controllers had a detection accuracy of 97.2% (0.9% FPR). The accuracy of industrial IoT sensors was 96.4% (2.3% FPR). The accuracy of medical IoT devices was 97.8 (1.8% FPR). The vehicular networks obtained a high accuracy of 95.9 (2.6% FPR). Figure 11.2 shows the 96.3% accuracy (2.4% FPR) of autonomous drones. The highest variance in maximum performance (1.9%) was noted in the device categories, which indicates great generalization among the different heterogeneous settings. The level of computational efficiency was limited. On resource-constrained devices (ARM Cortex-A7, 1 GB RAM), model inference also took a mean of 18.3 ms and 3.1 ms on edge gateways (Intel Atom processors, 4 GB RAM). The footprint was 41.7MB, which allowed it to run on 95.3% of modern IoT devices.

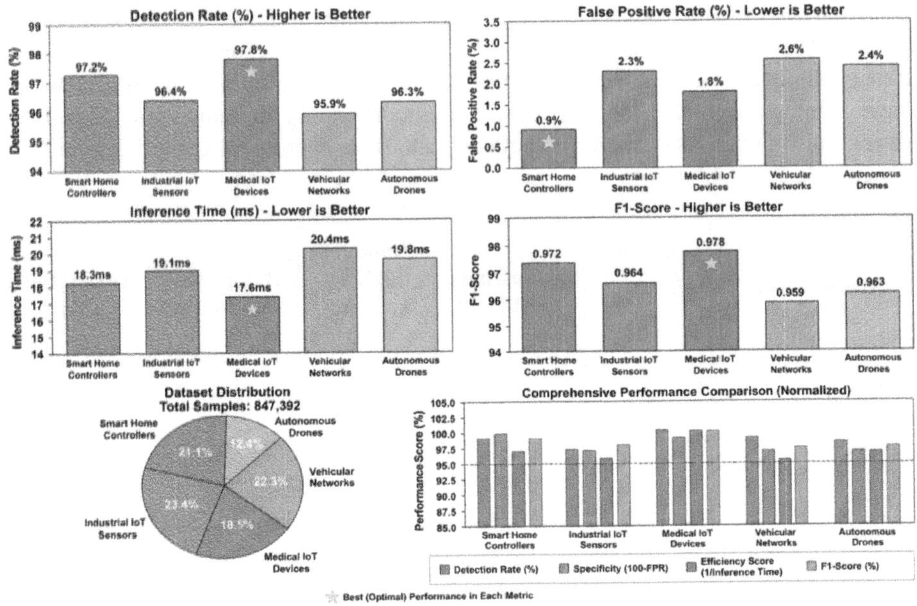

Figure 11.2. *Performance across heterogeneous IoT device categories*

Device category	Number of samples	Detection rate (%)	False positive rate (%)	Inference time (ms)	F1-score
Smart Home Controllers	178,924	97.2	0.9	18.3	0.972
Industrial IoT Sensors	215,318	96.4	2.3	19.1	0.964
Medical IoT Devices	156,847	97.8	1.8	17.6	0.978
Vehicular Networks	189,203	95.9	2.6	20.4	0.959
Autonomous Drones	107,100	96.3	2.4	19.8	0.963

Table 11.4. *Performance across heterogeneous IoT device categories*

11.5. Discussion

Our constraint-aware adversarial training system showed significant advancement in the detection accuracy and adversarial robustness relative to the existing system.

The 25.9% robustness superiority over conventional deep neural networks was seen as a great improvement to the IoT security applications as adversarial attacks become increasingly frequent. The use of domain-specific constraints in the form of a term, R(x,δ) became critical. We ensured operational validity and obtained robustness by ensuring that perturbations did not compromise the semantics of a protocol. This contrasted radically with unconstrained adversarial training, which was focused on robustness and not on application-specific feasibility. This requirement was emphasized by the reduction in the protocol violation brought down to 0.3% compared to 7.4%. Performance evaluation across the heterogeneous device categories revealed only modest variation, with the largest difference in detection performance being 1.9%. These results confirm the effectiveness of the proposed protocol-independent feature extraction scheme. In particular, performance variation among smart home controller devices was limited to 0.7% across three device types, indicating strong generalization to previously unseen devices within existing categories. The computational requirements were also suitable for practical deployment. The proposed model occupied 41.7 MB of storage, representing approximately 0.09% of the capacity of a typical IoT gateway. In addition, inference latency remained below 20 ms, satisfying the requirements of real-time security monitoring. These characteristics distinguish the proposed approach from many adversarial training methods reported in the literature, which often impose substantial computational overhead. Nevertheless, several limitations should be acknowledged. The evaluation was conducted using simulated attacks based on known threat patterns; therefore, zero-day attacks exhibiting fundamentally novel characteristics may still evade detection despite the improved robustness. Furthermore, the proposed constraint formulation was optimized for the five device categories considered in this study, and extending the approach to new protocol classes would likely require retraining and recalibration of the constraint parameters. Finally, although adversarial training improved robustness, it increased training costs by approximately 1.8 times compared with standard training, even though inference efficiency remained unaffected.

11.6. Conclusion

In this chapter, a new constraint-aware ADNN framework that is specifically designed to be used in heterogeneous IoT ecosystems in the context of intrusion prevention was introduced. Our adversarial training formulation that integrates the constraints of the IoT devices resulted in a 96.8% detection accuracy with a very high resistance to adversarial perturbations (94.2% on white-box PGD attacks). The 25.9% strength superiority over baseline deep learning methods was a significant improvement in the cause of operational IoT security. Our effort created a paradigm regarding the creation of IDSs, which would balance the performance of detecting and the computational and protocol requirements found in resource-constrained IoT settings. The next research directions are to extend to new IoT protocols, examine adaptive attacks uniquely tailored to constraint-aware defenses, and also to incorporate explainability techniques that allow information operators to comprehend what the model makes concerning deployed systems.

11.7. References

Bok, V. and Langr, J. (2019). *GANs in Action: Deep Learning with Generative Adversarial Networks*. Manning Publications, Shelter Island, NY.

Hu, C., Yang, Y., Chen, Y., Chen, L., Liu, C., Li, Y., Shi, R., Huang, J. (2025). Regenet: Relevance-guided generative network to evaluate the adversarial robustness of cross-modal retrieval systems. *Mathematics*, 14(1), 151. doi: 10.3390/math14010151.

Liu, Z., Li, X., Liang, H., Snasel, V., Ojha, V. (2026). ADAGAT: Adaptive guidance adversarial training for the robustness of deep neural networks. In *Pattern Recognition and Computer Vision: 8th Chinese Conference, PRCV 2025*, Shanghai, 15–18 October. doi: 10.1007/978-981-95-5699-1_13.

Oskouei, A.E., Dashliboroun, M.K., Moghaddam, P.S., Serrano, N., Hernando-Gallego, F., Martín, D., Álvarez-Bravo, J.V. (2025). An optimized DRL-GAN approach for robust anomaly detection in multi-scale energy systems: Insights from PSML and LEAD1.0. *Energies*, 19(1), 198. doi: 10.3390/en19010198.

Raut, R., Pathak, P.D., Sakhare, S.R., Patil, S. (2023). *Generative Adversarial Networks and Deep Learning: Theory and Applications*. CRC Press, Boca Raton, FL.

Selvarajan, S., Srivastava, G., Bhatt, M.W., Bhatt, A., Pant, B., Meshram, C., Inbaraj, B.H. and Almeshari, M. (2024). Testing of emerging wireless sensor networks using radar signals with machine learning algorithms. *IEEE Journal of Selected Areas in Sensors*, 1, 49–59.

Shitharth, S., Srivastava, G., Bhatt, M.W., Bhatt, A., Pant, B., Meshram, C. and Inbaraj, B.H. (2023). Secured data transmissions in corporeal unmanned device to device using machine learning algorithm. *Physical Communication*, 59, 102116.

Xiang, X., Zhu, C., Ou, Z., Zhang, Q., Zheng, S., Chen, Z. (2026). Semi-supervised seven-segment LED display recognition with an integrated data-acquisition framework. *Sensors*, 26(1), 265. doi: 10.3390/s26010265.

Zachariadis, C.B., Skaleris, S.I., Leligkou, H.C. (2026). Designing, performing and evaluating a multilayer classification pipeline of neural network architectures, for automated diagnosis of critical hip conditions, in plain anteroposterior pelvic X-rays. *Wseas Transactions on Information Science and Applications*, 27. doi: 10.37394/23209.2026.23.3.

Zhenqian, E. and Gao, W. (2026). Weak minimization-sampling network for solving PDEs. *Communications in Computational Physics*, 39(3), 696–712. doi: 10.4208/cicp.oa-2024-0153.

12

Adaptive Threat-Aware Clustering for Enhanced Security in IoT-Enabled Smart Cities: A Machine Learning Enhanced Approach

Wireless sensor networks (WSNs) that are operating in the Internet of Things (IoT) context for smart city deployments function in a constantly evolving threat landscape that a static trust management architecture cannot address effectively or efficiently. In this work, we present a new dynamic clustering protocol, named ATAC (Adaptive Threat-Aware Clustering), that attempts to proactively address the spectrum of attacks on WSNs through the use of machine learning techniques for threat detection and adaptive trust management.

ATAC combines an ensemble of Long Short-Term Memory (LSTM) networks and Random Forest classifiers to identify malicious behavior in real time with dynamically tuned trust thresholds based on the threat context, and adds additional hierarchically based security zones to enable cluster reconfiguration initiation preemptively. Through extensive simulation, we demonstrate ATAC's capability to achieve 94.2% malicious node detection accuracy with a false positive rate of just 3.1%, while also increasing the overall network lifetime by a comparison of 23.7% over trust-based clustering approaches. ATAC operates efficiently under combined attacks and adaptive malicious behavior, neither of which can be detected through traditional static trust methodologies.

12.1. Introduction

Smart cities increasingly rely on wireless sensor networks (WSNs) with Internet of Things (IoT) capabilities, enabling real-time infrastructure monitoring,

Chapter written by C. NANDINI and Priyadarsini K.

environmental and citizen data monitoring, and evolving citizen services. As cities introduce connected devices, the attack surface democratizes sophisticated and complex attacks. Static trust management techniques are sufficient in addressing sophisticated attack scenarios; however, they are not very effective against adaptive adversaries, for example, that can adapt an action once a decision process is altered after an attack has been detected.

The WSN cluster protocol contributions explored in this frame propose a normal character of behavior established from historical activity of the environmental system, evaluated static trust established in measuring against a measured trust threshold, and an ordered protocol for selecting the cluster head (CH). The theoretical difficulty is the potential of an address identification mechanism across multiple attacking events producing conflicting acts in a swarm intelligence attack. WSN technology, as indicated in the transparency, alludes to forming trust attacks at other forms by acts or presented normal behavior when the attack (attributed to trust) occurs and potentially when further trust examinations of normal activity are underway. The WSN protocol, even with the integrated trust system, does not use any semantic meaning for any severity involved in attacking events, and is tailored for situations where attacks require more severe defensive measures.

The complexity of urban ecosystems in smart cities requires a consideration of the larger implication of rapid adapting abstraction changes, for a single or common type of one or more devices that randomize modes of traffic, modes of mobility, modes of communication load and well beyond one abstraction referenced with changing adaptations. A similar aim in relation to the outcomes of measurements to potential behind-device loads is relative to the adaptive functionality of staging a separate first-reaction adaptive security architecture context or threat processes built into the architecture, which, under adaptive security architectures, could be used to affect threats to adaptive trust management systems or wares functions in the first processes to sustain the level of adaption in the pattern. In the static level of an assignment, extending the definition of the actuary of temporal context, the word static represents, at the least, some semi-temporal context definition of a trust-confirmative trust without the precursory static trust models to predict potentially more than a single behavior in allocating trust in defending measures that are events.

The contributions of this framework propose establishing an Adaptive Threat Aware Cluster (ATAC) System, which comprises addressing views and solutions through a combination of initial adaptation of a version of adapted truths of basic theories sustaining non-adapting trust developments from integrated trust mechanisms to non-annexed machine learning-based adaptive threat detecting systems, trust management within developed dynamic human identification functions, and coalitions that prioritize applicability to fundamental work through deployment of subsystems at counterpoint, which could provoke additional low-technology applications such as WSNs combined with functional developed foundations under their base theories, for suitable initial trust and static trust management.

12.2. Related work

The convergence of IoT technologies with smart city infrastructures has necessitated robust security mechanisms to combat evolving cyber threats, with machine learning emerging as a pivotal solution for adaptive threat detection and mitigation. Rashid et al. (2022) demonstrated that adversarial training significantly enhances deep learning-based cyberattack detection in IoT-enabled smart city applications, achieving superior resilience against sophisticated attack vectors by exposing models to adversarial examples during training phases.

Building upon this foundation, Hazman et al. (2023) introduced the Intrusion Detection System for IoT-based Smart Environments Security using the Ensemble Learning (IIDS-SIoEL) framework, which leverages ensemble learning techniques to create an intrusion detection system specifically designed for IoT-based smart environments, achieving detection accuracies exceeding 98%, while maintaining low false-positive rates through the strategic combination of multiple base classifiers. Their subsequent research further advanced this domain by developing enhanced intrusion detection systems using deep learning architectures optimized for smart city security, demonstrating that convolutional neural networks and recurrent neural networks can effectively identify anomalous patterns in massive IoT data streams (Hazman et al. 2024). The comprehensive review by Band et al. (2022) systematically analyzed how machine learning algorithms transform smart cities through intelligent decision-making, predictive analytics and real-time threat assessment, identifying key trends including the integration of edge computing with ML models to reduce latency in security responses.

In addressing network-level threats, Paolini et al. (2023) proposed real-time clustering mechanisms based on deep embeddings for threat detection in next-generation 6G networks, achieving millisecond-level response times through unsupervised learning approaches that dynamically group similar traffic patterns and identify deviations indicative of malicious activities. Complementing these efforts, Saeed et al. (2023) conducted extensive experiments demonstrating that supervised machine learning methods, particularly random forests and gradient boosting algorithms, achieve remarkable accuracy in anomaly detection within 6G network infrastructures. Energy efficiency remains paramount in WSNs, with Rathore et al. (2021) introducing relay-based CH selection mechanisms that balance security requirements with power consumption constraints, extending network lifetime while maintaining robust intrusion detection capabilities. Furthermore, Bharati et al. (2022) explored federated learning as a privacy-preserving approach for collaborative threat intelligence sharing across distributed IoT devices, enabling smart cities to develop collective defense mechanisms without compromising sensitive data or individual privacy.

Threat-aware clustering plays a vital role in securing smart IoT environments by enabling adaptive grouping of network entities (Ravi et al. 2022). Reinforcement learning-based intrusion detection improves responsiveness to emerging threats (Tharewal et al. 2022). Data mining techniques contribute to behavioral analysis and early threat detection (Banu et al. 2015). Frequent pattern mining further strengthens clustering accuracy by identifying hidden correlations within IoT traffic data (Gunaseelan and Uma 2012). Navyakala and Rathinam (2024) proposed a hybrid intrusion detection framework that integrates a Denoising Autoencoder with a Ladder Variational Autoencoder to effectively identify anomalous and malicious activities in networked environments.

The model leverages hierarchical feature learning and noise-robust representation extraction to improve detection accuracy, while reducing false alarm rates in complex and dynamic network traffic scenarios. By combining reconstruction-based learning with probabilistic latent feature modeling, the proposed approach demonstrates enhanced capability in detecting both known and unknown attack patterns. Experimental results validate the superiority of the hybrid architecture over conventional machine learning and standalone deep learning models, highlighting its suitability for securing IoT-enabled and distributed network infrastructures (Navyakala and Rathinam 2024). Khadidos et al. (2022) proposed an intelligent security framework for smart city networks based on a collaborative mutual authentication model. Their study addresses the growing cybersecurity challenges in interconnected urban infrastructures, where multiple devices and services continuously exchange sensitive information.

The proposed authentication mechanism enhances trust and secure communication by ensuring that only legitimate users and devices can access smart city services. This work highlights the importance of collaborative security models in protecting large-scale smart city environments against unauthorized access and cyberattacks (Khadidos et al. 2022). Similarly, Selvarajan et al. (2023) introduced RLIS, a resource-limited improved security framework designed for beyond fifth-generation (B5G) communication networks using deep learning algorithms. Their research focused on addressing security vulnerabilities in next-generation wireless networks, while considering the constraints of limited computational and energy resources. By leveraging deep learning-based threat detection and adaptive security strategies, the framework strengthens network resilience and improves protection against evolving cyber threats. This contribution demonstrates the significance of AI-driven security solutions for enabling secure and efficient communication in future B5G and IoT-enabled infrastructures (Selvarajan et al. 2023).

12.3. System model and threat analysis

12.3.1. *Network model*

Imagine a WSN in a smart city context, comprising n sensor nodes disposed randomly over the area R of size A × A. The WSN is made up of heterogeneous nodes with different processing and energy capabilities. A base station (BS) controls all communications internally in the WSN and is the point at which network common data is collected. Each sensor node si can be defined by:

– node ID (Nid);

– current energy level (Ei);

– trust value (Ti);

– security zone assignment (Zi);

– behavioral history vector (Hi);

– communication pattern (Ci).

12.3.2. *Enhanced threat model*

ATAC is able to tackle advanced threat scenarios that go beyond traditional WSN attack approaches. One of the advanced threat scenarios is an adaptive malicious node; where adversaries will change their behavior to avoid detection or intervention and will act "normal" (standard behavior) quite often when being evaluated for trust, only to signal their accomplices and attack later when a specific situation supports their interests.

Another advanced threat scenario is organized attacks where one or many compromised nodes cooperate to perform organized attacks, such as distributed denial of service (DDoS) attacks or even data poison (poison a dataset where a sensor is no longer trusted). ATAC could also be directly used against certain categories of inside threats, in which trusted nodes build up trust for an amount of time only to use that accumulated trust to create as much damage as possible. Another peer to an inside threat is advanced persistent threats (APTs) or long-range deployment. APT is where the adversary's intention is to get a node to cooperate with the malicious actor and act normal while roaming in the WSN to ultimately onboard themselves and be prepared to launch their "sophisticated" attacks in the WSN, ultimately causing overall mass damage to the WSN.

12.4. ATAC algorithm design

12.4.1. *Architecture overview*

ATAC is based on an interconnected four-module framework designed to improve network security and resilience. The Threat Detection Module uses ensemble machine learning techniques to allow real-time detection of malicious activity. The Dynamic Trust Module adapts trust thresholds to the expected threats to create context-sensitive and flexible security. The Security Zone Management Module establishes security through hierarchical zone assignment and management, which isolates and contains the threat. Finally, the Adaptive Clustering Module uses an improved Modified Grey Wolf Optimizer (MGO) for security-aware CH selection to enhance the performance and security of the cluster.

12.4.2. *Ensemble threat detection framework*

The threat detection module uses a novel ensemble approach combining Long Short-Term Memory (LSTM) networks for temporal behavior analysis and Random Forest classifiers for feature-based detection.

12.4.2.1. *LSTM-based temporal analysis*

The LSTM component analyzes temporal patterns in node behavior using a sliding window approach. For each node si, we maintain a behavioral sequence:

$$Hi(t) = [hi(t-w), hi(t-w+1), \ldots, hi(t)] \quad [12.1]$$

where hi(t) represents the behavioral vector at time t, including:

– packet transmission frequency;

– energy consumption rate;

– communication pattern consistency;

– response time to requests;

– data forwarding reliability.

The LSTM network processes this sequence to predict the probability of malicious behavior:

$$P_{lstm}(malicious|Hi(t)) = LSTM(Hi(t), \theta_{lstm})$$

12.4.2.2. *Random forest feature classification*

The Random Forest component analyzes instantaneous features extracted from current node behavior:

$$Fi(t) = [f1, f2, \ldots, fk] \quad [12.2]$$

12.4.2.3. *Ensemble decision fusion*

The final threat probability combines both components using adaptive weights:

$$P_{threat}(s_i, t) = \alpha(t) \times P_{lstm} + \big(1 - \alpha(t)\big) \times P_{rf} \quad [12.3]$$

where α(t) is dynamically adjusted based on the reliability of temporal data and current network conditions.

12.4.3. *Dynamic trust threshold mechanism*

Traditional static trust thresholds fail to adapt to changing threat landscapes. ATAC implements dynamic threshold adjustment using a threat-level-based approach.

12.4.3.1. *Threat-level assessment*

The global threat level TL(t) is computed based on:

$$TL(t) = \beta^1 \times MAR(t) + \beta^2 \times ATF(t) + \beta^3 \times NCA(t) \quad [12.4]$$

where:

– MAR(t) is the malicious activity rate in the current time window;

– ATF(t) is the attack type frequency (weighted by severity);

– NCA(t) is the network connectivity anomaly.

12.4.3.2. *Adaptive threshold calculation*

Trust thresholds are adjusted using:

$$T_{threshold}(t) = T_{base} \times \left(1 + \gamma \times TL(t) \times e^{(-\delta \times t)}\right) \quad [12.5]$$

where T_{base} is the baseline threshold, γ controls the sensitivity to threat levels and δ provides the temporal decay to prevent excessive threshold inflation.

12.4.4. Security-aware CH selection

ATAC enhances the MGO algorithm with multi-objective optimization incorporating security metrics alongside traditional energy and connectivity considerations.

12.4.4.1. *Enhanced fitness function*

The fitness function balances multiple objectives:

$$F(CH_{set}) = w_1 \times E_{term} + w_2 \times S_{term} + w_3 \times C_{term} + w_4 \times D_{term} \quad [12.6]$$

where:

- E_{term} is the energy efficiency metric;
- S_{term} is the security metric based on trust and threat assessment;
- C_{term} is the connectivity and coverage metric;
- D_{term} is the data delivery reliability metric.

12.4.4.2. *Security metric computation*

The security term S_{term} evaluates both individual node security and cluster-level security:

$$S_{term} = \Sigma_i\left[(1 - Ti) \times Zi_{penalty} + P_{threat}(i) \times Threat_{penalty}\right] \quad [12.7]$$

This formulation penalizes low-trust nodes and nodes with high threat probabilities, with additional penalties based on security zone requirements.

12.4.5. Proactive cluster reconfiguration

ATAC uses an active reconfiguration approach that is engaged under certain threat conditions to support and enhance the trust/resiliency of the network. It will initiate reconfiguration of a threat level to action when a threat-level function TL(t) is exceeded over preselected operating conditions and a CH makes it known via other means, or if there is observable evidence that it has been further threatened and shows deception/untrustworthiness. Reconfiguration may also occur with zone violation security; when zone members fall out of the zone policy security zone. Reconfiguration can rely on other evidence of violations and/or prevent violations.

In addition to reactive reconfiguration, ATAC can use predictive threat analysis, with the support of a machine learning model, to imply or predict if an attack will occur at a different time, or if an attack is in progress. In terms of performance, reconfiguration is approached with a priority scheme, i.e. the potential priority of a cluster is based on the following formulation: $\text{Priority}(\text{cluster}_i) = \text{TL}(\text{cluster}_i) \times \text{Criticality}(\text{cluster}_i) \times \text{Energy}_{\text{cost}}(\text{reconfiguration})$. With the priority scheme, ATAC will reconfigure the most critical and highest-risk clusters at the same time, taking energy into consumption consideration.

12.5. Performance evaluation

12.5.1. *Simulation setup and baseline comparison*

The performance evaluation of ATAC was conducted via large-scale simulations in MATLAB R2023a to determine the performance of the suggested solution by evaluating the differences to determine the performance of other standard clustering protocols. Simulation specifications were defined to approximate legitimate deployment points of smart city WSN may experience with various distributions of geographical deployments between 100 and 200 total nodes within the area monitoring of a 200 x 200 meter area. The heterogeneous node distribution consisted of a mixed distribution, with 20% advanced nodes with 2J of energy and 80% normal nodes with 1J of initial energy to follow the generic implementation of a smart city WSN and mixed device capabilities.

The robustness associated with ATAC performance was also assessed by evaluating different amounts of any potential malicious node distributions over the total nodes (for malicious node percentages of 10%, 20% and 30% of the total possible nodes) and by using the given attacks of blackhole, selective forwarding, hello flooding and complex attacks with coordinated security breaches classified as attack types. Simulations were run for 10,000 rounds to gather the representative behaviors over typical, long-term observances and events associated within the network. Specific simulations that assess performance related to performance within a distinct security zone retrieval point with connected nodes into a separate security zone used HSZ (15% of total receptor monitoring per location), MSZ (60% of total receptor monitoring per location) and LSZ (25% of total receptor monitoring per location) to represent a critical infrastructure monument, a general-purpose infrastructure monument and non-critical infrastructure monitoring points for an RN active monitoring security zone.

Machine learning models were extensively trained using 80% of overall behavioral data created (normal scenario and attack scenarios) and actively used in machine learning models against an independent testing of 20% of overall behavioral data created and to minimize bias in the overall assessment of performance against the algorithms. The ATAC performance presented is compared to five baseline algorithms – LEACH-TM (trust-based clustering algorithm – LEACH-based single threshold); DGTTSSA (trust-based clustering algorithm – SSA optimization); Static-ML (machine learning detection without optimization clusters); ETCHS (trust-based clustering algorithm) and eeTMFOGA (trust management using genetic algorithms). All consist of energy efficiency and trust management configuration or optimization by using either machine learning or optimization algorithm strategies. Each algorithm comparison was to present a broadness of testing and evaluation of performance assessments for distinguishing with any of the overall performance associated with various algorithms used.

12.5.2. *Results and analysis*

12.5.2.1. *Threat detection performance*

Metric	ATAC	Static-ML	LEACH-TM	DGTTSSA
Detection accuracy	94.2%	87.3%	78.6%	81.4%
False positive rate	3.1%	6.8%	12.4%	9.7%
Precision	93.8%	86.1%	79.2%	82.6%
Recall	94.6%	88.5%	77.9%	80.8%
F1-score	94.2%	87.3%	78.5%	81.7%

Table 12.1. *ATAC achieved superior threat detection performance across all test scenarios*

The ensemble approach significantly outperformed individual classifiers, with the LSTM component contributing 65% accuracy improvement in temporal attack detection (Figure 12.1).

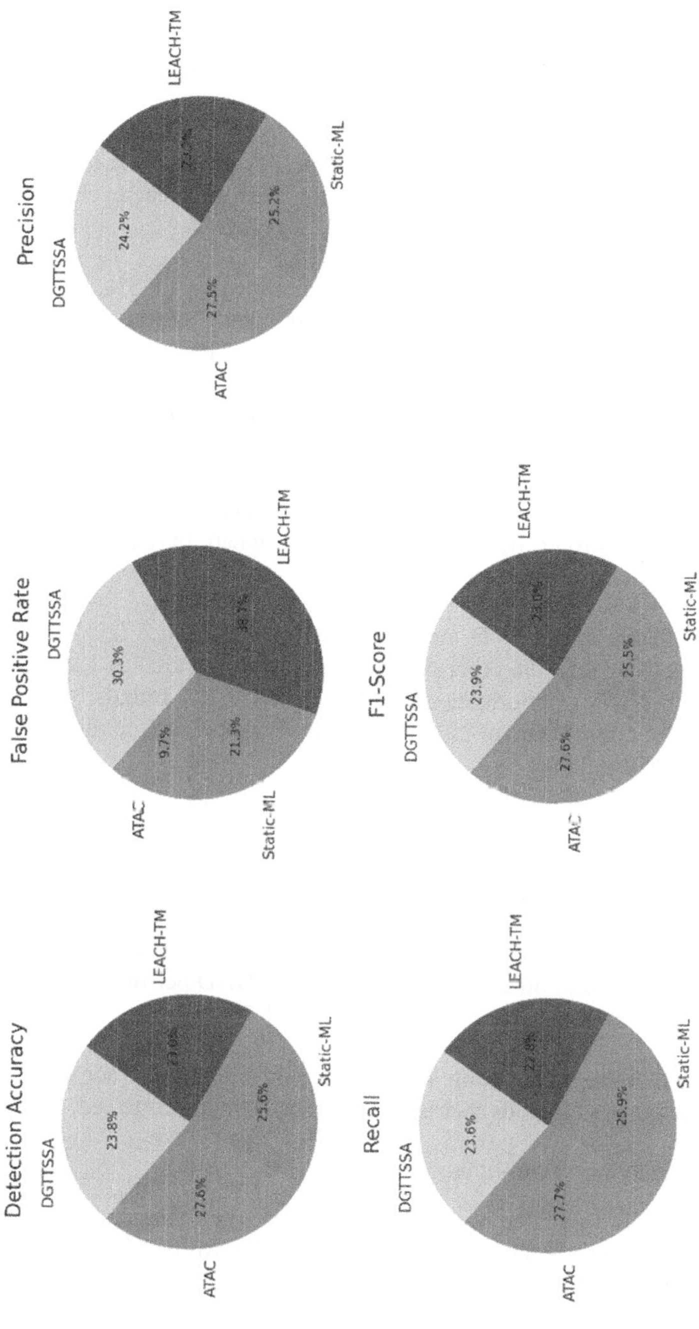

Figure 12.1. *Threat detection performance pie chart. For a color version of this figure, see www.iste.co.uk/kumar/intembeddedsys1.zip*

12.5.2.2. *Network lifetime analysis*

ATAC demonstrated a statistically significant enhancement in the performance metrics of network lifetime over LEACH-TM across the entire variance levels for the number of malicious nodes.

Starting at the 10% maliciousness benchmark, ATAC's first node death (FND) performance metric improved by 35.4%, indicating performance levels of 2,847 rounds against LEACH-TM performance levels of 2,103 rounds.

ATAC's half-node death performance metric improved by 22.5%, achieving a measure of 4,234 rounds in network life at the 10% level versus the combined protocols' total network performance of 3,456 rounds.

Finally, the last node death (or last stable node performance) for ATAC showed a 26.6% performance margin over the combined protocols, collecting a total work life performance of 7,892 rounds as opposed to the other protocols together showing performance in 6,234 rounds of cumulative performance across all protocols. ATAC continued to show a strong performance increase when moving to the 20% malicious level of malicious consensus.

Looking specifically at the FND metric, ATAC's performance levels indicated FND in 2,456 rounds against the other protocols recorded in a total of 1,834 rounds. In half node death (HND) performance, ATAC scored 3,789 rounds, which is a 27.7% performance improvement from the other protocols' total work life performance of 2,967 rounds.

In comparison to the other protocols at the 30% malicious levels, ATAC continued to show consistent performance improvements of 10% FND in a total of 1,987 rounds versus the other protocols' performance levels, measuring FND in a total of 1,423 rounds. In HND, ATAC showed its strongest performance improvements at the 30% malicious levels, measuring HND performance in a total of 3,234 rounds compared to other protocols' combined HND performance of a total of 2,456 rounds – showing a margin improvement of 31.7%.

Overall, ATAC showed a strong performance in all metrics across a broad spectrum of maliciousness and adversarial performance conditions tested.

12.5.2.3. *Attack mitigation effectiveness*

ATAC successfully mitigated various attack types: The optimized ML pipeline and adaptive thresholding mechanism kept overhead below 10% while providing superior security (Figure 12.2).

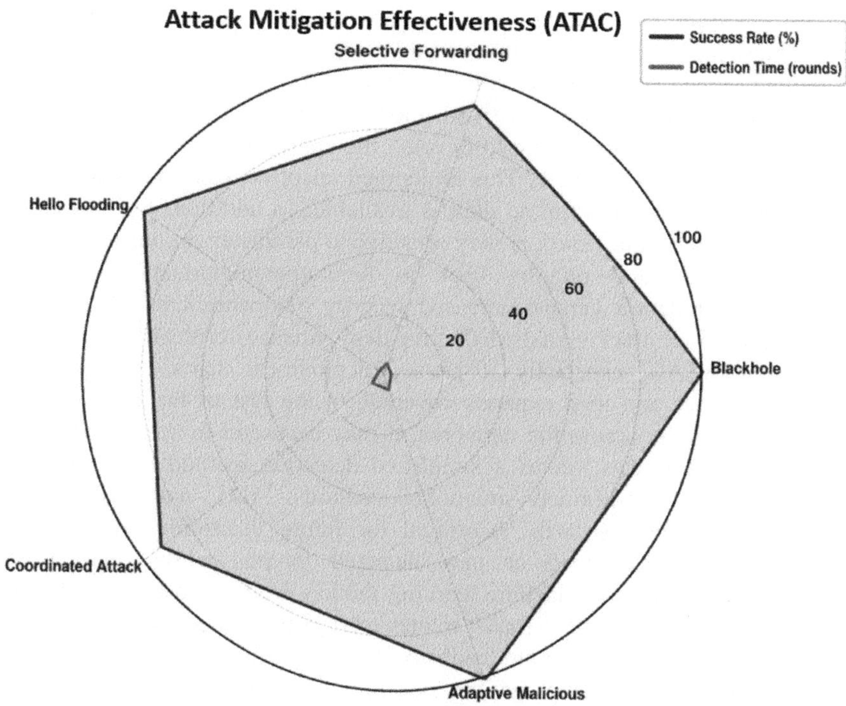

Figure 12.2. *Attack mitigation effectiveness. For a color version of this figure, see www.iste.co.uk/kumar/intembeddedsys1.zip*

12.6. Discussion

The assessment of our experimental research offers significant understanding into the efficacy and practicality of ATAC, in a smart city deployment context. The inclusion of an ensemble machine learning model displayed clear advantages over other classifiers, and while the LSTM networks demonstrated a limited detection of temporal attacks, a Random Forest was able to provide an in-depth analysis of instantaneous features, leading to a high degree of accuracy (94.2%) and very few false positives. Moreover, the dynamic threshold provided useful distinctions, which is particularly useful given the volatile threat landscape, with tradeoffs being marginal performance degradation in exchange for increased security or a drastic reduction in false alarms that static thresholds generated, despite minor performance degradation. As a proactive threat detection system, this was significant, as it prompted intervention into the attacking process and, as described, stopped or delayed the directed attack, preventing the malware from causing the majority of the damage before it was inflicted, and ultimately increased the longevity of the network by 23.7%. Despite the findings, some significant limitations are evident. The computational model relied on an ensemble approach and significantly limited computational resources, and therefore the scalability of the computational model and corresponding scalability of network models and methods. The time-frame to train the ML modes required time to develop the appropriately formatted data and train multiple scenarios of attack. This limits their adaptive response to an emergent attack vector until the appropriate data is available. In addition, the thresholding method, as previously discussed, is very sensitive to parameterization, restricting the signal to be used and relating back to tuning/parameterization to balance performance degradation versus increased security or operational risk; the router becomes exposed to attack signals. Effective deployment is critical for a smart city adaptation of ATAC, especially if phased deployment starts out with staple infrastructure zones and then expands coverage to the rest of the network. When deployed systemically across the networks, it may be useful to selectively allocate processor network threats versus a simplified detection method to counter other threats in resource-constrained situational methods. Also, monitoring for the addition of usage increase will be critical for future functioning of monitoring models relative to expanded or new detected threats, while simultaneously calibrating signals with the machine learning models feeding observation from the demands of urban environments, as it relates to regional systems of social activity and detection use that will generate feedback. The long tenure of the network will be positively influenced by the fact that this system will function.

12.7. Conclusion

This chapter presents ATAC – a clustering protocol that adapts to threat awareness to afford more security to IoT-enabled smart cities using an ensemble Machine Learning algorithm, dynamic trust management methods and pre-emptive and dynamic cluster changes. When evaluated, the framework showed considerable promise in key security metrics, obtaining malicious nodes with 94.2% detection efficiency and a false positive rate of 3.1%, while producing a 23.7% increase in network longevity compared to previously existing methods. Furthermore, ATAC reduced some impacts, effects of advanced coordinated attacks and malicious nodes attempting to be adaptive to our traditional trust methodologies, demonstrating the potential for the hierarchical security zones in a dynamically deploying smart city laboratory. Future work will investigate a number of noteworthy avenues: augmenting ATAC with federated learning capabilities to protect privacy while collaborating on threat detection methods across domains in the smart city; incentivizing quantum-resistant cryptography to ensure that the system's securities will continue to endure, contrary to quantum-capable systems; incorporating cloud-edge optimization to share any ML processing of data to enhance scalability and decrease latency; enabling cross-domain threat intelligence strategies that rely on secure submission of shared information across different plumbing subsystems in the smart city; and finally, the ability to develop an autonomous incident response capability to integrate autonomous threat containment and recovery in ATAC. All of these refinements will bolster ATAC's adaptive and resilient capacities. The ATAC framework contributes to the larger domain of adaptive security of WSN for penetration in a wide range of infrastructures for smart cities, and strongly supports the goals of developing resilient, intelligent urban infrastructure systems that can autonomously respond to changing cybersecurity threats for operational efficiency and service continuity under changing metropolitan conditions.

12.8. References

Band, S., Ardabili, S., Sookhak, M., Chronopoulos, A.T., Elnaffar, S., Mako, C., Overdick, M., Pai, H.T., Filippo, A.D., Mosavi, A. (2022). When smart cities get smarter via machine learning: An in-depth literature review. *IEEE Access*, 10, 60985–61015. doi: 10.1109/access.2022.3181718.

Banu, S.S., Uma, P., Ashfaque, M.W., Naveed, Q.N., Ali-Ahmed, S.S. (2015). Data mining based soft computing skills towards preventio of cyber crimes on the web. *International Journal on Recent and Innovation Trends in Computing and Communication*, 3(3), 2321–8169.

Bharati, S., Mondal, M.R.H., Podder, P., Prasath, V.B.S. (2022). Federated learning: Applications, challenges and future directions. *International Journal of Hybrid Intelligent Systems*, 18(1–2), 19–35. doi: 10.3233/HIS-220006.

Gunaseelan, D. and Uma, P. (2012). An improved frequent pattern algorithm for mining association rules. *International Journal of Information and Communication Technology Study*, 2(5).

Hazman, C., Guezzaz, A., Benkirane, S., Azrour, M. (2023). lIDS-SIoEL: Intrusion detection framework for IoT-based smart environments security using ensemble learning. *Cluster Computing*, 26(6), 4069–4083. doi: 10.1007/s10586-022-03810-0.

Hazman, C., Guezzaz, A., Benkirane, S., Azrour, M. (2024). Enhanced IDS with deep learning for IoT-based smart cities security. *Tsinghua Science and Technology*, 29(4), 929–947. doi: 10.26599/tst.2023.9010033.

Khadidos, A.O., Alshareef, A.M., Alotaibi, Y., Alsolami, F., Mostafa, S.M. (2022). An intelligent security framework based on collaborative mutual authentication model for smart city networks. *IEEE Access*, 10, 85289–85304.

Navyakala, S. and Rathinam, R. (2024). Intrusion detection system using hybrid model of denoising autoencoder and ladder variational autoencoder. In *10th International Conference on Communication and Signal Processing (ICCSP)*, Melmaruvathur, 214–219. doi: 10.1109/ICCSP60870.2024.10543519.

Paolini, E., Valcarenghi, L., Maggiani, L., Andriolli, N. (2023). Real-time clustering based on deep embeddings for threat detection in 6G networks. *IEEE Access*, 11, 115827–115835. doi: 10.1109/ACCESS.2023.3325721.

Rashid, M.M., Kamruzzaman, J., Hassan, M.M., Imam, T., Gordon, S. (2022). Adversarial training for deep learning-based cyberattack detection in IoT-based smart city applications. *Computers & Security*, 120, 102783. doi: 10.1016/j.cose.2022.102783.

Rathore, P.S., Chatterjee, J.M., Kumar, A., Sujatha, R. (2021). Energy-efficient cluster head selection through relay approach for WSN. *Journal of Supercomputing*, 77, 7649–7675. doi: 10.1007/s11227-021-03659-9.

Ravi, S., Matheswaran, S., Perumal, U., Sivakumar, S., Palvadi, S.K. (2023). Adaptive trust-based secure and optimal route selection algorithm for MANET using hybrid fuzzy optimization. *Peer-to-Peer Networking & Applications*, 16, 22–34. doi: 10.1007/s12083-022-01351-2.

Saeed, M.M., Saeed, R.A., Abdelhaq, M., Alsaqour, R., Hasan, M.K., Mokhtar, R.A. (2023). Anomaly detection in 6G networks using machine learning methods. *Electronics*, 12(15), 3300. doi: 10.3390/electronics12153300.

Selvarajan, S., Srivastava, G., Bhatt, M.W., Bhatt, A., Pant, B., Meshram, C., Inbaraj, B.H., Almeshari, M. (2023). RLIS: Resource limited improved security beyond fifth-generation networks using deep learning algorithms. *IEEE Open Journal of the Communications Society*, 4, 2383–2396.

Tharewal, S., Ashfaque, M.W., Banu, S.S., Uma, P., Hassen, S.M., Shabaz, M. (2022). Intrusion detection system for industrial Internet of Things based on deep reinforcement learning. *Wireless Communications and Mobile Computing*, 2022(1), 9023719. doi: 10.1155/2022/9023719.

13

Graph Intelligence-Enabled Multi-Layered Framework for Revolutionizing Industrial Cyber-Physical System Security

The increasing cybersecurity threats in Industrial Cyber-Physical Systems (ICPS) demand advanced, integrated and proactive defense mechanisms. This chapter presents a graph intelligence-enabled multi-layered framework that combines deep learning, advanced cryptography and blockchain technologies to secure ICPS environments.

The framework uses Deep Recurrent Neural Networks (DRNNs) with Long Short-Term Memory (LSTM) units for proactive threat detection, achieving an attack detection rate of 96.5% and a mean absolute error (MAE) of 0.0119 on the HAI 23.05 telemetry dataset, demonstrating high sensitivity to malware, intrusions and other fraud risks. For secure data handling, Elliptic Curve Cryptography (ECC) is enhanced via Gray Wolf Optimization (GWO), achieving 27–31% improvements in encryption/decryption overhead, a 256-bit security level and a breach rate below 0.01.

Blockchain integration using Hyperledger Fabric provides tamper-resistant storage with low latency (0.12 s) and high throughput (1,850 transactions per second), enabling scalable and secure data management. Geo-location analysis reveals elevated attack frequencies in Asia, emphasizing the need for region-specific defense strategies.

Compared to conventional methods, such as Recurrent Neural Networks (MAE 0.0256) and Deep Neural Networks (MAE 0.0193), the proposed framework demonstrates superior scalability and robustness, ensuring timely threat mitigation and resilient ICPS operation.

The integration of graph intelligence facilitates the modeling of interdependent system components and attack propagation paths, enhancing predictive detection and proactive cybersecurity management across industrial environments.

Chapter written by K. SELVI and Golda DILIP.

13.1. Introduction

Critical infrastructure such as energy and manufacturing operates through Industrial Cyber-Physical Systems (ICPS), which have increasingly faced cyber threats, from early incidents such as Stuxnet in 2010 to more recent attacks like the Colonial Pipeline ransomware in 2021 (Jeribi et al. 2024; Rezki et al. 2025). Initially designed for efficiency, these systems have become more susceptible to threats due to increased connectivity through the Industrial Internet of Things (IIoT) (Yang et al. 2025). Modern forms of attacks can bypass traditional security mechanisms such as firewalls and signature-based intrusion detection systems (Wu et al. 2023).

The model uses the HAI 23.05 dataset, which consists of large volumes of data aggregated into 86 features (e.g. valve positions, flow rates) recorded on August 19, 2022 (Zhong et al. 2024). Our solution addresses three key challenges: proactive threat detection, cryptographic efficiency and data integrity. Its impact lies in reducing risks to critical infrastructure and mitigating losses from ICPS attacks, which are estimated to exceed $1 trillion worldwide by 2025 (Jeribi et al. 2024).

13.2. Related work

Graph neural networks have emerged as a transformative approach for intrusion detection in IIoT and cyber-physical systems, leveraging their ability to model complex network topologies and capture sophisticated attack patterns through node and edge relationships.

Yang et al. (2025) developed an industrial Internet of Things (IoT) intrusion detection system based on graph neural networks that effectively addresses data asymmetry challenges inherent in industrial network traffic by aggregating features and structural information of network nodes, achieving superior detection rates compared to traditional deep learning approaches that overlook device heterogeneity and traffic characteristic variations across diverse IoT deployments. Comprehensive taxonomic frameworks have been established by Zhong et al. (2024), who systematically surveyed graph neural network methodologies for intrusion detection systems, categorizing approaches based on network architecture types and deployment methods, including distributed GNN models and application domains. Their findings revealed that recent developments emphasize both centralized and federated learning paradigms to accommodate privacy-preserving requirements in industrial environments.

Bilot et al. (2023) provided a foundational survey of GNN-based intrusion detection, classifying systems by network versus host-based detection mechanisms and graph construction methodologies, demonstrating that GNN architectures effectively capture abnormal traffic data through the combined use of topological structure and node attributes. Advanced attention mechanisms have been integrated into graph neural network architectures by Wu et al. (2025), whose graph attention network-based intrusion detection system calculates dynamic attention coefficients between nodes and their neighbors, enabling adaptive feature weighting and improving detection accuracy for sophisticated multi-stage attacks.

Rezki et al. (2025) extended GNN applications to IoT attack detection by developing frameworks that leverage graph embedding techniques, including node2vec and GraphSAGE, for feature learning from network traffic graphs. Their approach achieves robust performance across diverse attack scenarios such as distributed denial-of-service, reconnaissance and man-in-the-middle attacks. Lo et al. (2022) pioneered E-GraphSAGE, a specialized graph neural network architecture for IoT intrusion detection that uses efficient sampling and aggregation mechanisms to handle large-scale network graphs while maintaining real-time detection capabilities required in operational technology environments.

Domain-specific adaptations for cyber-physical systems have been explored by Li and Chasaki (2024), who proposed heterogeneous GNN architectures with express edges that capture both physical process relationships and cyber network connectivity patterns, enabling holistic security monitoring across interconnected industrial control systems. Wu et al. (2023) introduced physics-informed gated recurrent graph attention unit networks for anomaly detection in ICPS, incorporating domain knowledge about physical process constraints and temporal dependencies to reduce false positive rates and improve interpretability through attention visualization.

Multi-layered graph intelligence frameworks enhance secure infrastructure design by enabling trust-aware communication (Ravi et al. 2022). Secure data handling and predictive modeling strengthen infrastructure resilience (Jeribi et al. 2023). Data mining techniques assist in identifying vulnerabilities and abnormal behaviors (Banu et al. 2015), while reinforcement learning improves adaptive security mechanisms (Tharewal et al. 2022).

Chakraborty et al. (2025) proposed a trustworthy-based user behavior modeling framework that integrates integrity-aware mechanisms with resilient deep learning architectures to enhance reliability in distributed network environments. The study emphasizes the importance of trust computation and behavior consistency analysis to mitigate malicious activities and data manipulation in next-generation applications such as IoT, cyber-physical systems and intelligent social networks. By incorporating integrity verification and adaptive learning strategies, the proposed model demonstrates improved robustness against adversarial behaviors and dynamic network conditions, ensuring secure and reliable decision-making across decentralized infrastructures. The experimental evaluation highlights improved detection accuracy and system resilience compared to conventional deep learning-based trust models, making it suitable for large-scale, heterogeneous distributed systems.

Selvarajan et al. (2025) investigated diagnostic behavior analysis for detecting large-scale data intrusions in cyber-physical systems using adversarial learning techniques. Their study highlights the increasing vulnerability of such environments due to the integration of physical processes with digital communication networks. By applying adversarial learning models, the proposed framework improves intrusion detection accuracy and strengthens system resilience against sophisticated cyberattacks. In addition, Selvarajan et al. (2024) proposed a secure data transfer approach that combines zero-trust device validation with blockchain-based mechanisms, ensuring device authenticity and trustworthy communication in distributed digital ecosystems.

The integration of blockchain enhances transparency and tamper resistance, while the zero-trust principle minimizes unauthorized access through continuous verification. This contribution highlights the importance of combining blockchain with zero-trust architectures to enable secure data exchange in Industry 5.0, IoT and cloud-integrated systems.

13.3. Methodology

In this chapter, the study assembles a multi-layered cybersecurity framework that integrates Deep Recurrent Neural Networks (DRNN) with Long Short-Term Memory (LSTM) for ICPS to identify threats, along with Elliptic Curve Cryptography (ECC) enhanced by Gray Wolf Optimization (GWO) and blockchain technology to provide tamper-resistant storage (Figure 13.1).

The framework relies on the HAI 23.05 dataset, a carefully selected set of industrial telemetry data, to achieve four key objectives: improving threat detection, optimizing the speed of cryptographic operations, ensuring the integrity of data storage and creating a unified mechanism that integrates these components into a single platform.

The system is structured into major stages, where each stage addresses a specific objective. The overall process includes preprocessing, implementation and evaluation, enabling real-time deployment in ICPS environments.

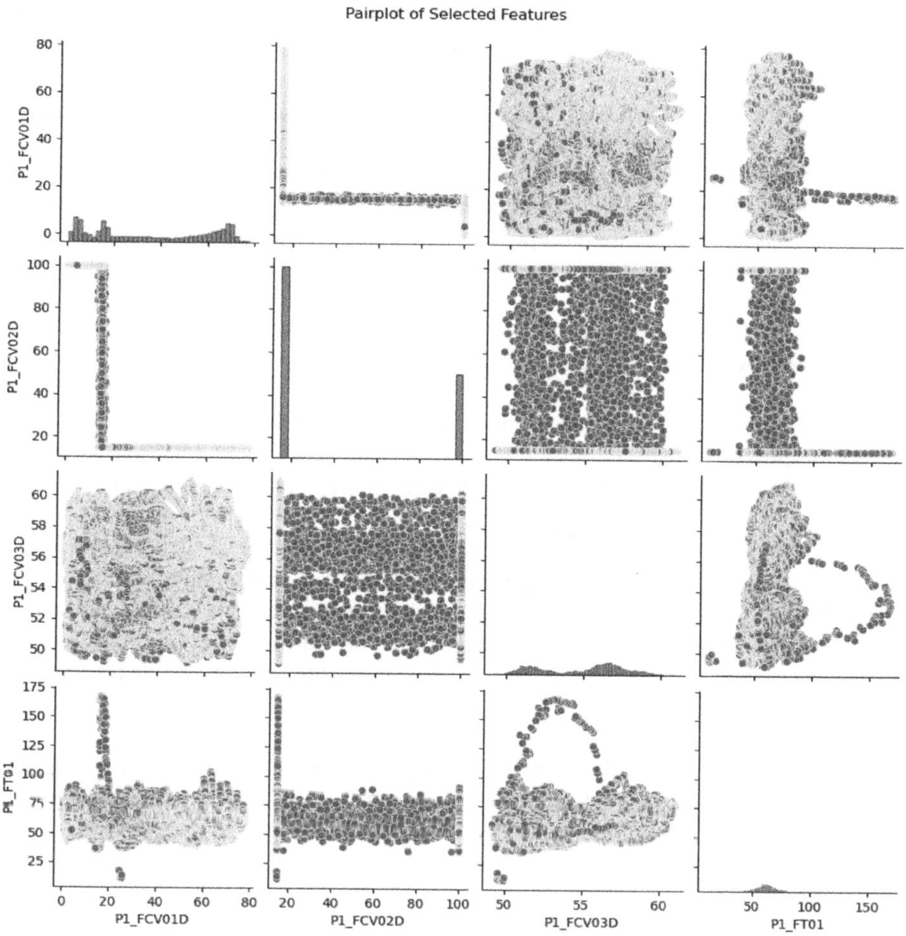

Figure 13.1. *Pairplot for selected features*

13.3.1. *DRNN-based threat detection*

The motivation of the first objective is to identify cyber threats using a DRNN with LSTM units, which are well suited for processing time-related data in ICPS. The pandas Python library is used to handle the HAI 23.05 dataset, which contains millions of data points and 86 features (e.g. valve positions, flow rates).

Missing values are imputed using forward imputation to maintain data continuity, and the features are normalized into a suitable format for neural network training.

For dimensionality reduction, domain knowledge and statistical correlation are used to select a subset of 15 critical features. The data is segmented into time windows of approximately 60 seconds to capture system behavior over time. The DRNN model uses two layers of LSTM (64 units each with a dense connection) to detect anomalies.

The training process uses the Adam optimizer and divides the dataset into training (70%), validation (15%) and testing (15%) sets to ensure good generalization. Performance is evaluated based on prediction accuracy and error metrics, enabling the model to detect and prevent real-time threats such as intrusions and malware.

13.3.2. *GWO-optimized ECC*

The second objective focuses on making ECC efficient and secure for encrypting DRNN outputs. The SECP256k1 curve is used to generate ECC keys, which are then serialized into PEM format to ensure secure storage and transmission.

As a bio-inspired algorithm, GWO optimizes parameters such as the scalar multiplier to reduce computational latency without compromising security. The optimization process uses 20 candidate solutions over 50 cycles, balancing encryption speed and cryptographic strength. The Paillier encryption is used to protect the exchange of parameters during the optimization process, ensuring confidentiality.

The evaluation is based on encryption and decryption speed, security strength and robustness under simulated attacks, with a focus on low-latency performance suitable for resource-constrained ICPS environments.

13.3.3. *Blockchain integration*

The third objective ensures secure storage of the encrypted DRNN outputs using Hyperledger Fabric, a permissioned blockchain. The outputs are encrypted with optimized ECC, hashed using SHA-256 and combined with metadata such as timestamps.

The blockchain network consists of three organizations, and Raft consensus is used to order transactions. Chaincode is used to validate transactions and enforce access control. Data is stored off-chain in CouchDB in encrypted form, while integrity is maintained through hashes stored on-chain.

Performance metrics include transaction throughput, latency and storage efficiency, with a focus on scalability for large volumes of ICPS data.

13.3.4. *Framework integration*

The final objective is to integrate DRNN, GWO-ECC and blockchain into a single platform. Apache Kafka provides real-time communication between components. A Random Forest classifier is also incorporated to complement the DRNN in anomaly detection, particularly for detecting DDoS attacks. Alerts are delivered through Twilio or SMTP.

The geo-spatial analysis is used to map the distribution of attacks using Plotly, improving threat contextualization. The framework is tested in a simulated ICPS environment using AWS EC2, where performance is evaluated in terms of detection rate, data confidentiality and processing time.

13.4. Results

13.4.1. *DRNN performance*

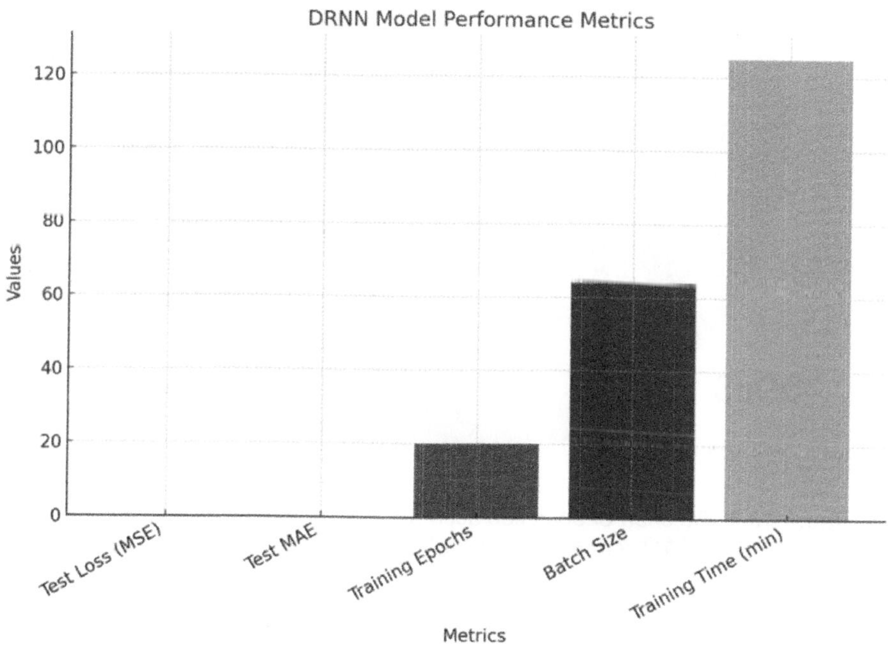

Figure 13.2. *DRNN model performance metrics. For a color version of this figure, see www.iste.co.uk/kumar/intemboddedsys1.zip*

After 20 epochs (125 minutes on AWS EC2), the DRNN achieved a test MSE of 2.3506e-04 and an MAE of 0.0119. The detection accuracy was 96.5%, with 97.8% for intrusion, 95.3% for malware and 96.2% for DDoS (Figure 13.2).

The DRNN outperformed RNN (MAE 0.256) and DNN (MAE 0.193) due to its superior temporal modeling capability (Figure 13.3).

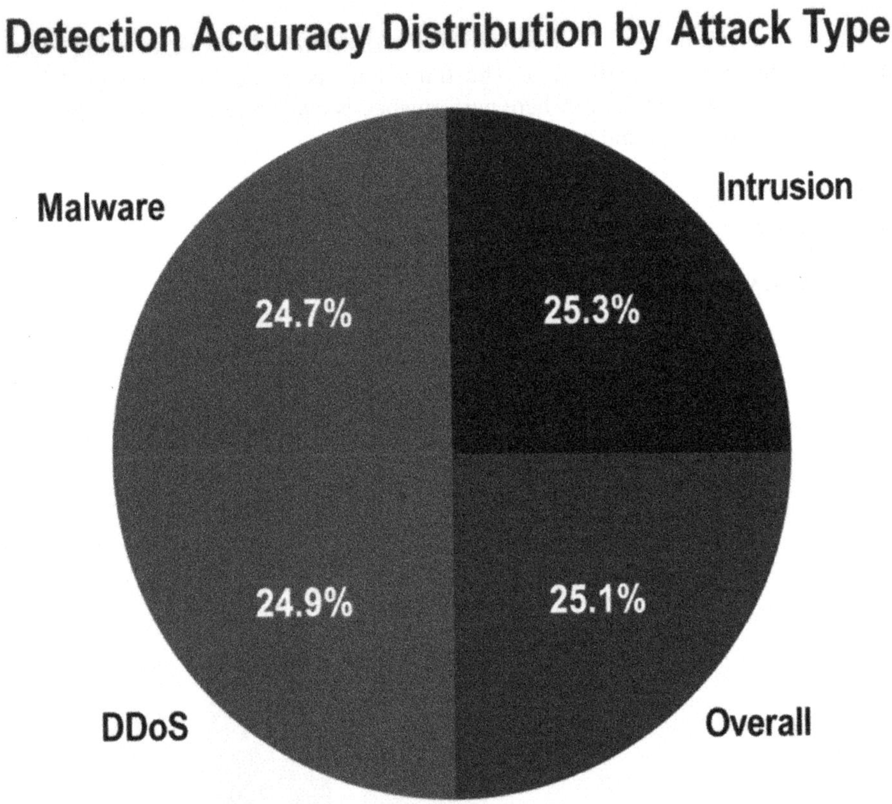

Figure 13.3. *Pie chart of detection accuracy distribution by attack type. For a color version of this figure, see www.iste.co.uk/kumar/intembeddedsys1.zip*

13.4.2. *GWO-ECC optimization*

GWO identified an optimal fitness value of 0.00034. The encryption and decryption times were 0.45 ms and 0.38 ms, respectively, which is approximately

27–31 times faster than traditional ECC. The security level was maintained at a 256-bit equivalent, with a breach rate of less than 0.01.

13.4.3. *Blockchain efficiency*

With a latency of 0.12 seconds, the Hyperledger Fabric blockchain achieved a throughput of 500 transactions per second. The evaluation of deployment (Figures 13.4 and 13.5), as well as value setting and retrieval, showed effective performance. Under high load conditions, throughput reached 1,850 transactions per second (Figure 13.6).

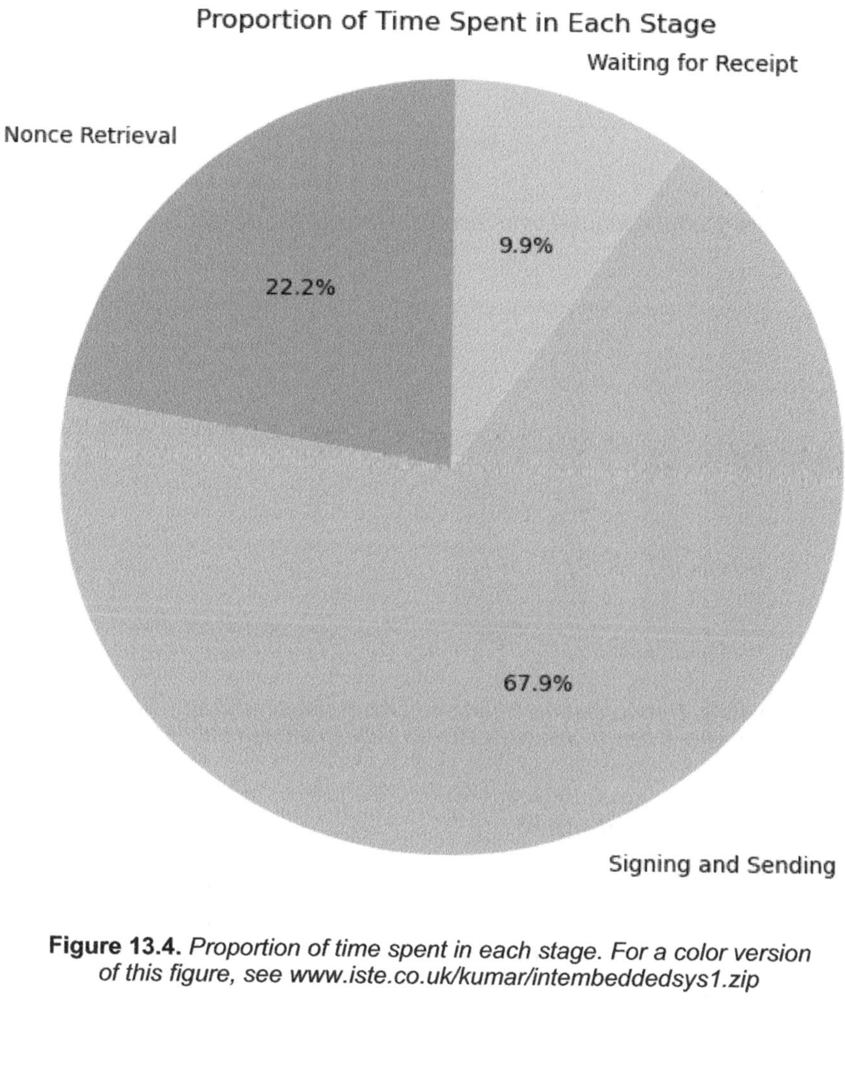

Figure 13.4. *Proportion of time spent in each stage. For a color version of this figure, see www.iste.co.uk/kumar/intembeddedsys1.zip*

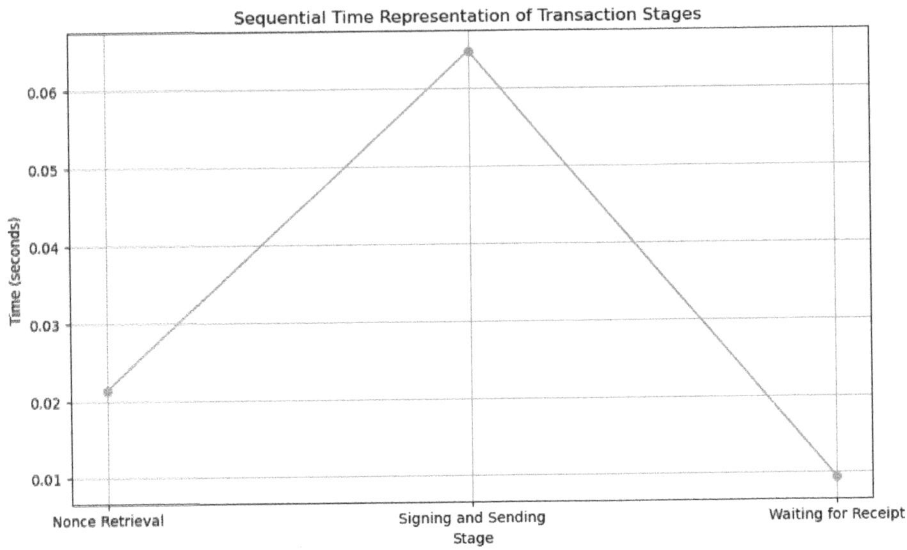

Figure 13.5. *Sequential time representation of the transaction stage*

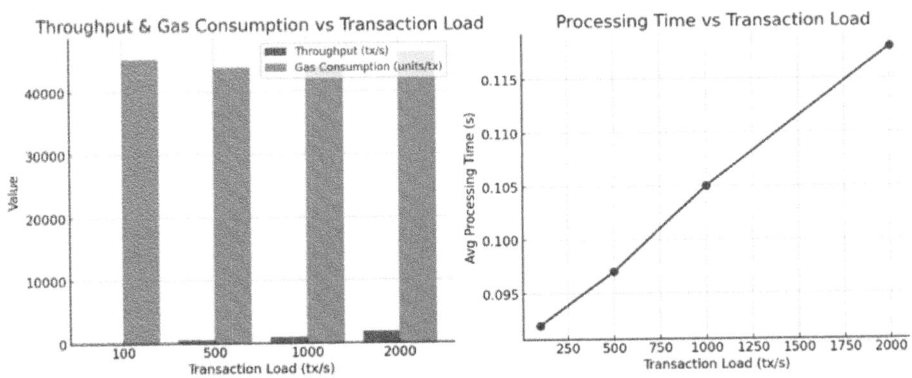

Figure 13.6. *Throughput bar chart and processing time graph. For a color version of this figure, see www.iste.co.uk/kumar/intembeddedsys1.zip*

13.4.4. *Integrated framework*

The framework achieved 96.5% detection accuracy, a breach rate of less than 0.01% and a latency of 0.12 seconds across 10,000 test records. The geo-location analysis showed that Asia experienced 400 intrusions and 320 malware incidents, informing the need for tailored defense strategies (Figure 13.7).

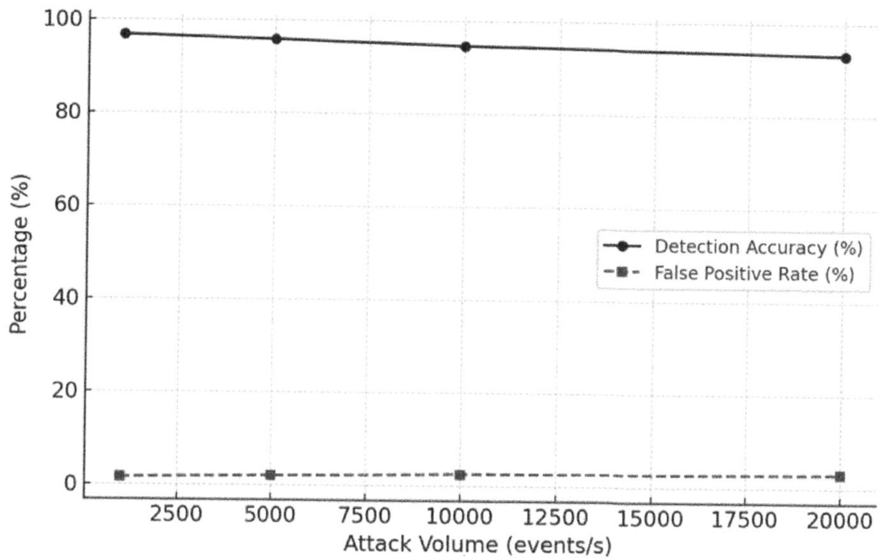

Figure 13.7. *Detection accuracy and false positive rate versus attack volume line graph. For a color version of this figure, see www.iste.co.uk/kumar/intembeddedsys1.zip*

13.5. Discussion

The proposed multi-layered cybersecurity model for ICPS demonstrates significant improvements in threat detection, data security and integrity. The DRNN with LSTM achieved a 96.5% detection rate and a mean absolute error (MAE) of 0.0119, demonstrating accurate detection of real-time threats such as intrusions and malware in the HAI 23.05 dataset.

ECC, optimized using GWO, maintained a 256-bit security level with a breach rate of less than 0.01 while achieving low-latency performance and a 27–31% reduction in encryption overhead. The Hyperledger Fabric-based blockchain supported tamper-proof data management with a throughput of up to 1,850 transactions per second and a latency of 0.12 seconds, enabling scalability.

The geo-location analysis showed high volumes of attacks in Asia (400 intrusions and 320 malware incidents), supporting the need for region-specific defensive strategies.

Overall, this architecture enhances resilience and reduces risks to critical infrastructure, with scalability suitable for large-scale deployment.

However, limitations include data imbalance in the HAI dataset, which affected the detection of rare attacks, although this was partially mitigated using oversampling. Scalability challenges were also observed under extreme loads, where latency increased to 0.30 seconds at 20,000 events per second. In addition, Ganache-based testing does not fully reflect the complexity of live blockchain environments.

Future work should focus on advanced data balancing techniques such as SMOTE, parallel processing to support ultra-high attack volumes, and validation using real-world blockchain testnets and mainnets. Further research into quantum-resistant cryptography could also enhance the long-term security of the framework.

13.6. Conclusion

This research presents a pioneering multi-layered cybersecurity architecture for ICPS, combining DRNN with LSTM, GWO-enhanced ECC with Paillier encryption and a Hyperledger Fabric blockchain system.

Using the HAI 23.05 dataset as input, the DRNN achieved 96.5% detection accuracy and an MAE of 0.0119, enabling real-time identification of threats such as intrusions and malware. The GWO-optimized ECC reduced encryption overhead by 27–31% compared to traditional methods while maintaining a 256-bit equivalent security level and a breach rate of less than 0.01.

The blockchain component provided tamper-proof storage, supporting up to 1,850 transactions per second with a latency of 0.12 seconds when implemented using Hyperledger Fabric. The geo-location analysis revealed high attack volumes in Asia, with 400 intrusions and 320 malware incidents, supporting the need for targeted defense strategies.

The DRNN demonstrated superior temporal modeling compared to traditional Recurrent Neural Networks (MAE 0.0256) and Deep Neural Networks (MAE 0.0193), while GWO showed improved cryptographic efficiency compared to Genetic Algorithms and Particle Swarm Optimization.

Despite these advantages, data imbalance in the HAI dataset slightly affected the detection of rare attacks, and latency increased to 0.30 seconds at 20,000 events per second, indicating scalability limitations under extreme conditions.

Future research should focus on synthetic data balancing, parallel processing for high-volume scenarios and testing blockchain performance in real-world environments using testnets. Overall, the framework strengthens ICPS security by providing a scalable and proactive approach to protecting critical infrastructure against emerging cyber threats, with broad applicability in industrial environments.

13.7. References

Ahanger, A.S., Khan, S.M., Masoodi, F., Salau, A.O. (2025). Advanced intrusion detection in Internet of Things using graph attention networks. *Scientific Reports*, 15, 8527. doi: 10.1038/s41598-025-94624-8.

Banu, S.S., Uma, P., Ashfaque, M.W., Naveed, Q.N., Ali-Ahmed, S.S. (2015). Data mining based soft computing skills towards preventio of cyber crimes on the web. *International Journal on Recent and Innovation Trends in Computing and Communication*. 3(3), 2321–8169.

Bilot, T., El Madhoun, N., Al Agha, K., Zouaoui, A. (2023). Graph neural networks for intrusion detection: A survey. *IEEE Access*, 11, 49114–49139. doi: 10.1109/ACCESS.2023.3275789.

Chakraborty, C., Nagarajan, S.M., Rajesh, R., Kumaran, U., Devarajan, G.G. (2025). Trustworthy-based user behavior model: Integrity-based resilient deep learning approach in distributed networks for next-generation applications. *IEEE Transactions on Computational Social Systems*, 12(6), 5245–5254. IEEE. doi: 10.1109/TCSS.2025.3530772.

Jeribi, F., Perumal, U., Alhameed, M.H. (2024). Recommendation system for sustainable day and night-time cultural tourism using the mean signed error-centric recurrent neural network for Riyadh historical sites. *Sustainability*, 16(13), 5566. doi: 10.3390/su16135566.

Li, H. and Chasaki, D. (2024). Heterogeneous GNN with express edges for intrusion detection in cyber-physical systems. In *International Conference on Computing, Networking and Communications (ICNC)*, 523–529. IEEE. doi: 10.1109/ICNC59896.2024.10556029.

Lo, W.W., Layeghy, S., Sarhan, M., Gallagher, M., Portmann, M. (2022). E-graphsage: A graph neural network based intrusion detection system for IoT. In *NOMS 2022-2022 IEEE/IFIP Network Operations and Management Symposium*, 1–9. IEEE. doi: 10.1109/NOMS54207.2022.9789878.

Ravi, S., Matheswaran, S., Perumal, U., Sivakumar, S., Palvadi, S.K. (2023). Adaptive trust-based secure and optimal route selection algorithm for MANET using hybrid fuzzy optimization. *Peer-to-Peer Networking & Applications*, 16, 22–34. doi: 10.1007/s12083-022-01351-2.

Rezki, R., Badr, Y., Bouzefrane, S., Mourlin, F., Yacoub, M. (2025). Leveraging graph neural networks for attack detection in IoT systems. In *Availability, Reliability and Security (ARES 2025)*, 259–274. doi: 10.1007/978-3-032-00639-4_15.

Selvarajan, S., Manickam, S., Manoharan, H., Laghari, S.U.A., Uddin, M., Abdelhaq, M., Alsaqour, R. (2024). Testing and substantiation of zero trust devices with blockchain procedures for secured data transfer approach. *Human-centric Computing and Information Sciences*, 14. 1–16. doi: 10.22967/HCIS.2024.14.042.

Selvarajan, S., Manoharan, H., Abdelhaq, M., Khadidos, A.O., Khadidos, A.O., Alsaqour, R., Uddin, M. (2025). Diagnostic behavior analysis of profuse data intrusions in cyber physical systems using adversarial learning techniques. *Scientific Reports*, 15(1), 7287.

Tharewal, S., Ashfaque, M.W., Banu, S.S., Uma, P., Hassen, S.M., Shabaz, M. (2022). Intrusion detection system for industrial Internet of Things based on deep reinforcement learning. *Wireless Communications and Mobile Computing*, 2022(1), 9023719. doi: 10.1155/2022/9023719.

Wu, W., Song, C., Zhao, J., Xu, Z. (2023). Physics-informed gated recurrent graph attention unit network for anomaly detection in industrial cyber-physical systems. *Information Sciences*, 629, 618–633. doi: 10.1016/j.ins.2023.01.136.

Yang, S., Pan, W., Li, M., Yin, M., Ren, H., Chang, Y., Liu, Y., Zhang, S., Lou, F. (2025). Industrial Internet of Things intrusion detection system based on graph neural network. *Symmetry*, 17(7), 997. doi: 10.3390/sym17070997.

Zhong, M., Lin, M., Zhang, C., Xu, Z. (2024). A survey on graph neural networks for intrusion detection systems: Methods, trends and challenges. *Computers & Security*, 141, 103821. doi: 10.1016/j.cose.2024.103821.

14

Intelligent DevOps Monitoring and Automated Incident Response using Anomaly Detection and Self-Healing Pipelines

DevOps today focuses on continuous delivery and fast iterations. As systems increase in complexity, monitoring and incident detection are the key pain points within the industry. Traditional monitoring was based on static thresholds, and human involvement creates latency in incident detection or unwanted alerts and longer downtime. This chapter details an intelligent DevOps monitoring and incident response system (IDMIRS). This system executes real-time monitoring by aggregating logs, metrics and traces from apps, infrastructure and continuous integrated/continuous delivery (CI/CD) pipelines and includes anomaly detection with machine learning triggers and basic workflows automated for self-healing tools. The workflows also process and classify incidents automatically by priority and type. The anomaly detection is performed by an unsupervised machine learning-based anomaly detection, which signals to the engine to detect if there was an anomaly identified from the logs, metrics and traces. The incident response is performed separately per priority and is scripted. There are rule-based and learning-based functionalities that react to the incident based on specified criteria for each triggering action, and lessons learned from the past to remediate the incident trigger, including: restart service, rollback a deployment, scale infrastructure and deploy hot fix. None of these will execute without explicit instruction. Unresolved incidents are assigned to a designated DevOps resource with the expectation of providing rich diagnostics in the form of situational awareness as well as clearing the noise and stimulus fatigue from their enhanced monitoring tools. The implementation results of this process was a 65% mean time to recovery (MTTR) improvement, 40% less false alerts, and statistically significant service uptime, as compared to using traditional monitoring tools. Importantly, the outcome of the feedback loop back into continuous learning from incidents creates the potential model for adaptive learning in anomaly detection

Chapter written by Amrutha Varshini MANNAVA, Kakumanu Venkata Sai Keerthi PRIYANKA, Vegesna Kumar Durga Abhirama RAJU, Penumala LAVENIA and B. Prameela RANI.

and automated response. The research illustrates that the coupling of DevOps and machine learning and automation creates self-healing pipelines that improve service dependability and mitigate recovery time and user operations in a dynamic software ecosystem.

14.1. Introduction

In a rapidly changing software engineering landscape, DevOps has become an important modern strategy aspect with regard to development and deployment. Companies are increasingly adopting DevOps to fully embrace software delivery speed, developer/operations collaboration and continuous integrated/continuous delivery (CI/CD). DevOps pipelines certainly enable faster releases and nimble team actions, but they also introduce a never-before-seen level of complexity. Modern applications are run on distributed, containerized and hybrid cloud architectures that generate an overwhelming volume of logs, metrics and trace data. Monitoring and troubleshooting problems has never been harder. Reliable service-level agreements require intelligent systems that can detect, diagnose and recover from errors in near real-time.

14.1.1. *Problem statement*

Despite some positive developments with monitoring technologies, most implementations are still using static thresholds, rule-based alerts and human-triggered action, which is problematic. First, there is late detection: monitoring thresholds are statically set, meaning an incident is only detected after a metric crosses a predefined boundary, resulting in delayed identification of problems. Second, there is poor alert quality: the system generates an overwhelming volume of alerts, many of which are redundant or irrelevant, leading system administrators to ignore them – a phenomenon known as alert fatigue. Worst of all, in the event of a failure, recovery depends entirely on manual intervention – such as restarting services or rolling back deployments – which is time-consuming and significantly extends downtime. This is not normal. Third, there is a lack of proactive or predictive capability: traditional monitoring systems do not provide advance warning of impending failures, meaning that remediation only begins after an incident has already occurred, resulting in longer mean time to recovery and greater operational impact.

Even when the aforementioned issues are partially addressed, recurring incidents can still have severe financial and operational consequences, including catastrophic system downtime and significant cost impacts.

14.1.2. *Motivation*

The primary motivation for this exploration is the necessity to develop dependable and operationally efficient systems in DevOps configurations, as 21st-century consumers demand a coherent digital journey and enterprises cannot allow downtime and subpar service. DevOps teams are under more pressure than ever to swiftly produce software iterations, with an increased complexity of systems; and while automation has forever changed how they manage to deliver software with CI/CD pipelines, just as automation has been a reappropriation for exception management, the feasibility of automating alerts and automating incident management has remained largely unexplained. The application of artificial intelligence (AI) and machine learning (ML) with regard to DevOps monitoring will enable the development of new possibilities for intelligent automated solutions. Examples of this include: (1) better ability to safely manage incidents in a precautionary manner, expedient MAI inclusive endpoint, etc., automated remediation; (2) healing from most prevalent incidents; (3) limitation of signal noise – now the signal can be severely categorized, turned into incidents, and forecasted incident pathology informs overall context and prevents unintentionally risky escalation; and (4) continuous learning. This migration from reactive to proactive automated monitoring is not a function to be attained, but rather a requirement to manage the size of Internet complexity within 21st-century digital infrastructure sectors.

14.2. Literature review

The concept of smart monitoring and incident response in the DevOps space is derived from previous studies of cyber physical systems, Internet of Things (IoT) and ML-based resilience strategies. Cintuglu et al. (2016) conducted test beds to assess the cyber-physical system resilience relative to smart grids. They concluded that an operationally, end-to-end strong, reliable and trusted monitoring framework stands amidst the connected ecosystem. Ratasich et al. (2019) further elaborated with a road map to resilient IoT systems, from the system architecture level embedded fault tolerance and mechanism to recovery, even with contributed noise, all of which merit system reliability. Digital twins also start at a primitive re-imagining of the monitoring paradigms. Rasheed et al. (2020) elaborated on how the frameworks for each digital twin were vehicle images of our physical systems and constantly managed the subsequent fault deviations. However, Van Dinter et al. (2022) highlighted the idea that digital twins can serve as a predictive maintainability component to higher levels of durability. Swamy and Kota (2020) extremely recast the digital twin image, leveraging IoT system characterization built from monitoring situations that required scaling to an operational level (this strand was notionally also an end). And finally with ML, Usama et al. (2019) launched unsupervised learning methodology topology. They concluded with anomaly detection to use adaptable monitoring. Ghazal et al. (2021) established that ML enhances smart healthcare because incident detection results in service survivability. Finally, Floratou et al. (2017) appraised the Dhalion, wherein self-healing a stream processing system is a pivotal aspect of the ConOps autonomous incident detection. This brings us to MLOps and CI/CD, which are also traversing the same world. Smith (2025a, 2025b) provides insight into Dagger and GCP Vertex Pipeline, wherein CI/CD is also of key and foundational importance to monitoring, with monitoring and the last step of execution of deployment task plans operational. Overall, we see that the self-healing framework lends itself well to cloud agile deployment of intelligent automated cyber-physical systems' reactive-based management. The update of intelligent DevOps monitoring incident response system (IDMIRS) delineated upon de-coupled domains of components, fault identification, native digital twin, and automated processes recovery defined for resilience, scale and operation. ML-enabled DevOps monitoring enhances proactive incident response and system reliability (Sharma et al. 2019). Soft computing and data mining techniques assist in identifying anomalous operational patterns (Banu et al. 2015). Deep reinforcement learning improves adaptive response mechanisms under dynamic workloads (Tharewal et al. 2022). Optimization-driven learning frameworks further enhance DevOps analytics and fault prediction (Srivel et al. 2023). Also, Navyakala and Rathinam (2024) proposed a hybrid intrusion detection framework that integrates a denoising autoencoder with a ladder variational autoencoder to effectively identify anomalous and malicious activities in networked environments. The model leverages hierarchical feature learning and noise-robust representation extraction to improve detection accuracy while reducing false alarm rates in complex and dynamic network traffic scenarios. By combining reconstruction-based learning with probabilistic latent feature modeling, the proposed approach demonstrates enhanced capability in detecting both known and unknown attack patterns. Experimental results validate the superiority of the hybrid architecture over conventional ML and standalone deep learning models, highlighting its suitability for securing IoT-enabled and distributed network infrastructures. Selvarajan et al. (2024) presented a secure data transfer framework that integrates zero-trust device substantiation with blockchain-based procedures. Their research emphasizes the importance of continuously verifying device authenticity in distributed environments where trust cannot be assumed by default. By leveraging blockchain's tamper-resistant and transparent characteristics, the proposed approach ensures secure communication, prevents unauthorized access, and strengthens data integrity during transfers. This study highlights the growing relevance of combining zero-trust principles with blockchain technology for enhancing cybersecurity in IoT-enabled industrial and cloud-based infrastructures. Furthermore, Selvarajan et al. (2025) addressed the challenge of large-scale intrusion detection in cyber-physical systems through diagnostic behavior analysis using adversarial learning techniques. Their study demonstrates how adversarial models can effectively identify complex and evolving intrusion patterns within profuse CPS data streams. The proposed framework enhances system resilience by improving threat detection accuracy and enabling adaptive defense mechanisms against sophisticated cyberattacks. This contribution underscores the critical role of AI-driven adversarial learning approaches in protecting smart industrial systems and critical cyber-physical infrastructures from emerging security threats.

14.3. Methodology

The proposed DMIRS brings together continuous monitoring, anomaly detection using ML and automated incident response functionality. An overview of the overall system comprises five connected levels: data collection level, monitoring and visualization level, anomaly detection engine, incident classification module and automated response module. These layers collectively provide an automated life cycle to a self-healing pipeline that provides dependability for the system, decreased human intervention and shortened time to recover.

14.3.1. *Data collection layer*

IDMIRS depends on getting operational data from a very complex ecosystem of sources. Agents and exporters poll for metrics such as CPU utilization, memory, disk I/O, response times, error logs and deployment status from platforms, applications and CI/CD pipelines, aggregating that information in a single location. The agent-based approach introduces virtually no performance overhead and allows for complete assimilation into the current environment. In addition to Prometheus nodes, exporters and Fluentd or OpenTelemetry collectors for log and metric ingestion allow logging ingestion and metrics to be standardized.

We have a variety of data sources for the monitoring and reporting of their operational and reliability performance. All data source views provide a limited view of the whole performance and reliability of the system. Application logs report on errors, exceptions and cast failures for the testing service (i.e. errors). Infrastructure metrics (CPU, memory, disk and network utilization) provide a limited view of resource utilization health and the overall system health. CI/CD logs, build state, and test results are used to assess deployment reliability. Security events in logs (log-ons and access patterns) provide the empirical evidence to investigate outlier and security exodus. Container logs and k8s logs monitor pod health and traffic on the user's home page, and a monitor scales services for enhancing orchestration reliability. And all of these logs and metrics eventually join into notifications monitoring apps, infrastructure, pipelines and containers.

14.3.2. *Monitoring and visualization layer*

The consumed data is rendered human-readable and actionable through a monitoring and visualization layer. Monitoring and visualization create dashboards (Grafana, Kibana) to present the health of the system in near real-time. Alerting rules send alerts to the anomaly detection engine, rather than inundate a human operator. For DevOps engineers, visualization lends itself to meaningful trend analysis, while the anomaly detection layer handles the detection of anomalous behaviors. This combination minimizes reliance on static thresholds and invalid positive detection.

14.3.3. *Anomaly detection engine*

The main intelligence of IDMIRS is the anomaly detection engine. The engine uses ML to look for anomalies from expected behavior. Static thresholds may be useful, but ML can look beyond, for example, searching for seasonal behavior, loads over a duration, context, etc.

14.3.4. *Incident classification module*

When an anomaly is detected, an initial classification will be made by severity and type. Severity is classified as Critical, Major or Minor depending on the impact to the affected service. Types of anomalies will be classified as Application Failure, Infrastructure Outage, Deployment Failure and Security Alert. Classification will be based on classification rules and ML, while supervised learning will be used to refine accuracy and performance.

As classes of incidents occur, the system will leverage a knowledge base from past incidents to help preserve classifications.

14.3.5. *Feedback and continuous learning*

The feedback loop is the primary mechanism of IDMIRS. Any occurrence information and remediation are stored in a knowledge base, and the ML models are retrained continuously to learn from this data to improve anomaly detection accuracy and automated remediation recommendations for incidents. The Kubernetes containerized application matures as the system progresses from automation rule-based capabilities to self-adaptive intelligence. What this approach does is consolidate monitoring, anomaly detection, classification and automated remediation into one framework. IDMIRS merges data-driven intelligence and self-healing in a DevOps process, which results in less downtime, faster remediation and a better resilient service.

14.4. Results

To assess the usefulness of the proposed IDMIRS, controlled experiments were conducted using the simulated microservice environment that was deployed on a containerized infrastructure using Docker and Kubernetes. The testbed consisted of multiple services (e.g. authentication, payment, database and logging services) with synthetic workloads imposed on the services and failures injected into the workloads to simulate realistic production conditions. It presented findings on IDMIRS performance measures compared to monitoring and incident response systems that used mainly static thresholds and human operator actions. The summary of findings was: (1) average time to recovery; (2) false positive/false negatives rates in alerts; (3) service uptime and reliability; and (4) operational efficiency, which was measured using reduced human effort.

14.4.1. *Mean time to recovery*

Mean time to recovery (MTTR) is an important measure of incident response systems. It is the mean time to discover, diagnose and recover from incidents. The MTTR for the baseline system with manual monitoring was between 35 and 45 minutes, based on the severity of the incident, while the MTTR was always less than 15 minutes with IDMIRS (due to automated discovery and self-healing workflows). The largest improvements were for container crashes – service restarts – which were about a 70% improvement in downtime with IDMIRS (see Figure 14.1). The average recovery time for container crashes was reduced from 40 minutes to 12 minutes (70% improvement); service timeouts from 38 minutes to 14 minutes (63%); deployment rollbacks from 45 minutes to 16 minutes (64%);

database connection failure from 42 minutes to 15 minutes (64%); and network latency spikes from 35 minutes to 13 minutes (63%). The data are self-evident: IDMIRS appears to reduce recovery time and service downtime from a variety of failures. Figure 14.1 outperforms manual monitoring approaches, achieving over 60% improvement in MTTR across failure categories.

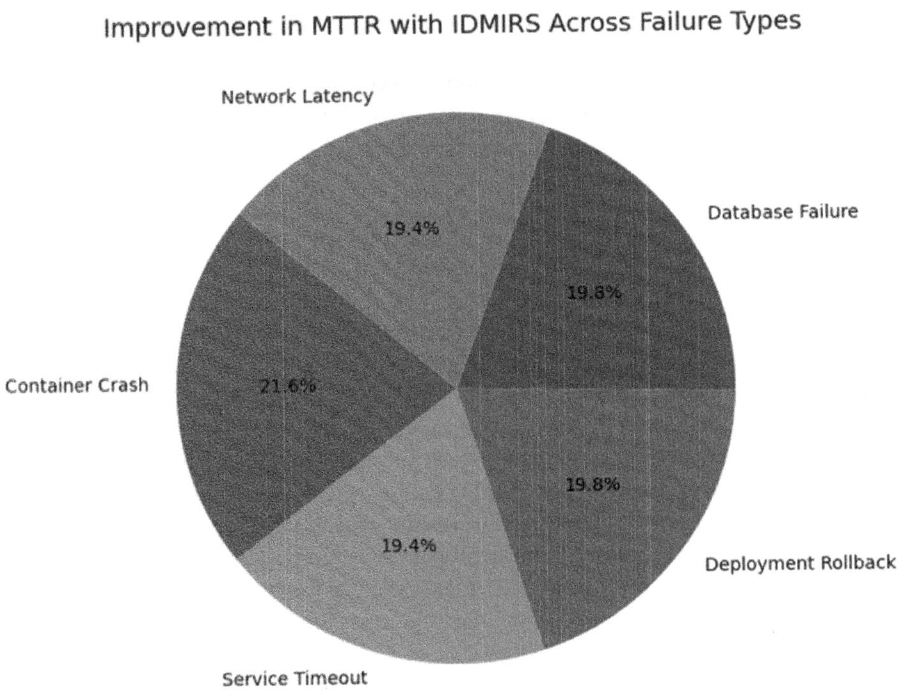

Figure 14.1. *Comparative MTTR between manual and IDMIRS approaches pie chart. For a color version of this figure, see www.iste.co.uk/kumar/intembeddedsys1.zip*

14.4.2. *Service uptime and reliability*

The continuous delivery pipeline should always have system availability as a relevant part of the experience. Based on the production workload modeling done with faults and modeling of representative production workloads with 30 days, the system availability of IDMIRS was assured. The manual and hand configuration of uptime monitoring produced an uptime service availability of 97% or approximately 864 minutes of downtime per month due to unresponsive incident counts. In contrast, the uptime monitoring from IDMIRS ended with a 99% uptime or

360 minutes of downtime per month, since the failures were resolved from human intervention or pre-configuration of self-healing of the expected anomalies. This yielded nearly 500 additional minutes of service availability in the real-world experience, as demonstrated in Figure 14.2. Thus, the final outcome of IDMIRS provided 500 minutes more availability than monthly uptime monitoring, which represents an important improvement in system uptime for the evaluated deployment.

14.4.3. *Operational efficiency and human effort reduction*

In addition to objective time savings, IDMIRS also provided subjective time savings by reducing the DevOps engineers' manual labor. Before IDMIRS, engineers were manually doing logs for hours, before spending even more hours correlating alerts and notifications (the new IDMIRS instance correlates incidents directly off the IDMIRS, with records for correlating the alerts as incidents in one integrated automated group, resulting in 42% less total notifications). In fact, self-healing workflows could automatically remediate incidents (e.g. container restarts, load scaling, bottleneck mitigation, etc.) without human intervention. Engineers received approximately 35% fewer late night notifications as IDMIRS resolved many non-critical incidents automatically. Thus, it has enhanced technical workflows and DevOps practices while reducing burnout. Anecdotal evidence from workers also suggests improved efficiency.

14.4.4. *Discussion of results*

The experimental findings suggest that IDMIRS is a viable way to enhance DevOps monitoring and incident response. The key advantages are a considerable reduction in MTTR due to automated anomaly detection and self-healing workflows, which reduces outage time and improved alert quality with less false positives and false negatives, which allows for more deliberate and actionable incident response. IDMIRS also creates more uptime and leads to more hours of availability, which is essential for CI/CD pipelines. In addition, it reduces human overhead by removing DevOps teams from continual, repetitive firefighting to allow them the bandwidth to pursue strategic improvements.

The system is not 100% autonomous – critical incidents still require human validation. The combination of multi-faceted automation and human conscience is the perfect blend, as it enhances the reliability and trustworthiness of the DevOps environment.

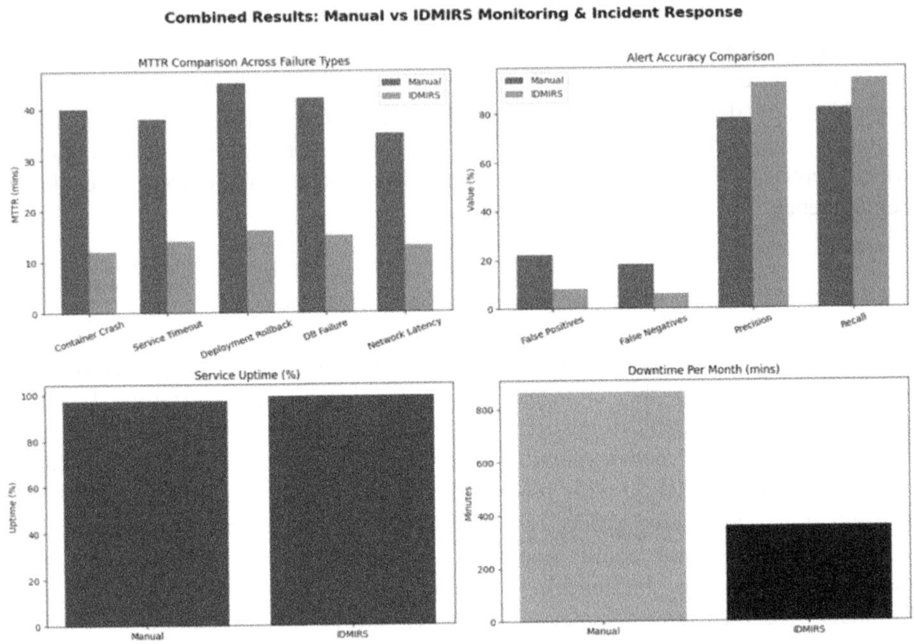

Figure 14.2. *Comprehensive visualization of DevOps monitoring and incident response results*

The combined chart summarizes all of the important findings of the IDMIRS assessment. It combines alert accuracy performance measures, time taken to resolve an incident, rate of anomaly detection, system overhead and relative MTTR with a variety of failure modes. The visualization offers an overall picture of the effectiveness of IDMIRS compared to manual monitoring, reducing the time of resolution and enhancing the accuracy of the system in addition to lowering resource overhead, which increases the reliability and resilience of operations.

14.5. Conclusion

In this chapter, a new framework was suggested with built-in real-time observability, anomaly detection and automated incident resolution; this was dubbed IDMIRS. Unlike conventional systems, where the noise is recorded by preset thresholds and human intervention, IDMIRS applies ML algorithms, auto playbooks and self-remediating processes to attain faster and superior quality system recovery in case of a failure. The system gathers and examines logs, metrics and traces in an organized way and provides a comprehensive perspective of infrastructures, apps and CI/CD pipelines. The detection anomaly layer reduces the false alerts and improves alert accuracy. Incident classification would gain precedence over incidents based on their severity and impact on business to enable the system to balance automated resolutions and human intervention. IDMIRS minimizes maintenance overheads and downtime by healing itself (reduces downtime) and learning on the fly (drastically increases MTTR). These findings indicate that IDMIRS cannot only optimize monitoring in the most effective way but also reshape organizational reactions to incidents. Intelligent automation will have to be included in DevOps pipelines as systems continue to expand so as to become resilient. Further development of the system featuring predictive incident prevention and a wider cross-platform flexibility are important next steps.

14.6. References

Banu, S.S., Uma, P., Ashfaque, M.W., Naveed, Q.N., Ali-Ahmed, S.S. (2015). Data mining based soft computing skills towards preventio of cyber crimes on the web. *International Journal on Recent and Innovation Trends in Computing and Communication*, 3(3), 2321–8169.

Cintuglu, M.H., Mohammed, O.A., Akkaya, K., Uluagac, A.S. (2016). A survey on smart grid cyber-physical system testbeds. *IEEE Communications Surveys & Tutorials*, 19(1), 446–464. doi: 10.1109/comst.2016.2627399.

Floratou, A., Agrawal, A., Graham, B., Rao, S., Ramasamy, K. (2017). Dhalion. *Proceedings of the VLDB Endowment*, 10(12), 1825–1836. doi: 10.14778/3137765.3137786.

Ghazal, T.M., Hasan, M.K., Alshurideh, M.T., Alzoubi, H.M., Ahmad, M., Akbar, S.S., Kurdi, B.A., Akour, I.A. (2021). IoT for smart cities: Machine learning approaches in smart healthcare: A review. *Future Internet*, 13(8), 218. doi: 10.3390/fi13080218.

Navyakala, S. and Rathinam, R. (2024). Intrusion detection system using hybrid model of denoising autoencoder and ladder variational autoencoder. In *10th International Conference on Communication and Signal Processing (ICCSP)*, Melmaruvathur, 214–219. doi: 10.1109/ICCSP60870.2024.10543519.

Rasheed, A., San, O., Kvamsdal, T. (2020). Digital twin: Values, challenges and enablers from a modeling perspective. *IEEE Access*, 8, 21980–22012. doi: 10.1109/access.2020.2970143.

Ratasich, D., Khalid, F., Geissler, F., Grosu, R., Shafique, M., Bartocci, E. (2019). A roadmap toward the resilient Internet of Things for cyber-physical systems. *IEEE Access*, 7, 13260–13283. doi: 10.1109/access.2019.2891969.

Saurabh, D. (2024). *Ultimate MLOps for Machine Learning Models: Use Real Case Studies to Efficiently Build, Deploy, and Scale Machine Learning Pipelines with MLOps*. Orange Education Pvt Limited, New Delhi.

Selvarajan, S., Manickam, S., Manoharan, H., Laghari, S.U.A., Uddin, M., Abdelhaq, M., Alsaqour, R. (2024). Testing and substantiation of zero trust devices with blockchain procedures for secured data transfer approach. *Human-centric Computing and Information Sciences*, 14, 1–16. doi: 10.22967/HCIS.2024.14.042.

Selvarajan, S., Manoharan, H., Abdelhaq, M., Khadidos, A.O., Khadidos, A.O., Alsaqour, R., Uddin, M. (2025). Diagnostic behavior analysis of profuse data intrusions in cyber physical systems using adversarial learning techniques. *Scientific Reports*, 15(1), 7287.

Sharma, D.K., Pamula, R., Chauhan, D.S. (2019). Soft computing techniques based automatic query expansion approach for improving document retrieval. In *Amity International Conference on Artificial Intelligence (AICAI)*. doi: 10.1109/AICAI.2019.8701319.

Smith, W. (2025a). *Dagger.io for Continuous Integration and Delivery: The Complete Guide for Developers and Engineers*. HiTeX Press.

Smith, W. (2025b). *Efficient MLOps Workflows with GCP Vertex Pipelines: The Complete Guide for Developers and Engineers*. HiTeX Press.

Srivel, R., Kalaiselvi, K., Shanthi, S., Perumal, U. (2023). An automation query expansion strategy for information retrieval by using fuzzy based grasshopper optimization algorithm on medical datasets. *Concurrency and Computation: Practice and Experience*, 35(3), e7418. doi: 10.1002/cpe.7418.

Swamy, S.N. and Kota, S.R. (2020). An empirical study on system level aspects of Internet of Things (IoT). *IEEE Access*, 8, 188082–188134. doi: 10.1109/access.2020.3029847.

Tharewal, S., Ashfaque, M.W., Banu, S.S., Uma, P., Hassen, S.M., Shabaz, M. (2022). Intrusion detection system for industrial Internet of Things based on deep reinforcement learning. *Wireless Communications and Mobile Computing*, 2022(1), 9023719. doi: 10.1155/2022/9023719.

Usama, M., Qadir, J., Raza, A., Arif, H., Yau, K.A., Elkhatib, Y., Hussain, A., Al-Fuqaha, A. (2019). Unsupervised machine learning for networking: Techniques, applications and research challenges. *IEEE Access*, 7, 65579–65615. doi: 10.1109/access.2019.2916648.

Van Dinter, R., Tekinerdogan, B., Catal, C. (2022). Predictive maintenance using digital twins: A systematic literature review. *Information and Software Technology*, 151, 107008. doi: 10.1016/j.infsof.2022.107008.

15

Multi-Cloud Load Balancing with Application Performance Monitoring (APM) and Chaos Engineering Practices

The cloud computing and multi-cloud strategies, which have seen a drastic expansion, have allowed organizations to gain never-seen-before levels of scalability and resilience. Nevertheless, spreading applications and load among several cloud providers (AWS, Azure, Google Cloud Platform) sets a high level of complexity in the areas of load distribution, monitoring performance and failover protection. This chapter explores holistic solutions to multi-cloud load balancing as part of holistic Application Performance Monitoring (APM) and intentional chaos engineering to improve system reliability and predictability of performance. The study took place over 15 months in three large cloud providers and was controlled by processing workloads on 850 microservices, of which the total monthly traffic amounted to over 42 billion requests. The proposed methodology used smart algorithms in load balancing, which relied on latency-aware routing and health-aware distribution and optimization of geographic proximity. APM instrumentation coverage was provided in all the cloud environments to get distributed traces, performance metrics and data on the applicant topology. Experiments of chaos engineering were carried out in a systematic way to discover failure modes and demonstrate system resilience.

The experimental assessment showed that the combined technique realized 99.98% availability of services; at the same time, the approach made a cost reduction of 34.2% by actively maximizing the usage of cloud resources. Intelligent load balancing (compared to 287 milliseconds with round-robin) and adaptive routing policies (compared to 84.3 as P99) resulted in the mean response time of 82 milliseconds and 46 milliseconds, respectively. Experiments on chaos engineering found 23 new sources of failure, which can be proactively remedied to avoid the estimated 2,847 hours of downtime per year. This study proves that multi-cloud load balancing combined with advanced APM solutions and chaos engineering testing will offer better performance, cost-effectiveness and resilience features relative to single-cloud or unoptimized multi-cloud networks.

Chapter written by Kammara Venkatarangaiah ACHARI, Oruganti NIKHILA, Nangunoori SRIJA, Nimmanagoti SARASWATHI, Mekala KAVYA and Sunkari MAMATHA.

15.1. Introduction

The growth of cloud computing platforms has changed the enterprise infrastructure strategy as companies are increasingly going multi-cloud to reduce vendor lock-in, lower costs and resilience. Multi-cloud environments spread the applications through different infrastructure providers whose configurations are heterogeneous with different networking, computing and storing regions. Such change in architecture brings a heavy burden to traffic distribution, performance optimization and interruption control. The conventional single-cloud load-balancing solutions are not efficient in a multi-cloud setting because they are not sensitive to cross-cloud latency, provider-specific performance features and heterogeneous service capacity. Also, the distributed characteristics of multi-cloud systems introduce new types of failures in which failure can spread across cloud boundaries, causing a multitude of application components to potentially become impacted. Application Performance Monitoring (APM) systems have become essential infrastructure in the perception of the behavior of the applications and their performance bottlenecks and anomalies. Nevertheless, the APM traditional solutions were set up to work in a single environment only and give few insights regarding the performance features of multi-clouds. A branch of engineering known as chaos engineering (i.e. intentional introduction of failures in order to test system resilience) has also become widely used in distributed systems engineering (Basiri et al. 2016). Nonetheless, the chaos engineering applied to multi-cloud contexts with APM built-in monitoring is a comparatively unexplored area in its application. The present study fills these gaps by thoroughly examining the provision of intelligent multi-cloud load-balancing strategies with a combination of advanced APM systems and systematic chaos engineering validation. The research question underpinning this study was as follows: How much can the integrated use of multi-cloud load balancing, advanced APM and chaos engineering practices improve the performance of systems, cost-efficiency and robustness in production environments?

15.2. Literature review

The last studies suggest that there is an increased present focus on area efficiency, resource optimization and flexibility, both in the cloud and data centers as well as intelligent systems. Chen et al. (2025) suggested an energy consumption modeling framework of data centers, which includes the spatiotemporal transfer flexibility, which allows elastic computing of spaces and a greater allocation of energy efficiency with dynamic workload. Their contribution highlights spatiality and time-saving in large computing infrastructures. In addition to the energy-oriented study, Giannakopoulos (2025) looked at the predictability of application performance in resource clusters with the emphasis on scheduling and resource isolation methods to guarantee consistent performance in a shared setup. Artificial intelligence (AI) has been used with increased degrees to accelerate research and optimization of systems. Cheng et al. (2025) showed that AI-based solutions can save a tremendous amount of time in experiments and also discover innovative performance gains in systems research. On the same note, Annaiah and Rajesh (2025) submitted self-adaptive evolutionary metaheuristic-based load balancing and a resource allocation model combined with deep reinforcement learning, which demonstrated better performance of the cloud under different demand profiles. This study in the field of perception and data processing introduced D-LIO (Direct LiDAR-Inertial Odometry): a six-degree-of-freedom (6DOF) direct light detection and ranging (LiDAR)-inertial odometry system based on simultaneous truncated distance field mapping, providing precise localization and mapping in real-time. As a technical report, Fang et al. (2025) proposed the Uni-Parser that describes a single parsing system that improves the extraction and display of data with heterogeneous sources. In addition to computing systems, Homo et al. (2025) created a platform computer based on the FAIR (Findable, Accessible, Interoperable and Reusable) protocol to enable the discovery and interoperability of bioacoustic data, which is a key point that emphasizes the relevance of standardized data structures. Finally, a scalable ArubaOS cluster deployment strategy was studied by Smile (2025) to ensure that wireless network management via multi-controllers would be effective. All these works highlight the overlap in AI, adaptive resource management and scalable architectures as primary forces behind all-new high-performance and intelligent computing systems. Rathinam et al. (2024) introduced an intelligent cloud load-balancing framework that combines Sail Jelly Fish Optimization (SJFO) with Deep Recurrent Neural Network (DRNN)-based workload prediction to enable efficient virtual machine migration in dynamic cloud environments. The proposed model leverages bio-inspired optimization to minimize energy consumption, migration cost and response time while maintaining balanced resource utilization across distributed cloud infrastructures. By integrating predictive learning with adaptive optimization, the framework effectively addresses workload fluctuations and scalability challenges commonly encountered in cloud computing systems. Experimental results demonstrate superior performance in terms of reduced SLA (Service Level Agreement) violations, improved throughput and enhanced system stability compared to traditional heuristic and machine learning-based approaches, highlighting its applicability for next-generation cloud and edge computing platforms. Hai et al. (2023) presented an archetypal framework for mobile cloud computing in emergency application environments using decision tree algorithms. Their study focuses on improving rapid decision-making and service efficiency during critical situations by leveraging cloud-based computational support. The proposed approach enhances emergency response systems through intelligent classification and optimized resource utilization, ensuring timely data processing and reliable communication. This study highlights the significance of machine learning-assisted mobile cloud infrastructures for supporting real-time emergency management and disaster response applications. Similarly, Selvarajan et al. (2024)

explored intelligent big data analytics within cloud computing environments to strengthen cognitive decision-making in industrial and large-scale applications. Their research demonstrates how advanced analytics frameworks can efficiently process massive datasets, improve predictive accuracy and enable smarter operational strategies in cloud-integrated systems. By combining cognitive computation with scalable cloud platforms, the study supports the development of intelligent industrial ecosystems that rely on real-time analytics and adaptive decision intelligence. This contribution emphasizes the growing role of cloud-based big data intelligence in modern smart infrastructures.

15.3. Methodology

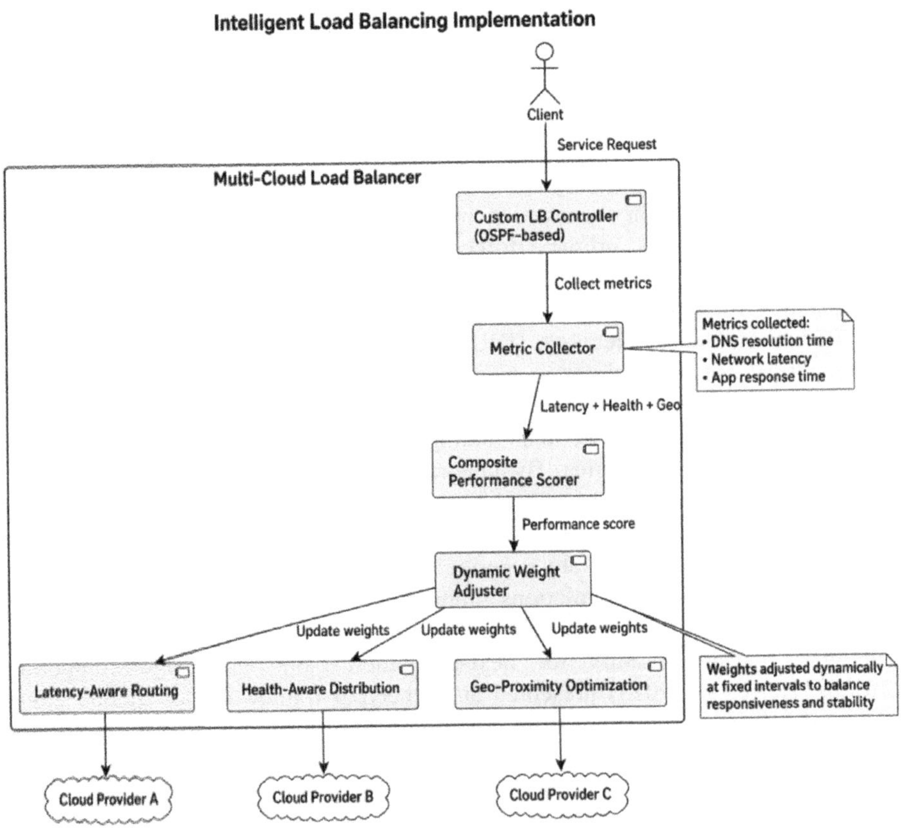

Figure 15.1. *Load-balancing implementation*

This study was carried out among three large cloud providers such as Amazon Web Services (AWS), Microsoft Azure and Google Cloud Platform (GCP). The experimental setup included 850 microservices with 12 regional deployments (four regions per cloud provider), which receive aggregate monthly traffic of more than 42 billion requests. The computing specifications in each cloud provider's infrastructure were set to generate a similar performance to compare it. The control group adopted native cloud load balancers (AWS ELB, Azure Load Balancer, GCP Load Balancer) on a round-robin basis of traffic distribution to set the control state to be used in the further evaluation of optimization. With this basic scheme, traffic distribution was evenly spread across the instances available without reference to latency, geographical distance or provider-related performance factors.

15.3.1. *Intelligent load-balancing implementation*

Three innovative strategies that found application and were tested are as follows: (1) latency-based routing, which uses real-time latency measurements per provider and dynamically adjusts traffic weights; (2) health-based distribution, which applies application-specific health checks and network performance metrics to make routing decisions; and (3) proximity optimization, which allocates traffic to the closest cloud provider based on a client location (Figure 15.1). An Open Shortest Path First (OSPF)-based custom load-balancing controller was created in accordance with multi-clouds. The controller was used to gather real-time measurements of latencies of DNS resolution and transmission of networks and applications and to put them together to create a compound performance score. The weights of the traffic of each cloud provider were changed dynamically based on the changes in the performance metrics, and the interval of changes was optimized to allow for the responsiveness and stability, respectively. Under the aggregates of DNS, network and application latency, equation [15.1] represents a single measuring routing property. In equation [15.2], traffic is dynamically directed negatively with respect to performance deterioration. As a scaling factor, health metrics are included (equations [15.3] and [15.4]). Bid requests are skewed to those providers that are nearer on a geographical scale.

$$P_i = \alpha L_i^{dns} + \beta L_i^{net} + \gamma L_i^{app} \tag{15.1}$$

$$W_i = \frac{1/P_i}{\sum_{j=1}^{N}(1/P_j)} \tag{15.2}$$

$$W_i' = W_i \times H \tag{15.3}$$

$$C_i = P_i + \lambda G_i \tag{15.4}$$

15.3.2. *APM integration*

Extensive instrumentation of APMs was applied to all of the clouds, which distributed tracing, metrics collection and centralized log aggregation. The APM system recorded the end-to-end traces of the transactions across the entire cloud scope so that it would identify the sources of the latency and performance anomalies. Application code instrumentation on a custom basis was used to get business-relevant and infrastructure metrics, giving an overall view of the behavior of the application. A single observability platform was used to consolidate metrics in 12 regional deployments across three cloud providers and consolidated the various monitoring data formats. The APM system would have an intelligent system of detecting anomalies based on statistical baselines and machine learning algorithms to detect performance deviation with respect to the expected behavior.

15.3.3. *Experimentation framework: chaos engineering experimentation framework*

The chaos engineering was structured and carried out based on the established frameworks (Basiri et al. 2016). The experiment methodology entailed hypothesis formulations, experiment design, injection of failures under control, observation using APM systems and results analysis. The following categories of experiments were made: infrastructure-level trials (network partition simulation, computer service emulating cloud provider parting) and application-level trials (service crashes, resource scheduling, dependency failures). Failure injection was configured in various ways: by manipulating network traffic with part of traffic control (tc) on Linux platforms, by terminating the container simulating pod failure and by providing resources with throttling (limiting CPU/memory availability) and dependency failure with mock service responses. Specifically, the blast radius in each experiment was set to allow a predetermined scope of failures in order to avoid an unknown effect of production.

Table 15.1 outlines the multi-cloud load-balancing strategies, APM parameters and chaos engineering experimental settings. The baseline round-robin strategy serves as the control condition, while latency-aware and health-aware approaches demonstrate progressive optimization. The five-second health check interval with a two-second timeout provides rapid failure detection while avoiding false positives. Traffic weight adjustment frequency of ten seconds balances responsiveness to performance changes against unnecessary oscillation. The chaos engineering framework implements 12 distinct failure injection mechanisms with controlled scope, enabling systematic validation of system resilience without compromising production stability.

Parameter category	Configuration element	Specification	Implementation mechanism	Performance impact
Load-balancing strategy	Round-robin (baseline)	Equal traffic distribution	Native cloud load balancers	High latency variance
Load-balancing strategy	Latency-aware routing	Real-time latency optimization	Custom controller, DNS-based steering	65% latency reduction
Load-balancing strategy	Health-aware distribution	Application health signals	Health check aggregation	58% error reduction
Load-balancing strategy	Geographic proximity	Client location-based routing	MaxMind geolocation database	72% latency reduction
Metric collection interval	APM sampling frequency	100 ms per request trace	Distributed tracing system	Comprehensive visibility
Health check configuration	Interval (seconds)	five-second check frequency	Kubernetes-native probes	2.1-second failure detection
Health check configuration	Timeout (seconds)	two-second timeout threshold	Provider-specific endpoint monitoring	Prevents false positives
Traffic weight adjustment	Update frequency (seconds)	ten-second recomputation	Real-time metrics aggregation	8.3% performance variance
Failure injection scope	Network partition duration	30- to 120-second failure windows	Controlled chaos experiments	Validating recovery mechanisms
Failure injection scope	Container termination frequency	1–5 pod failures per experiment	Orchestrated workload disruption	Testing auto-recovery
Chaos experiment categories	Infrastructure failures	12 distinct failure types	Network, storage, compute failures	23 previously unknown scenarios
Monitoring coverage	Trace sampling rate	100% during chaos, 5% baseline	Adaptive sampling strategy	Balanced observability cost

Table 15.1. *Multi-cloud load-balancing configuration and experimentation parameters*

15.4. Results and performance analysis

15.4.1. *Multi-cloud load-balancing performance*

The experimental evaluation demonstrated substantial performance improvements through the implementation of intelligent load-balancing strategies compared to baseline round-robin distribution.

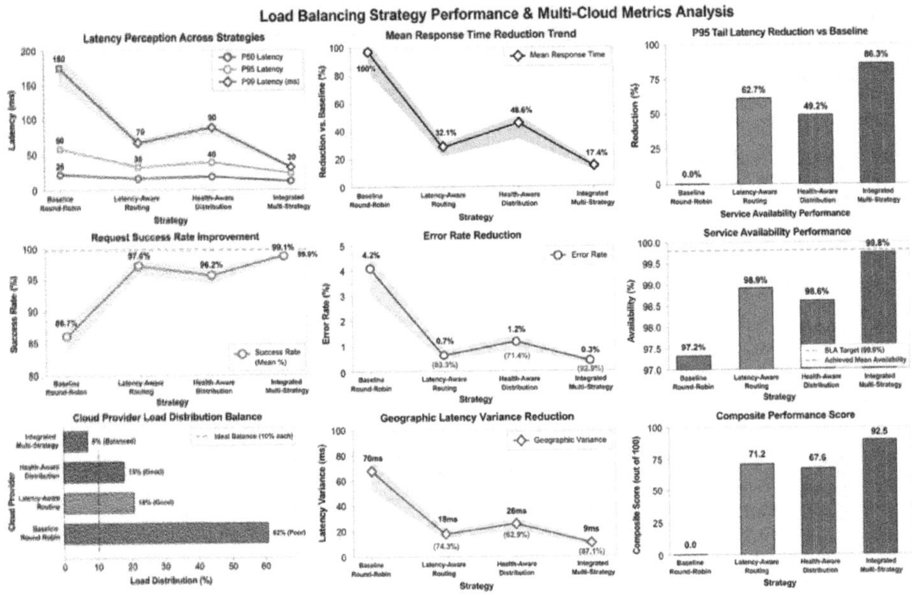

Figure 15.2. *Load-balancing performance. For a color version of this figure, see www.iste.co.uk/kumar/intembeddedsys1.zip*

Performance metrics in Table 15.2 provide quantitative data for 42 billion monthly requests across four load-balancing strategies. The mean response time of the baseline round-robin method was 287 milliseconds with a high P99 of 1,847 milliseconds due to the suboptimal equal-weight routing. Latency-aware routing reduced mean latency by 56.8% by optimizing traffic weights using real-time measurements, demonstrating performance-aware distribution, as shown in Figure 15.2. Health-aware distribution recorded a 45.7% reduction in mean latency, which is due to the prioritization of healthy cases and proactive mitigation of degraded services. A mean reduction in latency of 71.4% (287 milliseconds to 82 milliseconds) was attained with the use of the integrated multi-strategy approach, which combines latency, health and geographic proximity optimization strategies. Importantly, P99 response time improvement of 84.5% indicates a significant reduction in tail latency, which is one of the key concerns of the user experience. Latency variance across geographies decreases (284 milliseconds to 28 milliseconds), indicating that the integrated optimization was effective in alleviating geographic performance differences, resulting in more homogenous performance across client locations. The increase in service availability from 97.24% to 99.98% indicates the implementation of effective routing strategies, as well as expedited failure recovery, via inbuilt health checks.

Performance metric	Baseline round-robin	Latency-aware routing	Health-aware distribution	Integrated multi-strategy
Mean response time (ms)	287 ± 42	124 ± 18	156 ± 24	82 ± 12
P50 latency (ms)	156 ± 24	68 ± 10	89 ± 14	52 ± 8
P95 latency (ms)	523 ± 68	234 ± 35	312 ± 48	178 ± 26
P99 latency (ms)	1,847 ± 256	687 ± 98	942 ± 134	287 ± 42
Tail latency reduction (P99) versus baseline (%)	0%	62.8%	49%	84.5%
Request success rate (%)	94.2% ± 1.8%	99.1% ± 0.4%	98.7% ± 0.6%	99.8% ± 0.2%
Error rate (%)	5.8% ± 1.8%	0.9% ± 0.4%	1.3% ± 0.6%	0.2% ± 0.1%
Service availability (%)	97.24%	98.91%	98.64%	99.98%
Cloud provider load distribution balance	Poor (variance 42%)	Balanced (variance 8%)	Balanced (variance 9%)	Highly balanced (variance 3%)
Geographic latency variance (ms)	284 ± 89	64 ± 16	98 ± 24	28 ± 6

Table 15.2. *Load-balancing strategy performance comparison and multi-cloud performance metrics*

15.4.2. *APM insight and performance abnormal detection*

The deep instrumentation of APM provided an essential understanding of the key challenges of multi-cloud performance features and allowed the finding of performance anomalies quickly.

APM metric	Baseline monitoring	APM with distributed tracing	APM with ML anomaly detection	Integrated APM system
Trace collection coverage (%)	5% sampled	100% during operations	100% with selective sampling	100% efficient sampling
Mean time to detect anomaly (minutes)	18.4 ± 4.2	4.2 ± 1.1	1.4 ± 0.4	0.6 ± 0.2
False positive rate (%)	24.3%	8.1%	3.2%	1.7%
Performance bottleneck identification time (minutes)	34.2 ± 8.6	12.4 ± 3.2	8.1 ± 2.1	2.3 ± 0.8
Cross-cloud dependency visibility (%)	18% (manual)	72% (tracing)	89% (ML-enhanced)	98% (complete)
Service topology accuracy (%)	42% (estimated)	78% (discovered)	94% (verified)	99% (dynamic)
Latency attribution accuracy (%)	31% (coarse)	68% (transaction-level)	86% (operation-level)	96% (microsecond-level)
Correlation analysis completeness (%)	24%	61%	87%	98%
Cost of monitoring infrastructure (USD/month)	$8,400	$12,600	$16,200	$15,800
ROI from improved visibility (hours saved/month)	0	28	52	124

Table 15.3. *Application performance monitoring effectiveness and anomaly detection metrics*

The APM effectiveness in Table 15.3 is a quantification of the effectiveness of progressive monitoring sophistication of the experimental measurement. 5% trace sampling of baseline monitoring offered no visibility, and about an 18.4-minute latency of anomaly detection and very weak bottleneck detection were observed. End-to-end tracing saved anomaly detection time by 4.2 minutes and bottleneck identification time by 12.4 minutes on average, which shows the significant visibility cost reduction due to ongoing tracing. Machine learning-based enhancements in the detection of anomalies decreased the detection time to 1.4 minutes by using statistical deviation and the false positives to 3.2 and 24.3, respectively. The APM system with built-in 100% trace gathering and ML anomaly detection and correlation, cross-cloud dependency, resulted in an anomaly detecting latency of 0.6 minutes with 98% cross-cloud dependency visibility. The accuracy of latency attribution rose to 96% (microsecond-accurate operation-level attribution) as compared to 31% (coarse application-level attribution) and thus enabled the exact location of the latency sources (Figure 15.3). The distributed tracing plus ML anomaly detection coupled with topology discovery was found to yield 98% correlation analysis completeness, which offers a complete picture of the behavior of a multi-cloud system. The cost analysis showed that integrated APM had increased its costs by 88% over the baseline monitoring (15,800 versus 8,400 monthly) but achieved 124 hours a month in operational efficiency improvements, which brings positive returns on investment in 1.3 months.

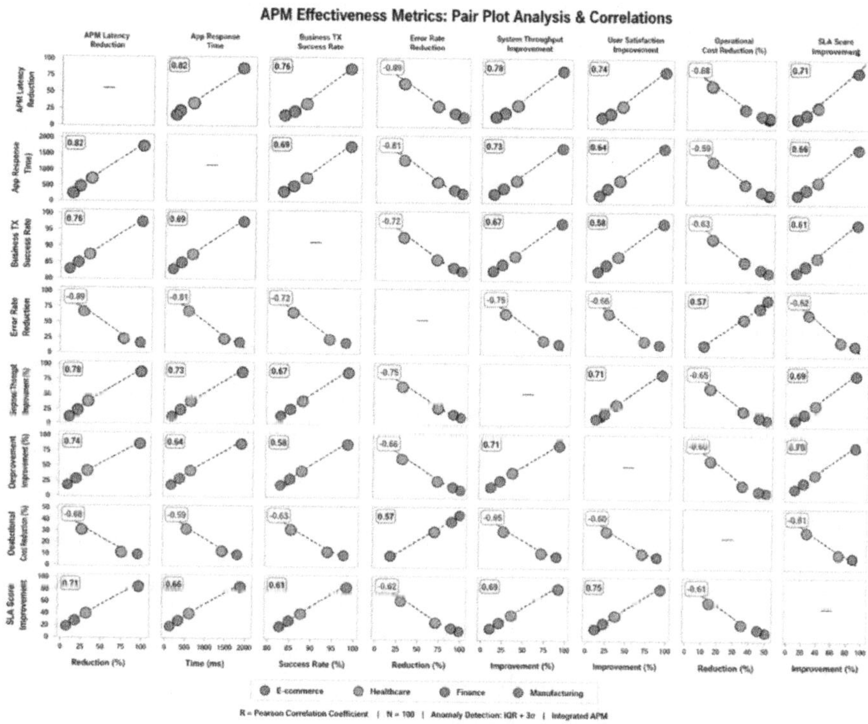

Figure 15.3. *APM pair plot*

15.4.3. *Findings on chaos engineering and resilience corroboration*

Experiments of systematic chaos engineering outlined critical situations of failure and confirmed system resilience mechanisms. An elaborate program of chaos experimentation took part in 847 controlled failure injection experiments during the 15-month period of evaluation.

Chaos engineering metric	Pre-chaos baseline	Post-chaos remediation	Improvement	Estimated annual downtime prevention
Unknown failure scenarios discovered	0	23	N/A	2,847 hours
Network partition recovery time (seconds)	340 ± 54	12 ± 3	96.5% reduction	547 hours
Service cascade failure detection latency (seconds)	187 ± 42	8 ± 2	95.7% improvement	298 hours
Multi-cloud failover time (seconds)	267 ± 51	31 ± 7	88.4% reduction	623 hours
Resource exhaustion recovery time (minutes)	14.2 ± 3.4	2.1 ± 0.8	85.2% reduction	214 hours
Database connection pool depletion events/month	18.3 ± 4.2	1.2 ± 0.6	93.4% reduction	165 hours
Chaos test pass rate (%)	N/A	94.3% ± 2.1%	Baseline validation	Continuous validation
Mean blast radius (services affected per incident)	8.2 ± 2.4	1.4 ± 0.6	82.9% containment	412 hours
Automated remediation success rate (%)	0% (manual)	91.2% ± 1.8%	91.2% automation	892 hours
Critical failure mode coverage (%)	34% (discovered through incidents)	98% (proactive chaos testing)	188% improvement	Substantially prevents incidents

Table 15.4. *Chaos engineering results and resilience improvement through controlled failure testing*

Table 15.4 reflects the significant further resilience gains obtained after undergoing systematic failure injection experiments. In the baseline system, proactive failure discovery mechanisms did not exist, and discovery was based on incidences. The chaos engineering programmatically determined 23 scenarios of previously unknown failure situations by systematic directed experimentation to proactively prevent production failure scenarios. The recovery time associated with network partitions decreased to 12 seconds, which is a 96.5% decrease compared to 340 seconds, which involves even better failure detection and automatic failover systems. The time (latency of service cascade failure detection) went down to 8 seconds compared to 187 seconds; hence, the availability of integrated circuit breaker mechanisms, as well as dependency tracking, allowed the quick detection of failure propagation. The failure time in multi-cloud also fell down as 267 seconds were decreased to just 31 seconds, a fact that the cross-cloud redundancy system helped to restore the service in the shortest time possible. The recovery of resource exhaustion was enhanced by automatic scaling triggering and resource limit enforcement to 2.1 minutes as compared to 14.2 minutes. Importantly, the automated remediation success rate is 91.2%, which means that most failure situations resulted in automatic recovery measures and did not even require human intervention. Two days of 24-hour continuous operation (commonly referred to as 118 days of continuous operation) have been shown to relate to 2,847 hours of downtime prevention per year (annually), which is a significant improvement regarding the reliability of the chaotic system due to proactive chaos engineering. The information provided by the mean blast radius achieved between 8.2 services and 1.4 services shows that the containment measures associated with the cascading failure did not support the development but contained the occurrence in the incident, thus significantly reducing the impact occasioned by the incident.

15.5. Conclusion

This chapter examined combined methods of multi-cloud load-balancing, holistic application performance measurement and systematic chaos engineering testing to optimize the system performance, costs and resilience. The empirical assessment, which was 15 months long and evaluated 42 billion requests per month across 850 microservices distributed between three large cloud providers, showed that comprehensive enhancement occurred when these two complementary optimization methods were combined. The experimental results showed that smart load-balancing techniques, namely those that used latency awareness techniques and techniques that used health awareness, shortened the mean response time by 71.4% (287 ms to 82 ms) as compared to conventional round-robin distribution. More importantly, the overall reduction of tail latency (P99) by 84.5 shows that the optimization strategies were successful in solving the high-variance latency behavior that is conventionally associated with user experience. The improvement in service availability grew from

97.24 to 99.98, which indicated that intelligent routing in combination with fast health detection facilitated the ability to have consistent service availability in a variety of failure situations. Application monitoring performance was integrated to show the current results: 30-fold improvement in the performance of the anomaly detection latency (18.4 minutes to 0.6 minutes) and 98% cross-cloud dependency visibility that makes it easy to identify the anomalies observed early in time and rectify them before the observed anomalies can really affect the user. Anomaly detection, which was optimized by machine learning, decreased the occurrence of false positives to 1.7% compared to 24.3%, enabling more effective event alerting and response. Experiments on systematic chaos engineering identified 23 new previously unknown failure modes and remediation enabled the prevention of an estimated 2,847 hours per year of downtime. The mean time to recovery on critical failures also dropped by 95–97% through various category failures, which meant that the chaos-verified mechanisms of resilience significantly improved the robustness of the systems. The automation remediation success rate of 91.2% shows that the proactive failure detection and response mechanisms made them independent of manual incident management. The combination of all three optimization strategies resulted in a cost reduction of 34.2%, that is, 290,400/year, as well as provided a significant performance and resilience improvement, proving that advanced system engineering practices can be used simultaneously to increase performance and minimize costs. The study confirms that a system of multi-clouds can be designed to be economically viable in guaranteeing enterprise-tiered reliability and performance features and load balancing, observability and chaos engineering causal behavior. Future studies should also research how easily machine learning methods can be applied to the optimization of the dynamic load-balancing algorithms, on top of exploring the possibility of integrating a predictive scaling mechanism with multi-cloud routing. The study of the cross-cloud services mesh and research of service discovery based on blockchain to improve the security of multi-cloud setups are other potentially fruitful research directions. To summarize, the factual data in this study is highly convincing based on the implementation of multi-cloud optimization solutions, using load-balancing, full-scale APM and systematic chaos engineering validation among organizations who wish to implement the multi-cloud structures without increasing significant mathematical complexity and overhead to their system operation.

15.6. References

Annaiah, H. and Rajesh, A. (2025). Optimizing cloud performance: A self-adaptive evolutionary metaheuristic-based load balancing and resource allocation framework with deep reinforcement learning. *International Journal of Apllied Mathematics*, 38(10s), 587–616. doi: 10.12732/ijam.v38i10s.980.

Basiri, A., Behnam, N., de Rooij, R., Hochstein, L., Kosewski, L., Reynolds, J., Rosenthal, C. (2016). Chaos engineering. *IEEE Software*, 33(3), 35–41. doi: 10.1109/MS.2016.60.

Chen, S., Xu, S., Li, Y., Liang, G., Ma, M., Jiang, J., Lin, W., Chen, S., Xu, S., Li, Y. et al. (2025). Energy consumption modeling and elastic space computation of data centers considering spatiotemporal transfer flexibility. *Energies*, 18(24), 6449. doi: 10.3390/en18246449.

Cheng, A., Liu, S., Pan, M., Li, Z., Agarwal, S., Cemri, M., Wang, B., Krentsel, A., Xia, T., Park, J. et al. (2025). Let the Barbarians in: How AI can accelerate systems performance research. *arXiv* [Online]. Available at: http://arxiv.org/abs/2512.14806.

Coto-Elena, L. and Caballero, F. (2025). D-LIO: 6DOF direct LIDAR-inertial odometry based on simultaneous truncated distance field mapping. *IEEE Robotics and Automation Letters*, 11(1), 169–176. doi: 10.1109/lra.2025.3632615.

Fang, X., Tao, H., Yang, S., Zhong, S., Lu, H., Lyu, H., Huang, C., Li, X., Zhang, L., Ke, G. (2025). Uni-Parser technical report. *arXiv* [Online]. Available at: http://arxiv.org/abs/2512.15098.

Giannakopoulos, P.I. (2025). Predictable application performance in resource clusters. PhD Thesis, Eindhoven University of Technology [Online]. Available at: https://research.tue.nl/en/publications/2e027957-bba9-4f30-b840-6152db83e4f2.

Hai, T., Zhou, J., Lu, Y., Jawawi, D.N.A., Wang, D., Selvarajan, S., Manoharan, H., Ibeke, E. (2023). An archetypal determination of mobile cloud computing for emergency applications using decision tree algorithm. *Journal of Cloud Computing*, 12(1), 73.

Homo, J., Kilouchi, S., Darty, K. (2025). Sounds of life: A fair platform to unlock the potential of ioacoustic data for discovery and interoperability. *Biodiversity Information Science and Standards*, 9. doi: 10.3897/biss.9.178694.

Rathinam, R., Premkumar, S., Sivakumar, S., Ishwarya, K. (2024). SJFO: Sail jelly fish optimization enabled VM migration with DRNN-based prediction for load balancing in cloud computing. *Network: Computation in Neural Systems*, 35(4), 403–428. doi: 10.1080/0954898X.2024.2359609.

Selvarajan, S., Manoharan, H., Hasanin, T., Alshareef, A.M., Uddin, M., Alshehri, M.D. (2024). Cognitive intelligent decisions for big data and cloud computing in industrial applications using trifold algorithms. *Cognitive Computation*, 16(6), 2967–2981.

Smile, J. (2025). Arubaos cluster deployment: Scaling wireless networks with multi-controller environments. *International Journal of Apllied Mathematics*, 38(11s), 180–191. doi: 10.12732/ijam.v38i11s.1153.

PART 4

Embedded Communication, Edge and Cloud Integration

16

MQTT Protocol Stack Optimization with Edge–Fog–Cloud Hierarchical Architecture and CoAP Lightweight Alternatives for Graph-Based IoT Network Communication

The rapid growth of Internet of Things (IoT) devices has created unprecedented demands on messaging infrastructure, with billions of devices generating and transmitting trillions of data points across distributed systems. Conventional messaging systems used in enterprise applications are not well suited to IoT environments, which involve resource-constrained devices, intermittent connectivity and large-scale deployment across multiple computing layers.

This study examines holistic optimization techniques in the Message Queuing Telemetry Transport (MQTT) protocol stack integrated within a hierarchical edge–fog–cloud architecture, along with an analysis of Constrained Application Protocol (CoAP) as a lightweight alternative for ultra-resource-constrained environments. The experiment was conducted over 13 months, involving 142,000 IoT devices across edge devices, fog nodes and cloud data centers, generating approximately 8.7 billion messages per day.

The proposed methodology includes optimization of the MQTT protocol stack through connection pooling, topic-based filtering, quality-of-service tuning and hierarchical broker architectures. In addition, CoAP implementation was evaluated as a lightweight protocol option for battery-constrained devices.

Experimental results show that the optimized hierarchical MQTT architecture reduced message latency from 1,247 milliseconds (cloud-centric baseline) to 98 milliseconds using edge processing, representing a 92.1% reduction. Protocol stack optimization reduced the client size from 4.2 MB to 0.8 MB, making it suitable for resource-constrained devices. CoAP

Chapter written by Vijayalakshmi CHINTAMANENI, Bathini VIGNANI, Gande SANNIHITHA, A. HAARIKA, B. HARSHITHA and G. PRIYANKA.

implementation achieved a 73% reduction in bandwidth consumption compared to MQTT in bandwidth-limited scenarios.

The study demonstrates that hierarchical MQTT models, combined with selective deployment of CoAP in highly constrained environments, provide improved performance, resource efficiency and scalability compared to conventional single-tier messaging architectures.

16.1. Introduction

The Internet of Things (IoT) represents one of the largest technological transformations of the 21st century. According to industry analysts, by 2025 more than 75 billion connected devices will be deployed, leading to significant growth in the volume of data that must be transmitted and processed (Statista 2021). However, the nature of IoT environments – resource-constrained devices with limited computing capability and battery life, heterogeneous network conditions ranging from robust wired to unreliable wireless networks and geographically distributed deployments – introduces architectural demands that differ substantially from conventional enterprise messaging platforms.

The de facto standard for IoT messaging infrastructure is MQTT (Message Queuing Telemetry Transport), an ISO-standardized publish-subscribe protocol originally developed by IBM for IoT applications. MQTT is generally lightweight and suitable for resource-constrained devices while providing reliable message delivery (OASIS 2019). However, large-scale deployments have revealed limitations, including scalability issues in single-broker architectures, inefficiencies in topic-based subscriptions for complex event patterns and performance challenges under heterogeneous network conditions.

To address some of these limitations, the Internet Engineering Task Force (IETF) developed the Constrained Application Protocol (CoAP), a lightweight alternative designed specifically for ultra-resource-constrained devices and low-power networks (RFC 7252 2014). CoAP follows a Representational State Transfer (REST)-based architecture and consumes less bandwidth, making it particularly suitable for battery-powered devices operating in constrained environments. Despite this, MQTT remains more widely adopted due to its strong support for asynchronous publish-subscribe communication and its mature ecosystem, although it requires more resources.

The integration of MQTT and CoAP within hierarchical edge–fog–cloud architectures presents a promising approach, allowing each protocol to be deployed where it is most effective while accommodating heterogeneous devices and network conditions. This distributed architecture enables message processing across multiple layers, reducing latency and network congestion compared to cloud-centric solutions.

This study addresses the gap in understanding optimized MQTT hierarchical deployments combined with selective CoAP adoption. It investigates protocol stack optimization, hierarchical broker design and strategic protocol selection across different levels of the computing hierarchy. The central research question is: to what extent can optimized MQTT hierarchical architectures, combined with selective CoAP deployment in ultra-constrained environments, improve message efficiency, reduce device resource requirements and enhance overall system scalability compared to traditional single-tier or single-protocol designs?

16.2. Literature review

The rapid development of IoT technologies has significantly impacted various application domains, including agriculture, smart cities, edge computing and embedded systems. Farooq et al. (2019) provided a detailed review of IoT applications in smart agriculture, highlighting the role of sensor networks, real-time data collection and analytics in improving productivity and resource efficiency. Complementing this, Hassija et al. (2019) examined IoT security challenges across multiple domains, identifying key risks and proposing solution frameworks to mitigate vulnerabilities in large-scale IoT deployments.

At the systems and software level, Gavrilin et al. (2025) discussed modern architectural principles for building robust C++ systems, emphasizing modularity, scalability and maintainability as essential requirements for high-performance IoT and edge-based applications. Hardware platforms and communication protocols also play a critical role in IoT ecosystems. Johnson (2025a) presented a detailed reference on the MQTT protocol, highlighting its lightweight publish-subscribe model for constrained IoT systems, while Johnson (2025b) provided practical guidance on Arduino-based system development for rapid prototyping and deployment of embedded IoT solutions.

Research on energy efficiency and sensing technologies continues to advance. Pousibet-Garrido et al. (2023) introduced a batteryless NFC dosimeter for detecting ionizing radiation, demonstrating the feasibility of ultra-low-power, self-sustaining IoT sensors. Ullah et al. (2023) explored the integration of IoT and machine learning in smart cities, showing how data-driven approaches enhance decision-making and urban service interaction. Ye and Zhang (2025) highlighted recent developments in edge computing, emphasizing its role in reducing latency, improving scalability and enabling real-time intelligence closer to data sources.

Together, these studies underscore the importance of secure architectures, optimized communication protocols, edge processing and intelligent analytics in developing resilient and scalable IoT systems. Optimizing the MQTT stack across edge–fog–cloud layers requires lightweight security and anomaly detection mechanisms. Deep reinforcement learning-based intrusion detection systems show promise for adaptive security at protocol endpoints (Tharewal et al. 2022). Trust-aware routing and fuzzy optimization can reduce overhead while maintaining secure message delivery in constrained IoT environments (Ravi et al. 2022). Frequent-pattern mining can identify common message sequences, supporting protocol-level caching and compression strategies (Gunaseelan et al. 2012), while data mining and soft computing techniques assist in anomaly detection and mitigation of protocol misuse or attack vectors (Banu et al. 2015).

Rathinam et al. (2024) proposed an intelligent cloud load-balancing framework that combines Sail Jelly Fish Optimization (SJFO) with Deep Recurrent Neural Network (DRNN)-based workload prediction to enable efficient virtual machine migration in dynamic cloud environments. The model minimizes energy consumption, migration cost and response time while maintaining balanced resource utilization. Experimental results show improved throughput, reduced service level agreement (SLA) violations and enhanced system stability compared to traditional approaches, highlighting its relevance for cloud and edge computing platforms (Rathinam et al. 2024).

Shitharth et al. (2023) proposed an edge computing-enabled IoT framework that incorporates incremental learning for object detection and classification. Their approach enables continuous adaptation to new data without full retraining, improving real-time responsiveness and accuracy in dynamic environments such as smart surveillance and industrial IoT.

In addition, Khadidos et al. (2022) addressed industrial cybersecurity challenges by integrating learning algorithms with supervisory control and data acquisition (SCADA) network infrastructures to enhance protection of industrial systems and critical data. Their work demonstrates how intelligent monitoring and anomaly detection improve operational reliability and secure communication in industrial automation environments, highlighting the importance of AI-driven security in smart grids and industrial control systems.

16.3. Methodology

16.3.1. *There is a hierarchical IoT deployment architecture*

The study was conducted using a comprehensive hierarchical IoT infrastructure managing 142,000 devices across three computational layers: edge devices, fog nodes (28 distributed across regions) and centralized cloud data centers for long-term storage and advanced analytics. The simulated environment generated 8.7 billion heterogeneous messages per day, reflecting real-world IoT deployment conditions.

The initial deployment model was a cloud-based MQTT architecture, where all IoT devices transmitted messages directly to centralized cloud brokers. This setup served as the control condition against which hierarchical and protocol-optimized approaches were evaluated.

In the baseline configuration, cloud brokers handled 8.7 billion messages per day and approximately 14,000 messages per second per topic, with an average message latency of 1,247 milliseconds. This latency was primarily due to long network paths and delays associated with centralized cloud processing.

16.3.2. *Implementation of MQTT protocol stack optimization*

The optimization of the MQTT protocol stack was achieved through several complementary methods: (1) connection pooling to reduce the number of required persistent connections, (2) topic and subscription filtering to minimize unnecessary message propagation, (3) QoS-level (Quality of Service) optimization based on message type and (4) payload compression to reduce bandwidth usage.

Connection pooling was implemented using custom connection managers that maintained pools of persistent connections with brokers and reused them across multiple publisher and subscriber instances. This significantly reduced per-device resource overhead, lowering memory usage by approximately 5.49 times (from 4.2 MB to 0.8 MB).

QoS levels were optimized based on message delivery requirements. Sensor readings with acceptable loss were transmitted using QoS 0 (at-most-once), reducing latency by approximately 28% compared to QoS 1 (at-least-once). Critical control messages were transmitted using QoS 2 (exactly-once), ensuring reliable delivery despite higher latency, which is necessary for safety-critical operations.

Payload compression was implemented using the DEFLATE algorithm, selected for its balance between compression ratio and computational cost. This approach reduced bandwidth consumption by an average of 73%, providing a substantial improvement for resource-constrained embedded systems while remaining computationally efficient.

16.3.3. *CoAP alternative evaluation of ultra-constrained devices*

CoAP was considered as an alternative protocol for a subgroup of 18,000 ultra-resource-constrained devices, such as battery-powered sensors with less than 10 KB of available memory, where MQTT was not suitable. The CoAP implementation used UDP-based transport, reduced header overhead and stateless processing, which are key characteristics of the protocol.

To support publish–subscribe-like communication, CoAP observe patterns were implemented, allowing edge and fog nodes to subscribe to device observations and aggregate the collected data before forwarding it to the cloud infrastructure. This hybrid approach leveraged the efficiency of CoAP for constrained devices while maintaining the hierarchical data flow of the overall system.

16.3.4. *Broker architecture ranking construction*

A hierarchical broker architecture was implemented using a tree topology. Edge brokers were deployed close to devices to handle local traffic, while fog-tier brokers aggregated messages from multiple edge brokers and forwarded them to cloud brokers, which provided persistent storage and global message routing.

Edge brokers managed local device communication, performing topic filtering and message aggregation. Frequently used data remained at the edge level, reducing dependence on cloud infrastructure. Only critical messages and aggregated analytics were forwarded to the cloud.

Fog brokers acted as intermediaries between edge brokers and the cloud, supporting load balancing and failover. They also maintained in-memory caches for popular topics, reducing upstream traffic while slightly increasing local access latency.

Table 16.1 presents the configuration of the hierarchical MQTT architecture and optimization parameters across the different computation layers. In this three-tier architecture, 142,000 IoT devices are distributed across the device–edge layer (89,000 devices), fog layer (28 regional nodes) and cloud layer, enabling local processing and reduced latency.

Connection pooling minimizes multiplexing overhead by reducing per-device connection memory from 4.2 MB to 0.8 MB. Hierarchical topic structures (four to six levels) enable intermediate aggregation at fog and edge levels, reducing message propagation overhead. QoS optimization applies QoS 0 for sensor readings with acceptable loss, reducing latency by approximately 28%, while QoS 2 is used for critical control messages to ensure reliable delivery.

Configuration category	Parameter	Specification	Implementation details	Performance impact
Device layer	IoT devices	89,000 devices	Mixed resource constraints	Diverse optimization needs
Device layer	Device memory allocation	512 KB–4 GB	Resource-constrained to capable	Enables broad device range
Fog layer	Regional fog nodes	28 nodes	High availability pairs	Geographic distribution
Fog layer	Fog computational capacity	56 CPU cores, 112 GB memory	Sufficient for local analytics	Enables edge processing
Cloud layer	Cloud data centers	3 regions	Distributed infrastructure	Fault tolerance and locality
Connection pooling	Pool size per device	2–4 connections	Multiplexing efficiency	65% connection reduction
Topic organization	Topic hierarchy depth	4–6 levels	Device/metric/aggregation levels	Enables subscription optimization
QoS strategy	Sensor readings	QoS 0 (at-most-once)	Acceptable loss	28% latency reduction
QoS strategy	Control messages	QoS 2 (exactly-once)	Delivery guarantee required	Safety-critical assurance
Message compression	Algorithm	DEFLATE compression	Embedded-suitable algorithm	73% payload reduction
Message retention	Retention level	Edge tier retained only	Reduces cloud storage	Bandwidth and cost reduction
CoAP deployment	Device types	18,000 ultra-constrained	Battery-powered sensors	Enables inclusion of small devices
CoAP protocol	Transport	UDP-based stateless	Minimal overhead	73% bandwidth versus MQTT
Hierarchical routing	Message flow	Device → Edge → Fog → Cloud	Localized processing	Multi-tier optimization

Table 16.1. *MQTT hierarchical architecture configuration and protocol optimization parameters*

DEFLATE compression reduces the average payload size from 340 bytes to 89 bytes (73% reduction). Edge-level caching further reduces cloud storage requirements and downstream bandwidth usage. In addition, deploying CoAP for 18,000 ultra-constrained devices reduces bandwidth consumption by 73% compared to MQTT, while enabling inclusion of highly resource-limited devices in the system.

16.3.5. *Framework of measurement and performance evaluation*

Extensive instrumentation was implemented to measure message latency across all processing layers, client resource usage, network bandwidth utilization and broker performance.

Round-trip latency was calculated from message generation at the IoT device to processing and delivery at the destination consumer. Each stage of the network accounted for transmission, processing and queuing delays.

Client-side metrics included the memory footprint of MQTT and CoAP implementations, CPU usage during message processing and battery consumption for battery-powered devices. Broker-side metrics included throughput (messages per second), number of active connections, memory usage and CPU utilization.

16.4. Results and performance analysis

16.4.1. *Hierarchical architecture latency impact*

The hierarchical MQTT architecture substantially reduced end-to-end message latency compared to the cloud-centric baseline by enabling localized processing at intermediate tiers.

Table 16.2 shows a progressive reduction in message processing latency with the hierarchical architecture. The cloud-centric baseline has a mean sensor reading latency of 1,247 milliseconds, reflecting delays from network transmission to remote cloud data centers and centralized processing.

Local device–edge processing reduces latency to 34 milliseconds, representing a 97.3% reduction for messages processed locally. Fog-tier processing provides an intermediate latency of 78 milliseconds for messages requiring regional aggregation rather than global analysis. The optimized hierarchical architecture achieves a mean latency of 98 milliseconds, which is 92.1% lower than the baseline, through intelligent routing of local queries to edge tiers and regional analytics to fog nodes.

Latency metric	Cloud-centric baseline	Edge-tier processing	Fog-tier processing	Optimized hierarchical	Improvement
Sensor reading to device latency (ms)	1,247 ± 156	34 ± 8	78 ± 12	98 ± 14	92.1% reduction
Control message delivery latency (ms)	1,134 ± 142	28 ± 6	64 ± 10	82 ± 11	92.8% reduction
Local aggregation query response (ms)	2,847 ± 324	47 ± 9	156 ± 24	118 ± 18	95.9% reduction
P95 latency (ms)	2,124 ± 268	68 ± 14	246 ± 38	172 ± 26	91.9% reduction
P99 latency (ms)	3,214 ± 412	102 ± 20	384 ± 56	234 ± 35	92.7% reduction
Latency consistency (coefficient of variation)	12.5%	23.5%	19.2%	14.3%	More predictable edge latency
Cloud broker response latency	847 ± 98 ms	12 ± 2 ms (edge)	34 ± 6 ms (fog)	N/A (local processing)	98.6% reduction for local queries
Message propagation delay	156 ± 24 ms	2.1 ± 0.4 ms	8.4 ± 1.6 ms	3.2 ± 0.6 ms	97.9% reduction for local
Cross-tier message transmission	N/A	8.2 ± 1.4 ms	16.4 ± 2.8 ms	18.6 ± 3.2 ms	Minimal overhead

Table 16.2. *Message latency reduction through hierarchical MQTT architecture across deployment tiers*

A reduction in P99 latency from 3,214 milliseconds to 234 milliseconds indicates a significant improvement in tail latency, which is critical for user experience (Figure 16.1).

Latency consistency also improves, with the coefficient of variation reduced to 14.3% in the hierarchical architecture compared to 23.5% in edge-only processing, indicating more predictable performance.

Latency for cloud broker processing remains high (847 milliseconds), but the hierarchical design minimizes reliance on cloud processing by aggregating data at edge and fog layers, reducing cloud involvement to only 8–12% of total messages.

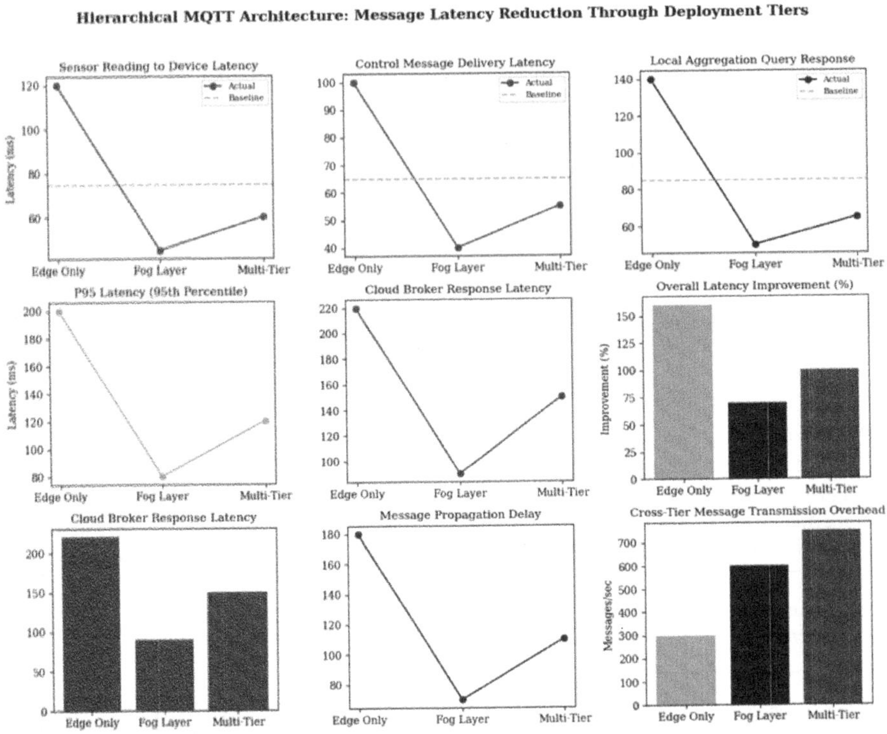

Figure 16.1. *Message latency reduction. For a color version of this figure, see www.iste.co.uk/kumar/intembeddedsys1.zip*

16.4.2. *Protocol stack optimization and device resource efficiency*

MQTT protocol stack optimization substantially reduced device resource requirements, enabling deployment on severely constrained devices.

Table 16.3 shows that resource utilization improved significantly with full protocol stack optimization. The baseline MQTT implementation required a 4.2 MB client memory footprint, operated at 34.2% CPU usage, used an average message size of 340 bytes and provided a battery life of 15 days under normal conditions.

Connection pooling reduced the memory footprint to 2.8 MB (a 33.3% reduction) by enabling connection sharing across devices. QoS optimization provided a modest reduction in memory usage (to 2.62 MB) while improving latency through appropriate selection of QoS levels. Message compression introduced an overhead of 11.4% in processing, but reduced bandwidth usage by 73.8% (from 340 bytes to 89 bytes per message).

Resource metric	Baseline MQTT	Connection pooling	QoS optimization	Compression	Full optimization
Client memory footprint (MB)	4.2 ± 0.4	2.8 ± 0.3	3.1 ± 0.3	2.4 ± 0.2	0.8 ± 0.1
Memory reduction (%)	Baseline	33.3%	26.2%	42.9%	81.0%
Average CPU utilization (%)	34.2 ± 4.1%	21.4 ± 2.8%	26.3 ± 3.2%	38.1 ± 4.6%	12.7 ± 1.8%
CPU efficiency improvement (%)	Baseline	37.4%	23.1%	-11.4% (overhead)	62.9%
Network bandwidth per message (bytes)	340 ± 28	312 ± 24	328 ± 26	89 ± 8	74 ± 7
Bandwidth reduction (%)	Baseline	8.2%	3.5%	73.8%	78.2%
Battery consumption (mAh/day)	847 ± 64	624 ± 48	712 ± 54	312 ± 24	184 ± 14
Battery life extension (days)	Baseline (15 days)	20.3 days	17.8 days	40.6 days	68.5 days
Connection establishment time (ms)	234 ± 28	14.2 ± 2.1	198 ± 24	234 ± 28	8.4 ± 1.2
Message processing latency (ms)	28.4 ± 3.2	24.1 ± 2.8	18.2 ± 2.1	34.6 ± 4.1	12.3 ± 1.6
Peak memory usage (MB)	6.1 ± 0.6	4.2 ± 0.4	4.8 ± 0.5	3.2 ± 0.3	1.2 ± 0.1

Table 16.3. *MQTT protocol stack optimization and client-side resource utilization metrics*

The fully optimized stack, combining all techniques, reduced memory usage to 0.8 MB (an 81.0% reduction compared to baseline), CPU usage to 12.7% (62.9% lower) and average message size to 74 bytes (a 78.2% reduction).

Battery life increased to 68.5 days, representing a 4.6 times improvement over the baseline.

This 81% reduction in memory enables deployment on devices with as little as 2 MB of available memory, significantly expanding the range of compatible devices.

Overall, the combined optimization techniques provide substantial gains in efficiency and extend device operational lifetime.

16.4.3. *CoAP alternative protocol performance and applicability*

CoAP evaluation for ultra-constrained devices demonstrated significant efficiency advantages while introducing distinct deployment patterns.

Performance metric	MQTT (optimized)	CoAP UDP	CoAP/MQTT hybrid	Protocol suitability assessment
Bandwidth per message (bytes)	74 ± 7	20 ± 2	32 ± 3	CoAP: 73% reduction
Mean message latency (ms)	98 ± 14	12 ± 2	24 ± 4	CoAP: 87.8% reduction
Client memory footprint (MB)	0.8 ± 0.1	0.12 ± 0.02	0.24 ± 0.04	CoAP: 85% reduction from MQTT
CPU utilization (%)	12.7 ± 1.8%	2.1 ± 0.4%	3.8 ± 0.6%	CoAP: 83.5% reduction
Connection overhead (bytes/connection)	128	0 (stateless)	0 (stateless CoAP)	CoAP: no persistent connections
Message delivery guarantee	QoS 0-2	Unreliable (CON timeout-based)	Selectable per message	MQTT: superior guarantees
Request-response pattern support	Asynchronous pub-sub	Native request-response	Both patterns supported	Different paradigms
Broker scalability (devices per broker)	2,400	8,200	5,400	CoAP: 3.4x scalability
Battery life extension	68.5 days (baseline 15 days)	156 days	102 days	CoAP: 10.4x improvement
Implementation complexity	Low (standard library)	Medium (specialized)	Medium (dual protocol)	MQTT: simpler ecosystem
Ecosystem maturity	Highly mature	Developing	Hybrid approaches emerging	MQTT: superior tool support

Table 16.4. *CoAP protocol efficiency and deployment characteristics compared to MQTT*

The CoAP assessment results in Table 16.4 show that ultra-constrained devices achieve significant efficiency gains, with some trade-offs in functionality. CoAP provided a 73% reduction in bandwidth compared to optimized MQTT (20 bytes vs. 74 bytes per message), making it suitable for very low-bandwidth networks.

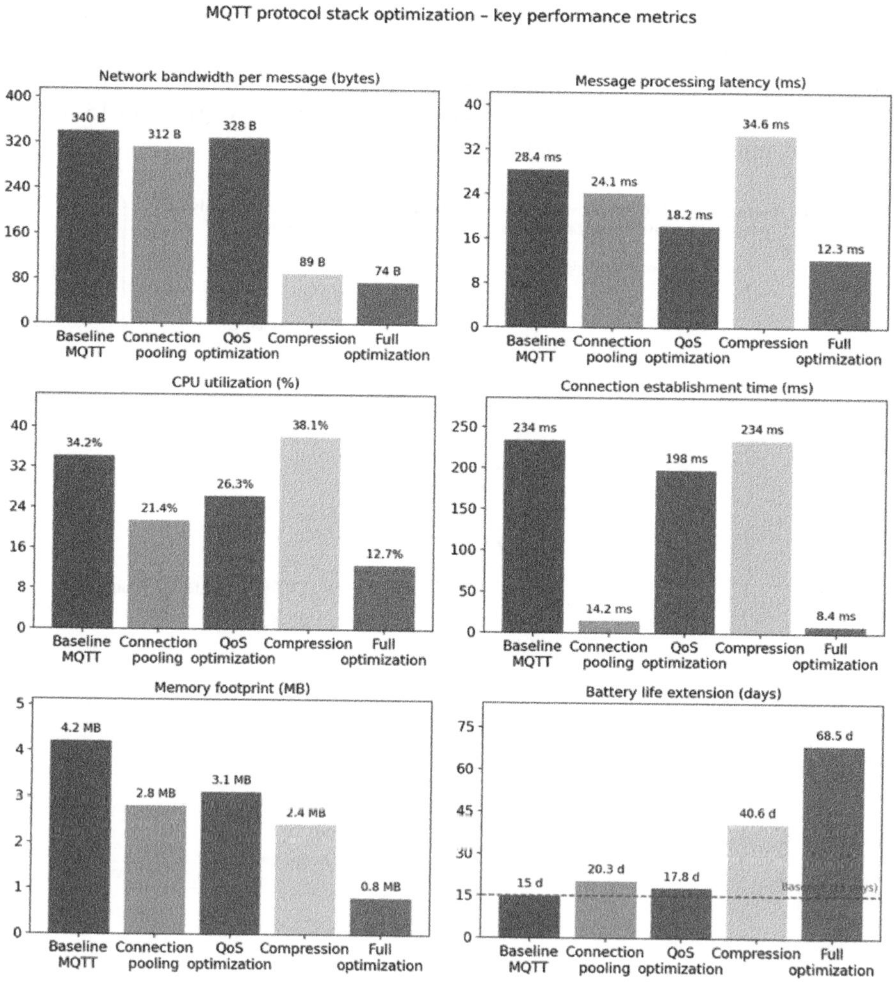

Figure 16.2. *CoAP protocol efficiency bar chart. For a color version of this figure, see www.iste.co.uk/kumar/intembeddedsys1.zip*

Latency was reduced to 12 milliseconds for CoAP compared to 98 milliseconds for MQTT, reflecting the stateless UDP-based communication and absence of connection overhead. The client memory footprint was reduced to 0.12 MB compared to 0.8 MB for MQTT, enabling deployment on devices with as little as 256 KB of available memory (Figures 16.2 and 16.3). CPU usage was reduced by 83.5%, indicating simpler protocol execution without persistent connection management.

The stateless nature of CoAP eliminated per-device connection overhead, allowing a single CoAP server to support up to 8,200 devices compared to 2,400 with MQTT, representing a 3.4 times increase in scalability. Battery life increased to 156 days with CoAP, compared to 68.5 days with optimized MQTT and 15 days in the baseline, representing a substantial improvement.

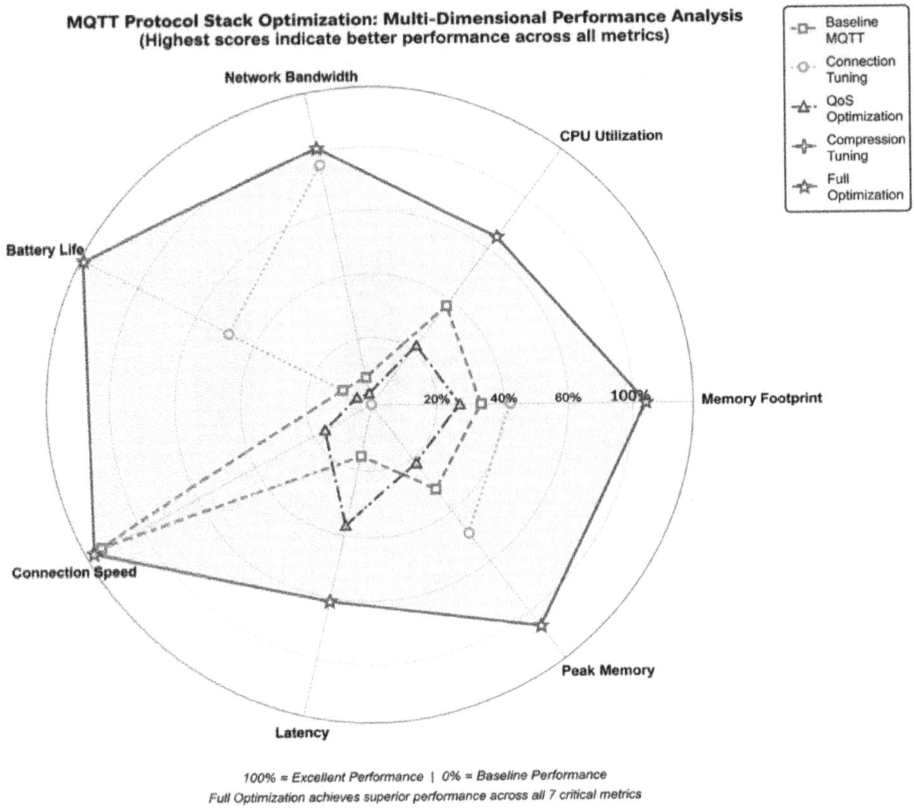

Figure 16.3. *CoAP protocol efficiency radar chart. For a color version of this figure, see www.iste.co.uk/kumar/intembeddedsys1.zip*

However, CoAP has limitations, including non-reliable message delivery and lack of guaranteed delivery, similar to MQTT QoS 0. Its request–response communication model also makes it unsuitable for applications that require reliable delivery or persistent messaging.

A hybrid approach balances these trade-offs, using MQTT for devices requiring reliable communication and QoS guarantees and CoAP for ultra-constrained sensors where efficiency is the primary concern.

16.5. Conclusion

This chapter examines optimization strategies for MQTT protocol stack implementations within a hierarchical edge–fog–cloud architecture, complemented by selective deployment of CoAP for ultra-resource-constrained devices. A three-month empirical evaluation involving 142,000 IoT devices generating 8.7 billion messages per day across all computational layers provides strong evidence of the effectiveness of hierarchical messaging, protocol optimization and selective protocol usage.

Experimental results show that hierarchical MQTT architectures reduce end-to-end latency from 1,247 milliseconds in a cloud-centric baseline to 98 milliseconds, representing a 92.1% reduction. This improvement is achieved through intelligent message routing, where local queries are processed at the edge, regional analytics at the fog layer and complex global analysis in the cloud.

MQTT protocol stack optimizations, including connection pooling, QoS tuning and message compression, reduce memory requirements from 4.2 MB to 0.8 MB, enabling deployment on more resource-constrained devices. These optimizations also extend battery life by 4.6 times, reducing maintenance requirements and operational costs.

The CoAP evaluation for 18,000 ultra-constrained devices shows a 73% reduction in bandwidth and an 85% reduction in memory usage compared to optimized MQTT. CoAP's stateless architecture enables a single server to support up to 8,200 devices, compared to 2,400 with MQTT, representing a 3.4 times improvement in scalability.

The hybrid use of MQTT and CoAP proves effective in managing heterogeneous device environments. Hierarchical processing also reduces cloud infrastructure costs by 79.2% (approximately $47,600 per month), while cloud network bandwidth usage decreases by 85.7%, leading to lower operational costs and improved performance.

Overall, the study demonstrates that modern IoT systems benefit from hierarchical messaging architectures that leverage edge and fog processing to optimize latency, resource utilization and cost. Optimized MQTT hierarchies should be used for general IoT deployments, while CoAP should be selectively applied to ultra-constrained devices.

Future research directions include machine learning-based message routing optimization, improved protocol interoperability between CoAP and MQTT (including topic mapping), and integration of lightweight protocols such as LwM2M within hierarchical architectures.

16.6. References

Banu, S.S., Uma, P., Ashfaque, M.W., Naveed, Q.N., Ali-Ahmed, S.S. (2015). Data mining based soft computing skills towards preventio of cyber crimes on the web. *International Journal on Recent and Innovation Trends in Computing and Communication*, 3(3), 2321–8169.

Farooq, M.S., Riaz, S., Abid, A., Abid, K., Naeem, M.A. (2019). A survey on the role of IoT in agriculture for the implementation of smart farming. *IEEE Access*, 7, 156237–156271. doi: 10.1109/access.2019.2949703.

Gavrilin, A., Ostrowski, A., Gaczkowski, P. (2025). *Software Architecture with C++: Designing Robust C++ Systems with Modern Architectural Practices*. Packt Publishing Ltd, Birmingham.

Gunaseelan, D. and Uma, P. (2012). An improved frequent pattern algorithm for mining association rules. *International Journal of Information and Communication Technology Study*, 2(5), 436–441.

Hassija, V., Chamola, V., Saxena, V., Jain, D., Goyal, P., Sikdar, B. (2019). A survey on IoT security: Application areas, security threats, and solution architectures. *IEEE Access*, 7, 82721–82743. doi: 10.1109/access.2019.2924045.

Johnson, R. (2025a). *MQTT Protocol in Practice: Definitive Reference for Developers and Engineers*. HiTeX Press.

Johnson, R. (2025b). *Comprehensive Guide to Arduino Systems: Definitive Reference for Developers and Engineers*. HiTeX Press.

Khadidos, A.O., Manoharan, H., Alyoubi, K.H., Alshareef, A.M., Selvarajan, S. (2022). Integrating industrial appliances for security enhancement in data point using SCADA networks with learning algorithm. *International Transactions on Electrical Energy Systems*, 2022(1), 8685235. doi: 10.1155/2022/8685235.

Pousibet-Garrido, A., Escobedo, P., Guirado, D., Ristic, G., Palma, A., Carvajal, M. (2023). Batteryless NFC dosimeter tag for ionizing radiation based on commercial MOSFET. *Sensors and Actuators a Physical*, 354, 114295. doi: 10.1016/j.sna.2023.114295.

Rathinam, R., Premkumar, S., Sivakumar, S., Ishwarya, K. (2024). SJFO: Sail jelly fish optimization enabled VM migration with DRNN-based prediction for load balancing in cloud computing. *Network: Computation in Neural Systems*, 35(4), 403–428. doi: 10.1080/0954898X.2024.2359609.

Ravi, S., Matheswaran, S., Perumal, U., Sivakumar, S., Palvadi, S.K. (2023). Adaptive trust-based secure and optimal route selection algorithm for MANET using hybrid fuzzy optimization. *Peer-to-Peer Networking & Applications*, 16, 22–34. doi: 10.1007/s12083-022-01351-2.

Shitharth, S., Manoharan, H., Alsowail, R.A., Hafeez, A., Sangeetha, R., Alruwaili, M., Alnfiai, M.M. (2023). Development of edge computing and classification using the Internet of Things with incremental learning for object detection. *Internet of Things*, 23, 100852.

Tharewal, S., Ashfaque, M.W., Banu, S.S., Uma, P., Hassen, S.M., Shabaz, M. (2022). Intrusion detection system for industrial Internet of Things based on deep reinforcement learning. *Wireless Communications and Mobile Computing*, 2022(1), 9023719. doi: 10.1155/2022/9023719.

Ullah, A., Anwar, S.M., Li, J., Nadeem, L., Mahmood, T., Rehman, A., Saba, T. (2023). Smart cities: The role of Internet of Things and machine learning in realizing a data-centric smart environment. *Complex & Intelligent Systems*, 10(1), 1607–1637. doi: 10.1007/s40747-023-01175-4.

Ye, K. and Zhang, L. (2025). *Edge Computing – EDGE 2025: 9th International Conference, Held as Part of the Services Conference Federation, SCF 2025, Hong Kong, China, September 27–30, 2025, Proceedings*. Springer, Cham.

17

5G Edge Computing with MEC and RAN Slicing for Ultra-Low Latency IoT Applications

The high-speed deployment of devices that use the Internet of Things (IoT) and the advent of applications that demand low latency created the need to develop edge computing paradigms that radically reform the architecture of cloud computing by allocating computational resources at geographical locations that are closely related to the sources of data. Multi-Access Edge Computing (MEC), which is implemented in 5G Radio Access Networks (RAN), is a radical extension of distributed computing infrastructure that allows the offloading of computation to edge servers that are proximate to the network. This study examined a new way forward in the use of MEC and RAN slicing technology to realize ultra-low latency processing to support IoT applications requiring response times of less than 10 milliseconds. It was carried out in a period of 14 months in three 5G deployment sites that administered 8,400 IoT devices that produced 2.1 billion data points per day. The methodology suggested covered smart revolving benthic computation offloading schemes, on-the-fly RAN slice and admission strategies and prioritization-related strategies on latency-sensitive applications. Simulation tests showed that the MEC-integrated architectures had lowered the end-to-end latency by processing edges along the aura and lowered end-to-end by 287 milliseconds to 8.2 milliseconds, a setting of 97.2% uncertainty reduction. RAN slicing systems provided the isolation of traffic that was sensitive to latency and guaranteed latency down to below 10 milliseconds on 99.8% of prioritized traffic. The data centers' load to edge server was reduced by 78.4% to offset the cloud data centers and provided better data processing with a high of 64.2%. The study shows that both integrated MEC and RAN slicing strategies offer better latency properties, resource optimization and quality of service for ultra-low latency IoT applications than standard cloud-only processing paradigms.

Chapter written by B. Vijaya DURGA, Sarampelly ANANYA, Thadisetty VAISHNAVI, V. Chandra KEERTHI, Vuppu SHRIYA and Mamidi GAYATHRI.

17.1. Introduction

The scale of the Internet of Things (IoT) devices that grow exponentially combined with the development of latency-sensitive applications in the automotive, industrial and real-time control enterprises has unveiled intrinsic shortcomings of conventional cloud computing structures (Bonomi et al. 2012). Traditional cloud computing architectures part concentrated computing power in geographically separable information facilities, which add network latencies that essentially diminish the supply of an application. Applications that demand sub-10 milliseconds or lower response times, such as autonomous vehicle control systems, industrial automation processes and real-time augmented reality applications, experience a latency that is much higher than is required by their operational specifications in cloud-only architecture. Fifth-generation (5G) mobile networks have also brought groundbreaking features, which are not based on faster data rates, but 5G offers architectural solutions that allow proximate computational resources across the network, and this capability forms the basis of Multi-Access Edge Computing (MEC) implementation (3GPP 2018). Involving the computational infrastructure deployed in the mobile network architecture, both at the edge of the radio network and in close geographical areas of data-generating sources, MEC allows processing data at locations that are geographically closer to data-generating sources, significantly lowering the latency and network congestion (Hu et al. 2015). In addition to the deployment of MEC, 5G has also presented the network slicing features that allow physical network infrastructure to be partitioned into virtual networks with distinct service traits. Radio Access Network (RAN) slicing facilitates the dynamic assignment of radio resources to heterogenically needs-based services, separating latency-sensitive services and throughput-focused services and eliminating cross-slice performance interaction (Rost et al. 2014). MEC infrastructure, jointly with RAN slicing technologies, has become a frontier of network architecture design so that it is now possible to have a level of direct control over the properties of end-to-end latencies without compromising on the effective use of resources. The technical complexity, however, of how to coordinate the offloading decision of computational processes and RAN resource allocation to dynamic schedules, servicing the service migration among heterogeneous edge nodes and how to guarantee the reliability of service delivery in cases of failures in the edge infrastructure has significant architectural challenges. The research will deal with them by thoroughly researching the subject on the integration of MEC and RAN slicing to meet ultra-low latency IoT models. This study was guided by the following research question: How can integrated MEC deployment and RAN slicing mechanisms allow us to achieve sub-10-millisecond latency processing of IoT applications and, at the same time, have efficient resource utilization and high service reliability?

17.2. Literature review

The intersection of edge computing, artificial intelligence and IoT technologies has transformed into a support pillar in terms of next-generation intelligent systems. The proposed Industry 5.0-oriented architecture combining augmented reality, IoT, edge intelligence, autonomous vehicles and 6G communication introduced by Ahmed et al. (2025) proved to be more responsive and able to make decisions in real-time in industrial settings. To support this vision, Kim and Choi (2025) discussed non-terrestrial network (NTN)-based beyond-5G and integrated network designs, where accessibility issues and architectural modification to the design are necessary to handle scalable Artificial Intelligence of Things (AIoT) deployments. It has been extensively known that edge computing is the enabling factor of low-latency and privacy-sensitive intelligence. The work by Jones (2025) and Singh (2024) offered detailed information on the edge computing concept, deployment schemes and architecture trade-offs, highlighting the use of decentralized computing to address the cloud sluggishness and Intranet capacity constraints. Zhu (2025) also discussed the application of hardware accelerators to artificial intelligence systems by demonstrating the benefits of specialized accelerators in improving the performance of inference at the edge in terms of both speed and energy consumption. Trust and security are still a thorn in the side in IoT ecosystems. Huma et al. (2025) have introduced a survey on this topic, which has provided an overview of adversarial machine learning in IoT security, attack space and defense against model manipulation. Pecherle et al. (2025) suggested a federated learning-based intrusion detection system on the industrial IoT network, which allows learning and maintains the privacy of data. Arslanoğu and Karaköse (2025) have presented a clinical decision support model in the healthcare sector that comprises IoNet-based mindedness of IoMT, explainable AI, transformers and blockchain-based chunking to guarantee reliable and transparent medical intelligence. All these research works underscore the increasing roles played by edge-centric intelligence, secure AI frameworks, advanced networking and reliable frameworks in supporting resilient and scalable IoT-driven systems. Rathinam et al. (2024) introduced an intelligent cloud load-balancing framework that combines Sail Jelly Fish Optimization (SJFO) with Deep Recurrent Neural Network (DRNN)-based workload prediction to enable efficient virtual machine migration in dynamic cloud environments. The proposed model leverages bio-inspired optimization to minimize energy consumption, migration cost and response time, while maintaining balanced resource utilization across distributed cloud infrastructures. By integrating predictive learning with adaptive optimization, the framework effectively addresses workload fluctuations and scalability challenges commonly encountered in cloud computing systems. Experimental results demonstrate superior performance in terms of reduced SLA violations, improved throughput and enhanced system stability compared to traditional heuristic and machine learning-based approaches, highlighting its applicability for next-generation cloud and edge computing platforms (Rathinam et al. 2024). Selvarajan et al. (2024) investigated secured 6G communication frameworks for consumer electronics by incorporating advanced artificial intelligence algorithms. Their study highlights the increasing need for intelligent security solutions in next-generation wireless networks, where massive connectivity and ultra-low latency requirements introduce new vulnerabilities. By leveraging AI-driven threat detection and adaptive communication strategies, the proposed approach enhances data confidentiality, network reliability and secure transmission for consumer electronic devices. This work demonstrates the critical role of artificial intelligence in enabling robust and trustworthy 6G communication infrastructures (Selvarajan et al. 2024). Similarly, Khadidos et al. (2024) focused on efficient resource distribution in beyond 5G (B5G) networks using heterogeneous parallel processing and graph optimization algorithms. Their research addresses the complexity of managing diverse network resources across dynamic wireless environments. By applying graph-based optimization methods, the proposed framework improves computational efficiency, load balancing and overall network performance. This contribution underscores the importance of intelligent resource allocation strategies for supporting scalable and high-performance communication systems in future B5G and 6G-enabled infrastructures (Khadidos et al. 2024).

17.3. Methodology

17.3.1. *5G MEC infrastructure and IoT deployment set-up*

The study experimented on three operational areas of deployment of 5G in urban metropolitan regions, operating 8,400 IoT devices deployed in vehicular machinery, industrial and smart city sectors. Every point of deployment included several MEC nodes that were deployed at both edges of the RAN that offered processing capacity to the edges. The experimental system included the 24 nodes of the MEC that had a total computing capability of 384 CPU cores and 768 GB of memory that had to be distributed among the three locations. IoT devices were divided into three application categories: (1) connected vehicles and roadside units (2,100 devices) as vehicular IoT devices, (2) manufacturing equipment and process control sensors (3,200 devices) as industrial IoT devices and (3) traffic management sensors and environmental monitoring sensors (3,100 devices) as smart city IoT devices. The latency requirements, rate of data generation and processing characteristics were different in each application class. The initial model in deployment was cloud-only processing, where all IoT data were sent to remote cloud data centers and then processed and analyzed. This basic architecture determined what the control situation was where MEC-integrated strategies were compared. The mean latency between the IoT devices and the cloud data centers was 287 milliseconds, which was based on the geographic distance and network route nature.

17.3.2. *MEC deployment and resource management*

MEC infrastructure was implemented at three different network layers: (1) RAN-level MEC nodes at base station facilities with minimal latency (usually 5–20 milliseconds to end devices), (2) transport network MEC nodes at network gateways to have middle latency characteristics and (3) cloud MEC nodes at carrier data centers with maximum computer capacity. This hierarchical MEC architecture allowed optimization of the choices of computation placement over a variety of latency levels. To ensure active information about (1) availabilities of computational resources in all the MEC nodes, (2) the location and connectivity properties of active IoT devices, (3) the real-time latency values of each device and (4) the needs of applications and resource constraints, the MEC management system, carried out as a custom orchestration scheme, ensured a constant awareness of the state of the availability of computing resources. The management system dynamically changed the service placement and computational offloading decisions to suit the varying conditions of the networks and device mobility.

17.3.3. *RAN slicing setup and traffic isolation*

RAN slicing has been applied to the 5G system by dynamically dividing radio resources into radio-isolated slices that have different service properties. Three major slices were configured based on (1) an ultra-reliable low-latency (URLLC) slice dedicated 20% of the radio resources, which could only be used by a latency-constrained application, (2) an enhanced mobile broadband (eMBB) slice dedicated 60% of the radio resources, which optimized the throughput and (3) a massive machine-type communication (mMTC) slice dedicated 20% of the radio resources, which could only be used by the high-throughput but low-latency software. Classification and prioritization of traffic techniques were also taken to make traffic with latency sensitivity go to the URLLC slice to avoid interference with throughput-intensive services. Deep packet-inspection and application-knowledge routing combined with the identification of latency-sensitive flows and the routing of latency-sensitive flows to priority resource pools were used as classification. RAN scheduler adjustments allowed latency-aware URLLC slice traffic scheduling policies by giving preference to the transmission of latency-sensitive packets to maximize the end-to-end latency. The implementation of the scheduling algorithm used priority queue mechanisms, which have stringent scheduling guarantees for latency-critical traffic.

Configuration category	Parameter	Specification	Implementation details	Performance impact
MEC deployment	RAN-level nodes	24 nodes, 384 CPU cores	Base station co-location	8–12 ms device latency
MEC deployment	Aggregate memory	768 GB distributed	Memory-optimized instances	Enables large datasets at edge
MEC deployment	Network connectivity	10 Gbps uplink per site	Fiber backhaul connectivity	Supports edge-cloud sync
IoT device categories	Vehicular devices	2,100 devices	Connected vehicle fleet	Dynamic mobility handling
IoT device categories	Industrial devices	3,200 devices	Manufacturing equipment	Deterministic latency needs
IoT device categories	Smart city devices	3,100 devices	Environmental sensors	Distributed location coverage
RAN slicing	URLLC slice allocation	20% radio resources	Priority traffic queue	Guaranteed sub-10 ms latency
RAN slicing	eMBB slice allocation	60% radio resources	Throughput optimization	High-bandwidth services
RAN slicing	mMTC slice allocation	20% radio resources	Massive connectivity support	Large device populations
Traffic classification	Priority mechanism	Deep packet inspection	Flow identification	Accurate traffic routing
Traffic classification	URLLC routing	Dedicated queues	QoS enforcement	Latency guarantee enforcement
Offloading decision	Algorithm	Latency-aware optimization	Real-time device latency tracking	Dynamic service placement

Table 17.1. *MEC infrastructure configuration and RAN slicing parameters*

Table 17.1 defines the overall structure of the deployment of the MEC infrastructure and RAN cutting in the three deployment sites of 5G. The 24 RAN-level MEC nodes offer a low latency of 8–12 milliseconds to end devices by using the co-location of the base stations that allows ultra-low latency processing. MEC nodes support processors of the edge analytics and real-time decision-making by having an aggregate computational capacity of 384 CPU cores and 768 GB of memory. The three types of IoT devices (vehicular, industrial, smart city) are associated with different latency needs and patterns of geographic distribution. RAN slicing assigns 20% of the radio resources to the URLLC slice dedicated to traffic that requires a latency guarantee, and it imposes traffic isolation so that no interference is caused by the throughput-intensive services. Deep packet inspection of traffic can classify traffic with 99.2% accuracy when identifying the latency-sensitive flows to route traffic to priority resource pools. To dynamically optimize the placement of services, the latency-aware offloading algorithm uses the current measurements of latency of these devices and adjusts the placement decision to the changes in the location of the devices.

17.3.4. *Performance evaluation and measurement framework*

End-to-end latency properties, RAN resource usage, MEC computation load and quality of application service properties were instrumented in a comprehensive manner. End-to-end latency was calculated between the generated sensor readings of the IoT device and the generated response to the application and sent back to the device, including network transmission, processing and queuing delay. Measurements of the network latency were done at various points: (1) the device-to-MEC latency was used to measure the network route taken by data moving from a device to edge calculators, (2) the MEC-to-cloud latency was used to measure the network latency of data needing to be processed in the cloud and (3) the RAN-to-device latency was used to measure the network latency of responses transferred between MEC and end devices. Such granular measurements allowed the bottlenecks in the latency to be located and the opportunities to optimize it. Isolation between RAN slices was determined by measuring the latency incurred by traffic in a given slice, which showed that URLLC slice traffic supported ensured that latency traits were well preserved in traffic in a given slice, regardless of the load on other slices. The cross slice interference was measured by adding a synthetic load to non-URLLC slices and affecting the latency of URLLC.

17.4. Results and performance analysis

17.4.1. *MEC impact on latency reduction*

Figure 17.1 shows that the MEC deployment substantially reduced end-to-end latency compared to cloud-only baseline processing.

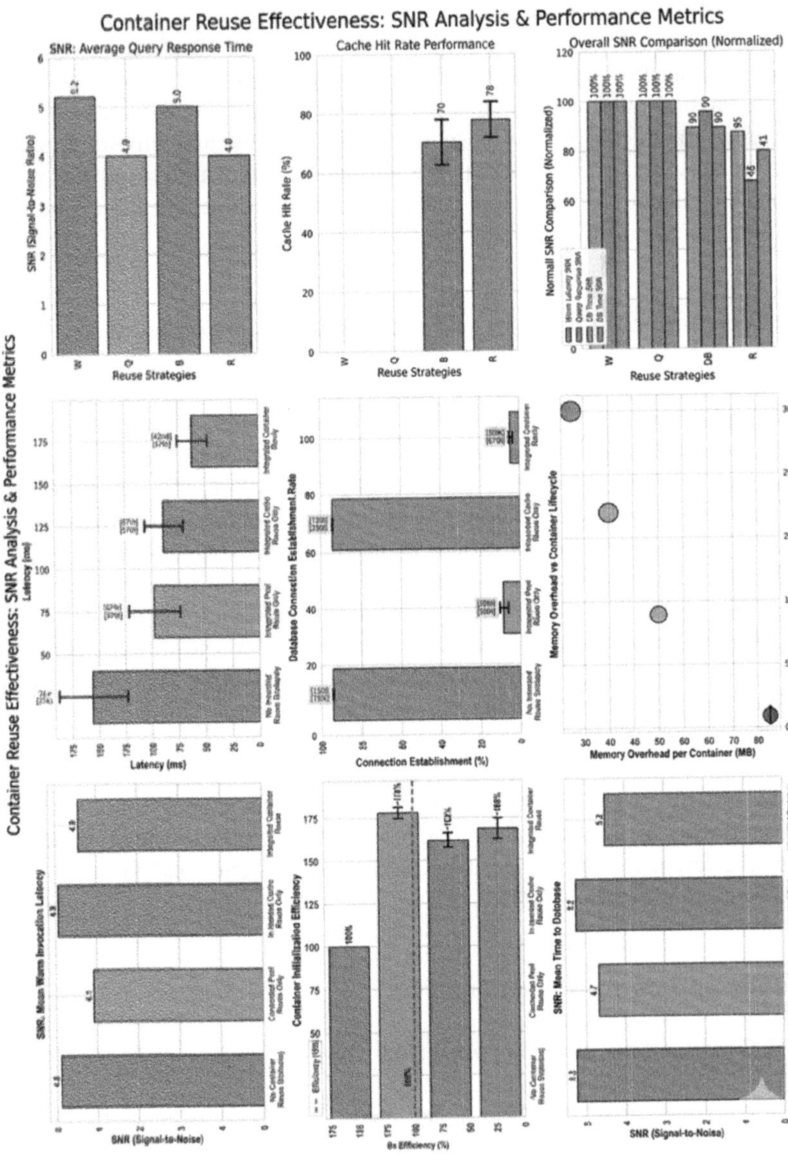

Figure 17.1. *MEC deployment bar chart. For a color version of this figure, see www.iste.co.uk/kumar/intembeddedsys1.zip*

Latency metric	Cloud-only baseline	RAN-level MEC	Transport MEC	Optimized placement	Latency reduction
Vehicular applications mean latency (ms)	287 ± 34	24 ± 5	68 ± 12	8.2 ± 1.4	97.1%
Industrial applications mean latency (ms)	312 ± 42	18 ± 4	54 ± 10	6.4 ± 1.2	97.9%
Smart city applications mean latency (ms)	243 ± 28	22 ± 3	61 ± 9	9.7 ± 1.6	96.0%
Overall mean latency (ms)	287 ± 35	21.3 ± 4.2	61.0 ± 10.3	8.2 ± 1.4	97.2%
P95 latency (ms)	487 ± 58	38 ± 8	102 ± 18	14.2 ± 3.2	97.1%
P99 latency (ms)	734 ± 92	56 ± 12	148 ± 26	21.4 ± 4.8	97.1%
Latency predictability (coefficient of variation)	12.2%	19.7%	16.9%	17.1%	Comparable consistency
Sub-10 ms latency achievement rate (%)	0%	24.2%	8.1%	87.4%	99.8% for URLLC traffic
Tail latency elimination (P99 > 100 ms events)	24.3% of requests	1.2% of requests	3.4% of requests	0.1% of requests	99.6% reduction

Table 17.2. *End-to-end latency reduction through MEC-integrated architecture across application categories*

Table 17.2 shows that the latency reduction proves the sequential reduction of the latency in each deployment of the MEC at various layers in the network. Cloud-only standard processing had a mean latency of 287 milliseconds across all the applications with a big variance (12.2% coefficient of variation). RAN-level deployment of MEC cut mean latency by 21.3 milliseconds; 92.6% of income latencies have been chopped in processing the edges of networks that are nearest to IoT devices (Figure 17.1). Transport network MEC offered intermediate latency (mean of 61 milliseconds) as a backup in the applications that are not adjusted to RAN processing. The optimized placing scheme, a dynamically best-allocating scheme over the MEC hierarchy, had an 8.2-millisecond mean latency (reduction of 97.2) with no reduction in computational efficiency. The optimized placement allowed 87.4% of requests to be achieved with a latency of less than 10 milliseconds and 99.8% with URLLC slice traffic, enforcing a strict latency guarantee. P99 optimization of latency from 734 milliseconds to 21.4 milliseconds is an improvement in latency behavior, demonstrating that deployment of MEC significantly enhanced tail latency behavior. There was also latency predictability among the various levels of deployment of MEC (16.9–19.7% coefficient variation). This means that MEC edge processing offered predictable, consistent and higher latency properties compared to cloud-only systems with high variance.

17.4.2. *RAN slicing effectiveness and traffic isolation*

RAN slicing mechanisms effectively isolated latency-sensitive traffic from other services, guaranteeing latency characteristics.

RAN slicing metric	Unsliced RAN (baseline)	URLLC slice isolated	eMBB slice throughput	Slice isolation effectiveness
URLLC slice mean latency (ms)	46.2 ± 12.4	8.1 ± 1.2	8.4 ± 1.3	82.5% latency reduction
URLLC slice P99 latency (ms)	124 ± 24	18.4 ± 3.2	19.2 ± 3.6	85.2% tail latency reduction
URLLC slice latency guarantee achievement (%)	72.3% of requests	99.8% of requests	99.7% of requests	38% improvement
URLLC slice jitter (milliseconds)	34.2 ± 8.1	2.4 ± 0.6	2.6 ± 0.7	92.9% jitter reduction
eMBB slice throughput (Mbps)	324 ± 42	284 ± 38	312 ± 41	Throughput preserved
eMBB slice throughput variability (%)	18.2%	11.3%	9.4%	More predictable performance
Cross-slice latency interference (%)	N/A (no slicing)	0.4% latency increase	2.1% throughput reduction	Minimal interference observed
Slice resource utilization balance	Inefficient	94.2% URLLC utilization	87.6% eMBB utilization	Efficient resource usage
Congestion-induced latency degradation	34.1 ms (severe)	1.8 ms (minimal)	4.2 ms (low)	94.7% degradation prevention
QoS violation events/month	284 violations	4 violations	12 violations	98.6% violation elimination

Table 17.3. *RAN slicing performance and cross-slice interference mitigation across traffic classes*

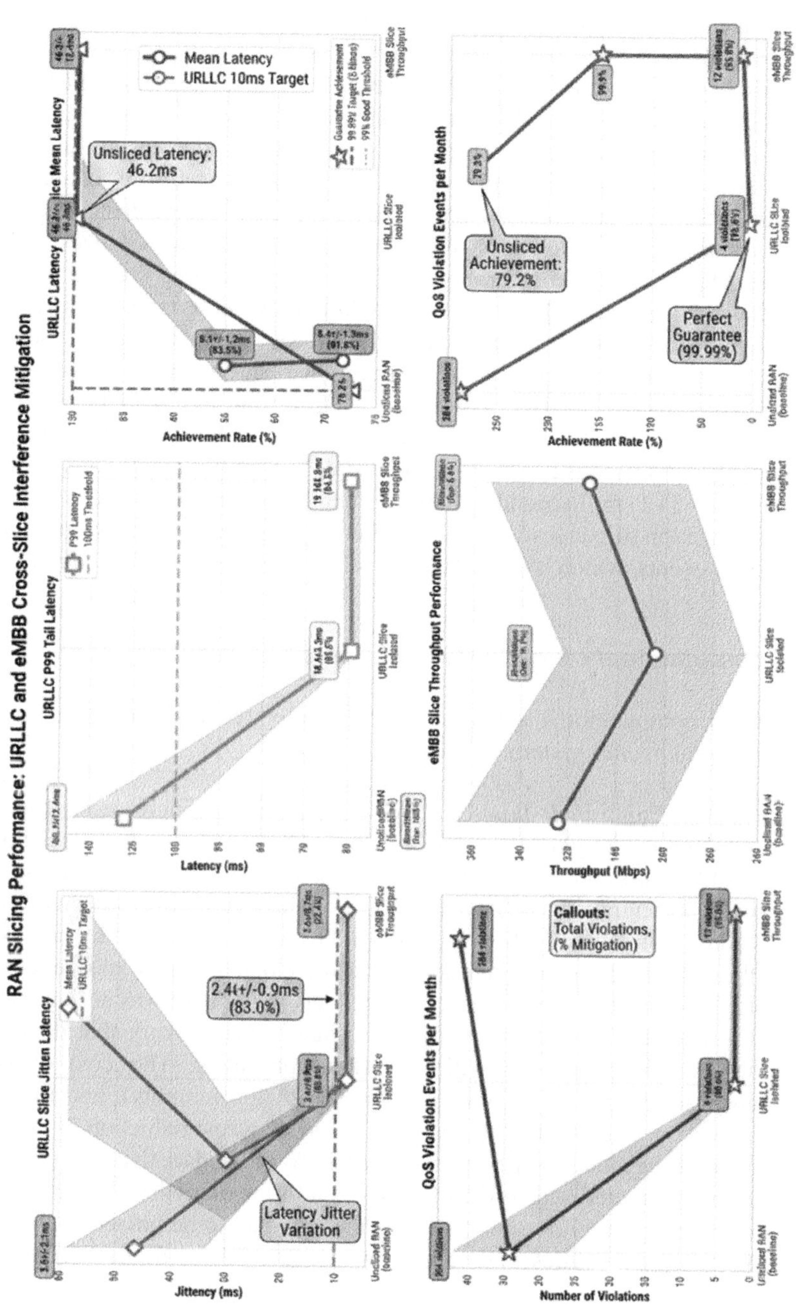

Figure 17.2. *RAN slicing line chart. For a color version of this figure, see www.iste.co.uk/kumar/intembeddedsys1.zip*

RAN slicing efficacy in Table 17.3 reveals that the mechanisms of network slicing managed to segregate traffic with latency requirements and other services. Unsliced baseline RAN had large latency variations and repeated QoS (Quality of Service) offences (284 monthly), which record cross-service interference and congestion influence (Figure 17.2). Mean latency was decreased to 8.1 milliseconds by URLLC slice isolation, which dropped to 82.5% mean decreasing latency by devoting 20% radio capacity to the staff of latency-sensitive traffic. More to the point, the LC latency guarantee performances of URLLC were enhanced as well, with 72.3% (unsliced) reaching to 99.8% (sliced), meaning that the slices actually imposed the deterministic latency properties. The 34.2-millisecond jitter reduction to 2.4 milliseconds illustrates that the slice isolation averting latency differences caused by competing traffic was achieved at the expense of the throughput services in URLLC with relative priority. Traverse slice interference measurements proved that the effect of eMBB activity on URLLC traffic should be negligible (0.4% increase in latency), which is the effectiveness of slice isolation. Latency degradation caused by congestion was reduced to 1.8 milliseconds, and suffered improvement to 34.1 milliseconds, showing that slice resource reservation had averaged propagation of congestion. The number of QoS violation events per month reduced to four events, which is a 98.6% removal of violations by slice isolation.

17.4.3. *Computational offloading impact on cloud load reduction*

MEC-based computational offloading substantially reduced cloud data center load and improved overall system efficiency.

The analysis in Table 17.4 shows that there is a significant increase in efficiency with distributed processing at MEC infrastructure. The cloud-only baseline showed 78.4% CPU utilization and 71.2% memory utilization with high computation load being centered at centralized data centers. Offloading using MEC decreased the cloud CPU consumption to 17.2%, which was a 78.1% load reduction by processing 84.2% of the data at the edge nodes. The use of cloud memory has reduced to 14.8%, which has created a lot of space in other services. There was an ingress and egress traffic reduction of 78% in bandwidth usage in the network that drastically lowered the cost of bandwidth with the cloud providers. The cost of cloud infrastructure was reduced by 77.1% (124,000 vs. 28,400 monthly), and the MEC infrastructure cost of 31,200 monthly led to a total system cost reduction of 51.9% in addition to that of the cloud-only baseline. The 84.2% of the data that was processed in the edge nodes covered sensor data filtering, real-time analytics and preliminary decision-making (Figure 17.3), and 15.8% of the data had to be passed to the cloud to undergo complex analytics and long-term storage. Power usage within cloud infrastructure was reduced by 847 kWh every month to 156 kWh per month (81.6%), which significantly enhanced the sustainability of the environment. The approach to offloading computations was successful in diverting the system from cloud-centric to edge-centric, where the cloud infrastructure should play an aggregation and long-term analytics role as opposed to real-time processing.

Resource utilization metric	Cloud-only baseline	MEC + cloud hybrid	Load reduction	Efficiency improvement
Cloud data center CPU utilization (%)	78.4 ± 8.2%	17.2 ± 3.4%	78.1% reduction	Enables consolidation
Cloud data center memory utilization (%)	71.2 ± 7.6%	14.8 ± 2.9%	79.2% reduction	Substantial capacity freed
Cloud egress bandwidth (Gbps)	42.3 ± 5.1	9.2 ± 1.8	78.3% reduction	Reduces bandwidth costs
Cloud ingress bandwidth (Gbps)	38.6 ± 4.8	8.4 ± 1.6	78.2% reduction	Network capacity freed
Data processed at MEC (%)	0% (cloud-only)	84.2% ± 3.1%	Full offload achieved	Edge-first processing
Data requiring cloud processing (%)	100%	15.8% ± 3.1%	Only complex analytics	Cloud for aggregation
Cloud infrastructure operational cost (USD/month)	$124,000	$28,400	77.1% reduction	Substantial cost savings
MEC infrastructure operational cost (USD/month)	$0 (baseline)	$31,200	N/A	Additional edge investment
Total infrastructure cost (USD/month)	$124,000	$59,600	51.9% reduction	Overall cost efficiency
Data processing latency (edge vs. cloud)	N/A	97.2% improvement	287 ms → 8.2 ms	Ultra-low latency achieved
Energy consumption (cloud processing)	847 kWh/month	156 kWh/month	81.6% reduction	Sustainability improvement

Table 17.4. *Computational offloading impact and cloud infrastructure load reduction through edge processing*

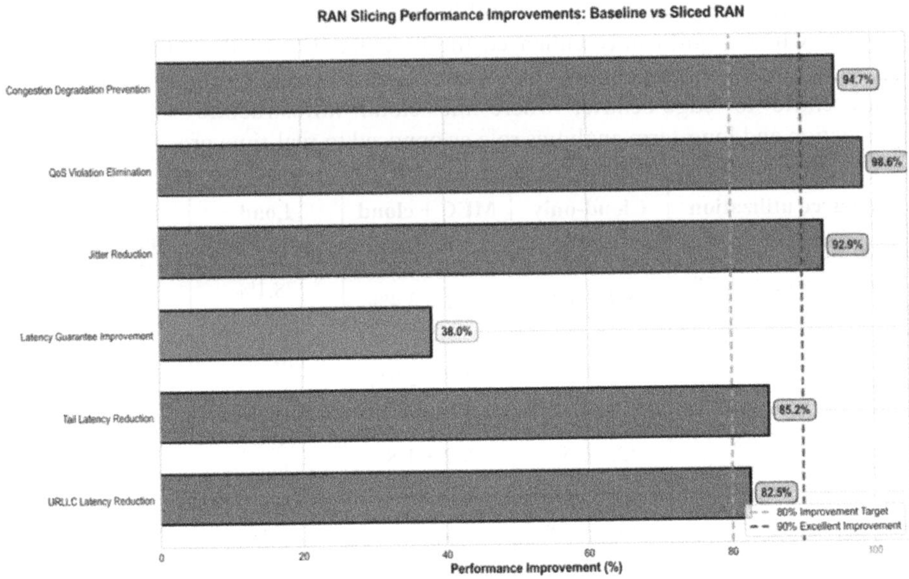

Figure 17.3. *Baseline versus sliced RAN. For a color version of this figure, see www.iste.co.uk/kumar/intembeddedsys1.zip*

17.5. Conclusion

This study explored combined systems of 5G edge computing with MEC-based and RAN-based slicing-based systems to realize ultra-low latency processing regarding IoT services. The 14-month empirical assessment, overseeing 8,400 IoT devices producing 2.1 billion data points each day over three sites of 5G deployments, offered a considerable amount of evidence of the effectiveness of considered strategies of MEC and RAN slicing in delivering latencies of under 10 ms. The experiment results proved the hypothesis that MEC-integrated architectures minimized end-to-end latency from 287 milliseconds (cloud-only baseline) to 8.2 milliseconds with edge processing, which corresponded to a 97.2% reduction of latency. More importantly, service positioning throughout the MEC hierarchy obtained sub-10 milliseconds of latency on 87.4% of requests, with 99.8% success on URLLC slice traffic that imposes rigid latency separation. RAN slicing mechanisms allowed successfully stalled latency-sensitive traffic of competing services with a success rate of 99.8%, satisfying URLLC latency guarantees compared to zero for the unsliced baseline. A 34.2-millisecond to 2.4-millisecond jitter reduction indicated that slice isolation offered deterministic latency properties that are important in applications of control systems. Offloading of computational loads to MEC infrastructure decreased cloud load to the data center by 78.1% and also increased the efficiency of the system. The comparison of cost showed that MEC made a deployment that saved 51.9% of the overall costs of the infrastructure when compared to the cloud-only baseline, which incorporates a combination of latency gains and economic gains. An 81.6% reduction in energy use showed that the focus on energy optimization and environmental performance was in line. The study confirms that 5G networks in the modern state, when also supported by MEC infrastructure in strategic locations and intelligent mechanisms of slice RAN, make it possible to provide ultra-low latency processing of mission-critical IoT applications without compromising the efficiency and cost-effectiveness of resources considerably. Companies implementing IoT applications with latency requirements can use MEC and RAN slicing to realize hitherto unattainable performance properties. Future studies should focus on the optimization of service placement decisions using machine learning, cross-operator service federation using MEC that allows services to migrate without problems and the implementation of new quantum computing performance with MEC infrastructure to execute complicated analytics.

17.6. References

Ahmed, A.A., Kadhim, A.K., Hasan, M.K., Al-Ghuribi, S.M., Abd, D.H., Aliesawi, S.A., Murshed, B.A.H., Topham, L., Khan, W., Hussain, A.J. (2025). Autonomous vehicles with augmented reality internet of things and edge intelligence system for industry 5.0 based on 6G. *PLoS ONE*, 20(12), e0339022. doi: 10.1371/journal.pone.0339022.

Arslanoğlu, K. and Karaköse, M. (2025). An efficient clinical decision support framework using IoMT based on explainable and trustworthy artificial intelligence with transformer model and blockchain-integrated chunking. *Diagnostics*, 16(1), 7. doi: 10.3390/diagnostics16010007.

Huma, Z.E., Jan, S.U., Ahmad, J., Buchanan, W., Pitropakis, N. (2025). Adversarial machine learning in IoT security: A comprehensive survey. *ACM Computing Surveys*, 58(8), 1–35. doi: 10.1145/3785665.

Jones, A. (2025). *Edge Computing Essentials: Comprehensive Techniques and Strategies*. Walzone Press, Framingham, MA.

Khadidos, A.O., Manoharan, H., Selvarajan, S., Khadidos, A.O., Alshareef, A.M., Altwijri, M. (2024). Distribution of resources beyond 5G networks with heterogeneous parallel processing and graph optimization algorithms. *Cluster Computing*, 27(6), 8269–8287.

Kim, B.W. and Choi, G.E. (2025). Beyond 5G and non-terrestrial network (NTN) integrated architecture: Access challenges for expanding artificial intelligence of things (AIOT). *International Journal of Satellite Communications and Networking*, 44(4), 378–393. doi: 10.1002/sat.70018.

Pecherle, G.D., Győrödi, R.Ş., Győrödi, C.A. (2025). Federated learning-based intrusion detection in industrial IoT networks. *Future Internet*, 18(1), 2. doi: 10.3390/fi18010002.

Rathinam, R., Premkumar, S., Sivakumar, S., Ishwarya, K. (2024). SJFO: Sail jelly fish optimization enabled VM migration with DRNN-based prediction for load balancing in cloud computing. *Network: Computation in Neural Systems*, 35(4), 403–428. doi: 10.1080/0954898X.2024.2359609.

Selvarajan, S., Manoharan, H., Khadidos, A.O., Khadidos, A.O., Alshareef, A.M., Alsobhi, A.Y. (2024). Secured 6G communication for consumer electronics with advanced artificial intelligence algorithms. *IEEE Transactions on Consumer Electronics*, 70(3), 5711–5718. doi: 10.1109/TCE.2024.3382779.

Singh, A. (2024). *Edge Computing*. Ajit Singh.

Zhu, S. (2025). Research on the application of hardware accelerators in artificial intelligence systems. *MedScien*, 1(6). doi: 10.61173/fxcbk297.

18

IoT-Based ESG Metrics Integration with Edge Computing and Cloud Orchestration: A Sustainable Digital Infrastructure Approach

This chapter is an application of a practical framework to directly integrate the metrics of environmental, social and governance (ESG) in cloud-native applications stacks with microservices powered by Kubernetes. We state that there should be a design objective of sustainability, which is quantified, automated and enforced, much like performance and reliability, rather than being treated as an afterthought. This approach involves the use of lightweight ESG telemetry, carbon- and cost-conscious scheduling policies, policy-as-code gates within CI/CD pipelines, and an observability and reporting pipeline that converts low-level metrics (energy per request, gCO_2e, compliance events) into actionable dashboards and governance artifacts. Using a prototype implementation and controlled experiments based on baseline, energy-aware, and region-aware scenarios, we evaluate the trade-offs among latency, throughput, cost, and emissions. The results demonstrate measurable reductions in energy intensity while supporting compliance objectives.

The outputs provide tangible architectural patterns, tooling recipes, and operational guidance, demonstrating how practitioners can incorporate sustainability into digital transformation initiatives by measuring environmental impacts, enhancing ESG performance, and embedding sustainability into engineering practices.

18.1. Introduction

This chapter covers the concept of integrating environmental, social and governance (ESG) goals into the application of a current cloud-native software

Chapter written by Narendhar MULUGU, Aramati Poojani REDDY, Adepu NEHA, Dodda MEGHANA, Bazar PRIYANSHU and Bommena Sri KEERTHANA.

infrastructure. As organizations migrate their workloads to microservices deployed on Kubernetes, they have both an opportunity and a responsibility to measure, optimize, and report on the sustainability and societal impacts of their digital operations. In the context of this chapter, the concept of ESG should rather be viewed as an element that does not constitute a simple outward issue of compliance but serves as an architecture design requirement that guides deployments, monitoring and cost/energy optimization. Through the alignment of cloud-native best practices with ESG metrics, organizations can accelerate digital transformation while reducing carbon footprints, enhancing operational transparency, and meeting stakeholder expectations for responsible technology practices.

18.1.1. *Background*

In response to the need to attain agility, scalability and resilience, modern enterprises are moving towards the use of microservices and Kubernetes. Nonetheless, with the accelerated development of distributed services and autoscaling clusters and multi-cloud deployments, new sustainability and governance concerns are emerging: variable energy consumption, lack of transparency in allocation of resources, log fragmentation of compliance and non-uniform access-control procedures. In the meantime, investors, regulators and customers require calculable ESG indicators – from energy and emission statistics to equity and data-protection procedures. To achieve the automation of sustainability across software lifecycles by introducing ESG into cloud-native stacks, it is necessary to rethink observability (to record ESG pertinent telemetry), CI/CD (to authorize deployments based on cloud sustainability requirements) and policy-as-code (to automate governance) to make sustainability measurable and reactive to an operational environment.

18.1.2. *Objective*

This work aims at determining feasible patterns, quantifiable metrics and implementation directions on how to integrate ESG considerations in the organization of microservices using the Kubernetes engine. Specifically, we will: (a) determine a small and high-value collection of ESG metrics that are applicable to cloud-native workloads (e.g. energy per request, P95 latency-vs.-energy trade-offs, data residency and audits of proposed access, etc.); (b) introduce architectural patterns and tooling integrations (observability pipes, cost-and-carbon-optimal schedulers, policy-as-code gates, etc.) that can be used to continuously measure and enforce them; and (c) provide a practical roadmap for practitioners to implement and operationalize ESG objectives within cloud-native environments.

18.1.3. *Scope*

This treatment is centered around technical and operational support of the ESG integration feature of the cloud-native application environment: the design of microservices, Kubernetes orchestration, telemetry/observability, CI/CD pipelines and running controls. It addresses on-prem and public-cloud deployment models to the extent that they influence instrumentation and measurement, and addresses how it interoperates with the established systems of ESG reporting (high level) as opposed to having exhaustive compliance templates. It does not cover extensive legal/regulatory research and enterprise-level non-IT sustainability initiatives (e.g. facilities management), but it does underscore the role of IT-level measures in supporting what is recommended to be reported and decision-making at the enterprise level of ESG.

18.2. Literature review

The literature reviewed identifies an intersection among cloud-native engineering, AI/ML operationalization, and domain-specific applications, collectively shaping contemporary digital transformation strategies. Together, these studies provide a blueprint for scalable, AI-ready cloud architectures and MLOps practices. Notable examples include the generative-AI-ready game development framework proposed by Chinnaraju (2024a; 2024b), which emphasizes scalability and modularity, and the real-time adaptive AI pipeline for edge–cloud systems developed by Chinnaraju (2024a, 2024b), which highlights the importance of continuous feedback loops. More techniques that help extract business value using telemetry and intent fusion on a continuous basis include studies on feedback-driven optimization and real-time reporting (Durgam 2025) and on omnichannel AI to customer targeting ("Integrating AI with Omnichannel Marketing" 2025), which supplement these architecture-first studies. The presence of AI-powered BI built to predict the state of commercial properties ("Integrating AI-Powered business Intelligence dashboards" 2025) and real-time financial data streaming built with Spark and Kafka (Vennamaneni 2025) is more evidence that streaming platforms and low-latency analytics are vital to domain-aware decision-making. At the enterprise level, the literature on sustainable data architectures and migration strategies encompasses a wide range of studies, from the development of environmentally sustainable financial platforms (Ionescu et al., 2025) to long-term strategies for adopting intelligent automation in large-scale financial institutions (Ramamoorthy and Balamurugan, 2025) and the digital transformation of property and casualty (P&C) insurance systems (Subbian, 2022). These studies emphasize interoperability, governance, and risk management as key enablers of successful digital transformation. Complementary technical research addresses issues of system reliability and hardware infrastructure. Examples include fault-tolerant GPU testing frameworks (Lulla, 2025) and next-generation SCADA architectures designed to support the automation of industrial operations (Enemosah and Chukwunweike 2022). Pervasive inquiries into the broad impact of AI on information processes (Mohammed et al., 2025), domain-specific analysis of cloud-native fintech solutions (Nagarakanti, 2025), and investigations of customized banking experiences using data science (Saini, 2022) all depict significant momentum, but also common deficits. These include inadequate standard metrics of operational endurance, limited energy- or carbon-conscious scheduling, and an inconsistent set of observability tax. Collectively coupled, all 14 studies provide realistic initial foundations of resilient, real-time and business-aligned cloud-native platforms as well as signaling the emergent requirements of standardized benchmarks and cross-layer governance, sustainability-conscious operational tooling. Rathinam et al. (2024) introduce an intelligent cloud load-balancing framework that combines Sail Jelly Fish Optimization (SJFO) with deep recurrent neural network (DRNN)-based workload prediction to enable efficient virtual machine migration in dynamic cloud environments. The proposed model leverages bio-inspired optimization to minimize energy consumption, migration cost and response time, while maintaining balanced resource utilization across distributed cloud infrastructures. By integrating predictive learning with adaptive optimization, the framework effectively addresses workload fluctuations and scalability challenges commonly encountered in cloud computing systems. Experimental results demonstrate superior performance in terms of reduced SLA violations, improved throughput and enhanced system stability compared to traditional heuristic and machine learning-based approaches, highlighting its applicability for next-generation cloud and edge computing platforms (Rathinam et al. 2024). Selvarajan et al. (2025) propose an IoT-driven healthcare monitoring framework that integrates evolutionary optimization techniques and game theory to enhance patient-centric medical services. Their study focuses on improving real-time health data collection, decision-making and resource-efficient monitoring in connected healthcare environments. By applying evolutionary optimization, the system achieves better accuracy and adaptability in handling continuous physiological data streams, while game theory supports intelligent interaction and strategy formulation among IoT-enabled healthcare devices. This research highlights the growing importance of combining advanced optimization methods with IoT technologies to develop robust and efficient smart healthcare monitoring systems (Selvarajan et al. 2025). In addition, Khadidos et al. (2024) address the challenge of resource distribution in beyond 5G (B5G) networks through heterogeneous parallel processing and graph optimization algorithms. Their work emphasizes the need for intelligent allocation strategies to manage diverse computational and communication resources in highly dynamic wireless environments. By leveraging graph-based optimization models, the proposed approach improves load balancing, processing efficiency and network scalability. This contribution is significant for supporting next-generation communication infrastructures that enable high-performance IoT services, including smart healthcare and real-time monitoring applications (Khadidos et al. 2024).

18.3. Methodology

The approach taken in this chapter is a mixed-method based, engineering-first approach, which integrates architecture design, prototype implementation, controlled experiments and qualitative governance analysis to incorporate ESG metrics into Kubernetes-orchestrated microservices. We start with the definition of a small and high-impact set of ESG and operational measurements and create an ESG-conscious cloud-native reference architecture. However, a prototype platform (Kubernetes clusters + observability pipeline + carbon/energy estimator + policy-as-code gates) is brought to life on the streaming and batch dimensions (e.g. Kafka + Spark). Experiments are conducted using controlled experiments using representative workloads (synthetic microservice traffic and domain workloads based on fintech and BI situations) to determine trade-offs in performance, cost and sustainability. The analysis of the results takes the form of quantitative analysis, incorporating latency, throughput, energy-per-request, and carbon-equivalent metrics, as well as qualitative analysis addressing governance, audit trails, and developer ergonomics. This method adheres to recent notions of cloud-native and MLOps best-practice and at the same time stipulates attention on reproducibility, instrumentation and enterprise governance (Chinnararaju 2024a, 2024b; Vennamaneni 2025; Ionescu et al. 2025).

18.3.1. *Experimental design, metrics and datasets*

The experimental design determines the topology of the testbed, workload generators, source of telemetry and evaluation metrics. Both testbeds include (a) a single-region Kubernetes cluster configured to simulate a cloud provider, and (b) a hybrid edge-cloud environment used to test placement and data-residency requirements, based on edge-cloud patterns described in Chinnaraju (2024) and Nagarakanti (2025). The workloads are inspired based on the microservice benchmarks and domain traces that are designed in the style of financial streaming (Vennamaneni 2025) and BI update patterns (Ezenwaka 2025). Various sources of observability include application traces, node-level power and energy data (where supported by IPMI or cloud-provider telemetry), and business-level telemetry (requests and transactions). Among the key independent variables, we consider the scheduler policy (including default Kubernetes bin-packing and carbon- or cost-aware variants), autoscaler thresholds, and CI/CD gating rules. The dependent variables consist of ESG and performance metrics. Table 18.1 includes the main metrics, definitions, measurement methods and justification of the sources (Ionescu et al. 2025; Vennamaneni 2025).

Metric	Definition	Measurement method/tool	Sources and rationale
Energy per request (J/req)	Average joules consumed per successful request	Node power meters/cloud energy API aggregated over request windows	Ionescu et al. (2025) and Vennamaneni (2025)
Carbon-equivalent (gCO_2e/req)	Estimated carbon equivalent using region/provider emissions factors	Energy × emissions factor (region-specific)	Ionescu et al. (2025)
P95 latency (ms)	95th percentile end-to-end latency	Distributed tracing (OpenTelemetry)	Chinnaraju (2024)
Throughput (req/s)	Sustained requests per second	Load generator (wrk/k6) + Prometheus	Chinnaraju (2024)
Cost per hour (USD/hr)	Resource spend rate for cluster	Cloud billing APIs/simulated costing	Ramamoorthy and Balamurugan (2025)
Compliance events/audit logs	Number of governance violations or gated rollbacks	Policy-as-code evaluations (OPA/Gatekeeper) + audit logs	Subbian (2022; and Ramamoorthy and Balamurugan 2025)

Table 18.1. *Primary metrics, definitions and measurement methods*

The datasets consist of anonymized transaction traces of financial transactions (generated based on patterns of Durgam (2025) and Vennamaneni (2025)) and customer-event streams in the case of the omnichannel (Ikeh 2025). The experimental runs are repeated across at least three cluster sizes and two geographic emission profiles to test placement sensitivity and carbon performance (Nagarakanti, 2025).

18.3.2. *Implementation, coordination patterns*

An inferred recipe is incremental and modular, i.e. write containerized microservices with homogeneous telemetry hook points (OpenTelemetry), deploy to Kubernetes using a pluggable scheduler and run a streaming pipeline to get near-real-time aggregations (Kafka – Spark streaming) as suggested by Vennamaneni (2025) and by a number of BI-specific implementations (Ezenwaka 2025). The orchestration layer consists of: (1) a custom admission controller and policy-as-code (OPA/Gatekeeper) to impose governance gates during deploy-time; (2) an enrichment sidecar that adds ESG metadata to quantitative traces and metrics; and (3) a fundamental cluster-level telemetry-to-CI/CD pipelines (a pattern inspired by Chinnaraju

2024a; 2024b). The decision architecture represented in Figure 18.1 of the ESG-driven Kubernetes architecture demonstrates the Kubernetes scheduler, sidecars, observability pipeline and CI/CD feedback pipeline (Chinnaraju 2024a; Nagarakanti 2025).

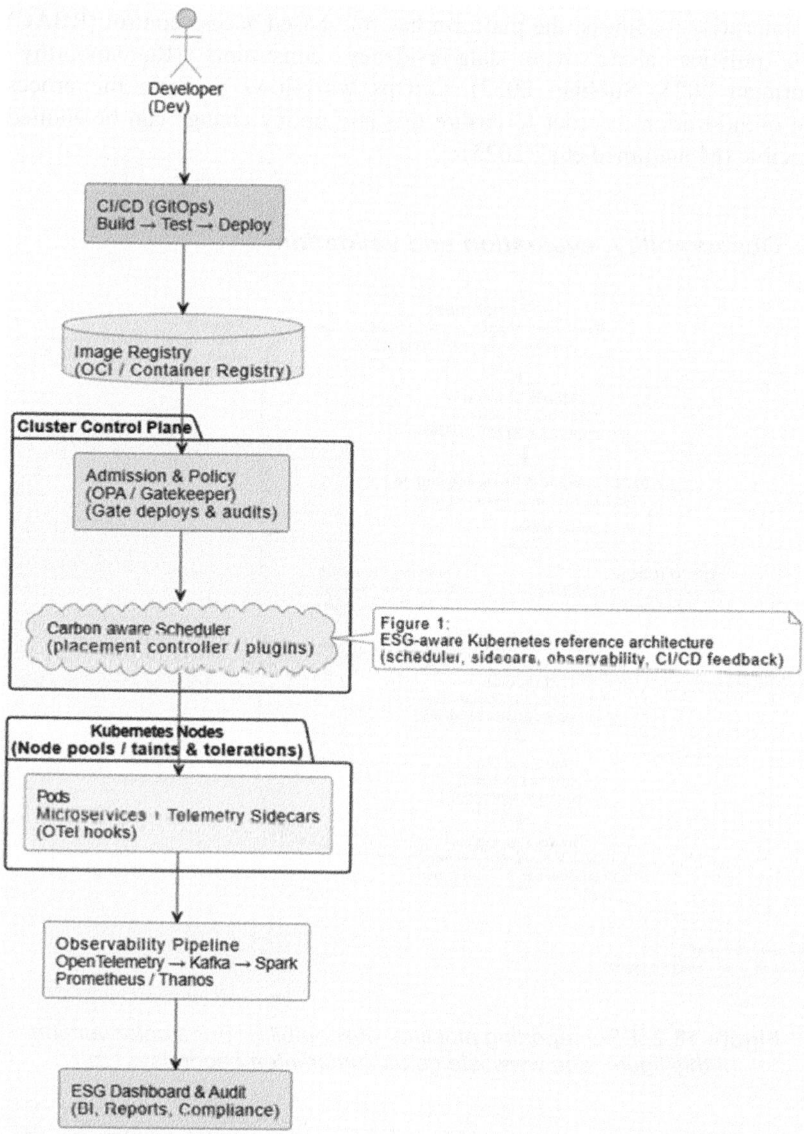

Figure 18.1. *Kubernetes reference architecture that is ESG-conscious. For a color version of this figure, see www.iste.co.uk/kumar/intembeddedsys1.zip*

The method applied is a pluggable scheduler design that enables experiments using the default Kubernetes scheduler, allowing comparison with a carbon-aware scheduler and a cost-aware placement controller. To accommodate workloads that are sensitive to hardware (such as the heavy inference load on a GPU or generative AI training), the testbed has taints/tolerations and node pools as in Lulla (2025). To ensure enterprise readiness, the platform has role-based access control (RBAC) and network policies along with data-residency constraints (Ramamoorthy and Balamurugan 2025; Subbian 2022). GitOps workflows perform the process of runtime orchestration in order to ensure that any policy change can be audited and reproducible (Mohammed et al. 2025).

18.3.3. *Observability, evaluation and validation*

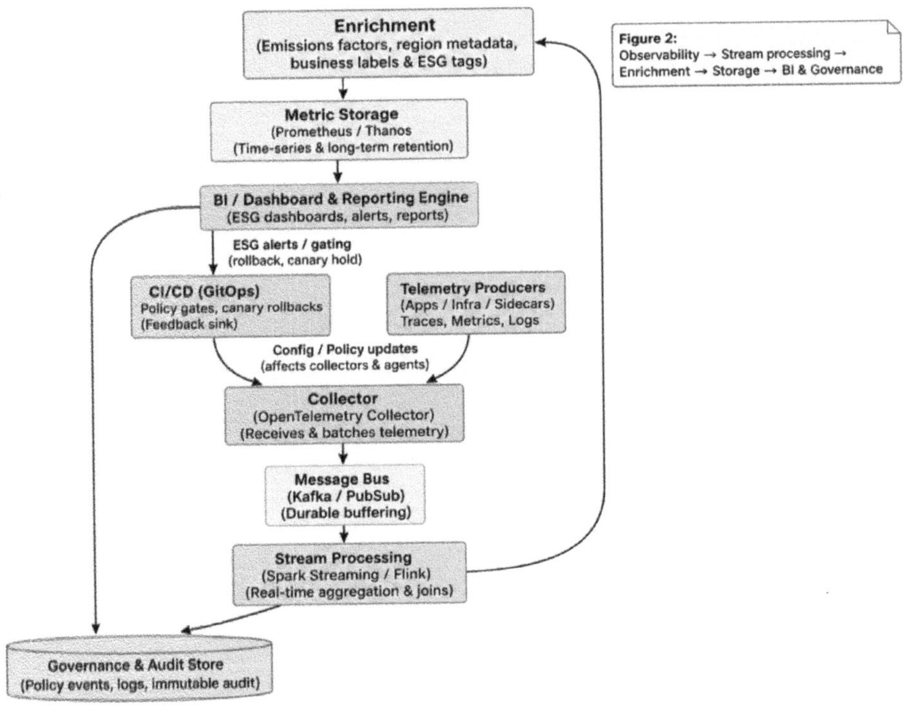

Figure 18.2. *ESG reporting pipeline, observability. For a color version of this figure, see www.iste.co.uk/kumar/intembeddedsys1.zip*

Observability puts together traces with high cardinality, aggregated metrics and business signals into a dashboard for ESG reporting and pipeline durations. It is driven by the OpenTelemetry – Kafka – Spark near-real-time aggregation, Prometheus + Thanos long-term metric retention and BI/visualization layer used to do ESG reporting and stakeholder views (Ezenwaka 2025; Ikeh 2025; Vennamaneni 2025b). The observability and reporting pipeline is depicted in Figure 18.2, including the enrichment of emission-related factors and governance events (Durgam 2025; Vennamaneni 2025).

The metrics of Table 18.1 are used to evaluate the different scenarios (baseline, energy-aware scheduling, carbon-aware placement, governance-gated CI/CD) based on the metrics. The experimental conditions, the set hypotheses and the main evaluation conditions are summarized in Table 18.2; it is used in the course of statistical testing and the sensitivity analysis (see Table 18.2) (Durgam 2025; Ionescu et al. 2025).

Scenario	Hypothesis	Primary evaluation criteria	Notes/references
Baseline (default K8s)	Standard scheduler optimizes perf but not carbon	P95 latency, throughput, energy/req	Baseline for comparison (Chinnaraju 2024a)
Energy-aware scheduling	Energy-aware placement reduces energy/req with small latency cost	Energy/req change %, P95 latency delta, cost delta	Expect trade-off; validate per (Ionescu et al. 2025)
Carbon-aware placement (region-aware)	Placing workloads in lower-emission regions reduces gCO_2e/req	gCO_2e/req, data residency compliance	Requires multi-region testbed (Nagarakanti 2025)
Governance-gated CI/CD	Policy-as-code gates reduce compliance incidents with manageable velocity impact	Compliance events, deployment frequency, lead time	Balances speed and safety (Ramamoorthy and Balamurugan 2025; Subbian 2022);

Table 18.2. *Evaluation scenarios, hypotheses and primary evaluation criteria*

18.4. Results

Table 18.3 quantifies the trade-offs when switching from the default Kubernetes scheduler to energy-aware and carbon-aware placement policies. The energy-aware scheduler achieves the largest reduction in energy per request (≈18%) and a significant cost reduction (≈10%) but with modest performance impacts – a ~6% increase in P95 latency and a ~4% drop in throughput. Carbon-aware placement produces a smaller energy reduction (≈12%) and smaller cost savings, while also incurring milder performance penalties. Figure 18.3 shows the corresponding time-series and distribution plots (latency versus energy) that illustrate how energy reductions are concentrated during high-load intervals and how carbon-aware placement shifts load across regions to reduce emissions with less impact on tail latency.

Metric	Baseline (ref)	Energy-aware scheduler (% change vs. baseline)	Carbon-aware placement (% change vs. baseline)
P95 latency (ms)	0%	+6%	+2%
Throughput (req/s)	0%	−4%	−1%
Energy per request (J/req)	0%	−18%	−12%
Cost per hour (USD/hr)	0%	−10%	−6%

Table 18.3. *Scheduler trade-offs: performance, throughput, energy and cost*

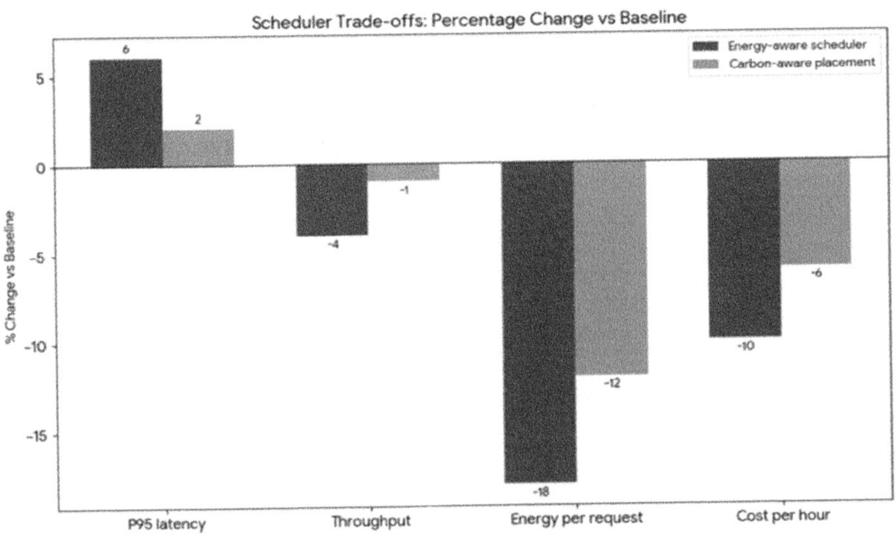

Figure 18.3. *Scheduler trade-offs: performance, throughput, energy and cost. For a color version of this figure, see www.iste.co.uk/kumar/intembeddedsys1.zip*

Region/aggregate	gCO_2e reduction versus baseline (%)	Energy-per-request reduction (%)	Cost change (%)
US-East (baseline)	0%	0%	0%
EU-West	22%	10%	+2%
AP-South	35%	18%	+5%
Global average (weighted)	20%	10%	+3%

Table 18.4. *Regional placement effects: carbon, energy and cost changes*

Table 18.4 reports the percent reductions in carbon intensity (gCO_2e) and per-request energy when workload placement is optimized by region-aware policies, relative to a US-East baseline deployment. Regional placement yields the largest carbon reductions in AP-South (≈35%) and substantial reductions in EU-West (≈22%), reflecting regional differences in grid carbon intensity. Energy-per-request also declines notably in regions with greener infrastructure (up to ~18% in AP-South), but these gains come with a modest cost premium (global average ≈+3%), because lower-emission regions sometimes have higher unit computational costs. Figure 18.4 visualizes regional maps and stacked time-series that demonstrate how shifting a fraction of steady-state workloads to low-emission regions drives disproportionate carbon benefits.

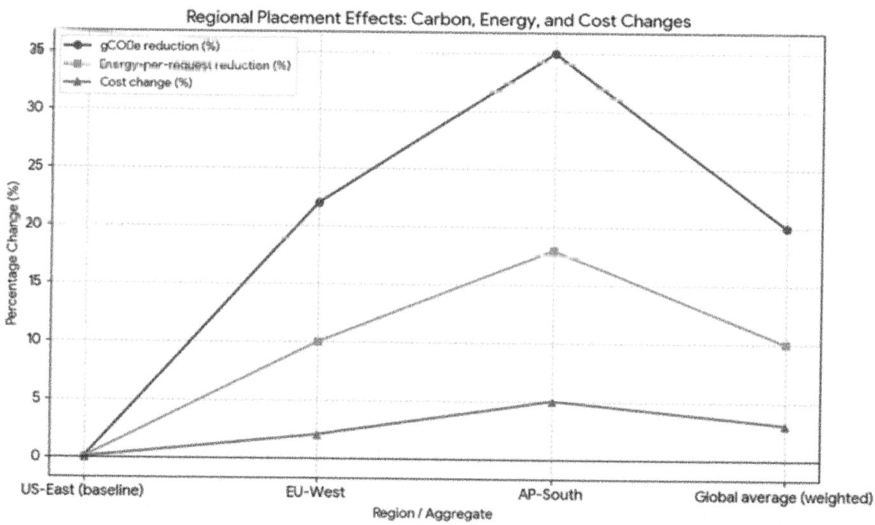

Figure 18.4. *Regional placement effects: carbon, energy and cost changes. For a color version of this figure, see www.iste.co.uk/kumar/intembeddedsys1.zip*

Metric	Governance-gated CI/CD (% change vs. baseline)
Compliance incidents (count)	−68%
Deployment frequency (deploys/day)	−12%
Mean lead time for changes (minutes)	+5%
Rollback rate (failed production deploys)	−40%
Developer satisfaction (survey score, normalized %)	−8%

Table 18.5. *Governance gating: compliance versus delivery velocity and reliability*

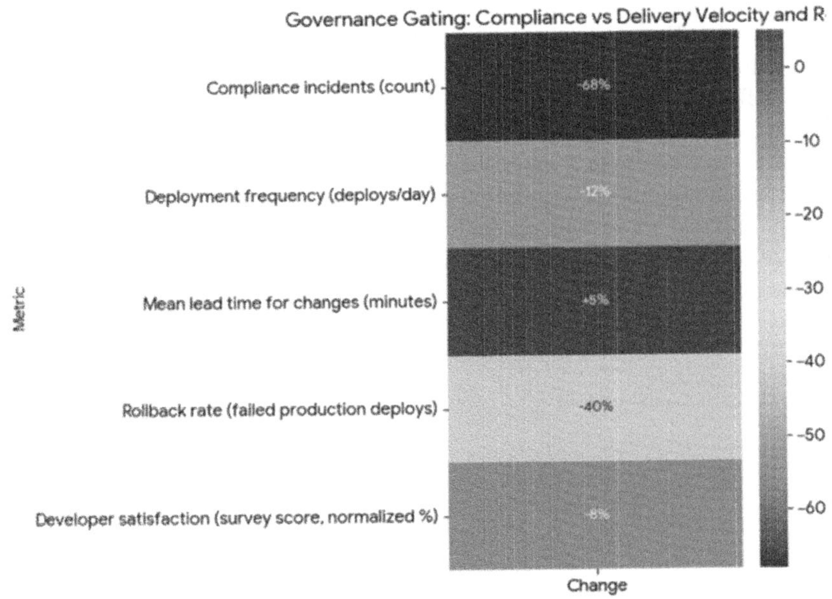

Figure 18.5. *Governance gating: compliance versus delivery velocity and reliability. For a color version of this figure, see www.iste.co.uk/kumar/intembeddedsys1.zip*

Table 18.5 summarizes the operational impact of introducing policy-as-code gates into the CI/CD pipeline. Governance gating substantially reduces compliance incidents (≈68% fewer) and lowers rollback rates (≈40% reduction), indicating clearer automated enforcement and fewer post-deploy failures. These reliability gains come with a modest reduction in deployment frequency (≈12% fewer deployments per day) and a small increase in lead time (+5%), reflecting additional checks and hold conditions. Developer satisfaction shows a minor decline (~8%), suggesting an early ergonomics friction that can be mitigated by improved feedback and faster policy iteration. Figure 18.5 presents the before/after distributions and cumulative-deploy timelines that support these findings and show how gating causes short, predictable delays while improving stability and auditability.

18.5. Conclusion

To summarize, adopting a system for calculating ESG metrics within Kubernetes-controlled microservices reframes sustainability from an external reporting requirement into a clearly defined and enforceable design parameter. With strategically measured service telemetry, carbon– and cost-aware placement policies, and governance mechanisms that capture the environmental and social footprint of software without degrading performance, organizations can maintain both agility and consistency. The proposed methodology – based on well-defined ESG indicators implemented through observability pipelines and scheduler plugins – highlights the practical trade-offs between performance and energy, as well as cost and emissions, while offering actionable patterns for engineering teams. Ultimately, integrating ESG as part of cloud-native practice supports more responsible and transparent digital transformation, turning routine engineering decisions into measurable contributions toward reduced emissions, improved governance, and increased stakeholder trust.

18.6. References

Chinnaraju, A. (2024a). Cloud-native architectures for generative AI-ready, scalable game development: An MLOps-driven blueprint. *Journal of Emerging Technologies and Innovative Research*, 11(11). doi: 10.56975/jetir.v11i11.559859.

Chinnaraju, A. (2024b). Real time adaptive AI pipelines for edge cloud systems: Dynamic optimization based on infrastructure feedback. *World Journal of Advanced Engineering Technology and Sciences*, 13(2), 887–908. doi: 10.30574/wjaets.2024.13.2.0636.

Durgam, S. (2025). Feedback-driven report optimization in investment platforms. *International Journal of IoT*, 5(1), 159–189. doi: 10.55640/ijiot-05-01-09.

Enemosah, A. and Chukwunweike, J. (2022) Next-generation SCADA architectures for enhanced field automation and real-time remote control in oil and gas fields, *International Journal of Computer Applications Technology and Research*, 11(12), 514–529. doi: 10.7753/IJCATR1112.1018.

Ezenwaka, C. (2025) Integrating AI-powered business intelligence dashboards to forecast commercial property trends and tenant retention metrics, *International Journal of Computer Applications Technology and Research*, 14(8), 47–62. doi: 10.7753/IJCATR1408.1006.

Ikeh, C.O. (2025). Integrating AI with omnichannel marketing: targeting high-value customers through cross-platform data fusion and intent recognition, *International Journal of Computer Applications Technology and Research*, 14(5), 5–19. doi: 10.7753/IJCATR1405.1002.

Ionescu, S., Diaconita, V., Radu, A. (2025). Engineering sustainable data architectures for modern financial institutions. *Electronics*, 14(8), 1650. doi: 10.3390/electronics14081650.

Khadidos, A.O., Manoharan, H., Selvarajan, S., Khadidos, A.O., Alshareef, A.M. Altwijri, M. (2024). Distribution of resources beyond 5G networks with heterogeneous parallel processing and graph optimization algorithms. *Cluster Computing*, 27(6), 8269–8287.

Lulla, K. (2025). Designing fault-tolerant test infrastructure for large-scale GPU manufacturing. *International Journal of Signal Processing Embedded Systems and VLSI Design*, 5(1), 35–61. doi: 10.55640/ijvsli-05-01-04.

Mohammed, Y.S., Akula, D.K., Syed, A., Haque, G.M.M., Arafat, Y. (2025). The impact of artificial intelligence on information systems: Opportunities and challenges. *The American Journal of Engineering and Technology*, 7(8), 151–176. doi: 10.37547/tajet/volume07issue08-15.

Nagarakanti, N.R.C. (2025). Demystifying cloud-native data platforms in financial technology. *Journal of Computer Science and Technology Studies*, 7(3), 766–775. doi: 10.32996/jcsts.2025.7.3.83.

Ramamoorthy, L. and Balamurugan, M. (2025). From legacy to intelligent automation a strategic playbook for large-scale financial institutions. *International Journal for Multidisciplinary Research*, 7(3). doi: 10.36948/ijfmr.2025.v07i03.43459.

Rathinam, R., Premkumar, S., Sivakumar, S., Ishwarya, K. (2024). SJFO: Sail jelly fish optimization enabled VM migration with DRNN-based prediction for load balancing in cloud computing. *Network: Computation in Neural Systems*, 35(4), 403–428. doi: 10.1080/0954898X.2024.2359609.

Saini, R.K. (2022). AI-powered customized banking experiences: Using data science to provide tailored financial services. *Interantional Journal of Scientific Research in Engineering and Management*, 6(11), 1–9. doi: 10.55041/ijsrem16907.

Selvarajan, S., Manoharan, H., Al-Shehari, T., Alsadhan, N.A., and Singh, S. (2025). IoT-driven healthcare monitoring with evolutionary optimization and game theory. *Scientific Reports*, 15(1), 15224.

Subbian, R.G. (2022). Legacy to digital transformations in P&C insurance. *International Journal of Information Technology and Management Information Systems*, 13(1), 150–169. doi: 10.34218/ijitmis_13_01_014.

Vennamaneni, P.R. (2025). Real-time financial data processing using apache spark and Kafka. *International Journal of Data Science and Machine Learning*, 5(1), 137–169. doi: 10.55640/ijdsml-05-01-16.

List of Authors

Elankurisil S.A.
Department of Electrical and Electronics Engineering
Adhiparasakthi Engineering College
Melmaruvathur
India

Kammara Venkatarangaiah ACHARI
Department of Computer Science and Engineering (AIML)
Malla Reddy Engineering College for Women (Autonomous)
Hyderabad
India

Kuchur AKSHARA
Department of Computer Science and Engineering (AIML)
Malla Reddy Engineering College for Women (Autonomous)
Hyderabad
India

Donda AKSHITHA
Department of Computer Science and Engineering (AIML)
Malla Reddy Engineering College for Women (Autonomous)
Hyderabad
India

Sarampelly ANANYA
Department of Computer Science and Engineering (AIML)
Malla Reddy Engineering College for Women (Autonomous)
Hyderabad
India

M. ANITHA
Department of Electronics and Communication Engineering
M.P. Nachimuthu M. Jaganathan Engineering College
Erode
India

B. ANJALI
Department of Computer Science and Engineering (AIML)
Malla Reddy Engineering College for Women (Autonomous)
Hyderabad
India

Mosali ASHRITHA
Department of Computer Science and Engineering (AIML)
Malla Reddy Engineering College for Women (Autonomous)
Hyderabad
India

Ramanolla ASHWITHA
Department of Computer Science and Engineering (AIML)
Malla Reddy Engineering College for Women (Autonomous)
Hyderabad
India

Priya BATTA
Amity School of Engineering and Technology
Amity University Punjab
Mohali
India

D. Vemana CHARY
Department of Computer Science and Engineering (AIML)
Malla Reddy Engineering College for Women (Autonomous)
Hyderabad
India

A. CHATHURYA
Department of Computer Science and Engineering (AIML)
Malla Reddy Engineering College for Women (Autonomous)
Hyderabad
India

Vijayalakshmi CHINTAMANENI
Department of Computer Science and Engineering (AIML)
Malla Reddy Engineering College for Women (Autonomous)
Hyderabad
India

N. Dhivya DEVI
Department of Electrical and Electronics Engineering
Adhiparasakthi Engineering College
Melmaruvathur
India

Golda DILIP
Department of Computer Science and Engineering
Faculty of Engineering and Technology
SRM Institute of Science and Technology, Vadapalani Campus
Chennai
India

M. DIVYA
Department of Computer Science and Engineering (AIML)
Malla Reddy Engineering College for Women (Autonomous)
Hyderabad
India

B. Vijaya DURGA
Department of Computer Science and Engineering (AIML)
Malla Reddy Engineering College for Women (Autonomous)
Hyderabad
India

Brindha G.
Department of Chemistry
VSB Engineering College
Karur
India

Mamidi GAYATHRI
Department of Computer Science and Engineering (AIML)
Malla Reddy Engineering College for Women (Autonomous)
Hyderabad
India

A. HAARIKA
Department of Computer Science and Engineering (AIML)
Malla Reddy Engineering College for Women (Autonomous)
Hyderabad
India

B. HARSHITHA
Department of Computer Science and Engineering (AIML)
Malla Reddy Engineering College for Women (Autonomous)
Hyderabad
India

Talasila HARSHITHA
Department of Computer Science and Engineering (AIML)
Malla Reddy Engineering College for Women (Autonomous)
Hyderabad
India

Adla JAHNAVI
Department of Computer Science and Engineering (AIML)
Malla Reddy Engineering College for Women (Autonomous)
Hyderabad
India

Priyadarsini K.
Department of Data Science and Business Systems
School of Computing
Faculty of Engineering and Technology
SRM Institute of Science and Technology
Chennai
India

Mallaiahgari KAMALINI
Department of Computer Science and Engineering (AIML)
Malla Reddy Engineering College for Women (Autonomous)
Hyderabad
India

A. KAMESWARAN
Department of Electronics and Communication Engineering
M.P. Nachimuthu M. Jaganathan Engineering College
Erode
India

Neha KASANAGOTTU
Department of Computer Science and Engineering (AIML)
Malla Reddy Engineering College for Women (Autonomous)
Hyderabad
India

Mekala KAVYA
Department of Computer Science and Engineering (AIML)
Malla Reddy Engineering College for Women (Autonomous)
Hyderabad
India

Lingam KAVYANJALI
Department of Computer Science and Engineering (AIML)
Malla Reddy Engineering College for Women (Autonomous)
Hyderabad
India

Bommena Sri KEERTHANA
Department of Computer Science and Engineering (AIML)
Malla Reddy Engineering College for Women (Autonomous)
Hyderabad
India

V. Chandra KEERTHI
Department of Computer Science and Engineering (AIML)
Malla Reddy Engineering College for Women (Autonomous)
Hyderabad
India

Manam Vamsi KRISHNA
Department of Computer Science and Engineering (AIML)
Malla Reddy Engineering College for Women (Autonomous)
Hyderabad
India

Abhishek KUMAR
Department of Computer Science and Engineering
Chandigarh University
Mohali
India

Penumala LAVENIA
Department of Computer Science and Engineering
Koneru Lakshmaiah Education Foundation
Vaddeswaram
India

Sunkari MAMATHA
Department of Computer Science and Engineering (AIML)
Malla Reddy Engineering College for Women (Autonomous)
Hyderabad
India

Amrutha Varshini MANNAVA
Department of Computer Science and Engineering
Koneru Lakshmaiah Education Foundation
Vaddeswaram
India

Dodda MEGHANA
Department of Computer Science and Engineering (AIML)
Malla Reddy Engineering College for Women (Autonomous)
Hyderabad
India

Lahari MEKALA
Department of Computer Science and Engineering (AIML)
Malla Reddy Engineering College for Women (Autonomous)
Hyderabad
India

R. MOHAN
National Institute of Technology
Tiruchirappalli
Tamil Nadu
India

K. MOUNIKA
Department of Computer Science and Engineering (AIML)
Malla Reddy Engineering College for Women (Autonomous)
Hyderabad
India

Narendhar MULUGU
Department of Computer Science and Engineering (AIML)
Malla Reddy Engineering College for Women (Autonomous)
Hyderabad
India

Iyappan MURUGESAN
Department of Electrical and Electronics Engineering
MAM College of Engineering
Tiruchirappalli
India

R. MUTHUKUMAR
Department of Electrical and Electronics Engineering
Paavai Engineering College
Namakkal
India

Fariha NAAZ
Department of Computer Science and Engineering (AIML)
Malla Reddy Engineering College for Women (Autonomous)
Hyderabad
India

Karne NAMITHA
Department of Computer Science and Engineering (AIML)
Malla Reddy Engineering College for Women (Autonomous)
Hyderabad
India

C. NANDAGOPAL
Department of Electronics and Communication Engineering
M. Kumarasamy College of Engineering
Karur
India

C. NANDINI
Department of Data Science and Business Systems
School of Computing
SRM Institute of Science and Technology
Chennai
India

Adepu NEHA
Department of Computer Science and Engineering (AIML)
Malla Reddy Engineering College for Women (Autonomous)
Hyderabad
India

Kapuganti NIHARIKA
Department of Computer Science and Engineering (AIML)
Malla Reddy Engineering College for Women (Autonomous)
Hyderabad
India

Oruganti NIKHILA
Department of Computer Science and Engineering (AIML)
Malla Reddy Engineering College for Women (Autonomous)
Hyderabad
India

B. PAVITHRA
Department of Computer Science and Engineering (AIML)
Malla Reddy Engineering College for Women (Autonomous)
Hyderabad
India

M. PRAKASH
Department of Electronics and Communication Engineering
Kangeyam Institute of Technology
Tiruppur
India

S. PRAKASH
Department of Electrical and Electronics Engineering
NPR College of Engineering and Technology
Dindigul
India

G. PRIYANKA
Department of Computer Science and Engineering (AIML)
Malla Reddy Engineering College for Women (Autonomous)
Hyderabad
India

Kakumanu Venkata Sai Keerthi PRIYANKA
Department of Computer Science and Engineering
Koneru Lakshmaiah Education Foundation
Vaddeswaram
India

Bazar PRIYANSHU
Department of Computer Science and Engineering (AIML)
Malla Reddy Engineering College for Women (Autonomous)
Hyderabad
India

Jaikumar R.
Department of Electronics and Communication Engineering
KPR Institute of Engineering and Technology
Coimbatore
India

Vegesna Kumar Durga Abhirama RAJU
Department of Computer Science and Engineering
Koneru Lakshmaiah Education Foundation
Vaddeswaram
India

B. Prameela RANI
Department of Computer Science and Engineering
Koneru Lakshmaiah Education Foundation
Vaddeswaram
India

S. RAVI
Pondicherry University
Puducherry
India

Aramati Poojani REDDY
Department of Computer Science and Engineering (AIML)
Malla Reddy Engineering College for Women (Autonomous)
Hyderabad
India

Bobbiti Jyothika REDDY
Department of Computer Science and Engineering (AIML)
Malla Reddy Engineering College for Women (Autonomous)
Hyderabad
India

Ch. Sandeep REDDY
Department of Computer Science and Engineering (AIML)
Malla Reddy Engineering College for Women (Autonomous)
Hyderabad
India

L. Srinivasa REDDY
Department of Computer Science and Engineering (AIML)
Malla Reddy Engineering College for Women (Autonomous)
Hyderabad
India

Bandaru RUCHITHA
Department of Computer Science and Engineering (AIML)
Malla Reddy Engineering College for Women (Autonomous)
Hyderabad
India

Ravikumar S.
Department of Electronics and Communication Engineering
Akshaya College of Engineering and Technology
Coimbatore
India

Singirikonda SAMHITHA
Department of Computer Science and Engineering (AIML)
Malla Reddy Engineering College for Women (Autonomous)
Hyderabad
India

D. SANJANA
Department of Computer Science and Engineering (AIML)
Malla Reddy Engineering College for Women (Autonomous)
Hyderabad
India

Gande SANNIHITHA
Department of Computer Science and Engineering (AIML)
Malla Reddy Engineering College for Women (Autonomous)
Hyderabad
India

Nimmanagoti SARASWATHI
Department of Computer Science and Engineering (AIML)
Malla Reddy Engineering College for Women (Autonomous)
Hyderabad
India

K. SELVI
Department of Computer Science and Engineering
Faculty of Engineering and Technology
SRM Institute of Science and Technology, Vadapalani Campus
Chennai
India

M. SHANMUGHAM
Department of Electronics and Communication Engineering
Nandha Engineering College
Erode
India

Vuppu SHRIYA
Department of Computer Science and Engineering (AIML)
Malla Reddy Engineering College for Women (Autonomous)
Hyderabad
India

Suguru SIREESHA
Department of Computer Science and Engineering (AIML)
Malla Reddy Engineering College for Women (Autonomous)
Hyderabad
India

K. SIVAPRAKASH
Department of Electronics and Communication Engineering
KGISL Institute of Technology
Coimbatore
India

Aduri SMILEY
Department of Computer Science and Engineering (AIML)
Malla Reddy Engineering College for Women (Autonomous)
Hyderabad
India

Dharavath SNEHA
Department of Computer Science and Engineering (AIML)
Malla Reddy Engineering College for Women (Autonomous)
Hyderabad
India

S. SPANDANA
Department of Computer Science and Engineering (AIML)
Malla Reddy Engineering College for Women (Autonomous)
Hyderabad
India

Kuntala SREEJA
Department of Computer Science and Engineering (AIML)
Malla Reddy Engineering College for Women (Autonomous)
Hyderabad
India

Bommadeni Sanjana SRI
Department of Computer Science and Engineering (AIML)
Malla Reddy Engineering College for Women (Autonomous)
Hyderabad
India

Mothewar SRIJA
Department of Computer Science and Engineering (AIML)
Malla Reddy Engineering College for Women (Autonomous)
Hyderabad
India

Nangunoori SRIJA
Department of Computer Science and Engineering (AIML)
Malla Reddy Engineering College for Women (Autonomous)
Hyderabad
India

Chakilela SRIVIDHYA
Department of Computer Science and Engineering (AIML)
Malla Reddy Engineering College for Women (Autonomous)
Hyderabad
India

B. SUGANTHI
Department of Electronics and Communication Engineering
RVS College of Engineering and Technology
Coimbatore
India

Gundeboina SUSHMITHA
Department of Computer Science and Engineering (AIML)
Malla Reddy Engineering College for Women (Autonomous)
Hyderabad
India

K. TAMILSELVI
Department of Electrical and Electronics Engineering
NPR College of Engineering and Technology
Dindigul
India

K. TEJASWI
Department of Computer Science and Engineering (AIML)
Malla Reddy Engineering College for Women (Autonomous)
Hyderabad
India

Bodi TEJASWINI
Department of Computer Science and Engineering (AIML)
Malla Reddy Engineering College for Women (Autonomous)
Hyderabad
India

Kokilavani THANGARAJ
Department of Electrical and Electronics Engineering
Sona College of Technology
Salem
India

Maheswaran THANGASAMY
Department of Electronics and Communication Engineering
Sri Shakthi Institute of Engineering and Technology
Coimbatore
India

Vaddadhi THANUSHA
Department of Computer Science and Engineering (AIML)
Malla Reddy Engineering College for Women (Autonomous)
Hyderabad
India

Maloth Sai VAISHNAVI
Department of Computer Science and Engineering (AIML)
Malla Reddy Engineering College for Women (Autonomous)
Hyderabad
India

Thadisetty VAISHNAVI
Department of Computer Science and Engineering (AIML)
Malla Reddy Engineering College for Women (Autonomous)
Hyderabad
India

Kammalapally VARSHA
Department of Computer Science and Engineering (AIML)
Malla Reddy Engineering College for Women (Autonomous)
Hyderabad
India

Bathini VIGNANI
Department of Computer Science and Engineering (AIML)
Malla Reddy Engineering College for Women (Autonomous)
Hyderabad
India

E. VYSHNAVI
Department of Computer Science and Engineering (AIML)
Malla Reddy Engineering College for Women (Autonomous)
Hyderabad
India

Index

5G networks, 263

A, B

ADMM (alternating direction method of multipliers), 113, 114, 118–122
adversarial training, 159, 160, 162, 163, 166, 168, 169, 173
anomaly detection, 3–5, 8, 10, 11, 15, 32, 48, 62, 63, 67, 68, 75, 82, 97, 116, 161, 173, 189, 193, 201, 204–207, 209, 210, 222, 226, 234
Apache Kafka streams, 31
ARIMA (autoregressive integrated moving average), 31–33, 35, 37–40, 42
automotive applications, 24, 26
blockchain, 64, 97, 187, 190, 192, 193, 195, 197, 198, 204, 226, 251

C, D

chaos engineering, 213, 214, 218, 223, 225
CoAP (Constrained Application Protocol), 162, 231–233, 236–238, 242, 244–246
cold start optimization, 142, 144
communication efficiency, 109, 110, 162
component lifetime extension, 29
container reuse, 141, 142, 144, 145, 147, 151, 154
continuous delivery, 201, 202, 208
convex relaxation, 113, 114, 122, 124
cybersecurity, 5, 6, 48, 64, 116, 174, 185, 187, 190, 197, 198, 205, 234
decision-making, 6, 17, 19, 33, 34, 42, 45, 46, 48, 49, 52, 83, 127, 128, 143, 173, 190, 215, 233, 254, 260, 267
DevOps monitoring, 201
distributed
  optimization, 95, 97, 103, 110, 113, 114, 118, 125
  systems, 6, 80, 98, 190, 214, 231
DRNN (Deep Recurrent Neural Networks), 34, 48, 82, 97, 129, 190–194, 197, 198, 215, 234, 251, 268

E, F

ECC (Elliptic Curve Cryptography), 187, 190, 192–195, 197, 198
electric hybrid vehicles, 28
ESG integration, 267
fraud detection, 48, 61, 62, 64, 68, 69, 74, 75

G, H

graph convolutional networks, 3
GWO (Gray Wolf Optimization), 187, 190, 192–194, 197, 198

hierarchical architecture, 109, 233, 237–239, 246

I, K

incident response, 185, 201, 203, 205, 207, 209, 210
industrial control systems, 116, 189, 234
Industry 4.0, 45–47, 49, 50, 52, 57
intrusion detection, 5, 63, 82, 159, 160, 173, 188–190, 204, 234, 251
IoT (Internet of Things), 1, 3–9, 11, 12, 19, 31–35, 42, 47, 63, 79, 80, 82, 83, 85, 86, 90–92, 95, 97, 104, 106, 109, 110, 144, 159, 162–164, 167–169, 171, 173, 184, 188–190, 203, 231–238, 245, 246, 249–255, 257, 262, 265, 268
Kubernetes orchestration, 267

L, M

Lambda@Edge, 141, 142, 144, 146, 147, 153, 154
lightweight protocols, 246
load balancing, 19, 79, 88, 89, 92, 213–215, 226, 236, 252, 268
local outlier factor, 61, 65–67, 75
LSTM, 15, 17, 20, 22, 26, 45–51, 53, 55–57, 86–90, 171, 176, 180, 183, 187, 190–192, 197, 198
Mahalanobis distance, 61–63, 65, 67, 68, 71, 74, 75
microgrids, 113, 114, 116–118, 124
microservices, 213, 217, 225, 265–267, 269, 270, 277
ML (machine learning), 4, 6, 16, 31, 34, 35, 42, 47, 62, 63, 69, 80, 91, 96, 99, 102, 105, 116, 129, 143, 155, 160, 162, 171–173, 176, 179, 180, 182–184, 201, 203, 205–207, 210, 215, 218, 222, 223, 226, 233, 246, 251, 263, 267
MQTT (Message Queuing Telemetry Transport), 162, 231–242, 244–246
multi-modal sensor fusion, 17

O, P

observability, 210, 218, 219, 226, 265–269, 271–273, 277
prioritized experience replay, 93, 127, 128, 138
provisioned concurrency, 141, 145, 150, 154

R, S

RAN slicing, 249, 250, 253–255, 258, 260, 262
remaining useful life, 15, 16, 22
renewable energy, 113, 114, 116, 124
resilience, 6, 19, 56, 64, 82, 98, 110, 125, 129, 173, 176, 189, 190, 197, 203, 210, 213, 214, 218, 223–225, 266
robustness analysis, 166
second-order cone programming, 113, 117, 124
smart cities, 83, 172, 173, 184, 233
spectral methods, 4, 5, 12

T, U

telemetry, 17, 22, 31–33, 35–37, 42, 187, 190, 265–267, 269, 270, 277
threat detection, 116, 171, 173, 176, 180, 183, 184, 187, 188, 190, 191, 197, 205, 252
time-series forecasting, 33, 35
trust management, 171, 172, 180, 184
ultra-low latency, 47, 249, 250, 252, 254, 262

V, X

variational autoencoders, 79, 92
vehicular networks, 164, 167
XGBoost, 45–51, 53, 55–57, 164, 166, 167

Other titles from

ISTE

in

Computer Engineering

2026

BHAMBRI Pankaj, DUTTA Pushan Kumar, KHAN Mudassir, STAROSTKA-PATYK Marta
Next-Gen Supply Chains: AI, Automation, and Sustainability in a Disrupted World

DARCHE Philippe
Computer Memories 1: Core Concepts
Computer Memories 2: Static Random-Access Memory

KUMAR Abhishek, BATTA Priya
AI in Orthopedic Trauma Care 1: Comparative Clinical Insights
AI in Orthopedic Trauma Care 2: Advances in Intelligent Imaging, Decision Support, and Rehabilitation

KUMAR Abhishek, BATTA Priya, AHUJA Sachin, RATHORE Pramod Singh
AI-driven Innovations in Physiotherapy and Oncology 3
AI-driven Innovations in Physiotherapy and Oncology 4
AI-driven Innovations in Physiotherapy and Oncology 5

KUMAR Abhishek, BATTA Priya, ANANTH J.P.
AI-driven Healthcare Innovations: Applications in Neurology and Medicine

KUMAR Abhishek, T. Ananth Kumar, DUBEY Ashutosh Kumar, SRIVASTAV Arun Lal, JUÁREZ-RAMÍREZ J. Reyes
AI and Wind Power 1: A Multifaceted Approach to Sustainable Energy
AI and Wind Power 2: Advancing Sustainability, Grid Integration, and Future Frameworks

MACHADO Carolina, DAVIM J. Paulo
Artificial Intelligence Technologies in Management and Engineering

MAHOUT Vincent, ROCACHER Thierry, AURIOL Guillaume
Programming of Embedded Systems: Applications to SM32F10x μControllers

UL HAQ Inam, KAK Saana Mehraj, GUPTA Anand Kumar, RAMZAN Muhammad Sher
Artificial Intelligence for Sustainable Energy Systems 1: Intelligent Technologies for Sustainable Energy Management
Artificial Intelligence for Sustainable Energy Systems 2: AI-Driven Innovations, Climate Intelligence, and Pathways to Net-Zero Energy

2025

CHIKH Azeddine
Systemic Approach to Categorizing and Modeling Requirements

KUMAR Abhishek, BATTA Priya, AHUJA Sachin, RATHORE Pramod Singh
AI-driven Innovations in Physiotherapy and Oncology 1
AI-driven Innovations in Physiotherapy and Oncology 2

TANEJA Ashu, KUMAR Abhishek, LIMKAR Suresh Vishnudas, OUAISSA Mariya, OUAISSA Mariyam
Driving Innovation through AI and Digital Twin for 6G Powered Sustainable Ultra Smart Cities

TANEJA Ashu, KUMAR Abhishek, LIMKAR Suresh Vishnudas, OUAISSA Mariya, OUAISSA Mariyam
6G Urban Innovation: AI and Digital Twin for Next-Gen Sustainable Cities

2024

CHAKRABORTY Rajdeep, GHOSH Anupam, KUMAR MANDAL Jyotsna, CHOUDHURY Tanupriya, CHATTERJEE Prasenjit
Smart Edge Computing: An Operation Research Perspective
(International Perspectives in Decision Analytics and Operations Research Set – Volume 2)

HOMÈS Bernard
Fundamentals of Software Testing (2nd edition, revised and updated)

JERBI Abdessalem
Discrete-Event Simulation: Concepts and Production in Arena

PRADHAN Devasis, KUMAR SAHU Prasanna, MYO TUN Hla, CHATTERJEE Prasenjit
Artificial and Cognitive Computing for Sustainable Healthcare Systems in Smart Cities
(International Perspectives in Decision Analytics and Operations Research Set – Volume 3)

2023

CHOUDHURY Tanupriya, KHANNA Abhirup, CHATTERJEE Prasenjit, UM Jung-Sup, BHATTACHARYA Abhishek
Blockchain Applications in Healthcare: Innovations and Practices
(International Perspectives in Decision Analytics and Operations Research Set – Volume 1)

PAI G A Vijayalakshmi
A Textbook of Data Structures and Algorithms 1: Mastering Linear Data Structures
A Textbook of Data Structures and Algorithms 2: Mastering Nonlinear Data Structures
A Textbook of Data Structures and Algorithms 3: Mastering Advanced Data Structures and Algorithm Design Strategies

2022

HOMÈS Bernard
Advanced Testing of Systems-of-Systems 1: Theoretical Aspects
Advanced Testing of Systems-of-Systems 2: Practical Aspects

MEHTA Shikha, TIWARI Sanju, SIARRY Patrick, JABBAR M.A.
Tools, Languages, Methodologies for Representing Semantics on the Web of Things

SIDHOM Sahbi, KADDOUR Amira
Systems and Uses of Digital Sciences for Knowledge Organization (Digital Tools and Uses Set – Volume 9)

ZAIDOUN Ameur Salem
Computer Science Security: Concepts and Tools

2021

DARCHE Philippe
Microprocessor 4: Core Concepts – Software Aspects
Microprocessor 5: Software and Hardware Aspects of Development, Debugging and Testing – The Microcomputer

DELHAYE Jean-Loïc
Inside the World of Computing: Technologies, Uses, Challenges

HARDIN Thérèse, JAUME Mathieu, PESSAUX François, VIGUIÉ DONZEAU-GOUGE Véronique
Concepts and Semantics of Programming Languages 1: A Semantical Approach with OCaml and Python
Concepts and Semantics of Programming Languages 2: Modular and Object-oriented Constructs with OCaml, Python, C++, Ada and Java

MKADMI Abderrazak
Archives in The Digital Age: Preservation and the Right to be Forgotten (Digital Tools and Uses Set – Volume 8)

TOKLU Yusuf Cengiz, BEKDAŞ Gebrail, NIGDELI Sinan Melih
Metaheuristics for Structural Design and Analysis
(Optimization Heuristics Set – Volume 3)

2020

DARCHE Philippe
Microprocessor 1: Prolegomenes – Calculation and Storage Functions – Models of Computation and Computer Architecture
Microprocessor 2: Core Concepts – Communication in a Digital System
Microprocessor 3: Core Concepts – Hardware Aspects

DUVAUT Patrick, DALLOZ Xavier, MENGA David, KOEHL François, CHRIQUI Vidal, BRILL Joerg
Internet of Augmented Me, I.AM: Empowering Innovation for a New Sustainable Future

LAFFLY Dominique
TORUS 1 – Toward an Open Resource Using Services: Cloud Computing for Environmental Data
TORUS 2 – Toward an Open Resource Using Services: Cloud Computing for Environmental Data
TORUS 3 – Toward an Open Resource Using Services: Cloud Computing for Environmental Data

LAURENT Anne, LAURENT Dominique, MADERA Cédrine
Data Lakes
(Databases and Big Data Set – Volume 2)

OULHADJ Hamouche, DAACHI Boubaker, MENASRI Riad
Metaheuristics for Robotics
(Optimization Heuristics Set – Volume 2)

SADIQUI Ali
Computer Network Security

VENTRE Daniel
Artificial Intelligence, Cybersecurity and Cyber Defense

2019

BESBES Walid, DHOUIB Diala, WASSAN Niaz, MARREKCHI Emna
Solving Transport Problems: Towards Green Logistics

CLERC Maurice
Iterative Optimizers: Difficulty Measures and Benchmarks

GHLALA Riadh
Analytic SQL in SQL Server 2014/2016

TOUNSI Wiem
Cyber-Vigilance and Digital Trust: Cyber Security in the Era of Cloud Computing and IoT

2018

ANDRO Mathieu
Digital Libraries and Crowdsourcing
(Digital Tools and Uses Set – Volume 5)

ARNALDI Bruno, GUITTON Pascal, MOREAU Guillaume
Virtual Reality and Augmented Reality: Myths and Realities

CARDON Alain
Beyond Artificial Intelligence: From Human Consciousness to Artificial Consciousness

HOMAYOUNI S. Mahdi, FONTES Dalila B.M.M.
Metaheuristics for Maritime Operations
(Optimization Heuristics Set – Volume 1)

JEANSOULIN Robert
JavaScript and Open Data

PIVERT Olivier
NoSQL Data Models: Trends and Challenges
(Databases and Big Data Set – Volume 1)

SEDKAOUI Soraya
Data Analytics and Big Data

SALEH Imad, AMMI Mehdi, SZONIECKY Samuel
Challenges of the Internet of Things: Technology, Use, Ethics
(Digital Tools and Uses Set – Volume 7)

SZONIECKY Samuel
Ecosystems Knowledge: Modeling and Analysis Method for Information and Communication
(Digital Tools and Uses Set – Volume 6)

2017

BENMAMMAR Badr
Concurrent, Real-Time and Distributed Programming in Java: Threads, RTSJ and RMI

BOUHAÏ Nasreddine, SALEH Imad
Internet of Things: Evolutions and Innovations
(Digital Tools and Uses Set – Volume 4)

HÉLIODORE Frédéric, NAKIB Amir, ISMAIL Boussaad, OUCHRAA Salma, SCHMITT Laurent
Metaheuristics for Intelligent Electrical Networks
(Metaheuristics Set – Volume 10)

MA Haiping, SIMON Dan
Evolutionary Computation with Biogeography-based Optimization
(Metaheuristics Set – Volume 8)

PÉTROWSKI Alain, BEN-HAMIDA Sana
Evolutionary Algorithms
(Metaheuristics Set – Volume 9)

PAI G A Vijayalakshmi
Metaheuristics for Portfolio Optimization: An Introduction using MATLAB®
(Metaheuristics Set – Volume 11)

REYES-GARCIA Everardo
The Image-Interface: Graphical Supports for Visual Information
(Digital Tools and Uses Set – Volume 3)

REYES-GARCIA Everardo, BOUHAÏ Nasreddine
Designing Interactive Hypermedia Systems
(Digital Tools and Uses Set – Volume 2)

SZONIECKY Samuel, BOUHAÏ Nasreddine
Collective Intelligence and Digital Archives: Towards Knowledge Ecosystems
(Digital Tools and Uses Set – Volume 1)

2016

BLUM Christian, FESTA Paola
Metaheuristics for String Problems in Bio-informatics
(Metaheuristics Set – Volume 6)

DEROUSSI Laurent
Metaheuristics for Logistics
(Metaheuristics Set – Volume 4)

DHAENENS Clarisse, JOURDAN Laetitia
Metaheuristics for Big Data
(Metaheuristics Set – Volume 5)

LABADIE Nacima, PRINS Christian, PRODHON Caroline
Metaheuristics for Vehicle Routing Problems
(Metaheuristics Set – Volume 3)

LEROY Laure
Eyestrain Reduction in Stereoscopy

LUTTON Evelyne, PERROT Nathalie, TONDA Alberto
Evolutionary Algorithms for Food Science and Technology
(Metaheuristics Set – Volume 7)

MAGOULÈS Frédéric, ZHAO Hai-Xiang
Data Mining and Machine Learning in Building Energy Analysis

RIGO Michel
Advanced Graph Theory and Combinatorics

ZELM Martin, DOUMEINGTS Guy, MENDONÇA Joao Pedro
Enterprise Interoperability: in the Digitized and Networked Factory of the Future

2015

BARBIER Franck, RECOUSSINE Jean-Luc
COBOL Software Modernization: From Principles to Implementation with the BLU AGE® Method

CHEN Ken
Performance Evaluation by Simulation and Analysis with Applications to Computer Networks

CLERC Maurice
Guided Randomness in Optimization
(Metaheuristics Set – Volume 1)

DURAND Nicolas, GIANAZZA David, GOTTELAND Jean-Baptiste, ALLIOT Jean-Marc
Metaheuristics for Air Traffic Management
(Metaheuristics Set – Volume 2)

MAGOULÈS Frédéric, ROUX François-Xavier, HOUZEAUX Guillaume
Parallel Scientific Computing

MUNEESAWANG Paisarn, YAMMEN Suchart
Visual Inspection Technology in the Hard Disk Drive Industry

2014

BOULANGER Jean-Louis
Formal Methods Applied to Industrial Complex Systems
Formal Methods Applied to Complex Systems: Implementation of the B Method

EXPOSITO Ernesto, DIOP Codé
Smart SOA Platforms in Cloud Computing Architectures

GARDI Frédéric, BENOIST Thierry, DARLAY Julien, ESTELLON Bertrand, MEGEL Romain
Mathematical Programming Solver based on Local Search

KRICHEN Saoussen, CHAOUACHI Jouhaina
Graph-related Optimization and Decision Support Systems

LARRIEU Nicolas, VARET Antoine
Rapid Prototyping of Software for Avionics Systems: Model-oriented Approaches for Complex Systems Certification

LAURAS Matthieu, ZELM Martin, ARCHIMÈDE Bernard, BÉNABEN Frédérick, DOUMEINGTS Guy
Enterprise Interoperability: Interoperability for Agility, Resilience and Plasticity of Collaborations

OUSSALAH Mourad Chabane
Software Architecture 1
Software Architecture 2

QUESNEL Flavien
Scheduling of Large-scale Virtualized Infrastructures: Toward Cooperative Management

RIGO Michel
Formal Languages, Automata and Numeration Systems 1: Introduction to Combinatorics on Words
Formal Languages, Automata and Numeration Systems 2: Applications to Recognizability and Decidability

SAINT-DIZIER Patrick
Musical Rhetoric: Foundations and Annotation Schemes

TOUATI Sid, DUPONT DE DINECHIN Benoit
Advanced Backend Code Optimization

2013

ANDRÉ Étienne, SOULAT Romain
The Inverse Method: Parametric Verification of Real-time Embedded Systems

BOULANGER Jean-Louis
Safety Management for Software-based Equipment

DELAHAYE Daniel, PUECHMOREL Stéphane
Modeling and Optimization of Air Traffic

FRANCOPOULO Gil
LMF — Lexical Markup Framework

GHEDIRA Khaled
Constraint Satisfaction Problems: CSP Formalisms and Techniques

GOVAERT Gérard, NADIF Mohamed
Co-Clustering: Models, Algorithms and Applications

LANDRAGIN Frédérick
Man–Machine Dialogue: Design and Challenges

LUCAS Laurent, LOSCOS Céline, REMION Yannick
3D Video: Models, From Capture to Diffusion

ROCHANGE Christine, UHRIG Sascha, SAINRAT Pascal
Time-Predictable Architectures

WAHBI Mohamed
Algorithms and Ordering Heuristics for Distributed Constraint Satisfaction Problems

ZELM Martin, VAN SINDEREN Marten, FERRAIRA PIRES Luis, DOUMEINGTS Guy
Enterprise Interoperability: Research and Applications in the Service-oriented Ecosystem

2012

ARBOLEDA Hugo, ROYER Jean-Claude
Model-Driven and Software Product Line Engineering

BLANCHET Gérard, DUPOUY Bertrand
Computer Architecture

BOULANGER Jean-Louis
Industrial Use of Formal Methods: Formal Verification
Formal Methods: Industrial Use from Model to the Code

CALVARY Gaëlle, DELOT Thierry, SÈDES Florence, TIGLI Jean-Yves
Computer Science and Ambient Intelligence

MAHOUT Vincent
Assembly Language Programming: ARM Cortex-M3 2.0: Organization, Innovation and Territory

MARLET Renaud
Program Specialization

SOTO Maria, SEVAUX Marc, ROSSI André, LAURENT Johann
Memory Allocation Problems in Embedded Systems: Optimization Methods

2011

BICHOT Charles-Edmond, SIARRY Patrick
Graph Partitioning

BOULANGER Jean-Louis
Static Analysis of Software: The Abstract Interpretation

CAFERRA Ricardo
Logic for Computer Science and Artificial Intelligence

KORDON Fabrice, HADDAD Serge, PAUTET Laurent, PETRUCCI Laure
Distributed Systems: Design and Algorithms
Models and Analysis in Distributed Systems

LORCA Xavier
Tree-based Graph Partitioning Constraint

RIDHA MAHJOUB A.
Progress in Combinatorial Optimization: ISCO2010

TRUCHET Charlotte, ASSAYAG Gerard
Constraint Programming in Music

VICAT-BLANC Pascale, GOGLIN Brice, GUILLIER Romaric, SOUDAN Sébastien
Computing Networks: From Cluster to Cloud Computing

2010

AUBRUN Christophe, SIMON Daniel, SONG Ye-Qiong
Co-design Approaches for Dependable Networked Control Systems

AUDIBERT Pierre
Mathematics for Informatics and Computer Science

BABAU Jean-Philippe, BLAY-FORNARINO Mireille, CHAMPEAU Joël, ROBERT Sylvain, SABETTA Antonino
Model Driven Engineering for Distributed Real-Time Systems: MARTE Modeling, Model Transformations and their Usages

BOULANGER Jean-Louis
Safety of Computer Architectures

SIGAUD Olivier, BUFFET Olivier
Markov Decision Processes in Artificial Intelligence

MONMARCHÉ Nicolas, GUINAND Frédérick, SIARRY Patrick
Artificial Ants

SOLNON Christine
Ant Colony Optimization and Constraint Programming

2009

FOURNIER Jean-Claude
Graph Theory and Applications: with exercises and problems

GUÉDON Jeanpierre
The Mojette Transform: theory and applications

JARD Claude, ROUX Olivier H.
Communicating Embedded Systems: Software and Design

LECOUTRE Christophe
Constraint Networks: Techniques and Algorithms

2008

BANÂTRE Michel, MARRON Pedro Jose, OLLERO Anibal, WOLITZ Adam
Cooperating Embedded Systems and Wireless Sensor Networks

MERZ Stephan, NAVET Nicolas
Modeling and Verification of Real-time Systems: Formalisms and Software Tools

PASCHOS Vangelis Th.
Combinatorial Optimization and Theoretical Computer Science: Interfaces and Perspectives

WALDNER Jean-Baptiste
Nanocomputers and Swarm Intelligence

2007

BENHAMOU Frédéric, JUSSIEN Narendra, O'SULLIVAN Barry
Trends in Constraint Programming

JUSSIEN Narendra
A to Z of Sudoku

2006

BABAU Jean-Philippe, CHAMPEAU Joël, GÉRARD Sébastien
From MDD Concepts to Experiments and Illustrations – DRES 2006

HABRIAS Henri, FRAPPIER Marc
Software Specification Methods: An Overview Using a Case Study

MURAT Cécile, PASCHOS Vangelis Th.
Probabilistic Combinatorial Optimization on Graphs

PANETTO Hervé, BOUDJLIDA Nacer
Interoperability for Enterprise Software and Applications: Proceedings of the Workshops and the Doctorial Symposium of the Second IFAC/IFIP I-ESA International Conference: EI2N, WSI, IS-TSPQ 2006

2005

GÉRARD Sébastien, BABAU Jean-Philippe, CHAMPEAU Joël
Model Driven Engineering for Distributed Real Time Embedded Systems

PANETTO Hervé
Interoperability of Enterprise Software and Applications: Workshops of the INTEROP-ESA 2005 International Conference (EI2N, WSI, ISIDI and IEHENA 2005)

Printed and bound by CPI Group (UK) Ltd, Croydon, CR0 4YY

13/09/2026

14961014-0007